Performing Spanishness

History, Cultural Identity and Censorship in the Theatre of José María Rodríguez Méndez

Michael Thompson

For Jenn and Alex

Performing Spanishness

History, Cultural Identity and Censorship in the Theatre of José María Rodríguez Méndez

Michael Thompson

intellect Bristol, UK / Chicago, USA

First Published in the UK in 2007 by
Intellect Books, PO Box 862, Bristol BS99 1DE, UK

First published in the USA in 2007 by
Intellect Books, The University of Chicago Press, 1427 E. 60th Street, Chicago,
IL 60637, USA

Cover illustration: *Flor de Otoño*, Teatro Español (Madrid), December 1982.
Photograph by Manuel Martínez Muñoz.

A catalogue record for this book is available from the British Library.

Cover Design: Gabriel Solomons
Copy Editor: Holly Spradling
Typesetting: Mac Style, Nafferton, E. Yorkshire

ISBN 978-184150-134-5

Printed and bound by Gutenberg Press, Malta.

CONTENTS

LIST OF ILLUSTRATIONS

Introduction

Hay momentos en que uno se da cuenta de que la verdadera transición, la transición a una democracia normal, está aún por hacer. De hecho, pasamos del silencio del franquismo al silencio de hielo de una democracia que tenía demasiadas cosas que callar, demasiados fantasmas a los que era mejor no despertar, aunque quizá fueron menos los miedos y más los intereses no siempre confesables. El caso es que se ha hablado muy poco de nuestra historia reciente, como si mirar hacia atrás fuera perder pie en el camino del progreso. Así es como han quedado olvidados autores que, como José María Rodríguez Méndez, hubiesen debido vertebrar el resurgir posfranquista de la dramaturgia española (Ley 2003).[1]

Thirty years after the end of the Franco dictatorship, despite widespread public satisfaction with the outcome of the political, economic and social changes that have taken place in Spain, the lingering sense of unease about the past referred to by Pablo Ley in his review of a production of Rodríguez Méndez's *Flor de Otoño* is never far from the surface. Recent interest in locating the graves of people executed during and after the civil war, and in identifying those responsible for human rights abuses, has crystallized a general feeling that too many memories have been suppressed, too many compromises were made for the sake of stability, too many stories have remained untold, and a great deal of history still needs to be written. Fictional texts in narrative, theatrical and cinematic form have played a very important role – both during the dictatorship and since – in reviving those memories, questioning those compromises, telling those stories and exploring that history, but the political and economic structures that govern the process of finding an audience have frequently obstructed attempts to break the silence.

The 2003 revival of Rodríguez Méndez's *Flor de Otoño* (in the Teatre Artenbrut, Barcelona), despite being a small-scale production in an 'alternative' venue, prompted a number of reviews containing remarks similar to those quoted above, underlining both the importance of the fact that the play was finally being staged in the city that inspired it and lamenting the lack of recognition accorded to a writer who has made a unique contribution to challenging the historical and cultural amnesia of the nation. However, the notion of Rodríguez Méndez as a 'forgotten' playwright was already being substantially revised at that time. In February 2001, the city of Ávila had named a new drama studio after him and organized a tribute involving a series of talks and the premiere of the play *Última batalla en El Pardo*. Although the production never reached a Madrid theatre, it played successfully in Barcelona, Valencia and Alicante and prompted the publication of another edition of the text. Several other events in recent years have done a great deal to consolidate his reputation as one of the most significant playwrights of the second half of the twentieth century in Spain. The year 2004 saw the publication of a new edition of *El pájaro solitario* in the SGAE *Teatrohomenaje* series and the award of the prestigious Max prize for his life's work. In 2005, a major new production of *Flor de Otoño* (directed by Ignacio García) had a successful and well-reviewed run at the Centro Dramático Nacional, coinciding with the publication of a two-volume edition of selected plays (*Teatro escogido*).

Rodríguez Méndez's work has always been ambitious: he has aimed to reveal uncomfortable truths and engage with important social issues; to discredit official myths and rediscover alternative versions of national history; to speak on behalf of ordinary people and give expression to their cultural identities without falsifying or over-simplifying them; to celebrate, reinterpret and do justice to a great theatrical and literary tradition; to reconnect 'elite' (literary) culture with 'popular' (oral or folk) culture; to revitalize Spanish theatre and bridge the theatrical gulf between Madrid and Barcelona. Few other writers in the past fifty years have so explicitly and insistently made Spanishness the core of their work, and no other contemporary Spanish dramatist has built up a body of work so deeply rooted in the social and cultural history of Spain, her people and her languages. Rodríguez Méndez (born in Madrid in 1925) has been a key contributor to the development of Spanish theatre in the second half of the twentieth century, with an assured place in literary and theatrical histories of the period.[2] Yet his prestige as a 'national' playwright has been limited: for much of his career he has remained an isolated figure, marginalized by censorship, by the unevenness of his output and by his obstreperous self-exclusion from the political and artistic mainstream.

This book, the first in English on the work of José María Rodríguez Méndez, aims to evaluate and consolidate the importance of his theatre within the context of social and cultural change in Spain over the past half-century, and assess the extent to which it achieves the objectives set out in the preceding paragraph. Taking its cue from the dramatist's own declaration of the centrality of *lo español* (Spanishness) to his work, my study of his plays focuses on issues of identity, investigating what kinds of ideas of Spanishness they construct, how these evolve over time and are represented theatrically, and what the political and cultural implications of representing them in these ways are. Consequently, this is as much a case study of a central topic in Hispanic cultural studies as it is an analysis of the texts of a particular author. Rodríguez Méndez's work offers a uniquely passionate, provocative and independent perspective on the historical development of cultural identities in Spain. It is embedded in tradition but alert to contemporary conditions; steeped in popular culture yet respectful of literary heritage; politically ambiguous and arguably lacking in intellectual rigour at times, but undeniably consistent and valiant in its challenging of trends and dominant ideologies. It also has the added advantage of its own dual identity, having grown out of the contrasting social, linguistic and theatrical environments of Madrid and Barcelona.

My main argument is that the central concern of Rodríguez Méndez's work is the representation of Spanishness as a diverse and evolving collection of performances of cultural identity summed up in the concept of *machismo español*. In common usage, *machismo* means 'actitud de prepotencia de los varones respecto de las mujeres' (Real Academia Española 1992: 1287) ('dominant behaviour of men towards women'). Although Rodríguez Méndez's use of the expression *machismo español* to refer to a collective identity does not erase the gender implications or negative associations of the term, he expands its meaning in a variety of ways and invests it with a positive cultural value. As used by Rodríguez Méndez and applied critically to his texts, the notion of *machismo español* turns out to be a useful and surprisingly flexible tool for the analysis of social history, popular culture and the representation of identities based on nationhood, local community, class, gender and language. It emphasizes the centrality of popular culture in traditional, oral, participative forms as a marker of community identity, an enabler of individual self-expression and a means of resistance to the ideological and cultural control exercised by the state and by dominant social groups. Above all, I intend to show that the idea of *machismo español* and its dramatic realization in Rodríguez Méndez's plays represent Spanishness and other identities as cultural, bodily and linguistic performances partly scripted by sedimented habits and ideologies but also – crucially – open to innovation and transformation. My analysis is centred on Rodríguez Méndez's history plays, arguing that they show cultural identities to be most distinctive, creative and effective in resisting ideological control in circumstances not yet dominated by the alienating, homogenizing effects of post-war industrialization and consumerism.

The first two chapters lay the foundations for the analysis of Rodríguez Méndez's plays. Chapter 1 briefly locates the author within the context of contemporary Spanish theatre, particularly the 'Realist Generation' that emerged in the early 1960s, and identifies as the central aim of his work the realistic representation of Spanishness. The theoretical and political implications of such an aim are discussed with reference to the problems of defining theatrical realism (especially as articulated by Alfonso Sastre) and the development of ideas of national identity in Spain (drawing on a range of sources including Benedict Anderson's notion of 'imagined communities', Spanish school textbooks from the Franco period and statements made by Rodríguez Méndez during the dictatorship between 1939 and 1975 and since the death of General Franco). Chapter 2 relates these issues to Rodríguez Méndez's own discussions of cultural history in his most important essays, especially

'El teatro como expresión social y cultural', *Ensayo sobre la 'inteligencia' española* and *Ensayo sobre el machismo español*. The first of these essays proposes an important social role for theatre in the context of an overview of the history of popular and elite culture in Spain, which I discuss with reference to Althusser's and Gramsci's theories of ideology. The second looks at ways in which intellectuals have allied themselves either with the dissident (realist) spirit of popular culture or with the mystifying effect of official discourses. The third expounds the notion of *machismo español* as the core of popular national identity and traces it through a series of cultural archetypes from the seventeenth century to the twentieth. I relate this essay's suggestion that such identities are fundamentally performances to Clifford Geertz's view of human identity as inseparable from cultural practices, Victor Turner's notion of 'social performance', and Judith Butler's theory of gender as a performative act. A set of principles for the analysis of Rodríguez Méndez's approach to the dramatization of historical material is also set out, drawing on the theories of Lukács and Hayden White.

Chapters 3, 4 and 5 constitute the main body of the book, analysing in detail all Rodríguez Méndez's history plays, from *Vagones de madera* to *Soy madrileño*, divided into three groups. The first group comprises plays focusing on ordinary, humble characters forced into extreme situations that function as microcosms of wider historical processes. The enclosed, suffocating spaces in which the dramatic conflicts are played out also unavoidably hint at parallels with the oppressive environment of Francoist Spain. The second group, discussed in Chapter 4, also dramatizes 'history from below' but now using more open, dynamic theatrical forms and showing communities with a greater sense of confidence and flamboyance. Chapter 5 then analyses the third group of history plays, which are centred on individuals rather than communities – well-known historical figures who are in a sense part of the elite but are reinterpreted by Rodríguez Méndez in terms of their connection to the popular culture of *machismo español*.

The final chapter uses *Última batalla en El Pardo*, which takes a markedly different approach to history, as a link between the works set in the past and those set in contemporary Spain, which are then analysed more briefly than the history plays. These texts dramatize what is argued in *Ensayo sobre el machismo español*: that the defiant spirit of *machismo* – and therefore the creativity and power of resistance of popular culture – crumbles away after the civil war under the pressures of first authoritarianism then industrialization and consumerism. The plays of the post-Franco period show a society emptied of cultural energy, its people alienated and disorientated even if many of them are politically freer and materially more comfortable.

The best critical studies to date of Rodríguez Méndez's work are in the form of articles and introductions to editions, many of them by scholars in the USA, notably Martha Halsey. These will be referred to in the chapters that follow. There are two monographs on Rodríguez Méndez's theatre: José Martín Recuerda's *La tragedia de España en la obra dramática de José María Rodríguez Méndez* (1979) and Gonzalo

Jiménez Sánchez's *El problema de España. Rodríguez Méndez: una revisión dramática de los postulados del 98* (1998). Both of these contain a large amount of interesting biographical material, enriched in the case of the first book by the close friendship between the two playwrights. Consequently, I have not included an account of Rodríguez Méndez's life in this book, though I have where appropriate highlighted particular connections between episodes in it and his writings. Since Martín Recuerda's book was written at a time when some of Rodríguez Méndez's most important texts remained unpublished, it devotes a great deal of space to simply describing the action and ambience of selected plays. It is most valuable for its evocation of the spirit of *iberismo* (Iberianism) shared by the two dramatists and for its emphasis on the emotional impact of the plays. Jiménez Sánchez develops a more substantial, scholarly argument focusing on the religious dimension of the playwright's personality and work, and includes discussion of some texts written or published since Martín Recuerda's book was produced. Valuable and interesting though Jiménez Sánchez's study is, I find its approach highly selective and occasionally simplistic; his readings of particular plays are challenged in detail in Chapters 5 and 6.

The only other extensive study of Rodríguez Méndez's theatre is a chapter in César Oliva's *Disidentes de la generación realista: Introducción a la obra de Carlos Muñiz, Lauro Olmo, Rodríguez Méndez y Martín Recuerda* (1979), supported by the companion volume *Cuatro dramaturgos 'realistas' en la escena de hoy: sus contradicciones estéticas* (1978). Oliva focuses productively on theatrical technique and stylistic evolution, but in my view overstates and oversimplifies the argument that there is a clear trajectory from naturalistic realism to *esperpento* – an argument seriously undermined by later developments in the dramatist's work.

The present volume offers the most comprehensive study to date of Rodríguez Méndez's work, and the first to take full account of the author's essays, particularly the crucial *Ensayo sobre el machismo español*. The analysis of the texts is informed by extensive investigation of the cultural and social environment in which they were written, the historical and literary background to plays set in earlier periods, and their staging and reception as evidenced by contemporary reviews and as recalled by the author himself and some of the people who have directed productions.

A further distinctive feature of my approach is its frequent reference to the evidence contained in censorship files, which throws fascinating light on the reception of the texts within the Franco regime and on the processes and circumstances that had a devastating effect on the development of Rodríguez Méndez's career in the late 1960s and early 1970s. Studies of theatre during the dictatorship have always made assumptions about the impact of censorship on the writing and staging of plays; investigation of the censors' reports reveals exactly what they thought about the texts and why they banned, cut or allowed them.[3] The Francoist system of censorship, set up during the war under the 1938 Ley de Prensa (Press Law) and extended in the post-war years to police all forms of publication, performance, broadcasting and public utterance, was strict and all-embracing. Newspapers and magazines were subject to tight controls affecting all stages of the newsgathering and publishing process. No book could be published without prior approval (until 1966), and the importation and translation of texts published abroad was strictly controlled. Film scripts required approval before production could start and prior to distribution; in the case of foreign cinema, dialogue was censored during dubbing and offending images, usually of a sexual nature, were cut.

The criteria for censorship were political, religious and moral. Material likely to be censored for political reasons included direct or implied criticism of the regime and the outcomes of its policies; expressions of rebellion against authority or rejection of patriotism; indications of sympathy for the Republic, for non-Spanish nationalisms or for liberal and left-wing ideologies. The untouchability of ecclesiastical institutions and teachings was ensured by a substantial contingent of censors appointed by the Church, and most censors paid obsessive attention to defending the public against eroticism and bad language. In the last ten years of the dictatorship the moral and religious factors began to be given less weight, while challenges to the political criteria were becoming more frequent and were being handled increasingly erratically. The Ley de Prensa introduced by Manuel Fraga in 1966 liberalized the system in so far as it removed the requirement for approval prior to publication and abolished press directives, but resulted in an increase in prosecutions against publishers who misjudged what they would be able to get away with.[4]

Until 1963, theatre censorship was governed by the law of 15 July 1939 which laid down regulations based on those already established for book and film censorship. Prior approval was required for all forms of performance: the producer would submit an application declaring the genre of the proposed production and providing details of the cast and venue, accompanied by three copies of the script. Falangists, priests, writers, theatre critics, journalists, military officers and others were employed as readers to produce reports summarizing the action of each play, commenting on specific aspects ('literary value', 'theatrical value', 'political implications' and 'religious implications'), and recommending one of the following verdicts:

1. Autorizada para todos los públicos.
2. Autorizada para mayores de ... años.
3. Autorizada únicamente para sesiones de cámara.
4. Prohibida.[5]

If authorization was recommended, the censor was required to mark any cuts or amendments considered necessary, and specify whether permission was subject to an inspection of the dress rehearsal. Censors often underlined this last condition if they suspected that problematic details might become more conspicuous or be introduced in performance. The inspection of the dress rehearsal by an official of the ministry could result in the last-minute banning of a show and the loss of all the effort and money invested in it.

My analysis of censorship reports on Rodríguez Méndez's plays will show that as well as following the political, religious and moral priorities set out above, the censors also tended to be concerned with aesthetic criteria. Seeing their role as a positive one of promoting high quality, they set themselves the task of rescuing promising but flawed scripts by suppressing material that would have spoiled them, while ensuring that badly written plays were not inflicted on the public: 'Aunque a muchos pueda parecerles sorprendente, la verdadera misión de esta Censura es creadora' (González Ruiz 1987: 173).[6] The trouble was that these aesthetic judgements were not properly distinguished from the other criteria, and tended to be highly subjective and conditioned by very conventional assumptions about theatrical genres. It was not necessarily a matter of rejecting innovation – some censors were well disposed to experimental theatre in principle – but of being suspicious of texts that did not fit neatly into generic categories. Such nervousness about ambiguity obstructed performances of several of Rodríguez Méndez's plays.

Reforms introduced by Manuel Fraga in 1963 brought greater consistency and transparency to the process by setting up a new Junta de Censura Teatral (Board of Theatre Censorship), which was required to carry out fuller consultation amongst its members. This did not make theatre censorship any less restrictive, but the resulting disagreements did in some cases bring out the contradictions and arbitrariness inherent in the system, as we shall see when we look at the impact of censorship on some of Rodríguez Méndez's plays, especially *Historia de unos cuantos*. Although the 1966 Ley de Prensa brought a slight loosening of control over the publishing industry, it did not remove the requirement for prior approval of theatrical productions. In practice, the political uncertainties of the last year or so of Franco's dictatorship and the high turnover at the top of the Ministerio de Información y Turismo between 1974 and 1977 meant that the system was already beginning to break down some time before the formal abolition of censorship in January 1978. Responsibility for censorship passed in 1977 to the new Ministerio de Cultura set up by Adolfo Suárez, who had begun to introduce liberalizing measures soon after coming to power in July 1976, resulting in the overturning of bans that had been in force for years. The institution of censorship did not disappear altogether in 1978, however. For another seven years many of the former members of the Junta de Censura Teatral continued to work as censors within the Ministerio de Cultura. Their task now, in a period marked by an explosion of sexual permissiveness in Spanish culture (*el destape*, literally 'uncovering'), was limited to the setting of minimum age limits for theatre and other performances, and it was clear that few of the standards previously applied were relevant any longer.

The book does not assume extensive knowledge of the Spanish language or of Spanish theatre and culture. All terms and cultural references are explained, and translations of quotations in Spanish are given in the notes at the end of each chapter.

The research for this book has been supported in invaluable ways by the University of Durham, the Arts and Humanities Research Council and the British Academy. I am grateful to the staff at the Archivo General de la Administración in Alcalá de Henares, who have always provided willing and cheerful assistance to my searches through the censorship files (and struggles to decipher the handwriting of censors who did not have access to a typewriter). My thanks also go to John Lyon, who first set me off on this journey, and, above all, to José María Rodríguez Méndez, whose friendship and unwavering support have been educational and inspirational.

Notes

1. 'There are moments when you realize that the real transition, the transition to a normal democracy, hasn't taken place yet. We passed from the silence of Francoism to the icy silence of a democracy with too many things to be kept unsaid, too many ghosts it was better not to wake, although perhaps it was less to do with real fears than with particular interests that couldn't always be owned up to. The fact is that our recent history hasn't been talked about much, as if looking back might make us lose our way on the road to progress. This has led to authors like José María Rodríguez Méndez, who should have been at the heart of the resurgence of Spanish drama after Franco, being forgotten.' All translations from Spanish are my own.
2. For general assessments of Rodríguez Méndez's work, see Blanco Aguinaga et al. (1983: 222–41); Oliva (1989: 221-26, 284–94); Pedraza Jiménez & Rodríguez Cáceres (1995: 301–46); Pérez-Stansfield (1983: 111–62, 231–47); Ragué-Arias (1996: 23, 29–32); Rebollo Sánchez (1994); Ruiz Ramón (1989: 487-90, 509-16); and Miras (2005). For biographical information, see Martín Recuerda (1979), Jiménez Sánchez (1998) and Thompson (2004b).
3. Theatre censors' reports can be consulted in the Archivo General de la Administración at Alcalá de Henares (Sección de Cultura).
4. Useful studies of the censorship of various media during the dictatorship include: Abellán (1987), Neuschäfer (1994), Labanyi (1995a), Gubern (1981), Sinova (1989). On theatre censorship: Martínez-Michel (2003), Thompson (2004a), O'Leary (2005) and Muñoz Cáliz (2005). Writers' responses to censorship are discussed in Perriam et al. (2000: 3–6, 15–17 and 118–25).
5. '1. Authorized for audiences of all ages. 2. Authorized for audiences over … years of age. 3. Authorized exclusively for studio productions. 4. Prohibited.'
6. 'Although it may appear surprising to many people, the true mission of this [Department of] Censorship is a creative one.' The document is reproduced without a date in Abellán (1987); I am grateful to Derek Gagen for pointing out that it was originally published in Nicolás González Ruiz's *La cultura española en los últimos veinte años: El Teatro* (Madrid: S. Aguirre, 1949).

1

DRAMATIZING SPANISHNESS

José María Rodríguez Méndez first achieved national recognition in Spain with the success of his play *Los inocentes de la Moncloa* in Barcelona in 1961 and Madrid in 1964. He was one of the authors identified by José Monleón as forming a new, dissident *Generación Realista* (Realist Generation): a group of playwrights aiming to represent the social reality of Spain in ways that were unprecedentedly direct and hard-hitting (Monleón 1962).[1] Rodríguez Méndez, José Martín Recuerda, Lauro Olmo and Carlos Muñiz (all born in the mid-1920s) had begun their writing careers in a theatrical world that was 'extremadamente pobre, chato y provinciano' (Rodríguez Méndez 1987: 5).[2] The theatrical mainstream of the 1940s and 1950s was socially conformist and aesthetically conventional. Its characteristic products were the continuing success of Jacinto Benavente, who before the civil war of 1936 to 1939, had dominated the bourgeois market for sophisticated comedy and dramas about moral dilemmas; the Benaventine inheritance maintained by Pemán, Luca de Tena and Calvo Sotelo; the trivial comedies of Torrado, López Rubio and Ruiz Iriarte; the endlessly successful but formulaic comedies of Alfonso Paso.[3] Above all, the everyday experiences of ordinary Spaniards and their memories of the terrible events of the preceding decades were not being represented on stage, partly as a result of draconian censorship but also because these writers and the companies that staged their work had little ambition to do so.

There were signs of change, though, such as the illogical, mildly subversive comedies of Miguel Mihura and Enrique Jardiel Poncela; the early existentialist allegories of Alfonso Sastre and the political dramas that followed in the 1950s; the unsettling absurdism of Fernando Arrabal; and, most influentially, the social tragedies of Antonio Buero Vallejo. The premiere of Buero's *Historia de una escalera* in 1949 has often been hailed as a mould-breaking moment, the beginning of a new era of serious realist theatre.[4] However, Rodríguez Méndez does not accept accounts that present Buero as the precursor or leader of the Realist Generation (1987: 5). He points out that Martín Recuerda's earliest works predate *Historia de una escalera* and

Rodríguez Méndez in Barcelona. *Photograph courtesy of J.M. Rodríguez Méndez.*

stresses the importance of the example of the 'Angry Young Men' of British theatre (1987: 3–4), whose texts were becoming known in Spain by 1960.[5] John Osborne's *Look Back in Anger* was first staged at London's Royal Court Theatre in 1956, and in 1959 a version in Spanish was performed in Madrid and Barcelona. Shelagh Delaney's *A Taste of Honey*, first performed by the Theatre Workshop in 1958, was published in Spanish in the journal *Primer Acto* (no. 20) in 1960. Moreover, Rodríguez Méndez asserts that the Realist Generation's main sources of inspiration go much further back, to the classics of Spain's Golden Age (the sixteenth and seventeenth centuries): 'Eso, más que el realismo – aunque éste venga a ser un importante ingrediente – era lo que a mí me impulsaba cuando empecé mi aventura literaria y creo que a algunos de mis compañeros: hacernos dignos de la gran tradición teatral española' (1987: 5).[6]

For these writers, 'realism' is as much to do with subject-matter and the social function of theatre as with dramatic technique. The works that originally defined the Realist Generation around 1960 are much more diverse in style than the label suggests, and each author developed his own brand of dramatic realism in highly distinctive and imaginative ways in the decades that followed. Ruiz Ramón, while identifying the group's shared commitment to bearing witness truthfully and directly as its defining preoccupation, nevertheless stresses their formal diversity and experimentation:

Su técnica realista de proyectar esa realidad en el escenario no es, por otra parte, ni simple ni pobre, sino compleja y rica en recursos y abierta siempre a la poesía en las situaciones y a la belleza en la expresión, como al humor, a la sátira y a lo grotesco, a la vez trágico y cómico, que trasciende siempre en doble plano de significante y significado el escueto documento (1989: 489).[7]

The authors of the Realist Generation had experienced the civil war as children, young enough to bear no responsibility for events but old enough to retain clear memories of bombardment, rationing, murder and the constant din of propaganda during and after the war. They completed their education and began to work towards establishing themselves as writers during the 1940s. These were hard, violent times in which the majority of the population suffered hunger, deprivation and fear while General Franco's regime exulted in its victory, carried out ruthless retribution against all those who had opposed it, and built an authoritarian state based on a rigid, traditionalist ideology of 'National-Catholicism' tinged with the revolutionary fervour of the Falange.[8] The inherent narrow-mindedness of the dictatorship was exacerbated by the diplomatic and economic isolation imposed on Spain between the end of the World War and the mid-1950s as a result of Franco's alliance with the Axis powers. Rodríguez Méndez evokes this period in which he and his fellow writers were beginning their careers in terms of intellectual frustration and cultural disorientation: at odds with the reactionary, triumphalist nationalism of the regime but resentful of the demonization of Spain by the liberal democracies, they sought ways of expressing 'nuestra derrota de españoles' ('our defeat as Spaniards') which could acknowledge the pain without renouncing a positive sense of national identity.

Soñábamos con incorporarnos a la dura y difícil tarea de levantar en los escenarios la presencia de España, de una España abofeteada y malherida. [...] Los 'redaños' de Iberia estaban sepultados y era vergonzoso sacarlos a la luz. Vergonzoso para aquellos que, de una manera directa o indirecta, los habían emponzoñado, y tratarán siempre de ocultarlos, mediante la exhibición de retablos más 'decorosos' y, por supuesto, confortables para ellos (Rodríguez Méndez 1969: 37–38).[9]

This summing-up of the representation of Spanishness as *redaños* (bravery, spiritedness, guts) is echoed by Martín Recuerda's definition of the project of the Realist Generation with the term *iberismo* (Iberianism): 'El iberismo, porque la mayor parte de nuestro teatro es violento, desgarrado, cruel, satírico, encerrado muy en sí mismo, orgulloso, vociferante. Piel de toro al rojo vivo, surgido de la tierra en que hemos nacido' (1969: 32).[10] The term *iberismo* is useful as a relatively neutral term connoting a broad pre-national ethnic identity associated with the geographical space of Iberia, as distinct from other similar terms with more specific right-wing connotations. It was used in the early twentieth century by Catalan proponents of a Spanish national identity strengthened by the diversity of the regions, although Martín Recuerda does not explicitly connect his use of the word to that tradition. *Españolismo* (Spanishness) suggests more of an association with the nation as a centralized political entity, while *casticismo* (related to *casta*, breeding) implies ethnic purity or exclusivity and has tended to be applied to Castilla as the supposed core of Spanishness, as articulated in Unamuno's *En torno al casticismo*: 'Lo castellano es, en fin de cuenta, lo castizo' (1943: 47).[11]

Both dramatists continue throughout their careers to emphasize their commitment to writing from within a particular culture, particular historical circumstances and a particular literary and dramatic tradition: 'Mi teatro se refiere siempre a la sociedad española. A la sociedad actual fundamentalmente, pero que a la vez es heredera directa de la sociedad del siglo pasado' (Rodríguez Méndez 1974a: 15).[12] They aim to create theatre that is not only about contemporary Spanish society and its historical roots – exposing truths suppressed by those in power – but also expresses a Spanish cultural identity through its tone, its language and its dramatic forms: 'Yo indago siempre en la piel ibérica, en la España nuestra, para sacar de ahí nuestra verdadera personalidad' (Martín Recuerda interviewed in Isasi Ángulo 1974: 253).[13] For both men, this concept of Spanishness is located primarily in the masses rather than in elite social groups or individuals, and is expressed most authentically in traditional popular culture in opposition to 'high' culture or modern mass-mediated culture. Above all, they see it as a liberating and empowering force, giving individuals a rooted sense of identity in a world becoming increasingly homogenized. A key term – roughly synonymous with *iberismo* – used by Rodríguez Méndez to sum up Spanish identity as embodied in popular culture is *machismo español*, a notion central to the view of the historical relationship between popular and elite cultures in Spain which he sets out in a series of essays. These essays and their theoretical implications will be discussed in detail in the next chapter.

Declarations such as these run a serious risk of oversimplifying complex historical and cultural processes. The problem is lucidly discussed in theoretical works by the playwright Alfonso Sastre, who argues from a Marxist standpoint for a dialectical 'realismo profundo' ('deep realism') capable of penetrating beneath the detailed texture of everyday life in order to represent 'la estructura de la sociedad y de la historia como totalidad' (1974: 145).[14] Since Sastre seeks ways of representing reality in terms of its underlying political and ideological structures, he advocates the avoidance of an unselfconscious naturalism that aims to reproduce the surface appearance of things and actions. Similarly, he advises caution in the use of realist representational strategies that are designed to reproduce cultural environments but amount to little more than artificial 'populismo' and are liable to act as unhelpful 'mixtificaciones del realismo' (1974: 95), including specifically Spanish settings, character types reminiscent of traditional popular comedies, and conspicuously colloquial language imitating particular dialects.[15] He argues that for as long as literature (and theatre in print and on stage) remains a relatively expensive commodity consumed almost exclusively by the middle classes, the sacrifice of literary style and intellectual substance involved in the imitation of proletarian or peasant speech patterns (usually by writers from middle-class backgrounds) is pointless: 'populist' literature offers its bourgeois readers 'una imagen de la realidad obrera, campesina y sub-proletaria, que [...] resulta pueril, falsamente patética o simplemente costumbrista (1974: 99).[16]

Sastre's wariness about the feasibility of representing the everyday life, cultural practices and idioms of the *pueblo* authentically and keeping them in critical perspective is shared by other critics. Monleón, for example, suggests that the dialogue in Rodríguez Méndez's plays is often 'amanerado' and that there is 'cierta retórica populista' in *Los quinquis de Madriz* (1968a: 53). Rodríguez Méndez is convinced, however, that he remains in touch with real popular culture. He and Martín Recuerda never renounce the importance of historical, cultural and linguistic specificity and are not afraid to use references to cultural forms that may be regarded as tainted by *costumbrismo* or by association with the manipulation of folklore by right-wing nationalsim. Rodríguez Méndez rejects suggestions that there is anything artificial about the colloquial language in his plays and insists that its authenticity is validated by his first-hand experience of the speech communities he portrays: 'Estas frases de las *Bodas*, de *Flor de Otoño*, son escuchadas en la calle. [...] Lo que pasa es que los críticos no callejean tanto como yo' (interview of April 1984, in Thompson 1989: 425–26).[17] He avoids the comic exaggeration with which some *sainetes* and *zarzuelas* ridicule their characters, especially the use of pretentious malapropisms and over-correction of grammatical anomalies.[18] As we shall see in our discussion of the plays in subsequent chapters, the main factors protecting his realism from populist 'mixtificación' are a very unsentimental sense of irony and the attention he pays to the political and cultural contexts in which he sets his characters and situations.

The Spanishness that the Realist Generation place at the heart of their aesthetic has been criticized from a different angle by the playwrights of the *Nuevo Teatro Español* (New Spanish Theatre), the symbolist avant-garde that became influential in the late 1960s (though it had been been anticipated by Fernando Arrabal and – in Catalan – by Salvador Espriu, Joan Brossa and Manuel de Pedrolo). Working alongside the performance groups that made up what came to be known as the Teatro Independiente movement and drawing on various influences from outside Spain, Francisco Nieva, José Ruibal, Luis Riaza, Alberto Miralles, Jerónimo López Mozo, Manuel Martínez Mediero and other playwrights experimented in various ways with symbolism, ritual, metatheatre, political allegory, the fragmentation of character and plot, and various non-naturalistic techniques inspired by Brecht, Artaud, Valle-Inclán, the Theatre of the Absurd, the Living Theatre, Grotowski and a cosmopolitan counterculture of pacifism, anti-Francoism, rock music and 'happenings'.[19] Most of the writers of the New Theatre explicitly define their work as anti-realist, rejecting geographical, cultural and historical specificity as a limiting factor that ties 'testimonial' theatre to the circumstances in which it is conceived. Ruibal, the most articulate proponent of theatre conceived as a 'totalidad poética' ('poetic totality') which creates its own verisimilitude, aims for a 'teatro sin Pirineos' ('theatre without Pyrenees') as a way of achieving enduring significance: his aim is to deal with general concepts rather than particular circumstances, and to 'trazar una síntesis poética, global por tanto, que atraviese el túnel o si se quiere la frontera del tiempo' (1984: 20).[20]

Ruibal also makes a political case against the cultivation of Spanishness, suggesting that it amounts to complicity with the reactionary chauvinism of Francoism and arguing that however critical *iberismo* may be of existing political and social structures, by using a discourse that has been manipulated to such an extent by the regime it risks falling into a 'trampa nacionalista' ('nationalist trap') (1977: 113). In this analysis, theatre that offers its audiences familiar images of their world can only promote passivity, while theatre that radically disrupts and defamiliarizes their perception of social reality is capable of stimulating greater awareness and prompting change.

Increasingly feeling that realism was being displaced by the methods of the *vanguardia*, Rodríguez Méndez published a series of virulent attacks on the New Theatre during the late 1960s and early 1970s, in *Ensayo sobre la 'inteligencia' española*, *Comentarios impertinentes sobre el teatro español* and *La incultura teatral en España*. He responds to the charge of reactionary localism by accusing the new dramatists of simply copying foreign trends. Alberto Miralles, one of the fiercest critics of the realists, has recently acknowledged that there was a tendency amongst the self-proclaimed avant-garde to 'adorar e imitar, con papanatismo deleitoso, todo lo que fuera extranjero, sin pensar en una creación propia' (2001: 186).[21] One of the results of this *colonización* (cultural colonialism) in Rodríguez Méndez's view is that the authors of the New Theatre 'siguen tan fielmente los modelos que hasta destrozan el lenguaje castellano [...] para que pierda toda jugosidad verbal y pueda identificarse con cualquier otro texto traducido y encontrado en otros países de tercera' (1972b: 100).[22]

The ideal of a 'lenguaje planetario' ('planetary language') formulated by Ruibal strikes Rodríguez Méndez as artificial and baroque. He contends that the most serious problem of language in the modern world is not so much the calculated manipulation of it to rationalize the essentially irrational as a general impoverishment: that the colourless, standardized vocabulary of technology, business and the leisure industry, efficiently disseminated by television, suppresses cultural individuality and invades literature. He concludes that the New Theatre, by incorporating the language of the mass media into an already artificial theatrical idiom, contributes to the dehumanization of language rather than combating it and, by sacrificing the representation of social reality to formal experimentation, ends up supporting the status quo and discouraging critical awareness.[23] In this context, grounding dramatic language in the authentic popular speech of particular communities becomes all the more important as an antidote to cultural homogeneity; dramatizing some form of concrete identity – national, regional or local – is a way of holding onto cultural distinctiveness.

Rodríguez Méndez's preoccupation with Spanish identity needs to be considered, therefore, in relation to three historical contexts: the development of competing nationalisms in Spain up to the 1930s, the Franco regime's attempt to consolidate by force an archaic and highly centralized Spanish nationalism between 1936 and 1975, and reactions against the Francoist project during and after the dictatorship.

When modern nationalisms as defined by Benedict Anderson (1991) – political projects based upon the cultural construction of 'imagined communities' – were emerging in nineteenth-century Europe, Spain was still characterized to a large extent by the survival of a traditionalist 'pre-national Spanish identity' founded upon the pre-eminence of Castilian as an administrative and intellectual lingua franca, reactionary religious uniformity, the standardization of legal and political institutions following Castilian models, and the involvement of people from all parts of Spain in the imperial project (Beramendi 2000: 80). The development of a centralized, reformist state under the Bourbons in the eighteenth century had encouraged the emergence of a Spanish 'proto-nationalism' (in which patriotism was beginning to be identified with the state more than with the monarchy itself), while opening up tensions between modernization and traditionalist aspects of the pre-national identity. This proto-nationalism, strengthened by the consequences of the Napoleonic invasion, gave rise to the liberal nationalism reflected in the 1812 Constitution (which contributed to the growth of independence movements in Spain's American colonies), yet its further development was impeded first by an absolutist counter-revolution reaffirming the pre-national identity and later by socio-economic underdevelopment. By 1868 the monarchy had been thoroughly discredited, but the First Republic of 1873 and 1874 was torn apart by conflict between radical federalists and a central government struggling to maintain order without a clear unifying discourse. The Bourbon Restoration that killed off the Republic at the end of 1874 promised economic and political stability, using the monarchy as a focus of national identity while subjecting it to the control of parliamentary constitutionalism. However, the liberalism of the Restoration regime was too cautious to prevent the growth of various reformist, revolutionary and centrifugal movements. The Spanish nationalism that consolidated itself in the late nineteenth century was therefore an unstable compromise between tradition and modernity: 'The final synthesis was therefore internally divided and conflictive, not only in an ideological-political sense (which was inevitable), but also in terms of identity' (Beramendi 2000: 84).

In the meantime, regional identities had survived, maintaining linguistic, cultural and institutional differences to varying degrees. The consolidation of ethnic pre-national identities had coincided with empire-building and in general did not challenge the authority of the Hapsburg state (apart from Catalan revolts in pursuit of political independence in the 1640s and 1705 to 1714). Catalan, Basque and Galician were the only regional identities to evolve in the late nineteenth century into true nationalisms in the sense expounded by Anderson. The emergence of these nationalisms was driven by various factors: the defence of traditional institutions against the centralized nation-building of the liberal state; economic development and the growth of communications and political mobilization (especially in Catalonia, where the loss of colonial markets caused the bourgeoisie to lose faith in the efficacy of the Spanish state); linguistic and cultural revivals inspired by Romanticism and by new philological theories. Basque nationalism became a largely reactionary separatist movement mythifying racial identity, while Catalanism, driven initially by middle-class interests and later by labour movements, tended to concentrate on building political structures and modernizing cultural and economic institutions, so that by the early twentieth century it had 'generated a widespread, deeply-rooted national consciousness' (Beramendi 2000: 91). Galician nationalism was much slower to develop, remaining politically insignificant until 1931. All three movements drew on reinvented cultural traditions, ideals of linguistic unity, and myths of ethnic origins and golden ages prior to Castilian domination in order to build their imagined communities.[24]

From the 1890s, and especially after the humiliating loss of Spain's colonies in Cuba, Puerto Rico and the Philippines in 1898, the most coherent discourse of Spanish nationalism was regenerationism – the reaffirmation in response to imperial collapse and the challenge of non-state nationalisms of 'an organic *españolismo*, intended to strengthen Spain's demoralized national identity' (Beramendi 2000: 92). Political thought was influenced by writers such as Joaquín Costa, Ricardo Macías Picavea, Rafael Altamira, Lucas Mallada, Francisco Giner de los Ríos and José Ortega y Gasset, who sought explanations for national decline which would be more soundly based in history, philosophy, science and ethnography than the orthodox Catholic narrative of Spain losing touch with her essential Christian destiny. While some of the proposals for regeneration looked towards the democratic and technological advances of northern Europe as a model, there was also a widespread preoccupation with identifying essential national qualities that might provide the foundations for regeneration from within. This search tended to focus primarily on Castilla as the supposed core of Spanishness, though up to the mid-1920s Enric Prat de la Riba's Catalanist party, Lliga Regionalista (later Solidaridad Catalana), argued the opposite: that the best hope for regeneration lay in the strength and diversity of the regional identities within Spain. The political agenda of regenerationism was not homogeneous: the Restoration regime was generally regarded as corrupt, capable of neither effective modernization nor the rediscovery of the cultural values that could lead to renewal, but the proposed programmes ranged from the democratic – embracing dialogue with the non-Spanish nationalisms – to the authoritarian, insisting on the essential unity of the nation-state.

Amongst the regenerationists and the Generation of 1898 there were those whose political instincts were fundamentally progressive and who played an important role in the development of republicanism in Spain.[25] However, the most influential ideas articulated by these groups about race and history were consonant with conservative myths of nationhood and were absorbed in a simplified form into the ideology of the Falange and the traditionalist dogmas of Francoism, as Labanyi (1989: 35–41 and 55–68) and Rodríguez Puértolas (1986: 59–72) demonstrate. Labanyi traces in various regenerationist writers and members of the Generation of 1898 an essentially Romantic urge to 'undo' history and return to origins through the construction of an essential national character, centred on Castilla, marked by intractability and stoical spirituality:

> By explaining Spanish history in terms of a mythical national character, the 1898 writers and their heirs necessarily end up advocating authoritarian solutions, for their appeal to racial determinism supposes that the people are incapable of improving themselves. Racial argument is invoked in a contradictory fashion: on the one hand it is claimed that the essential virtues of the race have been corrupted

by an inauthentic history, on the other it is suggested that the national character is congenitally flawed. In both cases a redeemer is needed to save the nation: the positivist concept of racial determinism leads to the mythical concept of *mesianismo* (1989: 61).

There are clear echoes of some of these late nineteenth-century and early twentieth-century ideas of nationhood and ethnicity in Rodríguez Méndez's plays and essays. The title of the play *El vano ayer* alludes to a poem from Machado's *Campos de Castilla*, *El círculo de tiza de Cartagena* contains references to Machado and Valle-Inclán, and in *Ensayo sobre la 'inteligencia' española* he devotes a chapter to the Generation of 1898: these links are discussed in detail in Chapters 3, 4 and 5. The approach to the representation of history characterized in Chapters 4 and 5 as 'history from below' is similar to Unamuno's notion of *intrahistoria*, which he defines with a metaphor: official, reported history is merely the movement of waves on the surface of the deep, silent sea of the everyday life of the masses (1943: 27–29). To some extent, Rodríguez Méndez's representations of the *pueblo* show a long-suffering population inhabiting a kind of repetitive *intrahistoria*, never benefiting from the convulsions taking place on the surface of public history, eternally distrustful of political agendas, clinging to folk traditions. However, collective identity is represented in terms of cultural practices rather than racial essences, and the classic nationalist myths are not reinforced but challenged: there is no evocation of a 'golden age' in the past, no rejection of history as a process of 'inauthentic' deviation from a true national destiny, and, above all, no call for an enlightened elite or messianic leader to 'save' the nation and recover that destiny.

Ultimately, Rodríguez Méndez's approach is sceptical, resistant to mythification and ideological inflexibility. If he repeats the regenerationists' and 1898 Generation's condemnation of the stagnation of the bourgeois Restoration, he does not see the problem as one of a lack of leadership over the increasingly insubordinate masses, as Ortega proposes in *España invertebrada* (1921): 'Cuando en una nación la masa se niega a ser masa – esto es, a seguir a la minoría directiva, – la nación se deshace, la sociedad se desmembra, y sobreviene el caos social, la invertebración histórica. Un caso extremo de esta invertebración histórica estamos ahora viviendo en España' (Ortega 1947: 93).[26] It is, rather, a simpler matter of the ruling class's indifference to the interests of the people: 'Las riendas del país, pese a la Gloriosa, eran llevadas por unos cuantos, mientras que el pueblo [...] quedaba a su albur, sin tener arte ni parte en los avatares de nuestra historia' (Rodríguez Méndez 1972b: 16).[27] While he might accept Ortega's suggestion that Spain's historical evolution has lacked outstanding individual contributions – everything has been done by the *pueblo* – he does not see this in the negative terms expressed by Ortega and would not go along with the argument that 'una nación no puede ser sólo "pueblo": necesita una minoría egregia, como un cuerpo vivo no es sólo músculo, sino, además, ganglio nervioso y centro cerebral' (Ortega 1947: 121).[28] The core of Rodríguez Méndez's plays and essays is the idea that the nation is the *pueblo*; when he focuses on prominent individuals (as in the plays discussed in Chapter 6), the emphasis is not on elite leadership but on the extent to which they are in tune with popular culture.

After the temporary ascendancy of authoritarian Spanish nationalism under the dictatorship of Miguel Primo de Rivera (1923–30), the Republic established in 1931 made a well-meaning attempt to achieve a compromise between the Spanish state and the three non-state nationalisms by means of a semi-federal structure. Article 1 of the 1931 Constitution defines Spain as a democratic workers' Republic based on principles of Liberty and Justice, which 'constituye un Estado integral, compatible con la autonomía de los Municipios y las Regiones' (cited in De la Granja et al. 2001: 297).[29] This did not fully satisfy the demands of any of the competing movements, but did 'begin to transform the dynamics of head-on antagonism into a possible – albeit conflictive – coexistence between Spanish (democratic) nationalism and the other nationalisms' (Beramendi 2000: 93). However, one of the weaknesses of the republican project that contributed to its disintegration was its neglect of the construction of a new version of Spanish nationalism:

> 1930s republicans [...] tended to assume that the republican nation already existed. Blind to the multiple local frames of meaning which underlay the popular celebrations of the fall of the monarchy in April 1931, they failed to understand the need actively to take on the political and cultural task of 'making the nation', as a dynamic project *vis-à-vis* the future (Graham 1996: 135–36).

The nationalism expounded by José Antonio Primo de Rivera as the core principle of the Falange (founded in 1933) was fiercely opposed to the semi-federal compromise, reaffirming Ortega's idea of the nation as an abstract mission or sense of destiny that brings together neighbouring peoples under inspirational leadership (but shifting the emphasis from moral and intellectual authority to messianic authoritarianism).[30] Primo plays down the contribution of 'spontaneous' ethnic factors (birth, inheritance, language, folk culture, topography) to the definition of nationhood, dismissing 'Romantic' concepts of the nation based on such factors as merely primitive, local and emotional:

> A people is not a nation because of anything physical or any local colour and flavour, but because it is 'another' in universal terms; that is to say, because its destiny is not that of other nations. Thus, not every people constitutes a nation, nor do all groups of peoples, but only those which accomplish a specific destiny in universal terms (Primo de Rivera 1972: 102).

This sense of a national destiny is equated by Primo with a unified authoritarian state, which inspires patriotic loyalty by transcending 'the disintegrating effect of local nationalisms' (103) and subsuming social, ideological and regional differences within a larger ideal: a *Patria* in harmony with Spain's unique historical mission, which demands sacrifices and obedience but promises a purer, more spiritual and universal form of collective identity than that offered by the insipid, bureaucratic relativism of liberal democracy or the fractious, vindictive materialism of socialism.

Primo's notion of Spain as 'una unidad de destino en lo universal' ('a body united by a universal destiny') was incorporated into the traditionalist nationalism of the Franco regime, but progressively emptied of its revolutionary implications.[31] Behind stirring Falangist rhetoric of charismatic leadership, youthful vigour, ascetic spirituality, cathartic cleansing and social transformation, Franco presided over a highly conservative restoration of the traditional hegemony of the Catholic Church, the armed forces, landowners and industrialists.[32] The nationalism that defined and united the coalition of forces that won the civil war of 1936 to 1939 was an extreme example of what Anderson terms 'official nationalism' – designed to preserve the territorial unity and centralized administration of a multi-ethnic state in response to the threat posed by separatist nationalisms within it. It incorporated deliberately archaic elements of 'dynastic' pre-nationalism: Catholicism as the eternal essence of Spanishness; Castilian as a kind of sacred universal language ('the language of Empire'); the divine right of monarchy absorbed into the cult of the military Caudillo ('by the grace of God'). This archaism was vividly enacted in the elaborate rituals and symbols favoured by the regime, especially in the so-called 'blue' period up to 1946: the obligatory raised-arm salute and the Falange anthem 'Cara al sol' ('Facing the Sun'); ostentatious parades blending military and religious pageantry; memorials to José Antonio and the other 'martyrs' of the civil war; the ubiquitous emblem of the yoke and arrows, derived from the arms of the Catholic Monarchs, Isabel and Fernando; men, women and children everywhere in uniform; heroic art and monumental architecture.[33] The 'undoing' of history – its immobilization and rewriting as national myth – was therefore crucial to the legitimization of the regime, as Labanyi (citing Bernard Lewis) argues:

> Revolutions and invasions have a special need to disguise their illegitimacy as 'usurpers' by spawning a historiography that postulates their descent from – and return to – some lost founding tradition, which they claim had been 'usurped' by their predecessors: the mythohistoriography of the Franco regime is a perfect example (1989: 33).

The regime's vision of national history combined the most reactionary elements of regenerationist theories with traditional Catholic orthodoxy, celebrating particular periods as divinely ordained stages in a national and imperial destiny, and using selected heroes of the past – El Cid, Columbus, the Catholic Monarchs, the conquistadors – as the focus for ideals of *Patria* (Fatherland), *Raza* (Race) and *Hispanidad* (a transatlantic community of Spanish-speaking peoples), usually directly linked with the personality cult of the *Caudillo* or with the memory of José Antonio Primo de Rivera. The myth of an eternal Spanish identity was projected right back to the earliest history of the Iberian Peninsula, assuming a more or less unified Celtic culture in pre-Roman times and considering the Roman occupation not so much the Romanization of Hispania as the Hispanicization of the Romans. The Gothic settlers of the fifth century and the Islamic invaders of the eighth were also supposedly absorbed into the Iberian essence, civilized and spiritualized by their contact with it. The patchwork of Christian kingdoms of the medieval period was then merely a transitional phase, destined in the course of the common struggle against Islam to give rise to the formation of a single nation, united by a single faith and led by Castilla. The mythology of this Crusade bound permanently together the elements of military conquest, religious unification and formation of the state, culminating in the reign of the Catholic Monarchs, who captured the last Muslim stronghold in 1492, brought together the kingdoms of Castilla and Aragón, and expelled the Jews from their united Christian realm.

The next stage is the expansion of the national destiny into a universal one. By providential coincidence, 1492 also marks the beginning of empire: the nation forged and sanctified by the Reconquest is chosen by God to carry the true faith into the new world. The high point of this heroic narrative – symbolized by the monastery palace of the Escorial – is the reign of Felipe II, when Spain controls Portugal as well as a European and American empire, plays the leading role in the Counter-Reformation and enjoys a cultural golden age. The subsequent decline was seen as having been brought about largely by foreign treachery and pernicious liberal ideas, distracting Spain from its Christian mission, eroding the authority of the Church and fomenting social turmoil, the ultimate humiliation being the loss of the last colonies in 1898. The only suitable manifestation of patriotism to be found in the intervening centuries was in the war against France (1808–14), simplified into a popular struggle for independence against Napoleon and his liberal-masonic collaborators within Spain. The Second Republic of 1931 was condemned for having threatened the very foundations of Church, State, family and traditional values, in response to which the military rebellion of 1936 had set in motion a new crusade that had saved Spain from anarchy and heresy.

Franco was therefore credited with leading the Spanish people to the rediscovery of their historic destiny and true identity, which were defined by national unity under firm leadership, dedication to spiritual values, and the sacred mission of propagating those values to the rest of mankind. Catholicism was therefore the unquestionable core of Spanishness: 'Ser cristiano y ser español es una y la misma cosa, porque España es el único país de la Historia donde no puede haber ni ha habido ni hay diferencia alguna entre la constitución moral y religiosa y la constitución histórica nacional' (Manuel García Morente, *Ser y vida del caballero cristiano* (Madrid, 1945), quoted in Rodríguez Puértolas 1987: 993–94).[34] The early 1940s even seemed to offer the possibility, on the back of Hitler's successes, of repeating the leap from domestic crusade to imperial expansion. For a short time, Falangists relished heady fantasies not only of the restoration of spiritual and cultural *Hispanidad* but of real conquest.[35]

Clearly, the ideas, myths and symbolism of Francoist nationalism were not new. What was new was the triumphalism with which they were now imposed and tied inescapably to an autocratic, militarized state structure: 'Sólo existe una nación cuando tiene: un Jefe, un Ejército que la guarda y un Pueblo que la asiste. Nuestra Cruzada demostró que tenemos el Jefe y el Ejército. Ahora necesitamos el pueblo, y éste no existe más que cuando logra tener unidad y disciplina' (Francisco Franco in a speech of 1942, quoted in Blanco Aguinaga et al. 1979: 74).[36] Spanish nationalists were no longer lamenting the decline of Spain but trumpeting its permanent salvation, claiming that history had been brought full circle, the apotheosis had been reached, no other discourse was conceivable. Military victory had resolved all arguments about the identity and destiny of the nation, and the violent purging of the enemies of that destiny continued long after the end of hostilities in March 1939. Those found guilty of supporting the Republic militarily, politically or intellectually were executed, imprisoned or forced out of their jobs, and the cultural legacy of those who had fled into exile was systematically denigrated and suppressed. The vision was brutally Manichaean, imposing exclusive categories of Spain and anti-Spain, *vencedores* and *vencidos*, Christian civilization and communist (or Jewish or masonic) barbarism, Iberian spirituality and foreign materialism, unity and disintegration, order and chaos, obedience and treachery, good and evil.

The victors of the civil war were particularly determined to punish the non-Spanish nationalisms, condemning them as a sickness to be eradicated (Richards 1996: 158). The statutes of autonomy established under the Republic were abolished and a highly centralized state administration was put in place. The Catalan, Basque and Galician languages were treated as inferior dialects; their use was denounced as unpatriotic and eliminated from official business, the communications media and public utterances. Publications and theatrical productions in these languages were completely banned until 1946, and continued to be tightly restricted until the mid-1960s. Many regional symbols and customs were banned, yet at the same time the regime (especially through the Falange, in line with its idealization of traditional rural life) encouraged forms of folk culture that could be separated from nationalist sentiments, claiming to celebrate a degree of cultural diversity while in practice ruthlessly subordinating it to the political ideal of the *Patria*. Luis Díaz points out that such manipulation of folk culture by governments or nationalist movements is not an uncommon phenomenon, but suggests that Francoist Spain was an extreme case, using folklore 'como almacén de trajes, bailes y canciones que, para decirlo en la jerga de entonces, "contribuía a dar brillante y variopinto colorido a la indisoluble unidad de la Patria"' (Díaz 1989: 99).[37]

The official nationalism constructed by the regime was also bound up with its isolationist economic policies, conditioned by and contributing to autarky: 'Economic protectionism, integrist Catholicism and a bastardised form of regenerationism combined with fascistic and militaristic ideas about punishment and social engineering to produce a nationalist creed which was above all violent and repressive' (Richards 1996: 164). Nationalism, or more specifically, *nacionalcatolicismo*, therefore embraced all the concerns – ideological, cultural, religious, moral, military and economic – of the otherwise disparate coalition of forces that made up the 'families' of Francoism, constituting a monolithic, hierarchical model of identity within which the regime set out to subsume all other identities.

Spanish society was defined as a 'vertical' structure, which meant that all allegiances and processes of identification were to operate in relation to the state, along the strictly hierarchical axis of patriotism, rather than along a horizontal axis of solidarity through participation in political parties, trade unions or other associations. The individual was seen primarily as a member of a family with a structure that matched that of the state, under the absolute authority of the father.[38] The family, in turn, was subject to the moral supervision of the Church, not only at worship but also at school and through Catholic community organizations. In parallel, boys and girls were inducted into the service of the *Patria* through Falange youth organizations, followed by military service for young men and social service for young women through the Sección Femenina. Workers and employers were integrated into *sindicatos verticales*, supposedly eliminating class conflict by subordinating the interests of both parties to patriotism. Public administration at local, provincial and national levels was bound together by the Movimiento Nacional (the single party formed by Franco as a way of absorbing the Falange into the state), backed up by the armed forces. And at the top of the pyramid of national identity, the dictator was not only immovably installed as head of state, government, armed forces and Movimiento, but also idealized as father of the nation, patriotic hero and model of Catholic piety.

The centrality of the family to the Francoist conception of social structure and national identity meant an insistence on rigidly fixed gender roles. The cultures of the armed forces and the Falange idealized strength and virility as national characteristics regained thanks to the crusade that had restored the backbone to *la España invertebrada*. The identity of women was defined exclusively with reference to their subordinate position within the Catholic family. Through the Church, the education system and the Sección Femenina, the regime 'promoted an "ideal" image of womanhood as "eternal", passive, pious, pure, submissive woman-as-mother for whom self-denial was the only road to real fulfilment' (Graham 1995: 184). This conditioning was materially enforced by a range of legal and economic measures designed to keep women at home devoting themselves primarily to childcare: 'The Franco regime's object, similar to that of Italian and German fascism, was to obliterate women as independent social beings' (Graham 1995: 184).[39]

The education system was purged of the liberal, secular values (and personnel) associated with the Republic, and placed in the hands of the Church and the Falange with the task of perpetuating the hegemony of *nacionalcatolicismo*: 'Sin duda, el franquismo realizó el más poderoso intento adoctrinador de toda nuestra historia' (Cámara Villar 1997: 16).[40] In addition to the daily diet of explicit *formación política* (political training), the teaching of all subjects was tailored to the orthodoxies of Catholicism, patriotism and authoritarianism. The patriotic lessons for the young to be drawn from history were insistently spelled out.[41] Children were exhorted by textbooks to follow the example of the heroes of the distant past, reproduced in the heroes of the recent past and the present (José Antonio and Franco), 'cumpliendo fielmente las consignas del Gobierno y cultivando las virtudes morales y religiosas que hicieron famosos a nuestros antepasados en los tiempos imperiales' (Álvarez Pérez 1959: 607).[42] Primary school children were obliged to learn by heart and recite the responses contained in the *Catecismo patriótico español* to questions on the spirit and destiny of the Spanish people, the centrality of Catholicism to the identity of

Spain, linguistic and political unity, the glories of empire, national emblems, and the justification of the totalitarian nature of the state. How was the spirit of the Spanish people formed? 'El espíritu del pueblo español se ha formado en los amplios moldes del catolicismo, con los ideales supremos de una catolicidad imperial, que es la que ha civilizado al mundo' (Menéndez-Reigada 2003: 38).[43] What are the characteristic qualities of the Spanish people? 'Las notas que caracterizan al pueblo español son la religiosidad, la honradez, el señorío, el espíritu de sacrificio y el entusiasmo por todo lo grande y elevado' (2003: 39).[44] The essential qualities of Spanishness were supposedly already established in the culture of the ancient Celtiberians, and even the Muslims could be absorbed into the myth of eternal *Hispanidad*: 'Toda aquella civilización maravillosa es española; españoles sus libros, sus sabios, sus guerreros, sus artistas, sus poetas' (F. T. D. 1940: 302).[45]

Although much of this rhetoric belongs to the Falangist heyday of the 1940s, the materials and approaches used in Spanish schools changed very little until the late 1960s, as Cámara Villar (1997: 15) and Abós Santabárbara (2003: 375–76) emphasize. The famous Álvarez encyclopedias played such a prominent part in the early lives of several generations of Spaniards that a facsimile edition was published in 1997. Rodríguez Méndez's own recollections of secondary school in Barcelona immediately after the war are not entirely consistent. In an unpublished autobiographical document written in the 1970s, he recalls the Falangist rituals carried out each morning, the daily *consigna* (slogan) read out from the works of José Antonio by the headmaster, and above all the feeling that 'el condicionamiento político se erguía sobre nosotros – profesores y alumnos – como algo determinante e inevitable' (quoted in Jiménez Sánchez 1998: 22, note 12).[46] However, in more recent accounts he makes a point of contesting the new consensus reflected in works such as *El florido pensil*:

> Nunca podré olvidar aquel maravilloso bachillerato que inicié el mismo año de 1939 y concluí en 1945. Porque en aquella época tan dura y denostada tuve a los mejores profesores que nunca soñé. [...] Y me emociona todavía hoy la extraordinaria conducta de aquellos catedráticos de Instituto, procedentes unos del bando victorioso y otros del bando perdedor, pero que sobreponiéndose todos a sus creencias e ideologías particulares se esforzaron en formarnos humanísticamente, sólo humanísticamente, con una dignidad y una valentía que hoy por desgracia han desaparecido. Por eso me río mucho cuando hablan de eso de la *escuela nacional católica* y otras tonterías por el estilo (Rodríguez Méndez 1999: 46).[47]

These remarks are a reminder of the importance of not categorizing Rodríguez Méndez simply as an anti-Franco writer. His plays, journalism and essays written between 1958 and 1975 certainly constitute a powerful critique of aspects of the ideology of Francoism, the social outcomes of its policies and especially its manipulation of history, and as a result many of his plays were censored. After the promising start of the early 1960s, the development of his career was choked off just as he was producing his most impressive mature works. Directors were keen to stage *Bodas que fueron famosas del Pingajo y la Fandanga* (1965), *Los quinquis de Madriz* (1967), *Historia de unos cuantos* (1971) and *Flor de Otoño* (1972), but their attempts were repeatedly blocked or delayed by censorship, with the result that there was no premiere of a Rodríguez Méndez play between 1966 and 1975. Although the attentions of the censors earned him a degree of political credibility as a dissident, investigation of their judgements shows that they were frequently inconsistent and not always related to political factors. Only the blandest material escaped the attentions of the censors altogether, and authors did not need to be explicitly critical of the regime to find their work mutilated or banned. On learning recently of the contents of some of the censorship files on his texts, Rodríguez Méndez has declared himself to be surprised that the censors could have considered his work such a threat. He clearly believes that theatre has a social function, a responsibility to 'establecer una cierta radiografía de la sociedad en que me ha tocado la gracia de vivir' (1968b: 17) ('to produce a kind of X-ray of the society in which I find myself'), and my analysis of plays in Chapters 3 to 6 aims to show exactly what they imply about Francoism and how the censors interpreted their political relevance. At the same time, however, he resists the ideological instrumentalization of theatre:

> No creo en el teatro político, en el estricto sentido de la palabra. Me parece tan vacuo hacer una apología del marxismo como hacerla del fascismo. Me parece también absurdo pretender que el teatro sea un arma progresiva, cuando la realidad es multiforme y están en juego fuerzas activas y reactivas (1968d: 99).[48]

It was not only the effect of censorship that politicized Rodríguez Méndez's work during the Franco period. He also felt the need to resist left-wing demands that works of art should articulate clear ideological positions, regarding such pressure as a form of unofficial censorship and insisting that his theatre 'siempre ha carecido de tendencia política determinada' (1977: 93–94).[49] The picture that will emerge from discussion of his essays and plays, therefore, is politically ambiguous. The defence of Spanishness and the Spanish language risks complicity with right-wing nationalism (as indicated in the remarks by Sastre and Ruibal quoted earlier), but that Spanishness is represented as an identity embodied in the common people, always opposed to the political establishment and to political control. An instinctive sympathy for the poor, the oppressed, the marginalized and the powerless is a constant feature of his work, and yet there is at the same time a pervasive cynicism about political solutions to social problems, and an absence of characters endowed with a critical understanding of their socio-historical circumstances and a capacity for effective action.

Although the Franco regime's deployment of repressive and persuasive forces may sound overwhelming, it must be acknowledged that in the long run its effectiveness in winning hearts and minds was limited. Whilst official propaganda continued to celebrate the idea of Spain as the 'spiritual reserve' of Christian civilization and order, keeping itself pure in a world corrupted by communism on the one hand and liberal democracy on the other, in practice the drive towards economic modernization in the 1950s and 1960s had set in motion processes that made that uniqueness impossible to sustain. The Church, prompted by the liberalizing message of the Second Vatican Council (1962–65), began to distance itself from the regime, gradually undermining its claims to legitimacy. The attempt to eradicate ethnolinguistic nationalisms was if anything counterproductive: opposition to the regime coalesced around ETA and expressions of Catalan identity such as the *Nova Cançó*, and Basque and Catalan nationalist sentiments emerged from the dictatorship stronger than ever, while Spanish nationalism was thoroughly discredited, tainted by its association with militarism, religious fundamentalism and intolerance (De la Granja et al. 2001: 166–91). Censorship had a destructive effect on the careers of numerous writers, artists and film-makers, yet provoked an over-politicization of cultural production that was not entirely helpful to the regime. Audiences became hypersensitive to coded suggestions of dissidence, and in some ways the challenge of censorship acted as a creative stimulus, as argued by Neuschäfer (1994). The Francoist vision of history was so obviously partisan and mythified that it never convinced the majority of the population:

> Official history justified the regime as the heir to the 'true' Spanish tradition and as the remedy to more recent historical violations of that tradition, but this definition of Spanish identity was accepted only by those who already accepted the legitimacy of the Franquist state. When this became clear, the regime largely abandoned its efforts to mobilize the masses through history and ritual (Boyd 1989: 189).

Although many accounts of Spain's transition to democracy tend to stress the extraordinary rapidity with which political, social and cultural change took place after 1975, social and economic transformation from the 1960s onwards had combined with a long tradition of intellectual and cultural dissidence to undermine authoritarianism and prepare the ground for democratization.[50] The desire for profound change felt by the vast majority of the Spanish people in 1975 was due in large part to a 'long process of democratic cultural renewal which made the transition possible' (Díaz 1995: 285). There was overwhelming popular support not only for the restoration of political pluralism and civil liberties, but also for the relaxation of moral and religious restrictions and the pursuit of greater social and sexual equality. While the anachronistic rhetoric of *nacionalcatolicismo* could still be heard in the 1980s railing against democratization, secularization and separatism, such voices were increasingly isolated as right-wing political forces distanced themselves from the Francoist legacy and gradually came to terms with the irreversibility of the new situation (including the opportunities offered by decentralization), especially after the failure of the military coup of February 1981.[51]

The transition to democracy was marked above all by negotiation and compromise – over the pace of reform, the structure of the state, the status of nationalities and languages, the role of the Church and the armed forces, and the reconciliation of past enmities and grievances. This spirit of *convivencia* (peaceful co-existence) is enshrined in the calculated ambiguities of the 1978 Constitution, which establishes a semi-federal compromise similar to that of 1931 and echoes some of the language of the republican Constitution. Spain is defined in Article 1 as 'un Estado social y democrático de Derecho' ('a social democratic State subject to the rule of law'), whose powers are derived from 'el pueblo español'. The nation is no longer defined as Catholic, no longer conceived as an authoritarian, hierarchical structure. Article 2 simultaneously asserts the 'indisoluble unidad de la Nación española, patria común e indivisible de todos los españoles' ('the indissoluble unity of the Spanish Nation, common and indivisible homeland of all Spaniards') and recognizes 'el derecho a la autonomía de las nacionalidades y regiones que la integran' ('the right to autonomy of the nationalities and regions of which it is comprised'). Article 3 declares that Castilian is the official language of the Spanish state which all Spaniards have the duty to know and the right to use, but also allows for 'las demás lenguas españolas' ('the other Spanish languages') to have co-official status in the relevant Autonomous Communities and promises protection for the cultural heritage of 'las distintas modalidades lingüísticas de España' ('the various linguistic modalities within Spain') (cited in De la Granja et al. 2001: 298–99). Although this careful balancing of the familiar concepts of *Estado*, *pueblo español*, *Nación española*, *patria* and *lengua española* on the one hand against the slippery new terms *nacionalidades y regiones*, *lenguas españolas* and *distintas modalidades lingüísticas* has been the source of much uncertainty since 1978, it has helped to establish a large degree of consensus around the principle of devolution and the consolidation of the *Estado de las Autonomías*. The process led by the traditional nationalisms (Catalan, Basque and Galician) quickly turned into 'café para todos' ('coffee for everyone') – varying degrees of autonomy for all parts of Spain.

The PSOE (Partido Socialista Obrero Español – Spanish Socialist Workers' Party) governments in power between 1982 and 1996 did not make a serious effort to reclaim or regenerate Spanish nationalism as such, but did enjoy some success in projecting a modernizing national image of social justice, administrative reform, economic growth, cultural effervescence and a high international profile. The multiple celebrations of 1992 (the Olympics in Barcelona, the Expo in Sevilla, the Quincentenary of Columbus's first voyage to the Americas, and Madrid's year as European City of Culture) were meant to symbolize a prosperous, democratic nation comfortable with its past, in control of its present and confident about its future, but by then a range of economic and political failures were catching up with the PSOE. Between 1993 and 2000, national politics was dominated by regional issues and the ongoing problem of the consolidation of the powers and responsibilities of the Autonomous Communities. The Catalan nationalist coalition CiU (Convergència i Unió – Convergence and Unity) extracted important concessions from Madrid in exchange for its support for minority governments – first the PSOE, then the conservative PP (Partido Popular – People's Party). Various tentative moves were made towards negotiations with the Basque separatist organization ETA (Euskadi ta Askatasuna – Basque Homeland and Freedom). After being re-elected in 2000 with an absolute majority in the Cortes, the PP was relieved of the need to do deals with CiU and began to revive a nationalist discourse reminiscent of the party's roots in Francoism (De la Granja et al. 2001: 209).[52]

Although friction between the various levels of government continues, there is widespread acceptance amongst the population of the notion of dual identities and of Spain as a multinational, multilingual state. Opinion polls indicate a clear majority preferring to define their identity in terms of both Spain and their Autonomous Community.[53] Nevertheless, from the point of view of significant minorities resident in Catalonia and the Basque Country but not identifying themselves primarily as Catalan or Basque, especially those who are monolingual Castilian speakers, the nationalist discourses and policies surrounding them have felt more like those of an oppressive 'official' nationalism (in the sense used by Anderson) than of a liberationist 'popular' one. The resuscitation by ETA, and to some extent by democratic Basque nationalists, of Sabino Arana's ideology of racial purity and total repudiation of the Spanish 'invasion' of the Basque homeland threatens to categorize a large proportion of the population of Euskadi as unwelcome aliens. Although bilingualism is embedding itself more comfortably in Catalonia, there has been something of a backlash amongst Castilian speakers against the Generalitat's implementation of the principles of 'linguistic normalization' in education, stirred up by the conservative national press: *ABC*'s headline on 12 September 1993 was 'Igual que bajo Franco pero al revés: persecución del castellano en Cataluña' (Mar-Molinero 2000: 163).[54]

Complaints also began to be made during the 1990s, especially after the PP came to power in 1996, that under the control of regional governments the teaching of history in schools was being conducted in a way that was 'igual que bajo Franco pero al revés': almost as tendentious and chauvinistic but now neglecting the Spanish national vision in favour of narrowly defined regional perspectives. The Real Academia de la Historia published a report in 2000 criticizing reforms that had encouraged the abandonment of traditional methods based on the dates, facts and personalities of national political history and the promotion of new methods emphasizing the critical evaluation of sources, relevance to pupils' interests, and local and social history. In the Academy's view, such changes were not only pedagogically flawed but were being exploited in pursuit of nationalist agendas that seemed simply to be replacing the ideal of a singular 'unidad de destino en lo universal' with multiple 'unidades de destino en lo universal', each with its own myths of uniqueness and continuity (Real Academia de Historia 2000). On this issue it was not only the right-wing press that was critical. In 1997 *El País* had reported with sardonic dismay on the blinkered perspectives offered by textbooks tailored to the requirements of particular Autonomous Communities, quoting a warning by Joaquín Prat, Professor of Historical Education at the Universidad Central de Barcelona that 'se resalta lo que nos separa, todo aquello que en el pasado nos ha enfrentado a unos con otros' (Prades 1997: 8).[55]

Long before these controversies came to a head, Rodríguez Méndez had found himself at odds with the rise of Catalanism. Despite having lived in Barcelona since 1939 and having been a defender of the ideal of peaceful coexistence between cultural producers in Castilian and in Catalan, he had never felt entirely integrated into the city's cultural life.[56] Nevertheless, he declared in an interview of 1972 that 'mi estancia en Barcelona me ha dado un toque de universalidad; aunque parezca mentira, me ha hecho ser más comprensivo y ha reducido las diferencias' (Isasi Ángulo 277).[57] It is Barcelona's status as a stimulating cultural and linguistic melting pot that he celebrates in *Flor de Otoño* and on which he later feels the Catalanists are turning their backs. In the prologue to an edition of his play *Literatura española*, he grouchily declares his reasons for escaping to Ávila in 1978 and immersing himself anew in the Spanish classics:

> Resultaba que yo, trabajador de la lengua, me sentía extranjero, totalmente extranjero, en un trozo entrañable de tierra española. Este ambiente cultural es lo que me hizo abandonar Cataluña – no he sido el único, ni voy a serlo – y volverme a saborear la rica tradición literaria de nuestros maestros, esa tradición que a los niños en Cataluña y en Vascongadas se les va a escamotear. Harto y dolido estaba hasta las raíces de mis huesos de soportar una constante, implacable y demoledora ofensiva desde todos los estamentos contra mi lengua y mi literatura (Rodríguez Méndez 1989: 18–19).[58]

Statements such as this, chiming uncomfortably with the right-wing backlash against devolution, are a useful reminder of the fact that what Rodríguez Méndez's work resists is not the nationalist ideal in itself but its ideological manipulation – both the appropriation of patriotism by the dictatorship to legitimize itself and the subsequent rejection of Spanishness because of that appropriation. In various texts and statements, he has made clear that he is not convinced that Spain has made progress in any sense since the end of the dictatorship. He argues that democracy is a sham, that the crushing of human individuality by globalized consumer capitalism has accelerated, that Spain's integration into Europe and devolution of power to the Autonomous Communities are massive confidence tricks, and that cultural production becomes more trivial as it becomes more prolific.

On the surface, theatre in Spain was a major beneficiary of the consolidation of democracy in the 1980s. Rodríguez Méndez's own work was being staged with slightly greater frequency: there were high-profile productions of two plays written during the dictatorship, *Bodas que fueron famosas del Pingajo y la Fandanga* in 1978 and *Flor de Otoño* in 1982; performances in various places of *Teresa de Ávila* in 1981 and 1982; two reasonably successful provincial *estrenos* which did not transfer to Madrid (*La sangre de toro* in 1985 and *La marca del fuego* in 1986); and various adaptations and musical spectacles between 1983 and 1990. Censorship had been abolished in 1978, and under the PSOE government first elected in 1982, public funding was substantially increased, new venues were opened, cultural policy was devolved to regional governments (which opened their own *Centros Dramáticos*), new festivals were established, prizes for writers and performers proliferated, practical and academic training became more professional and more widely available, innovative directors were given high-profile public appointments, and a new wave of female dramatists emerged. The surge of cultural events in 1992 included a wealth of publicly funded theatrical spectacle: La Fura dels Baus's pageant at the opening ceremony of the Barcelona Olympics; festivals of theatre and dance associated with the Expo in Sevilla and with Madrid's year as European City of Culture; and various productions related to the quincentenary of Columbus's first transatlantic voyage. However, one aspect of theatrical activity that did not receive much benefit from enhanced official support was the staging of new work by contemporary Spanish playwrights: most of the landmark productions in publicly funded theatres were revivals of classics or adaptations of non-dramatic texts.[59]

Rodríguez Méndez is scornful of all this activity and lavish public expenditure. In his essay *Los despojos del teatro*, he declares that 'jamás se había visto el teatro tan postrado como en el mítico año de 1992' (1993: 5).[60] He describes the festivities of that year as an empty, gaudy disguise behind which the hyenas and vultures of the political and cultural establishment scavenge on the rotting remains of the divine art of theatre, the victim of abuse and exploitation throughout the preceding decade: 'Acuso a esos llamados "socialistas" de la destrucción del teatro español [...] y del genocidio cultural' (1993: 5–6).[61] He rails against empty ostentatiousness, trashy consumerism, pretentiousness, ignorance and hypocrisy. He deplores the corrupting effects of public subsidy, which he sees as turning artists into toadies, subordinating culture to public relations, and removing the healthy competitive pressure of audiences' judgement. The author, clearly feeling he has nothing to lose, names prominent directors, authors and actors among those he regards as responsible for the destruction of theatre, including Adolfo Marsillach, Gustavo Pérez Puig, Miguel Narros, José Carlos Plaza, Guillermo Heras, Lluis Pasqual, José Tamayo, Francisco Nieva, Antonio Gala and Nuria Espert: a fairly comprehensive roll-call of the most distinguished names in Spanish theatre.[62] The whole essay is hyperbolic, apocalyptic, sarcastic and almost entirely devoid of concrete evidence to support the personal accusations and general prophecies of doom. Unreliable though it may be as a source of information on contemporary Spanish theatre, it is nevertheless invaluable as an expression of Rodríguez Méndez's character and his jaundiced view from the margins of Spanish culture: 'Podemos tirar la primera piedra, porque afortunadamente nos dejaron al margen del necrofágico festín y para mirar al futuro con la cabeza alta debemos acusar y acusarnos' (1993: 6).[63]

In all his work, Rodríguez Méndez emphasizes the long view, seeing both Francoism and post-1975 democracy as variations on a constant historical theme of political and cultural hegemony being enjoyed by a minority, while no real improvement is made in the lives of the majority. Towards the end of *Los despojos del teatro*, he expresses the hope that underneath the degeneration and corruption of the present there remains a priceless cultural tradition, which constitutes a kind of national soul that is imperishable: 'Tras todo eso yace el ser español al que pertenecemos' (1993: 47).[64] He invokes Unamuno's concept of *intrahistoria* to suggest that there is always an alternative, dissident, 'real' Spain capable of exposing the fraud of 'official' Spain, although it may be deeply submerged. This notion of a 'real' Spain is not to be understood as an entirely fixed, ahistorical essence: it changes over time but is always different from the versions constructed by governments and elite social groups. From this perspective, el desastre teatral que ha convertido en despojos lo existente vendría a ser algo que pertenece a la historia y a la España oficial, la España de la monarquía socialista que bajo el pecado de 'hibris' ha corrompido cualquier actividad humana. Pero ¿por qué no pensar que pueda existir otra España y otra intrahistoria donde se puede desmentir lo que afirma la otra España oficialesca y negra? (1993: 48)[65]

Rodríguez Méndez's emphasis on humanism, *iberismo*, tradition and historical perspective is therefore as out of tune with the times as ever.[66] Nevertheless, despite the desolate picture painted in *Los despojos del teatro* of the state of Spanish theatre, Rodríguez Méndez acknowledges that there are talented actors, directors and playwrights waiting to be given their chance, and he ends on a hopeful note: 'No todo está perdido. España tuvo un gran teatro, tiene todavía una gran lengua contra la que nada, ni nadie podrá. De España ha surgido una enorme civilización' (1993: 53).[67] He invariably comes back to what he sees as the core of Spanishness: a language and a cultural heritage which have been manipulated and degraded but offer the only solid foundations for the future.

Notes

1. The other productions that defined the Realist Generation for Monleón were: Ricardo Rodríguez Buded's *La madriguera* (1960), Carlos Muñiz's *El tintero* (1961) and Lauro Olmo's *La camisa* (1962). After the staging of *Las salvajes en Puente San Gil* (1963), José Martín Recuerda was generally regarded as belonging to the same group, while Rodríguez Buded wrote very little after *La madriguera*. For later discussions of the Realist Generation, see: Rodríguez Méndez (1968a), Isasi Ángulo (1974: 267–79), O'Connor & Pasquariello (1976), Halsey (1977), Oliva (1978), Oliva (1979), Rodríguez Méndez (1987), Salvat (1995) and Cornago Bernal (2000: 279–98). Various other playwrights, including Antonio Buero Vallejo, Alfonso Sastre and Antonio Gala, have been considered members of the Realist Generation; my use of the term, however, is limited to the core group of Rodríguez Méndez, Martín Recuerda, Olmo and Muñiz.
2. 'Inferior, narrow-minded and provincial.'
3. Ruiz Ramón characterizes this kind of undemanding middle-class theatre as *teatro público* (1989: 297–319 and 422–31); see also Monleón (1971) and Pedraza Jiménez & Rodríguez Cáceres (1995: 119–86).
4. See, for example, Pérez-Stansfield (1983: 81–83), Ruiz Ramón (1989: 337–41) and Ragué-Arias (1996: 22–25).
5. Rodríguez Méndez (1987: 3) also mentions the work of John Arden and Arnold Wesker in the late 1950s. Wesker's attempt to establish a working-class theatre company at the Round House in London in the early 1960s offers an interesting parallel to Rodríguez Méndez's experience with the Barcelona group La Pipironda at the same time.
6. 'When I was first setting out on my adventure as a playwright, what motivated me and some of my fellow writers more than realism as such – though this was an important ingredient – was a desire to make ourselves worthy inheritors of the great tradition of Spanish theatre.'
7. 'The realist techniques with which they project this reality onto the stage are, moreover, neither simple nor impoverished, but complex and rich in their use of theatrical resources. By infusing poetry into the situations and beauty into the language, with elements of humour, satire and the grotesque, simultaneously comic and tragic, they transcend the merely documentary at the level of both the signifier and the signified.'
8. Richards (1998) gives a vivid account of the effect on the population of the repression of the post-war years.

9. 'We dreamt of getting to grips with the arduous task of putting the real Spain on stage, a Spain that was battered and badly wounded. [...] The "guts" of Iberia had been buried and it was unacceptable to bring them out into the open. Unacceptable for those who, directly or indirectly, had poisoned that spirit and will always attempt to conceal it by constructing images that are more decorous and, naturally, more reassuring for themselves.'

10. 'Iberianism, because most of our theatre is violent, wild, cruel, satirical, self-absorbed, proud and loud. Like a raw, bloody bull's hide, straight out of the land of our birth.'

11. 'Ultimately, Castilianness is the same as *casticismo*'.

12. 'My theatre is always about Spanish society. Fundamentally, the society of today, but at the same time about how it is a direct product of the society of the previous century.'

13. 'I am always exploring the hide of Iberia, our Spain, in the hope of extracting from it our true personality.'

14. 'The structure of society and history as a totality.'

15. *Mixtificación* is a variant spelling of *mistificación*. The sense of *mistificar* here is falsification or deformation (Real Academia Española 1992: 1382).

16. 'An image of working-class, peasant or subproletarian reality which [...] ends up being puerile, sentimentalized or simply *costumbrista*.' *Costumbrismo* refers to the depiction in literature, theatre or visual arts of the customs and dress of particular regions. The term has connotations of superficiality, conventionality and concentration on the merely picturesque.

17. 'Those phrases in *Bodas* and *Flor de Otoño* are things I've actually heard in the street. [...] The fact is the critics don't get out in the streets as much as I do.'

18. The *zarzuela* first flourished in the seventeenth century as a courtly spectacle combining singing and spoken dialogue, while the *sainete* was a short comic sketch, with or without music, performed between the acts of a play. In the eighteenth century, Ramón de la Cruz developed the *sainete* into a more substantial form of satirical theatre (usually set in lower-class communities of Madrid), at the same time as popularizing the *zarzuela* by using settings and characters similar to those of his *sainetes* and introducing elements of folk music. In the second half of the nineteenth century, the full-length *zarzuela grande* was largely displaced by the successful commercialization of the lighter, shorter *zarzuela chica*, which again brought the genre closer to the *sainete*. The term *género chico* ('small genre') embraces the various forms of popular spectacle (*zarzuelas*, *sainetes*, *revistas* and *operetas*) produced for bourgeois and working-class audiences in the late nineteenth century. Recent studies of the *zarzuela* and the *género chico* include Doménech Rico (1998), Versteeg (2000), Alier (2002) and Webber (2002). See also Christopher Webber's website *Zarzuela!* <http://www.zarzuela.net>.

19. Although the term *Nuevo Teatro Español* is used by Ruiz Ramón (1989: 485) and Pörtl (1986) to embrace both the Realist Generation and the non-realist *vanguardia*, its more restricted application to the latter group has become the norm, as originally used in Miralles (1977). Ruiz Ramón discusses these playwrights under the heading 'Del alegorismo a la abstracción' (1989: 527–71). See also Wellwarth (1970 and 1972), Oliva (1989: 337–424), Pedraza Jiménez & Rodríguez Cáceres (1995: 421–533), Ragué-Arias (1996: 39–95), Cornago Bernal (1996) and Perriam et al. (2000: 184–87).

20. 'To create a synthesis that is poetic and therefore global, in order to travel through the tunnel – or across the border – of time.'

21. 'Mindlessly adore and imitate everything that was foreign, neglecting their own creative priorities.'

22. 'Follow their models so slavishly that they end up destroying the Spanish language, [...] to the extent that it loses all its juiciness and becomes indistinguishable from any text translated for consumption in other third-rate countries.'

23. This argument is to some extent derived from Lukács's defence of critical realism in opposition to modernist literature's subjectivism and denial of meaning (1963).

24. See Conversi (1997) and Mar-Molinero & Smith (1996), especially 6–9, 16–17, 76–81 and 196–205.

25. The Generation of 1898: a group of writers born in the 1860s and 1870s who, influenced by regenerationism, conducted similar enquiries into the nature and destiny of Spanishness through essays, novels, poetry and drama. Lists of the membership of the Generation usually include include Azorín, Pío Baroja, Ángel Ganivet, Antonio Machado, Miguel de Unamuno, Ramiro de Maeztu and Ramón del Valle-Inclán. See Shaw (1975 or 1997) and Abellán (1968).
26. 'When within a nation the masses refuse to be masses, that is, to follow the governing minority, the nation comes apart, society fragments, and social chaos – the crumbling of the country's historical backbone – ensues. What we are experiencing in Spain at the moment is an extreme case of such historical invertebration.'
27. 'The reins of the country, in spite of the Glorious Revolution [of 1868], were firmly in the hands of a small elite, while the mass of the people [...] were left to their fate, without any say in the twists and turns of our history.'
28. 'A nation cannot be just a "people": it needs an outstanding minority, just as a body is not just muscle but also ganglions and a central nervous system.'
29. 'Constitutes an integral state, compatible with the autonomy of the Municipalities and the Regions.'
30. 'Las naciones se forman y viven de tener un programa para el mañana' (Ortega 1947: 57) ('Nations are formed and develop by having a programme for the future').
31. The definition of Spain as 'una unidad de destino en lo universal' appears in several of Primo de Rivera's speeches and writings, and was incorporated into Franco's Ley de Principios del Movimiento Nacional of 1958.
32. Good general accounts in English of the evolution of the Franco dictatorship include Carr (1980), Carr & Fusi (1981), Preston (1993), Grugel & Rees (1997) and Richards (1998). See also the various essays in Part III of Graham & Labanyi (1995a: 167–310) and parts of Perriam et al. (2000). In Spanish, Abella (1985), Fontana (1986) and Tusell (1988 and 1990) are particularly useful. Palacios Buñuelos & Rodríguez Jiménez (2001) is a comprehensive survey of bibliography in Spanish and English on the period.
33. The recruitment of the young into this culture of archaic, regimented ceremonial is critically evoked in Rodríguez Méndez's novel Los herederos de la promesa (1979a).
34. 'To be Christian and to be Spanish are one and the same thing, because Spain is the only country in History in which there cannot be, nor has there ever been nor is there any difference whatsoever between the moral and religious identity of the nation and its historical constitution.'
35. See, for example, the extract from Santiago Montero Díaz's Idea del Imperio (Madrid, 1943), quoted in Rodríguez Puértolas (1987: 1073–74).
36. 'A nation exists only in so far as it possesses: a Leader, an Army to guard it and a People to serve it. Our Crusade showed that we have the Leader and the Army. Now we need the people, which in order to exist must achieve unity and discipline.'
37. 'As a storehouse of costumes, dances and songs which, as the rhetoric of the time would put it, "added bright, varied colour to the indissoluble unity of the Fatherland".'
38. 'The patriarchal family was seen as representing the corporate order of the state in microcosm' (Graham 1995: 184). On the Francoist model of the family and texts from the 1940s to the 1970s which deconstruct it, see Perriam et al. (2000: 68–95).
39. On the changing circumstances of women in Spain during and after the dictatorship, see especially Brooksbank Jones (1997), Lafuente (2001: 81–106) and Palacios Buñuelos & Rodríguez Jiménez (2001: 148–63).
40. 'Without a doubt, Francoism carried out the most intense attempt at indoctrination of our entire history.'
41. The simplistic myths foisted upon primary school pupils are hilariously satirized in Andrés Sopeña Monsalve's El florido pensil (1994), which was turned into a stage show in 2001 and a film in 2002. The phrase 'florido pensil' comes from one of the unofficial lyrics of the (officially wordless) national anthem, in which Spain is exalted as 'de glorias florido pensil'

('a flower-filled garden of glories'). Lafuente's account (1999: 107–27) is also humorous, while Valls (1987) and Abós Santabárbara (2003) provide more serious, thoroughly documented studies of the teaching of history during the dictatorship.

42. 'Faithfully following Government directives and cultivating the moral and religious virtues that made our ancestors famous in the age of empire.'

43. 'The spirit of the Spanish people has been formed within the capacious mould of the Catholic faith, informed by the supreme ideals of an imperial Catholicism, which has civilized the world.'

44. 'The qualities that characterize the Spanish people are religiosity, sense of honour, capacity for command, spirit of sacrifice, and enthusiasm for all that is great and lofty.'

45. 'Those Muslims were almost all Spanish. […] That whole marvellous civilization is Spanish; their books, their scholars, their warriors, their artists, their poets, all Spanish.'

46. 'The political conditioning dominated our existences, teachers and pupils alike, overwhelming and inevitable.'

47. 'I'll never forget the wonderful secondary schooling I began in 1939 and completed in 1945. Because in that hard, much-criticized period I had the best teachers I could have dreamt of. […] And I still remember with emotion the extraordinary conduct of those schoolmasters, some of them from the winning side and some from the losing side, who all put aside their personal beliefs and ideologies in order to give us a humanistic, purely humanistic, education, showing the kind of dignity and courage that has unfortunately disappeared these days. That's why I find all this talk about "National-Catholic" schooling and the like ridiculous.' What was clear from a performance of *El florido pensil* which I attended was the degree of recognition being loudly voiced by older members of the audience. Concepción Carrero, whose word-for-word recall of one of the standard set texts of Spanish history as taught to her around 1950 is quoted by Abós Santabárbara (2003: 376), has confirmed in conversation with me that her experience was precisely as described by Cámara and Abós.

48. 'I do not believe in political theatre, strictly speaking. It seems just as pointless to me to write a defence of Marxism as a defence of Fascism. I also think it absurd to regard theatre as a politically progressive weapon, when reality is multi-faceted and so many active and reactive forces are in play.'

49. 'Has never adhered to a specific political tendency.'

50. Amongst the many histories of the transition and of the longer perspective up to the end of the century, I recommend the following: Carr & Fusi (1981), Preston (1986), Ramos Gascón (1991), Graham & Labanyi (1995a: 311–418), Juliá et al. (1996), Powell (2001), and Tusell (2001).

51. Rodríguez Puértolas's survey and anthology of 'Fascist' literature in Spain runs up to 1985, although he does diagnose a decline in both quantity and quality after 1975 (1986: 792).

52. León Solís (2003) provides a concise account of tensions between the competing discourses of Spanishness and Catalanness from the early twentieth century to 2000, especially as fought out in political rhetoric, the media and sport.

53. See, for example, De la Granja (2001: 248) and Centro de Investigaciones Sociológicas (2002).

54. 'The same as under Franco but the other way round: Castilian persecuted in Catalonia.'

55. 'What is being emphasised is what separates us, everything that in the past has created conflict between us.'

56. In an article about culture in Barcelona, Rodríguez Méndez expresses admiration for the literary and theatrical heritage of Catalonia and notes with satisfaction that the relaxation of the 'absurd prohibition' that had restricted theatre in Catalan is encouraging new and innovative work (1963: 7). He advocates collaboration and mutual respect between those working in Catalan and those in Castilian, but accuses the Young Turks of Catalan theatre of displaying an attitude of exclusivity and rejecting cooperation.

57. 'My time in Barcelona has given me a touch of universality; believe it or not, it has made me more understanding and has diminished the differences.'

58. 'As someone who works with language, I was increasingly being made to feel like a foreigner, a complete foreigner, on a piece of Spanish soil that's dear to me. It was this cultural atmosphere that made me leave Catalonia – I wasn't the first person to do so and I won't be the last – and go back to the joys of the rich literary tradition of our masters, a tradition that children in Catalonia and the Basque Country are going to be deprived of. I was fed up and deeply hurt at having to put up with constant, implacable and devastating attacks from all quarters on my language and my literature.' The theatre director Ricard Salvat, who has also found himself marginalized by the Catalan nationalist elite, offers a fascinating reflection on Rodríguez Méndez's relationship with Barcelona in his contribution to the recent *Teatro escogido* (Salvat 2005: 267–70).

59. Good general accounts of developments in Spanish theatre from the end of the dictatorship to the 1990s can be found in: Oliva (1989: 337–463), Villanueva (1992: 432–507), Aznar Soler (1996), Gabriele & Leonard (1996a and 1996b), Ragué-Arias (1996) and Medina Vicario (2003). O'Connor (1992) is a useful anthology of plays translated into English.

60. 'Never had theatre been brought so low as in the mythical year of 1992.'

61. 'I accuse those so-called "socialists" of the destruction of Spanish theatre [...] and of cultural genocide.'

62. Some of these names had already figured in a letter to the SGAE amongst the actors and directors prohibited by Martín Recuerda and Rodríguez Méndez from staging their work (1975).

63. 'We can throw the first stone, because we had the good fortune to be left out of the necrophagic binge, and in order to be able to face the future with our head held high, we must accuse and we do accuse.'

64. 'Behind all that lies the Spanish identity to which we all belong.'

65. 'The disaster that has left our present-day theatrical culture in ruins could be seen as part of history and of the official Spain, the Spain of the socialist monarchy whose hubris has led it to corrupt all forms of human activity. But why not imagine another Spain and another *intrahistoria* in which the discourse of the black, official Spain is overturned?'

66. He expresses trenchant opinions on the current state of the theatre in Spain in an interview of 2001, criticizing Sanchis Sinisterra, Pallín, Mayorga, the *salas alternativas* and audiences' lack of discrimination (Perales 2001: 42–43).

67. 'Not everything is lost. Spain once had a great theatre, and it still has a great language which no-one and nothing can destroy. Spain has given birth to a vast civilization.'

2

Rodríguez Méndez's essays: realism, *machismo español*, *inteligencia española* and historical theatre

The non-dramatic writing on which Rodríguez Méndez worked in the late 1960s and early 1970s in parallel with his most impressive plays provides a crucial context for the understanding of his entire dramatic output. In these essays he conducts a wide-ranging investigation of Spanish cultural history, tracing the construction of collective identity through various forms of both 'high' and 'low' cultural production. The key concept that runs through his work is realism, understood not as an aesthetic category in isolation but as a historically evolving range of demystifying cultural practices linking the intellectual work of artists and educators to the everyday culture of ordinary people. As an art form that is essentially public and immediate in its impact, theatre is potentially the most productive medium for maintaining the vitality of that link. However, Rodríguez Méndez recognizes that in an industrialized society in which the *pueblo* in the traditional sense has ceased to exist as a creative cultural force, converted into passive *masas* (masses), it is not an easy matter for theatre to connect with popular culture in any authentic way. In his article 'El teatro como expresión social y cultural' ('Theatre As Social and Cultural Expression', written in 1965), he identifies the creation of an authentic culture of the masses as the crucial challenge facing contemporary theatre: not a paternalistic, socialist or consumerist culture *for* the masses which merely serves to confirm its audience's status as a manipulable mass, but cultural forms designed to 'redimir al hombre, mediante una toma de conciencia, de su degradado papel de animal social o simple número, para poder regir su propio destino' and to 'sacar al hombre de la masa y hacerle consciente de sí mismo y solidario de sus semejantes' (1968d: 88 and 90).[1]

The essential function of contemporary theatre according to this analysis can be translated into Marxian terms as counteracting alienation, or more precisely combating the deindividualizing power of ideology as defined by Louis Althusser in his essay 'Ideology and Ideological State Apparatuses'. Althusser proposes that ideology is a continuous and ubiquitous process that constitutes individuals as subjects by 'hailing' or 'interpellating' them; that is, offering them imaginary ways of seeing themselves as subjects in relation to the world ('subject positions'), and thus recruiting them into a discursive system (Althusser 1984: 44–45). Playing on the dual meaning of the term 'subject' (grammatical subject of a sentence and person subjected to another), Althusser describes the constitution of the subject as 'doubly speculary': ideology invites individuals to identify themselves with (see themselves reflected in) an idealized 'Absolute Subject' (in fact, usually a combination of such concepts as God, leader, father, monarch, nation, community, democracy, morality), while at the same time assuring them that the Subject 'recognizes' (sees itself reflected in) them and confirms that they belong to the system (1984: 54). The interpellation and recruitment are materialized and rehearsed in a variety of cultural and social practices or rituals, with the result that the majority of individuals 'work all by themselves' (1984: 55) as subjects integrated into a state of affairs accepted by them as 'natural'. Althusser uses a theatrical metaphor to emphasize that these practices are performances, referring to 'the way the "actors" in this *mise en scène* of interpellation, and their respective roles, are reflected in the very structure of all ideology' (1984: 51). To some extent, the system relies upon the coercive action of public 'Repressive State Apparatuses' (government, armed forces, police, and judicial, penal and administrative structures) to keep in line those who fail to be properly constituted as obedient subjects, but consensus is mostly constructed through 'Ideological State Apparatuses' (ISAs), which operate in both the public and private domains creating the imaginary representations that construct subject positions: religious institutions, education systems, the family, legal institutions, political parties, trade unions, the mass media, cultural institutions (1984: 17).

Although he does not use Althusser's terminology, Rodríguez Méndez's plays and essays clearly show ideology at work throughout Spanish history, offering examples of Repressive and Ideological State Apparatuses enforcing and gaining consent for identification with a series of Absolute Subjects: monarchy and Crusade in the Middle Ages; empire and Catholic orthodoxy in the sixteenth and seventeenth centuries; reform and rationalization in the eighteenth century; social and technological progress in balance with traditional values in the nineteenth and early twentieth centuries; the will of the people during the two republics; social order, unity and prosperity under Francoism; and finally democracy and freedom after 1975. In all these cases, the construction of the ideological ideal is represented as oppressive, constraining the freedom of individuals and social groups to articulate alternative identities. Most of Rodríguez Méndez's early plays show groups of characters irredeemably subjugated to powerful discursive systems, partly coerced and partly conditioned into accepting the status quo: the recruits in *Vagones de madera*, the agricultural labourers in *La Mano Negra*, the factory workers in *El ghetto*, the immigrant families in Barcelona in *La batalla del Verdún*.

In 'El teatro como expresión social y cultural', Rodríguez Méndez argues that theatre can play an important social role in exposing and counteracting the ideological control exercised by elites, not by means of didacticism or political activism but through engagement with the everyday life of characters in their social and historical contexts.[2] He considers Chekhov's theatre closer to this liberating ideal than Brecht's, arguing that 'a Brecht le interesa más la conciencia del hombre en tanto permanece dentro de la masa' (1968d: 90).[3] In a brief survey of Iberian culture since the early Middle Ages, he identifies a fundamental tension between two modes of theatre. On the one hand, 'rhetorical' or heroic forms reflect the interests of ruling elites and promote conformity through mystification, with their origins in imperial Latin culture and their evolution conditioned successively by 'una cultura de formas y superestructuras franco-borgoñonas' ('a culture of Franco-Burgundian forms and superstructures'), the Italian Renaissance, rigid Neoclassicism, and the 'nefasto influjo del romanticismo' ('the disastrous influence of Romanticism') (1968d: 93–95). On the other hand, 'un enorme esfuerzo por conformar un teatro que sea fiel expresión del pueblo' (1968d: 92) produces realist forms that promote resistance to power, with Arabic rather than Latin roots, drawing their vitality from authentic popular involvement, but also borrowing some aspects of the learned tradition. The first current produces the canonical 'national' theatrical tradition; the second is 'acosada y perseguida' ('harassed and persecuted'), although it occasionally finds expression in the work of established authors (1968d: 95). The tension between the two currents is played out within La Celestina, but subsequently, as the official theatre becomes increasingly dominated by the bourgeoisie (in terms of the circumstances of performance as well as its style and content), it becomes more and more remote from ordinary people. Rodríguez Méndez singles out a few examples of dramatists whose work attempts to bridge the gap: Ramón de la Cruz; Valle-Inclán; Lorca and Casona; Buero Vallejo and some contemporary realist playwrights, including, by implication, himself.

In the second half of the twentieth century, however, as industrialization, technological development and social change provoke 'la disolución de lo que se entendía por popular' ('the dissolution of what used to be understood as popular') and the possibility of creating 'teatro popular' with any degree of authenticity recedes, the challenge of creating a liberating 'teatro de masas' becomes paramount (1968d: 98). Rodríguez Méndez recognizes that theatre cannot on its own reinvent the 'popular' or offer an all-encompassing solution to the problem of what a 'cultura de masas' should be like. In the meantime, its most useful function is the essential realist task of social observation and analysis:

> En tanto el problema de las masas esté en crisis, en tanto la cultura de masas no sea más que una aspiración, el teatro sólo puede, si quiere ser reflejo de la sociedad y la cultura de esa época, acusar de una manera realista, con un realismo minucioso, casi científico, esa crisis (1968d: 99).[4]

Rodríguez Méndez's own evolution as a playwright was profoundly influenced by his involvement in the community theatre group La Pipironda, an experiment in popular theatre aimed at working-class audiences in the suburbs of Barcelona (mostly Castilian-speaking immigrants from other regions of Spain), between 1959 and

1966. The project, led by Ángel Carmona, was a modest precursor of the *Teatro Independiente* (Independent Theatre) movement that became influential in the late 1960s. Using minimal resources, unconventional venues and a variety of performance styles, the collective set out to

> acercarse al pueblo, no para enseñarle, ni para redimirle, ni siquiera para distraerle, sino para 'investigar' una posible vía de comunicación. Para aprender de él su lenguaje, sus motivaciones y sus resortes. Para, después de esa investigación, realizar conjuntamente ese posible teatro popular que no acaba de surgir plenamente (Rodríguez Méndez 1974c: 202).[5]

Most of their performances were free and took place in community centres, bars or in the open air. They used short texts written by Rodríguez Méndez (especially *La tabernera y las tinajas*) and others, as well as adaptations of Lope's *Fuenteovejuna* and *entremeses* by Cervantes, usually enlivened by song and dance. The performances were complemented by discussions, workshops and pamphlets on community theatre. Rodríguez Méndez's accounts of these events are enthusiastic about the response of their audiences. He describes unsophisticated working people who identify apparently ingenuously with characters and situations, but then demonstrate impressive critical awareness; audiences not shy of shouting out spontaneous insults or encouragement to the actors, laughing and applauding with great enthusiasm. This was a festive, generous, intelligent public, very different from the usual consumers of conventional theatre, responding to strong characterization, simple stories and recognizable social situations.[6] He concludes: 'Si ese público se ganara para el teatro, el teatro estaba salvado' (1968c: 73). However, he had no illusions about the degree to which theatre can be truly 'popular' or about the sustainability of such initiatives in a society becoming rapidly dominated by industrialization and on the verge of the boom in consumerism and the mass media (a process examined in *La batalla del Verdún* and other short pieces written for La Pipironda). The final chapter of his essay *La incultura teatral en España* is entitled 'Esa imposibilidad llamada teatro popular' ('That impossibility known as popular theatre'), in which he simply advocates artistic humility and directness as the only routes to any kind of authenticity: a playwright must be willing to get his hands dirty and 'buscar al pueblo por sí mismo' (Rodríguez Méndez 1974c: 197) ('go out in search of the people on their terms, not his own').

The displacement of traditional forms of popular culture by modern, mass-mediated forms is seen by Rodríguez Méndez as a loss of diversity, creative energy and critical potential. He launches a fierce attack on the alienating effects of television (a relatively recent phenomenon for most of Spanish society in 1971) in *Los teleadictos*, deploring its degradation of language and its vulgarizing treatment of 'la cultura con mayúscula' ('Culture with a capital C') (Rodríguez Méndez 1971b: 45), identifying its main function as the promotion of social conformity through consumption, and highlighting its usefulness to the state as an instrument of ideological control (31–34).

This argument is similar to the Frankfurt School's critique of the 'false consciousness' generated by the contemporary culture industry, and parallels the defence of traditional working-class culture mounted in the late 1950s and early 1960s by British sociologists such as Richard Hoggart.[7] There is a tendency in contemporary cultural studies written in English to use the term 'popular culture' to refer to both traditional 'folk' forms and modern mass-mediated forms. It is important, however, to maintain in our discussion of Rodríguez Méndez's work a distinction between popular culture (primarily implying active participation) and mass culture (primarily implying consumption of mass-produced material), while acknowledging the evolution and complexity of these terms, the inevitable slippage or overlap between them, and their equally problematic relationship with the notion of 'high' or 'elite' culture – deftly summarized with reference to Spain in Graham & Labanyi (1995b: 5–9) and Labanyi (2002: 10–13).

Rodríguez Méndez's theatre and essays privilege forms of cultural production that predate or do not depend upon modern media technologies, especially oral communication (with an emphasis on creativity and dialectal diversity), poetry, theatrical performance, and traditional music and dance, but without romanticizing any of these as the pure, unmediated voice of the *pueblo*. The plays set in contemporary Spain (between the 1960s and the 1980s) represent the semiotic systems of contemporary society as impoverished, too homogenized and commercialized to form the basis of individualizing cultural practices since they are based primarily not on active participation but on passive mass consumption – of recorded music, television, films and advertising. Rodríguez Méndez therefore rejects the proposition that mass-mediated culture provides opportunities for individuals to articulate their own identities through the choices exercised in the processes of reception, decoding and reusing of media texts. Such arguments have come to form an influential strand of contemporary cultural studies, through Stuart Hall's (1980) emphasis on the multiplicity of ways of interacting with and decoding texts available to audiences and Michel de Certeau's theory of 'tactical' consumption, in which 'imposed knowledge and symbolisms become objects manipulated by practitioners who have not produced them' (1984: 32), to John Fiske's postmodernist celebration of the carnivalesque, transgressive nature of contemporary cultural practices, especially television (1987). For Rodríguez Méndez, however, the crucial task of *desmasificación* (separating the individual from the mass) (Rodríguez Méndez 1971b: 45) cannot be fulfilled by the mass media and consumer culture. The distinction to which his work continually returns is that between, on the one hand, cultural forms that promote conformity and uniformity, either because they are designed for passive consumption or, conversely, because they are clearly elitist and deliberately inaccessible to the masses; and on the other hand, those that promote *desmasificación* either through active popular participation or, in some examples of 'high' culture (poetry, narrative and theatre), through the stimulation of critical social awareness.

Rodríguez Méndez's scepticism about the liberating potential of mass culture does not mean, however, that he presents a one-sided picture of people helplessly subjugated by ideology in the Althusserian sense. On the contrary, there is room in his work for something more like Antonio Gramsci's model of ideological 'hegemony' as a negotiated, contested process. Building on Marx, Gramsci argues that elite groups consolidate their own class-based interests by universalizing them – that is, persuading subjugated groups (partly by the threat of violence but largely through the dissemination of ideas, values and beliefs) to accept them as natural and feel that they have a stake in maintaining them. Hegemony is thus negotiated by a variety of means – political, cultural, educational – and at various levels of society, rather than simply imposed from above, and therefore leaves open the possibility of being contested.[8]

Rodríguez Méndez's division of the history of Spanish theatre into 'realist' and 'rhetorical' currents may be oversimplified, but it at least constitutes a recognition that culture at all levels of society is always a site of ideological struggle. Two inter-related dimensions of the struggle against the hegemony of the powerful are examined again and again in his dramatic and non-dramatic writings: the everyday cultural practices of the people on the one hand and the literary and theatrical texts produced by intellectuals in a close relationship with popular culture. He celebrates certain artists whose work he sees as being close to the realist ideal of giving voice to the *pueblo*, notably Cervantes and San Juan de la Cruz. Even in those of his plays which present social groups as most helplessly subject to physical and ideological control there are ways in which the characters put up some kind of resistance, and the later plays (especially *Bodas que fueron famosas del Pingajo y la Fandanga*, *Historia de unos cuantos* and *La Chispa*) make communal resistance through popular culture the primary focus of the representation of history. Nevertheless, both the essays and the plays remain profoundly sceptical about the possibility in any period of real negotiation of hegemony or actual shifts in the balance of power in favour of the ordinary people: the contestatory gestures of the oppressed are significant in cultural terms but make little difference to economic and political power structures.

Rodríguez Méndez's most important pieces of cultural analysis are the pair of complementary essays he published in the early 1970s examining the history of the relationship in Spain between the two dimensions of culture. *Ensayo sobre la 'inteligencia' española* uses the word *inteligencia* in a dual sense: intelligence as an abstract quality of cultural activity, and the intelligentsia as a social group mediating between the masses and the elite groups in power, either contributing to ideological control through mystification or contesting it through realism. *Ensayo sobre el machismo español* traces the development of cultural forms that the author sees as representing a genuine connection with the popular in some way. Both *machismo* and *inteligencia* are presented as forces of popularly rooted realism which are capable of contesting official myths and ideological manipulation, but often fail to do so effectively.

Inteligencia española
Ensayo sobre la 'inteligencia' española uses figures from high-culture texts as representatives of the relationship between intellectuals and society in various periods (constituting in a sense a historical study of Althusserian 'cultural ISAs' or

Gramscian 'organic intellectuals'). The first embodiment of *inteligencia* is the no-nonsense *furriel* (quartermaster) from Cervantes's short play *El retablo de las maravillas*, who for Rodríguez Méndez represents objective reality challenging heroic myths that enslave the gullible. Cervantes's confidence tricksters, Chirinos and Chanfalla, are presented as opportunists who take advantage of a hegemonic culture obsessed with hierarchy and conformity, but the quartermaster who demolishes their deception remains obstinately outside the game so that he can denounce the hypocrisy. Rodríguez Méndez compares his 'aggressive intelligence' with that of the mystic poets of the period, the antiheroes of the Picaresque novels and realist writers, including Cervantes himself and the later Generation of 1898 (1972a: 31).

The next archetype is Sansón Carrasco, the *bachiller* (scholar) in Cervantes's *Don Quijote*, who poses as a knight errant in order to force the hero out of his delusions. He represents in Rodríguez Méndez's analysis a more subtle method of destroying a myth by undermining it from the inside. Don Quijote embodies 'todos los males del siglo heroico-imperial' ('all the ills of the heroic-imperial age'), deluding himself about past glories (1972a: 42). As the Sancho Panzas of the world are not practised in seeing through these fictions, and are liable to be taken in despite their natural scepticism, the *bachiller* is needed in order to bring the mad knight down to earth by beating him at his own game and thereby saving him. Again, a link is made with the Generation of 1898 – an intellectual elite setting itself the task of regenerating a deluded and decrepit nation by means of a 'violenta llamada a la realidad') ('violent reminder of reality') – and with the whole tradition of realist writers (1972a: 53–54). However, Carrasco can also be seen to be working on behalf of the Establishment, anticipating the benevolent despotism of the Enlightenment by using his persuasive skills to win over hearts and minds: 'Sólo nos asusta pensar que esas técnicas de alcahuetería persuasiva podrán utilizarse también para todo lo contrario: para dominar y enajenar a otros seres perfectamente sanos' (1972a: 51).[9]

In the eighteenth century, Fray Gerundio de Campazas (the bombastic preacher satirized in the eponymous novel by José Francisco Isla de la Torre y Rojo) uses intelligence to manipulate language for his own advantage. Under an Enlightenment regime that does no more than modernize the old social order while blinding the people with science, Gerundio exploits the credulity of a people still 'más inclinado a cualquier clase de devoción que a la más rudimentaria forma de razonamiento' ('inclined more towards any kind of devotion than the most rudimentary form of reasoning'), creating an impressive mystique by means of an elaborate, pedantic jargon designed to mask the vacuousness of the discourse (1972a: 62). Rodríguez Méndez sees Gerundio as exemplifying an anti-realist intellectual tendency (artificial, rhetorical, foreign-influenced) and identifies it with later literary avant-gardes, which ensure that culture remains for the majority of people 'un mundo exótico e inalcanzable' (1972a: 87) ('an exotic, unattainable world') rather than a means of acquiring understanding.

Rodríguez Méndez sees no single figure created in the late nineteenth century as clearly embodying the intellectual spirit of the time, so he takes the Generation of 1898 as a representative group, making some of them express their views on the state of the nation as characters in a short play. Their opinions are diverse, but they have one objective in common: 'Todos están convencidos de que hay que "salvar a España" y para salvarla se ha de utilizar el arma de la cultura y del progreso' (1972a: 102).[10] Lucas Mallada, José Ortega y Gasset, Miguel de Unamuno, Eugenio d'Ors and Ramiro de Maeztu talk cleverly and endlessly about underdevelopment, Europeanization, morality, *casticismo* and the regenerative role of an intellectual elite. Meanwhile, Ángel Ganivet and the character referred to as *el Poeta melancólico* (Antonio Machado) listen thoughtfully but sceptically to the inconclusive debate, intervening only occasionally to affirm their attachment to popular cultural roots and peasant communities. The Poet is given a final monologue in which he ponders the intellectual aridity of the discussion and its insignificance in comparison with the passing of time, the presence of death, and the eternal realities of Spanish rural life: 'La vida basta por sí misma' (1972a: 127) ('Life is enough in itself').

The influence of elements of 1898 thinking on Rodríguez Méndez's view of history and the nature of Spain is significant: the notion of *intrahistoria*, the focus on the everyday life of the people, the exposure of the falseness of the public face of the Restoration, and the belief in the social importance of culture. He signals a debt to Machado in the title of *El vano ayer* and in the lines quoted on the title page of *El círculo de tiza de Cartagena*. Nevertheless, he does not identify himself unreservedly with the movement. He values their contribution to the growth of a progressive spirit through their focus on the *pueblo* as 'la médula del país' ('the country's core'), but he is suspicious of their insistence on Europeanization, their despair at Spain's degeneration, and what he sees as their intellectual elitism (Rodríguez Méndez 1971a: 93–95).

The eponymous heroine of Alejandro Casona's play *Nuestra Natacha* (1936) is Rodríguez Méndez's representative of *inteligencia* during the Second Republic. She is a product of the influence of the Generation of 1898, and applies their principles through practical involvement with feminism, secular education and political mobilization. Inspired by the pioneers of women's emancipation in other parts of Europe and by the Russian revolution, Natacha sets out to change the mentality of a backward, patriarchal society and combat 'el oscurantismo, el atraso y la pobreza en todas sus formas' (Rodríguez Méndez 1972a: 153).[11] Rodríguez Méndez compares her to Victoria Kent (the Republican lawyer, politician and prison reformer) and Dolores Ibárruri (the Communist leader), offering a generally sympathetic portrait of an intellectual committed to democratic social change, but suggesting that her idealism is over-optimistic.

The author describes the spirit of realist *inteligencia* evaporating in the post-war period, in a world dominated by memories of violence, the break-up of families and the corruption of the black market. He considers a few characters from fiction of the 1940s (particularly Andrea from Carmen Laforet's *Nada* and Cela's Pascual Duarte) but concludes that they are too absorbed by the minutiae of the daily struggle for survival to stand as representatives of the action of intelligence in relation to their age. It is only certain writers of realist fiction and theatre who continue to embody the stubborn critical intelligence of the *furriel* and Carrasco. In addition to official hostility and the general decline of rationalist, humanistic culture, realism is also under attack from the elitist avant-garde successors of Fray Gerundio:

> Aquellos muchos que preferían la "imaginación", el "ensueño", la finura preciosista, las investigaciones más o menos informales, la "invención del lenguaje". [...] Una pléyade de escritores cabalísticos, mágicos prodigiosos, que se valían fundamentalmente de la inexistencia de un pueblo que pudiera rechazarlos violentamente (1972a: 167–68).[12]

The final threat to intelligence in the realist, dissident form valued by Rodríguez Méndez is the hegemony of the computer. He argues that a fascination with the possibilities of technology and the proliferation of statistical data end up inhibiting critical analysis of the world in much the same way as Gerundio's rhetoric did in the eighteenth century. Despite this general gloom, however, he manages to end on a positive note, affirming the dogged persistence amongst some writers, scientists and others of 'la idea de crear, inventar, descubrir aquello que sirva para liberar al hombre, para hacerlo más completo, para aumentar su salud y su discernimiento, en contra de otros artilugios que se crean para esclavizarlo más' (1972a: 175).[13]

Machismo español

Ensayo sobre el machismo español looks at a series of archetypal figures from literary and theatrical works that have a strong connection with popular culture in some form, each of which is taken to represent the essential spirit of the Spanish people in a particular period. Rodríguez Méndez places special emphasis on the creative capacity of the Spanish *pueblo*, and tracks a process of reciprocal influence in which the language and everyday cultural practices of ordinary people on the one hand, and literary or canonical culture on the other, feed into and transform one another. He makes clear in his introduction that he is not interested in mere folklore or *costumbrismo*; on the contrary, he asserts that his intention is to 'poner de manifiesto el desconocimiento que la burguesía tiene del pueblo y lo falso que ha resultado precisamente ese populismo' (1971a: 9–10).[14]

The aggressive Escarramán of the seventeenth century (from Quevedo's narrative poem 'Carta de Escarramán a la Méndez'), the more confident and flamboyant Manolo of the eighteenth century (from Ramón de la Cruz's eponymous *sainete*), the socially conscious Julián of the nineteenth (from Ricardo de la Vega and Tomás Bretón's best-known *zarzuela*, *La verbena de la Paloma*), and the hedonistic but doomed Pichi of the Second Republic (from Celia Gámez's revue *Las Leandras*) all embody, in different ways, the rebellion of the people against the manipulative tendencies of their rulers. Each of these popular archetypes simultaneously expresses arrogant individuality and the collective spirit of a particular community; each serves to define the *pueblo* at a different stage in its historical development; each represents a different popular response to changing and usually hostile circumstances. What they have in common is a stubborn rejection of attempts to recruit them into the dominant ideological system. They function in a subversive way as a force of realism that exposes the workings of that ideology.

The term *machismo español* is used in this text by Rodríguez Méndez to articulate a concept of identity which in a sense operates at a more basic level than ideology (though not totally outside it) and is similar to that expounded by Clifford Geertz in *The Interpretation of Cultures*. Geertz defines identity as a phenomenon formed by and inseparable from culture in a broad anthropological sense: 'Believing, with Max Weber, that man is an animal suspended in webs of significance he himself has spun, I take culture to be those webs' (1975: 5). Geertz rejects the kind of essentialist view of humanity that would separate identity from culture and conceive of 'human nature' as immutable and universal, underlying and independent of all the roles, customs, beliefs and institutions constructed by civilization: 'What man is may be so entangled with where he is, who he is, and what he believes that it is inseparable from them (1975: 35).

Geertz insists that there is no 'real person' who can step out of cultural roles and be simply natural. People 'may change their roles, their styles of acting, even the dramas in which they play; but [...] they are always performing' (1975: 35–36). What is essentially human are the cultural particularities: 'Humanity is as various in its essence as it is in its expression' (1975: 37). The scientific basis for these arguments is the theory that human culture has evolved at the same time as, and inseparably from, the evolution of human biology. In comparison with other animals, human beings are much less regulated by automatic responses and depend heavily upon extragenetic symbolic systems that guide and give meaning to their behaviour. The cultural patterns operate at various levels – family, institution, community, region, nation. While they may appear to an individual participant at a particular time to be given, fixed or 'natural', they are, as semiotic systems, essentially arbitrary in their meanings, which are socially negotiated and historically changeable. The symbolic devices and practices we use in order to be ourselves and to relate to one another take many forms: words, gestures, images, music, dance, ceremonies, institutions, physical objects. These things are not merely reflections or products of our collective and individual identities; they are their very substance: 'There is no such thing as a human nature independent of culture. [...] We are, in sum, incomplete or unfinished animals who complete or finish ourselves through culture – and not through culture in general but through highly particular forms of it' (1975: 49). And finally, the symbolic systems provide the link between the 'innate capacities' of the species and the 'actual behaviors' of individuals: 'Becoming human is becoming individual, and we become individual under the guidance of cultural patterns, historically created systems of meaning in terms of which we give form, order, point, and direction to our lives' (1975: 52).

The aspects of Geertz's theory of culture that are particularly useful for our purposes are the rejection of essentialism; the definition of identity at all levels in terms of semiotic production; the idea of human individuality developing within particular collective cultural patterns; and the emphasis on diversity, creativity and performance. The theatrical allusion is not merely metaphorical: the point is that human beings *are* the roles they perform, the words they utter, the gestures they make, the settings they create, the costumes they wear. Although role-playing and meaning-making are built into the biological make-up of the species, this does not imply that the roles are fixed or universal, since the particular cultural forms are endlessly variable (from place to place and over time). While many individual performances (cultural acts, social practices, articulations of self or group identity) consist of unselfconscious repetition of received patterns, some amount to deliberate pastiche of traditional forms and others of individually improvised variations on a recognized theme.

The 'performance paradigm' in the study of human cultures has been developed most completely by Victor Turner, building on Erving Goffman's analysis of social interaction as a process of self-presentation through ritual acts:

> If man is a sapient animal, a toolmaking animal, a self-making animal, a symbol-using animal, he is, no less, a performing animal, *Homo performans*, not in the sense, perhaps, that a circus animal may be a performing animal, but in the sense that man is a self-performing animal – his performances are, in a way, *reflexive*, in performing he reveals himself to himself (Turner 1988: 81).

Turner identifies three levels of reflexivity in performance. 'Daily living', although it is a kind of theatre, is relatively unselfconscious and largely to do with maintaining the status quo, while 'social drama' is a kind of metatheatre – the self-conscious playing out of a crisis within a social group, characterized by a break from normal patterns (1988: 76). The more formalized genres of 'cultural performance' (including theatre) are 'secreted from the social drama and in turn surround it and feed their performed meanings back into it' (1988: 90). This interdependence between everyday 'social performance' and the special practices and texts of 'cultural performance' will emerge as a key feature of Rodríguez Méndez's essays and plays, especially *Historia de unos cuantos*, in which existing cultural icons are recreated and inserted into a reconfigured historical context.

The modes of cultural identity summed up as *machismo español* in Rodríguez Méndez's essay and dramatized in his plays are essentially performative, the product of multiple acts of creative resistance to official versions of culture, each growing out of and adding to the distinctive cultural traditions of a community. Although the archetypes used by Rodríguez Méndez are in fact from a narrow cultural range (three of the four are essentially from the same Madrid tradition of cocky urban *majos*), they are intended to serve as models for the dynamic construction of a national identity based on the sum of the cultural practices of a multitude of communities evolving over time. Language is the crucial component of this process. Although Rodríguez Méndez tends to associate *machismo español* with the Castilian language (and frequently celebrates its literary heritage), it is language as spoken dialect and sociolect that is proposed as the primary focus of individual and collective identities, as performed *habla* (speech, or 'parole' in Saussurean terms) rather than regulated *lengua del imperio* (language of empire). The colourful speech of the author's native Madrid predominates in many plays, but various other dialects of Castilian also make an appearance and the foregrounding of Catalan in *Flor de Otoño* is a crucial development.

Escarramán embodies a 'tragic' *machismo*, consisting largely of a desperate struggle for survival in a hostile world. The hollow, tottering empire of the Hapsburgs is magnificent and ostentatious at the top, but for the mass of the population life is brutal, sordid and short. Escarramán is a ruffian, a petty criminal and a pimp, bound for the galleys but keeping up an arrogant sense of black humour. He belongs to a despised social class existing at the lowest level of society. However, Rodríguez Méndez regards marginalized groups at various levels (including the reformist mystics within the Church, the *pícaros* on the edges of respectable society, converted Jews and Muslims, as well as certain realist writers impelled to depict them) as rebels who represent the most authentic spirit of the Spain of their time: 'La *realidad* de España estaba en esta abigarrada humanidad y no en la pompa de los discursos eclesiásticos, ni en las empresas rutinarias de los conquistadores, ni en los devaneos palaciegos, ni en los palacios de los nobles' (1971a: 29).[15] The creativity demonstrated by Escarramán is rough, angry and defensive, but what is most interesting about it is that it responds to oppression with parody:

> Los escarramanes reflejarán en su propio mundo el mundo fastuoso que les rodea. Copiarán, en su deforme rostro y talante, los gestos y maneras de aquéllos, darán a sus frases solemnes un nuevo sentido ridículo, proyectarán sus 'lances de honor' en sus peleas tumultuarias, [...] traducirán sus citas y latinajos en sus frases de lenguaje germanesco, mimetizarán con trágico humor los actos solemnes de los nobles (1971a: 41).[16]

The reflection is grotesque, but it springs from a realistic awareness of the grotesqueness of the contrast between the splendid imperial façade and the harshness of the everyday life of the masses behind it (1971a: 42). The cultural performance consists simultaneously of rejection and mimicry (1971a: 45). It may work through ironic detachment, but is driven by fear and ultimately degrades the people.

Manolo is more confident and flamboyant than Escarramán, still asserting his manhood against authority but, under the relatively benevolent, paternalistic regime of the Bourbons, less desperately aggressive.[17] Instead of lashing out crudely at the Establishment, Manolo is largely indifferent to it, arrogantly self-centred, even contemptuous of the effete *afrancesados* (members of the middle or upper classes who affect French manners) who rule over him: 'Para el Manolo, su gente, los compadres de la taberna, los ociosos de la plazuela y sus compañeros, los forzados africanos, son infinitamente superiores a los que gobiernan y a los que mandan en virtud de los privilegios y el dinero' (1971a: 85).[18] He makes fun of those in power and, to his great amusement, finds that they begin to imitate aspects of his culture: duchesses dress in the popular costume of *majas*, painters portray picturesque folk customs and the bullfight becomes a spectacle for all classes, rooted in popular culture. Popular creativity thrives in contrast with the sterile classicism of official culture, and life is now a game, a *sainete*. Since the socio-economic reality is still harsh and oppressive, however, it is a 'sainete para llorar, o tragedia para reír'.[19] Nevertheless, the *pueblo* as represented by Manolo is beginning to assert its sense of identity, its vitality and creativity, especially through its enrichment of the Castilian language: 'Es un lenguaje lleno de chispeantes sinónimos, de giros inesperados, de adjetivos rimbombantes para calificar cosas cotidianas. Todo ello dentro de un tono viril en que la majeza se haga patente' (1971a: 69).[20] What is also developing is a kind of patriotism, identified not so much with the monarchy and traditional institutions as with a vague sense of popular collective identity which, in practice, focuses more on a region than on the nation, and in its most concrete form may narrow right down to the particular *barrio* (neighbourhood). The mobilization of this feeling against Napoleon's forces in the War of Independence (dramatized in *La Chispa*) is characterized by Rodríguez Méndez as an authentic 'explosión de fe y de entusiasmo' ('explosion of faith and enthusiasm'), later manipulated by the state and transformed into a new form of servitude (1971a: 78–79).

By the end of the nineteenth century, *machismo español* is becoming proletarianized and politicized: Julián represents 'reformist' *machismo*. The *Ensayo* characterizes the Restoration period in terms of growing conflict between the demands of an increasingly active, politically aware working class and the corrupt, bogus constitutionalism of a conservative oligarchy. The *cuestión social* ('social question') has become the dominant preoccupation of parliamentary and extra-parliamentary politics, and the masses are becoming a potent economic and political force, with an increasing awareness of their collective identity and needs. Rodríguez Méndez sees this situation reflected in the culture of the period on two levels. Firstly, the preoccupation of major writers and thinkers with the state of the nation and the welfare of working people helped to create a reformist climate of opinion. These ideas are then seen to have spread through society and influenced popular culture – in the *género chico* and the boom of printed political and fictional material. Thus Rodríguez Méndez finds, under the triviality of populist entertainment, a solid basis in the real lives and interests of ordinary people as well as a strong element of social concern. He argues that the ordinary working men and women of Madrid could identify with the short satirical plays set in their world, using a language similar to their own, and 'aprendía a hermanarse con sus semejantes' (1971a: 97).[21] He considers *La verbena de la Paloma* (first performed in 1894) one of the best examples of this phenomenon, and Julián the figure who best typifies the character of the period.

Rodríguez Méndez's defence of the social and linguistic authenticity of the *género chico* and his argument that it is embedded in popular culture are questionable, especially from a left-wing perspective. Monleón acknowledges that the popularization of *sainetes* and *zarzuelas* in the late nineteenth century made a refreshing change from the stuffy conventionality of mainstream bourgeois drama and brought onto the stage social environments previously considered unworthy of dramatization (1968a: 24). However, he asserts that the genre is essentially designed to serve the ideological interests of the petty bourgeoisie through its emphasis on light comedy and *casticismo*, offering a sentimentalized, *costumbrista* image of the lower classes: 'La "cuestión social" estaba en danza, y el sainete vino a ser una respuesta dada "desde arriba", la imagen de un pueblo gracioso y feliz en sus corralas y verbenas de organillo' (1971a: 24).[22] Ruiz Ramón similarly argues that although the *género chico* supplied a welcome antidote to the apoplectic rhetoric of neo-Romantic melodrama, its effect was essentially to depoliticize its representation of social conditions (1978: 150).

Rodríguez Méndez, in contrast, values precisely what Monleón sees as the main defects of this kind of theatre, 'su proceso casticista, su achulamiento verbal' (Monleón 1968a: 24).[23] Essentially, his response is that if the representation appears stylized or aestheticized, this does not necessarily indicate falsification but rather a reflection of the extent to which the actual cultural practices of the *pueblo* (in a distinctive setting such as the traditional working-class districts of Madrid) constitute an ironic, self-conscious performance of identity. Although it clearly does not tackle serious social issues directly, the *género chico* participates in the rebellious, satirical spirit of *machismo* and thus refers implicitly to the social conditions to which that spirit responds. The dramatization of the *Ensayo*'s arguments in *Historia de unos cuantos* (discussed in Chapter 4) not only sets characters and situations from *La verbena de la Paloma* and other *zarzuelas chicas* in a concrete socio-historical context but also emphasizes the self-consciousness of the interaction between such forms and the everyday culture of the communities they represent.

The Julián of *La verbena de la Paloma* is, according to this analysis, more integrated into a social order than his predecessors, performing a brand of *chulería* inflected by a new progressive political consciousness (1971a: 110).[24] In order to flesh out the enigmatic figure of Julián, Rodríguez Méndez inserts between the lines of *La verbena* his reading of the history of the Madrid working class of the nineteenth century. He imagines a childhood marked by hunger, disease, mass unemployment, the beginnings of the political mobilization of the proletariat, and the catastrophic waste of pointless colonial wars (1971a: 104). He argues that Julián's occupation of typesetter indicates that he would probably have been a member of the Socialist Party, and imagines him articulating his hostility to privilege in terms of social justice (but moderately, and with a streak of individualism):

> Que ca cual luche por lo suyo, por que sus hijos tengan qué comer, y tengan estrucción y por tener un buen vivir. Aquí hay que implantar, ni más, ni menos, una república de trabajadores de modo y manera que tenga que hincar el pico too Dios y el que no hinque el pico, pues ése que no coma (1971a: 110).[25]

Finally, Rodríguez Méndez adapts De la Vega's theme of a conflict between head and heart to express a duality in the social orientation of his *macho* of 1898. In the *zarzuela*, Julián is torn between challenging his middle-class rival for the affections of Susana, don Hilarión, and prudently keeping quiet – a conflict between the heart and the head (De la Vega 1943: 1100–01). The caution counselled by Rita is necessary because of the higher social position of don Hilarión. This makes Julián indignant and frustrated, prompting the best-known lines in the piece:

> También la gente del pueblo
> tiene su corazoncito
> y lágrimas en los ojos
> y celos mal reprimidos.
> (De la Vega 1943: 1082)[26]

His protest is a feeble one and is soon defused, but Rodríguez Méndez feels that it is a significant social statement on behalf of his class, a demand to be taken into account, giving him a kind of unexpected greatness (1971a: 122). So Julián's heart represents his collectivist instincts, and the head his individualistic ambition. This form of *machismo* is ambiguous: the proud sense of class and cultural tradition produces the socialist commitment, while the arrogant self-assertion leads to the unscrupulous opportunism, which then creates its own momentum:

> Porque es seguro que el Julián habrá de casarse con la Susana y fundar un hogar. Procurará ir mejorando de nivel social. Su socialismo irá evolucionando. Tal vez se establezca con imprenta propia. Y hasta quizá se convierta en patrón. Luego no dejará de oír ciertas sirenas – partidos democráticos radicales, y si me apuran falangistas – , el confort le irá moldeando. Puede que terminara sus años siendo uno de los propagadores del desarrollo económico de España, olvidado de sus viejos ideales (1971a: 107).[27]

Although the cautious reformism of Julián helps to make real political change possible in 1931, the figure chosen by Rodríguez Méndez as representative of the *machismo social* of the Republic is the more glamorous, irresponsible figure known as 'el Pichi'.[28] The character was created by Celia Gámez in a musical revue of 1931 called *Las Leandras*, by José Muñoz Román with music by Francisco Alonso. The most popular number was a *chotis* (a version of the scottische, a slow polka, particularly associated with Madrid) in which the star wore overalls and a flat cap for a caricature of a 'chulo que castiga del Portillo a la Arganzuela'.[29] The girls of the *barrio* pursue him but he treats them casually, interested only in enjoying the pleasure of the moment. As well as this cavalier manner, his attraction lies in his now fashionable status as a skilled manual worker, and an association with the glamorous images of American cinema. The attitude of the dominant classes towards the *macho* had been hostility in the seventeenth century, paternalism in the eighteenth, and indifference in the nineteenth. Now the young worker in his blue *mono* (overalls) is the darling of the new society, the hero of republican activism, particularly in Madrid. Widespread poverty, unemployment and hunger have not been eradicated, but are seen as problems to be overcome through political action. Pichi is proud of his occupation, is instinctively loyal to the Socialist Party, and devotes the remainder of his time to womanizing.

Rodríguez Méndez sees the period as 'preconsumerist' (1971a: 139), featuring a youth culture influenced by the cinema, advertising and the fashion industry, and anticipating the consumer culture of the 1960s – although in a primitive, ingenuous form, without a massive commercial and media apparatus. Pichi himself is attracted by some of the paraphernalia and jargon of modern life but is *castizo* to the core and fiercely patriotic – in a way focused primarily on his class and his *patria chica* (literally, 'little fatherland'), like Manolo, rather than in a right-wing mode focusing on an ideal of national destiny. He is, however, at the end of the line of descent of true *machismo español*, representing for Rodríguez Méndez the decadence of 'la chulería castiza y nacional' (1971a: 143). His only philosophy is one of *carpe diem*, with none of the sense of responsibility of Julián. Nor does he inherit Julián's optimism, for his pursuit of pleasure is ultimately driven by desperation. He throws himself into the political life of the Republic, but largely because this is part of the excitement of the time. His attitude is casual and irresponsible. Indeed, Rodríguez Méndez points out that the political orientation of Gámez's creation was ambiguous. Pichi's anti-feminism held strong appeal for men of the Right, and his real-life counterparts ended up on both sides in 1936 (1971a: 146).

The type represented by Pichi is destined to be destroyed by the violence and ideological polarization of the war, and not to revive in the bleak post-war world.[30] Rodríguez Méndez proposes that the authentic Spanish *macho* figure is exterminated with Pichi in the civil war, on both sides of the battle lines, and it is this doomed quality of Pichi and his era that interests him most: 'En esta euforia orgiástica hay una clara premonición de tragedia' (1971a: 135).[31] After the civil war, *machismo español* disintegrates. Individuality is crushed in the hard years of the 1940s and early 1950s, and the *pueblo* as a distinctive cultural entity effectively ceases to exist. The everyday life of the masses is lived in a cultural vacuum, in which authentic popular creativity is replaced by football and, later, television. Economic development in the 1950s and 1960s brings further alienation and *masificación*:

> El pueblo se volvió de espaldas a sí mismo, se desintegró totalmente, para avanzar a esa entelequia – hoy aún oscura – de la sociedad del bienestar y el consumo. Las largas horas de trabajo, el pluriempleo, la batalla interminable por una remuneración congruente a la necesidad del trabajo desplazado, etc., serían las preocupaciones fundamentales de este pueblo, desalojando y anulando por inservible cualquier otra (1971a: 158–59).[32]

The only popular role models now are hollow fantasy figures: football players, foreign film stars, comic-book heroes, cosmopolitan playboys. Rodríguez Méndez argues that the traditional *pueblo* collaborates with its own disappearance, seduced by the glamour and comforts of consumerism. It loses its Spanish specificity and its creative energy, becoming merely a mass of consumers, indistinguishable from the populations of other industrial nations, no longer fulfilling the *macho*'s anti-ideological function as a force of realism and demystification (1971a: 166). This contemporary picture of the people as an alienated, homogenized mass without the spark of rebelliousness, pride and creativity formerly provided by *machismo español* is dramatized in several of Rodríguez Méndez's plays, notably *Los quinquis de Madriz* (discussed in Chapter 6). It is a pessimistic – and, in a sense, reactionary or at least patronizing – view that ignores the extent to which economic development was by the end of the 1960s opening up some opportunities for political mobilization, better education and improvements in working conditions, accompanied by a widening of cultural horizons through the mass media which increasingly eroded the dictatorship's ideological control. Nevertheless, Rodríguez Méndez's scepticism about the benefits to working people of Franco's 'economic miracle' is understandable: the regime's model of economic development involved low wages, poor protection for workers' health and safety, inadequate housing and social security, and severe constraints on the organization of labour.

Although Rodríguez Méndez uses the term *machismo* in a way that embraces much more than its conventional sense of assertive masculinity or male dominance, the concept of *machismo español* clearly has gender implications. It centres a definition of cultural identity on men and on self-consciously masculine behaviour, and assumes – apparently uncritically – the permanence of patriarchy. *Ensayo sobre el machismo español* emphasises sexuality in each of the incarnations of the *macho español*, who constantly strives to assert his manhood. In the case of Escarramán, this implies the straightforward physical domination of women, who are useful to him economically (through prostitution) and psychologically (by giving him an opportunity to exercise control). The more confident Manolo takes a playful, cavalier attitude, enjoying his role as a 'chulo barriobajero que se deja querer, porque las arrebata' (1971a: 70).[33] Since Julián is a man with a sense of social responsibility and an inclination towards bourgeois values, his interest in women is monogamous and bound up with questions of social status. His contest with don Hilarión is essentially over a woman as a status symbol, a piece of property. He manfully stands up to his rival in the end, but along the way has agonized over the risk of jeopardizing his interests. Pichi reverts to a more arrogant, carefree kind of *chulería*, now glamorized by consumerist accessories and political liberalization. Commitment-free womanizing has become easier than ever before, thanks to the beginnings of social and economic emancipation of women and the general weakening of traditional constraints.

Ensayo sobre el machismo español says nothing about women's subjectivity, discussing them only in so far as they complement or put up with the egocentric performance of the *machos*. However, a more complex and more interesting picture will be seen to emerge from Rodríguez Méndez's plays, in which women are represented as active participants in the performance of identity. Although collective identities in the plays are defined primarily in terms of male characters, who frequently behave in ways that imply objectification or even abuse of women, their *machismo* tends to be revealed as a flawed and fragile performance, while it is the female characters who in most cases are presented as the lasting embodiment of the collective spirit of a community (and by extension, the nation). The men are flamboyant, self-centred and usually doomed; the women tend to be more responsible, more community-orientated and more likely to survive. My analysis of the plays in Chapters 3, 4, 5 and 6 seeks to demonstrate that both women and men (including two homosexual protagonists) are embraced in various ways by the concept of *machismo español*, which, though it may appear to consist of a conventional, politically incorrect fixing of gender roles, ends up questioning and unfixing them.

The notion of gender as a performance has been most persuasively formulated by Judith Butler. Starting from phenomenological theory, Geertz's and Turner's analyses of culture as performance, and a linguistic analogy with performative utterances that effect actions by being spoken, she argues that gender is not natural, essential or stable but socially constituted through 'the stylized repetition of acts through time', and that a body genders itself (or 'does gender') through the adoption of a signifying 'corporeal style' (Butler 1990: 271–72). These acts become sedimented over time, so that the complex of social values, conventions and restraints built around the concept of gender is naturalized or reified; the process of construction conceals itself and gender 'appears to the popular imagination as a substantial core which might well be understood as the spiritual or psychological correlate of biological sex' (1990: 279). The analogy between the bodily acts by which gender is constituted and acting in a theatrical sense is not just a way of affirming the constructed nature of gender. The assertion that gender is performative, existing only in so far as it is performed by and on a body, implies that, like all social performances, the acting of gender is both public and personal, both rehearsed and individually reinterpreted:

> The body is not passively scripted with cultural codes, as if it were a lifeless recipient of wholly pre-given cultural relations. But neither do embodied selves pre-exist the cultural conventions which essentially signify bodies. Actors are always already on the stage, within the terms of the performance. Just as a script may be enacted in various ways, and just as the play requires both text and interpretation, so the gendered body acts its part in a culturally restricted corporeal space and enacts interpretations within the confines of already existing directives (1990: 277).

The theatrical analogy does not imply that gender is merely a role adopted by (or imposed upon) a subject with an essential, pre-existing identity independent of the performance. Gender is not expressive but performative: it does not reveal or conceal a true self or an essential sex, but rather 'constructs the social fiction of its own psychological interiority' (1990: 279). From the point of view of feminist political practice, the aim of exposing gender as 'a performative accomplishment' is to contest its reified status and open up possibilities for acting in new ways. Just as theatrical roles are open to various interpretations and can be modified by improvisation, so 'gender is a basically innovative affair' which offers opportunities to 'expand the cultural field bodily through subversive performances of various kinds' (1990: 282). Nowhere does Rodríguez Méndez himself explicitly advance such a theory of gender, but his concept of *machismo español*, as discussed in the *Ensayo* and dramatized in the plays, clearly links collective cultural identity with gender identity and represents both as forms of performance, manifested in speech, gesture and other everyday cultural acts, and modified in response to changing social conditions. Like Butler's account of performativity, then, *machismo español* as a metaphor for collective identity is valuable for its emphasis on the bodily nature of the acts that constitute various forms of identity, and for its reminder that although such performances consist basically of the reiteration of prescribed or sedimented acts, they are also open to innovation and change.

Historical theatre

If Rodríguez Méndez's view of culture and society had been dramatized only in texts set in the present, a very limited and pessimistic vision would have emerged from his work. Just as the analysis presented in the two *Ensayos* is fundamentally historical and finds its most interesting material in the past, historical perspective is also central to Rodríguez Méndez's theatre. What ultimately becomes more important than the simplistic objective of recording contemporary social reality is the illumination of that social reality through the exploration of its historical roots. One of the crucial routes towards the goal of *desmasificación* is the awakening of an understanding of the present as the product of the past, and of history as a process of social and cultural change in which the masses can have as important a role as the elites – in determining the authentic character of a period if not in deciding the course of events. Consequently, the chapters of this book that analyse Rodríguez Méndez's dramatic work in greatest detail concentrate on plays with temporal settings that are clearly in the past in relation to the moment at which they were written, the gap ranging from several centuries (in plays set in the Middle Ages or the sixteenth and seventeenth centuries) to a couple of decades (in plays dealing with the civil war and its aftermath). Discussion of plays with contemporary settings (in Chapter 6) is much briefer and emphasizes ways in which they echo or contrast with the historical plays, generally dramatizing the disintegration of popular culture as traced in Rodríguez Méndez's essays and as a result offering a much more subdued social vision, which in my view is theatrically less dynamic and less interesting since it has been drained of much of the creative energy of *machismo español*. The texts that form the primary focus of this book can therefore be easily defined – in the straightforward sense of being set in the past – as 'historical theatre'. What Chapters 3, 4 and 5 will demonstrate, though, is that they are historical in a more complex sense, not merely using history as an exotic setting and source of biographical or mythical material, but subjecting it to critical examination and inviting audiences to consider its relevance to their present.

In the context of the Franco regime's manipulation and mythification of national history through education, propaganda and officially supported cultural production, dissident dramatists played an important role between the late 1950s and the 1970s in challenging its hijacking of ideas of national identity and in reasserting the problematic, constructed nature of history. In the early years of the dictatorship, pro-Francoist writers such as José María Pemán, Eduardo Marquina and Eduardo Juliá Martínez had turned particularly to the period of the Catholic Monarchs and imperial expansion for dramatic material with which to celebrate the restoration of authoritarian traditionalism.[34] Now, alongside Rodríguez Méndez, playwrights such as Antonio Buero Vallejo, José Martín Recuerda, Carlos Muñiz, Alfonso Sastre, Antonio Gala, Ana Diosdado, Manuel Martínez Mediero, Domingo Miras, Alberto Miralles and Jerónimo López Mozo began to write more critical forms of historical theatre. Using a variety of theatrical forms their plays open up Spanish history as a dynamic process demanding reassessment. Previously idealized elements are problematized or satirized, while neglected or despised elements are recuperated or vindicated.[35]

One advantage of using a historical setting in a time of strict political control is that it may afford a disguise under which specific criticisms can be smuggled past the censors. However, none of the history plays written by these authors during the dictatorship can be reduced to such a limited aim. History is never used merely as an innocuous backdrop, yet nor does it function simply as an analogy for current political or social concerns. As we shall see from examination of the censorship files on Rodríguez Méndez's work, the censors were not easily fooled by disguise of this kind; indeed, they tended to be either exaggeratedly vigilant in seeking out possible analogies with present circumstances or else happy to give many texts the benefit of the doubt on the grounds that the action was remote and of no concern to the present. The sort of historical theatre we are considering here has more sophisticated and far-reaching objectives: to interrogate the relationship between the past and the present; to generate alternative views of the past which may suggest alternative possibilities for the present and future; and to examine how attitudes and ideologies in the present rewrite the past. Buero Vallejo articulates such priorities very clearly: 'El teatro histórico ilumina nuestro presente cuando no se reduce a ser un truco ante las censuras y nos hace entender y sentir mejor la relación viva existente entre lo que sucedió y lo que nos sucede' (1980–81: 19).[36]

After 1975, when the urgency of reclaiming history from right-wing manipulation had diminished, a new generation of playwrights (notably Carmen Resino, Concha Romero, Ignacio Amestoy and Eduardo Galán) joined their older colleagues in rediscovering suppressed histories and using the dramatization of the past to explore issues of individual and collective identity, class and gender relations, myth and memory, power and resistance. Historical subject matter is valued in both periods as offering special opportunities for the creative exploration of tensions between temporal distance and aesthetic distancing, between historical time and stage time, between audiences' knowledge of recorded events and personalities and the re-presentation of these as dramatic action and characters.

History plays by these writers tend to deploy one or more of three different representational strategies: (a) the thoughtful re-evaluation of well-known personalities and their role in crucial historical episodes, sometimes in the form of tragedy (exemplified most completely by Buero Vallejo); (b) the debunking of established myths through satire and parody, using exaggeration, non-naturalistic staging and black comedy to bring out the political processes behind the personalities and events (for example, Miras's *De San Pascual a San Gil*); (c) 'history from below', focusing on *intrahistoria* rather than *Historia*, calling attention to marginalized or suppressed interests and voices, and sometimes foregrounding women's experience (for example, *Como reses* by García Matilla and López Mozo).[37] The second of these approaches is most likely to involve devices of anachronism or disruption of a Brechtian kind designed to draw attention to parallels with the present or to the process of re-enactment and reinterpretation. As for dramatic structure, it tends to take the form of either a concentrated examination of a single key episode or an extended chronicle of a series of events. The first type focuses on the essential collision of social forces at a particular moment, while the second tends to place more emphasis on change and causality.[38]

It is undoubtedly Rodríguez Méndez who has made the most substantial contribution to historical theatre in Spain in the second half of the twentieth century. Since he first became known with the premiere of *Vagones de madera* in 1958, he has written seventeen full-length plays with historical settings and ten texts for other kinds of performance referring to classical and traditional models (adaptations of Golden Age plays, poetry recitals, musical tributes to Barbieri and Muñoz Seca), compared with fifteen full-length plays with contemporary settings and six other non-historical pieces (short plays for La Pipironda). Although to some extent his history plays deploy all three of the strategies described above, he is above all the leading exponent of the third approach – putting on stage the suppressed social history of the *pueblo*, giving voice to the powerless and focusing on everyday cultural practices. In a recent discussion of his dramatic treatment of history, he defines his primary aim as 'investigar el papel del pueblo español en la historia de mi patria, frente al papel interpretado por unas minorías dominantes, usurpadoras no pocas veces del acontecer histórico de España' (1999: 40).[39] He does not single out the distortions of the Francoist period as the only official versions to be contested. On the contrary, he appears to be equally suspicious of the revisionism of the post-Franco period. The public may now have access to more information and in a sense be better equipped to judge discourses for themselves, but the increased persuasive power of the mass media means that historical theatre can still have an important function in questioning the consensus.

As noted in Chapter 1, Rodríguez Méndez denies that he was subjected to extreme National-Catholic indoctrination at secondary school in Barcelona immediately after the war, and insists that he was given a traditional, largely unpoliticized education in the humanities which allowed him to develop critical thinking: 'Creo que allí fue donde aprendí a amar la lengua y la literatura y a utilizar la Historia para poder desmentir la que no se usa certeramente sino con finales torcidos' (1999: 46).[40] On the other hand, he identifies the influence on his understanding of the nature of history of certain trends in historiography which are implicitly opposed to the models of history propagated by the dictatorship and by Spanish conservatism in general. He makes a distinction between *teatro histórico* ('history plays'), essentially a Romantic model aiming at a relatively straightforward 'reconstrucción de la Historia' ('reconstruction of History'), exemplified by Schiller, Zorrilla and García Gutiérrez, and *teatro historicista* ('historicist theatre'), a twentieth-century model in which 'la Historia es manipulada por el autor para definir sus tesis ideológicas o sus doctrinas de hoy' (1999: 39).[41] He traces the philosophical origins of modern historicist theatre back to Hegel's philosophy of history and Arnold J. Toynbee's monumental *Study of History* (1935–1961).[42]

Unfortunately, these definitions remain rather imprecise. Rodríguez Méndez qualifies the notion of 'reconstruction' by associating it with a Romantic tendency to impose on historical material 'un tratamiento subjetivo y especial' (1999: 39) ('a subjective, special treatment'). However, he does not acknowledge the extent to which this approach also implies the articulation of an ideological position or 'thesis'. Furthermore, he does not distinguish here between modes of representation that reinforce hegemonic ideologies by immobilizing history as myth and those that challenge them by treating history as a process of change in which, in Toynbee's terms, civilizations grow and decline in response to a variety of social, economic, cultural and religious challenges.

The term *historicismo* is defined in a narrow and apparently disapproving way by the Real Academia Española: 'Tendencia intelectual a reducir la realidad humana a su historicidad o condición histórica' (1992: 1114). Rodríguez Méndez's references to Hegel and the French Catholic dramatists Claudel and Bernanos indicate, however, that he does not exclude a spiritual dimension in historicism and is using the term in a more neutral sense, closer to more nuanced definitions such as those offered by the *Oxford English Dictionary* (or at least the first and second of these):

1. The attempt, found esp. among German historians since about 1850, to view all social and cultural phenomena, all categories, truths, and values, as relative and historically determined, and in consequence to be understood only by examining their historical context, in complete detachment from present-day attitudes.
2. A tendency in philosophy to see historical development as the most fundamental aspect of human existence, and historical thinking as the most important type of thought, because of its interest in the concrete, unique, and individual.
3. The belief that historical change occurs in accordance with laws, so that the course of history may be predicted but cannot be altered by human will; the resulting attitude to the social sciences, of regarding them as concerned mainly with historical prediction (OED 1994).

Rodríguez Méndez's insistence that his work is historicist rather than historical implies three things: firstly, that history is treated as a dynamic process of social and cultural development open to multiple interpretations; secondly, that he is more concerned with the interpretative relationship between the past and the present than with an analytical understanding of the historical material itself; and thirdly, that an awareness that drama does not fulfil the same functions as historiography is built into his texts. On one level, the point is simply to justify a degree of subjectivity and artistic freedom (and we shall see in subsequent chapters that he does indeed handle source material loosely): 'Teatro más historicista que histórico. Porque en él la historia nace de la vida y no de los cronicones y fuentes de archivo. Es una historia vivida o revivida al contrastarla con los tiempos que me ha tocado vivir' (1999: 48).[43]

What is also implied, though, is a reminder of what is distinctive about dramatizing historical subject matter, as opposed to narrating it either in fictionalized form or as analytical historiography. All these forms of representation involve selecting particular events, people and circumstances from the incoherent mass of historical records and collective memories, and structuring this material in such a way as to impose coherence upon it and make it meaningful to a target audience temporally remote from the events. An influential strand of historiographical theory has focused on the status of historical writing as a form of discourse that constructs explanations by means of narrative structures characteristic of fictional genres. Hayden White shows how the historian arranges the events of a chronicle 'into a hierarchy of significance by assigning events different functions as story elements in such a way as to disclose the formal coherence of a whole set of events considered as a comprehensible process with a discernible beginning, middle, and end', and how history is given meaning through 'emplotment' as much as by deductive argument; that is, by 'identifying the *kind of story* that has been told' – Romance, Tragedy, Comedy, Satire or Epic (1973: 7).[44]

Whatever the kind of story it communicates, theatre is necessarily even more selective and condensed than historical writing in narrative prose (either fictional or non-fictional), since it takes the form not of storytelling but of re-enactment, consisting primarily of dialogue and interaction between characters, in real time, in front of an audience. The priority is to generate a relationship with an audience, holding their interest throughout the duration of performance time and, by asking them to watch something clearly signalled as 'then' but presented as happening 'now', encouraging them to consider (and feel) the relevance of the past action to their present. Georg Lukács establishes a crucial distinction between what he regards as great historical novels (the 'epic' mode) and great historical theatre (especially tragedy). Both seek to convey a sense of the 'totality' of the world represented; in the epic, the goal is a 'totality of objects' (detailed depiction of human society in relation to 'the surrounding world of things forming the object of its activity'), while in drama the aim is a 'totality of movement' (concentration on 'what is indispensable to the dynamic working-out of the collision, to those social, human and moral *movements* in men, therefore, out of which the collision arises and which the collision dissolves') (1969: 105–108). This concentration on 'movement' is largely a matter of structure – the structuring of the plot and of the relationship between characters, but also, crucially, of the relationship between the performance and the audience: 'While the essence of a collision must remain historically authentic, historical drama must bring out those features in men and their destinies which will make a spectator, separated from these events by centuries, feel himself a direct participant of them' (Lukács 1969: 179).

Kurt Spang follows Lukács in highlighting condensation as one of the essential features of historical drama, which generates 'una especie de totalidad intensiva, no extensiva, en la que lo particular se convierte en ejemplificación impactante de lo general' (1998: 36).[45] He adds that as a result, the formal structuring of the material tends to be made more evident, drawing attention to the fact that the representation is much more coherent and ordered than direct experience (1998: 37).

Historical theatre selects and shapes its material in order to impose coherence and generate meaning, yet to some degree it also gives spectators, by means of present-time re-enactment, a sense of the incoherence and immediacy of lived experience. The management of the balance between the coherence of the overall story and the incoherence – or at least incompleteness – of the succession of events as seen from the particular points of view of characters and spectators is the key structural problem of all historical theatre. As a result of their focus on social and cultural history rather than political history, Rodríguez Méndez's plays tend not to make the overall story coherence explicit (by, for example, having a character articulate the significance of the action, or building in an element of extra-diegetic commentary or narrative); they allow a degree of incoherence and immediacy to persist. Nor do they fit easily into the archetypal story modes identified by White; instead, they combine elements of tragedy, satire, comedy and epic (but rarely romance). The common structural principle that generates overall meaning will turn out to be not one of the literary genres referred to by White but a broader notion of cultural production in the form of collective performances of identity – the performance of *machismo español*.

Another key focus of analysis that will be developed through Chapters 3, 4 and 5 will be the tension between a determinist or cyclical view of history (the sense that the 'story' must reach a foreseen conclusion or repeat itself) and a contingent, changeable, open-ended one. Lindenberger suggests that 'the historical dramatist is always walking a tightrope between a determinism which he needs to give his play its central momentum and a commitment to the individuality of particular moments and events', seeking a balance between 'the concrete details of specific historical situations and the larger processes, forces, and meanings to which they can be related' (1975: 99). The emphasis in Rodríguez Méndez's works on *intrahistoria* and lack of change at the level of the everyday lives of the masses often appears to suggest a deterministic, static or even ahistorical view. However, this impression is offset by other factors that point to a more dynamic vision of historical development, including the very fact of the constructed nature of the dramatization. As Ruiz Ramón points out, there is something inherently anti-deterministic in historical drama: 'Lo que fue pudo no ser, pero fue por una serie de razones o sinrazones que el drama asume; en cambio, lo que es […] podría no ser o ser otro del que es' (1978: 216–17).[46] My analysis of the texts examines how these productive tensions – between history and *intrahistoria*, change and immobility, determinism and open-endedness – develop over the course of the playwright's career and how shifts in the balance correspond to changes in theatrical form.

Summing up: the continuous 'play' of history, culture and power
Even if there may often be a degree of oversimplification in Rodríguez Méndez's analysis of Spanish cultural history, the essays discussed in this chapter are valuable for the illuminating historical and theoretical context they set up around the author's dramatic texts. They emphasize a number of principles that will be central to the discussion of the plays in subsequent chapters: that elite culture and popular culture must always be considered in relation to one another, and that collective identities are constituted by means of both of these; that the most important function of cultural

activity (both in the form of everyday social performance and of artistic production), which authenticates it as 'real' or 'popular', is to contest the ideological hegemony of the powerful; and that cultural identities change over time, influencing and responding to specific publicly recorded historical events as well as shaping and reflecting the longer-term evolution of *intrahistoria*. The principles on which Rodríguez Méndez's essays and plays are based can be summed up very effectively in the following terms used by Stuart Hall to introduce a study of Caribbean identities:

> Cultural identity [...] is a matter of 'becoming' as well as of 'being'. It belongs to the future as much as to the past. It is not something which already exists, transcending place, time, history and culture. Cultural identities come from somewhere, have histories. But, like everything which is historical, they undergo constant transformation. Far from being eternally fixed in some essentialised past, they are subject to the continuous 'play' of history, culture and power. Far from being grounded in a mere 'recovery' of the past, which is waiting to be found, and which, when found, will secure our sense of ourselves into eternity, identities are the names we give to the different ways we are positioned by, and position ourselves within, the narratives of the past (1990: 225).

The identities dramatized in Rodríguez Méndez's plays are grounded in culture and subject to historical change. They consist of, and are expressed through, symbolic practices that are to a large extent conditioned by ideology but are also reworked and contested by individuals and groups. They are, above all, performances using language and gesture: partly automatic reiteration of sedimented rituals, partly self-conscious pastiche of such rituals, and partly improvisation of variations on them. National identity is similarly a symbolic and ideological artefact, a cultural performance based on an 'imagined community' that links language, history and culture with power. In opposition to the fixed versions of Spanishness propagated by hegemonic groups, Rodríguez Méndez's representations of cultural identity value the distinctiveness of identities rooted in particular cultural traditions and communities, and reassert the importance of recognizing 'the continuous "play" of history, culture and power'.

Notes
1. 'To rescue man from his degraded role as a social animal or mere number by stimulating awareness of his condition and thereby empowering him to control his own destiny. [...] To lift the individual out of the mass and endow him with consciousness of self and solidarity with others.'
2. Althusser acknowledges the power of 'authentic art' to reveal the working of ideology from the inside: 'What art makes us *see* [...] is the *ideology* from which it is born, in which it bathes, from which it detaches itself as art, and to which it *alludes*' (1984: 174).
3. 'Brecht is more interested in the consciousness of man as part of the mass.'
4. 'As long as the the the problem of the masses continues to be in crisis and as long as a culture of the masses remains no more than an aspiration, all that theatre can do, if it is to reflect the society and culture of its time, is to make a record of that crisis in a realist manner, with a detailed, almost scientific realism.'
5. 'Get close to the people, not in order to teach them or redeem them, not even to entertain them, but to investigate a possible means of communication. In order to learn from them about their language, their motivations and their resources.'

6. The Taurus edition of *La tabernera y las tinajas* and *Los inocentes de la Moncloa* contains several accounts of the Pipironda experience: Monleón (1968b), Rodríguez Méndez (1968c) and Candel (1968).

7. See, for example, Adorno (1991) and Marcuse (1964), whose ideas are neatly summarized, contextualized and qualified in Lewis (2002: 87–92). Hoggart concludes that 'most mass-entertainments are in the end what D. H. Lawrence described as "anti-life". [...] They tend towards uniformity rather than towards anonymity' (1957: 277-78).

8. The concept of hegemony is discussed at various points in the *Prison Notebooks* (in particular, Gramsci 1971: 12 and 55-59), and with slightly different meanings at different times (as explained in Adamson 1980: 170-79).

9. 'What is alarming about this is that such techniques of persuasive seduction can also be used for the opposite purpose: to dominate and confuse those who are of perfectly sound mind.'

10. 'They are all convinced that it is necessary to "save Spain" and to do so by using the weapons of culture and progress.'

11. 'Obscurantism, under-development and poverty in all its forms.'

12. 'All those who preferred "imagination", "fantasy", stylistic elaboration, more or less informal experiments, the "invention of languages". [..] A horde of cabbalistic writers, artistic sorcerers, relying fundamentally on the absence of a people capable of casting them out.'

13. 'The idea of creating, inventing or discovering things that can help to liberate man, make him more complete, increase his health and understanding, rather than things devised in order to enslave him even more.'

14. 'To expose the bourgeoisie's ignorance of the *pueblo* and the falseness of that kind of populism.'

15. 'The *reality* of Spain was in this motley collection of humanity, not in the pomp of ecclesiastical speeches, nor in the business of empire-building, nor in courtly diversions or nobles' palaces.' The link between the delinquent underworld represented by Escarramán and the intellectual dissidence of San Juan de la Cruz is the basis of *El pájaro solitario* (discussed in Chapter 5).

16. 'Escarramán and his kind will reflect in their own world the pomp and circumstance that surrounds them. They will act out deformed copies of the gestures and behaviours of the powerful, give their solemn phrases a ridiculous twist, parallel their disputes of honour with street brawls, [...] translate their learned allusions and Latin phrases into slang, and mimic with a black sense of humour the solemnity of the aristocracy.'

17. Manolo is re-created in *La Chispa*, and is to some extent the inspiration for characters in *Bodas que fueron famosas del Pingajo y la Fandanga* and *Soy madrileño* (discussed in Chapters 4 and 5).

18. 'For Manolo, his people, his drinking partners, the idlers who hang about on the streets and their companions, the ex-convicts, are all infinitely superior to their rulers and those who are in charge thanks to money and privilege.'

19. 'A comedy to make you weep, or a tragedy to make you laugh.' The subtitle given by Ramón de la Cruz to *Manolo* (first performed in 1769).

20. 'It's a language full of sparky synonyms, unexpected turns of phrase, overblown adjectives to describe everyday things. All with a tone of cockiness and assertive virility.'

21. 'Were led to feel a fraternal bond with their fellow men and women.'

22. 'The "social question" was in the air, and the *sainete* came to be an answer handed down "from above", offering an image of a chirpy, cheerful people happy with their neighbourly tenements and their folk festivals.'

23. 'Its stylized *casticismo*, its verbal strutting.'

24. Since *chulo* as a noun can mean 'pimp' but as an adjective tends to be used familiarly as a term of approval, *chulería* has ambiguous associations – a masculine display of streetwise confidence, insolence and panache which may be charming but is more often intimidating. It is therefore close in meaning to *majeza* (both are particularly associated with popular culture in nineteenth-century Madrid) and to Rodríguez Méndez's use of the term *machismo*.

25. 'Every man should be looking after his own, making sure his kids get enough to eat and can go to school, fighting for a decent life. What we need to set up here is a workers' republic. That's the only way to make sure everyone does their bit, to make sure that anyone who doesn't work doesn't eat.'

26. 'Common people have hearts too, and tears in their eyes and jealousy that they struggle to keep under control.'

27. 'Because it is clear that Julián will end up marrying Susana and starting a family. He will strive to work his way up in society. His socialism will evolve. Perhaps he will set up his own printing business. Later, he will not be able to avoid feeling drawn towards certain political options – the radical democratic parties, perhaps even the Falange – and he will get more and more used to his comfortable lifestyle. He may well end up as one of the leaders of economic development in Spain, leaving his old ideals behind.' This is exactly the trajectory of Julián dramatized in *Historia de unos cuantos*.

28. Pichi also features in *Historia de unos cuantos* precisely as described in *Ensayo sobre el machismo español*.

29. 'A charmer with a string of girls the length and breadth of Madrid.' The show figures amongst the author's own childhood memories as a mixture of sequin-spangled glamour and the cheeky local appeal of 'el maravilloso "Pichi" cantado por Celia y vitoreado siempre. Los niños del barrio lo repetimos incansables durante años y años' (quoted in Martín Recuerda 1979: 16) ('the wonderful "Pichi" sung by Celia and invariably cheered by the audience. The kids in my neighbourhood sang it endlessly for years and years').

30. Celia Gámez presented an updated version of Pichi in 1945, but it aroused little popular interest.

31. 'In the midst of all this orgiastic euphoria there is a clear premonition of tragedy.'

32. 'The *pueblo* turned its back on itself and totally disintegrated in its march towards the hollow fantasy (still unfulfilled) of a welfare and consumer society. People would from now on be so preoccupied with long working hours, the need to do more than one job to make ends meet, the endless struggle for a fair wage and so on, that they would be unable to pay attention to anything else.'

33. 'A stud from the rough end of town who just lets himself be loved, because he bowls the women over.'

34. There are extracts from representative examples in Rodríguez Puértolas (1987). See also Perriam et al. (2000: 36–38).

35. For general discussion of the importance of historical theatre in Spain since the 1950s, see Jones (1977), Pérez-Stansfield (1983: 163–278), Halsey (1988a, 1988b and 1988c), Oliva (1988 and 1999), Vilches de Frutos (1999b), Perriam et al. (2000: 47–57) and Lyon (2001).

36. 'Historical theatre illuminates our present when it consists of more than just a ruse to evade censorship, when it makes us understand and feel more fully the vital relationship that exists between what happened then and what is happening to us now.'

37. The phrase 'history from below' is used by Lindenberger to characterize a modern mode of historical theatre that responds to a widening of 'our conception of what appropriately belongs to the domain of history' to take in 'the role of the powerless within the life of a culture' (1975: 147).

38. On the notion of a 'collision' of social forces as the fundamental structural principle of historical drama, see Lukács (1969: 111–14).

39. 'To investigate the role played by ordinary people in the history of my country, in contrast to the role played by a series of dominant minorities, which have frequently hijacked the historical development of Spain.'

40. 'I think that is where I learned to love language and literature, and to make use of a knowledge of history in order to be able to discredit the abuse of history for dishonest purposes.'

41. 'History is manipulated by the author in order to articulate ideological positions or present-day doctrines.'

42. 'Hegel insists that human history represents a rational process, which exhibits empirically, and in distinct stages, the working out of a certain idea, the "Idea of Freedom"' (Gardiner

1959: 59). Toynbee (1889–1975) sums up *A Study of History* (1935–1961) as an empirical study of 'the lives of societies in both their internal and their external aspects' (1935: 46), which sets out 'to explore the uniformities that come to light when one takes a synoptic view of the histories of a number of civilizations' (1961: 598).

43. 'Theatre that's more historicist than historical. Because the history in it comes from real life, not from chronicles and records in archives. It's history lived or relived in contrast to the times I've lived through.'

44. White derives his categories from Northrop Frye's *Anatomy of Criticism*.

45. 'A kind of totality of intensity rather than of extensiveness, in which the particular is turned into a striking exemplification of the general.'

46. 'What *was* could have *not been*, but it *was* as a result of particular reasons and unreasons explored by the drama; on the other hand, what *is* […] could *not be* or *be other than it is*.'

3

History from below (1): enclosed spaces

The new wave of historical drama that would be one of the most significant features of Spanish theatre in the 1960s and 1970s was heralded by two plays written in 1958. Antonio Buero Vallejo's *Un soñador para un pueblo* (first staged in 1958) establishes an influential model of critical historicism developed further in *Las Meninas* (1960), *El sueño de la razón* (1970), *La detonación* (1977) and *Misión al pueblo desierto* (1999). Each of these plays isolates a key moment in the political history of Spain, essentially seen in terms of a conflict between forces of change and forces of immobility. Their main characters are mostly well-known historical figures involved in public life: 'world-historical individuals' engaged in work of social significance whose personal crises and relationships intersect with the 'collision' of underlying social forces which Lukács sees as the fundamental structural principle of historical drama (1969: 119).[1] The heroes are close to the centre of significant public events, but their dramatic importance lies in their roles as exceptionally perceptive interpreters of events rather than as the prime movers of them. Although a relationship with an obscure representative of the *pueblo* tends to make a crucial contribution to the development of the protagonists' understanding of events and of themselves, the emphasis is on individual action and self-awareness. In *Un soñador para un pueblo*, for example, the positive role of the maidservant Fernandita in helping to bring about the resolution of the crisis is sharply contrasted with the blind intolerance and manipulability of the masses.[2] The issues that emerge from the dramatic situations are essentially ethical and philosophical, centring above all on questions of truth and social responsibility, and history is ultimately represented as tragedy: 'España como tragedia: he ahí el tema permanente, que es también, por supuesto, el tema del hombre y de la sociedad como tragedia' (Buero Vallejo 1994, vol. 2: 422).[3] Idealism and social progress are constantly frustrated by egotism, human weakness and abuse of power, yet small, moving acts of integrity and humanity are held up as examples to the future (that is, the audience's present).

In contrast, the model established by Rodríguez Méndez in *Vagones de madera* (first staged in 1959) and developed in *En las esquinas, banderas* (written in 1964) and

La Mano Negra (written in 1965) does not focus on 'world-historical individuals', nor does it dramatize political history directly. This is 'history seen "from below"' (Halsey 1987: 39).[4] The characters in these plays are fictional representatives of the powerless masses, the victims of history rather than its protagonists, struggling to understand the wider significance of the circumstances imposed upon them. Large-scale public events (war in Morocco, civil war, suppression of anarchism in Andalucía) take place in the background and have devastating effects on the characters, but any sense of what causes these events is subordinated to an emphasis on *intrahistoria*, experienced as repeated frustration and continuing oppression. *El vano ayer* (written in 1963 and staged in 1966), also discussed in this chapter, shifts to a bourgeois setting and features characters who have a closer involvement in and understanding of public events, yet ultimately emphasizes the point of view of the ordinary people outside who suffer the consequences of the protagonists' actions.

The key structural feature that these pieces have in common is the use of a confined space in which a group of people is brought together under pressure from some external force, which, combined with personal and ideological tensions within the group, produces a crisis. Ruiz Ramón has identified the symbolic use of enclosed dramatic spaces as one of the 'principios estructurantes fundamentales en la dramaturgia española de la era de Franco' (1978: 198).[5] He argues that this mode of '*Huis-clos*' theatre (a reference to Sartre's classic Existentialist drama of 1944) symbolizes the closed, oppressive nature of Francoist Spain, and at the same time expresses a protest against the stifling of theatre itself. The metonymical function of the small-scale interaction as a microcosm of larger social and historical processes is reinforced by various elements that emphasize a symbolic dimension and connect the onstage action to the offstage contexts. The connections suggested by Rodríguez Méndez's plays between enclosed spaces at particular moments in the past and the oppressive nature of the society in which they were written will be investigated in this chapter, but without suggesting that this is the only function of such structures.

For Martín Recuerda, the enclosed stage space of *Vagones de madera* brings to mind one of the most characteristic literary motifs of the 1940s and 1950s: human beings trapped in confined spaces, in which they gradually acquire self-knowledge through their relationship with the others. He takes the Sartre connection further, arguing that the influence of the French Theatre of the Absurd is obvious, bringing with it 'todas las ideas del vacío, náuseas, aburrimiento, etc., de la existencia humana, que constituyeron un revulsivo entre la gente joven de la Europa de los años cuarenta' (Martín Recuerda 1979: 77–78).[6] Although Martín Recuerda's reminder of the intellectual atmosphere of the period and its impact on Sastre and some other Spanish writers is useful, it seems to me that the essentially philosophical emphasis of Existentialist-inspired drama, with its focus on questions of individual guilt, responsibility and integrity in the face of an absence of moral value, is not an important factor in these plays by Rodríguez Méndez. They are more concerned with collective identity and social and historical processes than with individual identity and metaphysical dilemmas.

The performance of *machismo español* in these sombre plays is subdued and constrained in comparison with the more festive, expansive manifestations we shall explore in the next chapter. The central preoccupations of Rodríguez Méndez's work are already in evidence, though. The dramatic conflict that develops in the tense, stifling atmosphere of these plays is essentially a clash between the expression of cultural identity and the imposition of ideological control; between an impulse towards a relatively spontaneous process of group identification (based on shared experiences, cultural practices, and especially language) and the construction by an authoritarian force of a coercive, homogenizing collective identity. There are suggestions of an element of fatalism in the dramatic action – hints that the failure of the people to recognize their common interests and work together is determined to an extent by some kind of innate factiousness built into the ethnic make-up of Spain. However, this feeling never becomes predominant, since the workings of concrete political and economic causes are made clear.

Vagones de madera (Wooden Wagons)

A wooden rail wagon transporting conscripts from different parts of Spain towards the Moroccan war of 1921 provides a powerful dramatic focus for this drama. The setting throws together into a confined *Huis-clos* situation a group of young men from various backgrounds, encouraging a universalizing interpretation of the particular situation as a microcosm of general social processes. Remarks by the most articulate character, Valencia, bring out the feeling of having been removed from everyday existence into a special space that bears existential significance:

> Todo se ha quedado atrás: las penas y las alegrías. Ahora es como si fuéramos otros. Como si fuéramos nuevos. Como si naciéramos. [...] Y la vida de cualquiera de éstos, y cualquier vida de cualquier muchacho de España, hoy, es suficiente para que todos nos consolemos y nos sintamos hermanos (*Vagones de madera* 1963: 45).[7]

The eight recruits represent a cross section of the working-class *pueblo*: peasants from villages in Navarra and Castilla, workers from Sevilla, Valencia and Madrid. Finding themselves thrown together in a cramped railway wagon on their way to possible death, they pass the time with cards, wine, food, talk and song. At times a sense of camaraderie and shared experiences of hardship is established, but the sullen refusal of the mysterious Álvar González to join in wholeheartedly acts as the catalyst for a conflict of personalities and attitudes, leading to the accidental death of Valencia, who is stabbed while attempting to intervene in a scuffle between Álvar, Navaja and Torero. These three are arrested and, in the third act, the remaining men, although shocked by the unnecessary death, allow their anger to be defused and redirected by the corporal posted to watch over them. The dialogue and action in the first two acts leading up to the death partly serve a conventional dramatic function of building up the character conflicts between individuals that will precipitate the climax, but ultimately this function is less important than the collective process of searching for a common identity and sharing a common language.

From the beginning, the men compete to assert themselves and establish their credentials as working-class *machos* – proud, tough and rebellious. Their mocking defiance is directed not only at their prospective enemy (the Moroccan chieftain, Abd-El-Krim), but also at the king and other traditional representatives of authority in Spain. This defiance, clearly tinged with fear and despair, is matched by displays of aggression towards each other, as Valencia, Navaja and Torero compete for dominance. Valencia is the strongest advocate of companionship in the face of hostile circumstances. He vividly characterizes their situation with a telling simile prompted by the cattle wagon in which they are travelling: '¿Qué importa que vayamos al matadero? ¿Qué importa que nos encajonen como toros de brega? ¡Somos jóvenes y nos gusta vivir! ¡Venga, beber, hombre, beber y alegrarse!' (44).[8] The men's expressions of rebellion are vague, naive and inhibited: when one of the resented representatives of authority – a sergeant – appears, they are deferential and docile. There is a deep sense of anger at their position, but it is usually misdirected, as they lash out at each other. The men find temporary consolation in the simple pleasures of wine, song and companionship, and their only defence against fear and anger is to try to construct a common sense of identity – as men of the *pueblo* and as victims.

In the second act, a renewed split in the group after the temporary harmony at the end of the previous act prompts a revealing discussion of the implications of their situation. Several of the men agree on the importance of 'being intelligent' – avoiding conflict amongst themselves in order to come through their ordeal together (46–47). The representativeness of this group as a microcosm of the Spanish nation is made more explicit when the characters begin to discuss analogies with wider issues:

> TORERO – En todos los pueblos hay dos o tres tíos que se meten a caciques y no te dejan vivir...
> ESTELLA – Es nuestro destino, siempre tenemos que estar esclavos de alguien (47).[9]

However, their analysis is still naive. The idea of unity is a vague one of a community of suffering, a united front against a common – but undefined and intangible – enemy. When Torero attempts to offer a tentative political explanation in simple socialist terms, the others make fun of him, instinctively distrusting the jargon he uses:

> Torero – No hay manera de que nos entendamos unos con otros, porque siempre tiene que haber alguien que quiere separarse de la colectividad.
> Los otros – (*A coro.*) Ooo...lé.
> Valencia – Eres un tío hablando, Torero. Estás hecho un Canalejas. Vaya palabreja: colectividad (48).[10]

The men edge towards a more constructive view, with some appreciation of the relevance of political education and organization, yet are repelled by the catchwords of socialism: *colectividad, revolución, solidaridad*. They give their loyalty instinctively to the anti-monarchist parties, but just as instinctively mistrust organized politics, and are sceptical about the possibility of real change. So Torero finds his advice rejected, and joins the two dissidents in the opposite corner. The breakdown of the unity they have longed for is irreparable. Valencia and the four who remain with him plan another party, but without the others. Luis comments that they are splitting into two camps, just as the children in Church-run schools used to be divided into Romans and Carthaginians: 'Los romanos eran los buenos y los cartagineses los malos. Yo siempre fui cartaginés. En clase siempre teníamos los puestos peores, pero en cuanto salíamos a la calle, nos liábamos a pedradas y los que ganábamos éramos nosotros, los cartagineses' (49).[11]

This suggestive metaphor reveals the relevance of the lines from Lorca's poem 'Reyerta' (from the *Romancero gitano*), quoted on the play's title page: 'Aquí pasó lo de siempre:/ han muerto cuatro romanos/ y cinco cartagineses' (38).[12] What is important about Luis's account is that the division of the boys into favoured Romans and despised Carthaginians is deliberately determined by the priests in charge on the basis of social status. Luis is proud of the rebellion of the underdogs after school, and when the parallel is drawn with society in general, the men agree to 'stick together and cut all the Romans' throats' (49) – schoolmasters, priests, mayors and the rest of the Establishment. The battle lines are instinctively drawn. But when the conflict in the freight car comes, it is confused and pointless, ending in the accidental death of Valencia, who, as he dies pathetically, calls on his comrades to stay united. There has been no rebellion, no heroism. The situation has not been altered.

The parable of Romans and Carthaginians is central to the meaning of *Vagones de madera*, linking the situation on stage to wider issues on various levels. The division imposed upon the schoolboys by the priests (representatives not only of pedagogical and spiritual authority, but also of economic and political power) is fought out in a controlled, ritualized way inside the school, but fosters real divisiveness and violence outside, setting up social barriers at an early age. Although the separation into two hostile camps of the soldiers in the wagon is not directly engineered by the military authorities that control their lives, it is a result of the situation into which these authorities have thrust them.

What the Lorca reference seems to add to this is a suggestion of timeless inevitability, and perhaps a special relevance of this pattern of strife to the Spanish character. The *reyerta* (fight, brawl) of the poem appears to have no rational causes. It arises from blood, *casta*, fate. Dark natural and supernatural causes are pointed to by 'una dura luz de naipe' ('a harsh glare of playing cards'), 'el toro de la reyerta' ('the bull of the brawl') and 'ángeles con grandes alas/ de navajas de Albacete' ('angels with big wings of Albacete knives') (García Lorca 1943: 21). These three poetic elements are themselves echoed in the play. The game of cards at the beginning comes to suggest the hopelessness of the situation of the soldiers: '¿Crees que podemos ganar ni tú, ni yo, ni nadie?' (*Vagones de madera* 1963: 39).[13] The men compare themselves to fighting bulls (44), forced to fight a pointless battle and doomed to die. The knife used to kill Valencia is, of course, *albaceteña*.[14] It is the symbolic pivot around which the plot of the play turns, repeatedly referred to in the dialogue.

The name Álvar González, together with the fact that he is identified as coming from Castilla, connects the play to another well-known poetic text suggesting a determinist idea of national character: Antonio Machado's 'La tierra de Alvargonzález' (in *Campos de Castilla*). This ballad of envy and fratricide in rural Castilla celebrates the region as the heart of Spain but attributes to its inhabitants 'mucha sangre de Caín' (Machado 1998: 185) ('the blood of Cain'). In an interview with me in 1984, Rodríguez Méndez confirms his belief, derived to a large extent from Machado and other writers of the Generation of 1898, in the existence of an essential Castilian character, conditioned by history and landscape: 'Es un personaje misterioso y un poco sombrío. Es una idea que tengo yo de Castilla: una región un poco sombría y atormentada, deprimida, envejecida ya y decadente' (quoted in Thompson 1989: 442).[15]

The function of the references to 'Reyerta' and 'La tierra de Alvargonzález' is to emphasize an implicit sense of the inevitability of conflict, to suggest that an essential *sangre de Caín* flows through the *intrahistoria* of the Spanish people, underneath the turbulent surface of historical change: 'Aquí pasó lo de siempre.' However, both Machado (in other parts of *Campos de Castilla*) and Lorca set this fatalism off against a recognition of the effects of political, economic and ideological forces. The lines quoted by Rodríguez Méndez are spoken the judge in Lorca's ballad, addressed to the civil guards accompanying him (García Lorca 1943: 22). The poet sets up a dramatic tension between the mysterious power of the forces of blood, Nature and Fate, and the cruel indifference of the authorities. The judge dismisses the incident as unimportant and goes away satisfied. There is no threat to law and order – the law that allows the Civil Guard to practise the brutality described in another poem in the same collection, 'Romance de la Guardia Civil española'. Both 'Reyerta' and *Vagones de madera* challenge their readers to examine what has happened, to explore the real significance of allegedly unimportant deaths.

While acknowledging Álvar González's function as representative of a certain kind of collective character, Martín Recuerda is anxious to make this figure the focus of an Existentialist reading of *Vagones de madera*. The character's introversion and melancholy air of mystery seem at one point to be related to some deep-rooted personal crisis, as he begins to confide in Valencia: 'Pero a veces lleva uno detrás mucha carga... Y es imposible... No puede ser... Te digo que no puede ser olvidarse de la verdad. Es como una agonía' (*Vagones de madera* 1963: 45).[16] If this points towards the possibility of a profound existential anguish, it is the only such hint that emerges. Although Álvar, Navaja and Torero resentfully plot an attack on the others, it is between the three of them that the fight breaks out. Valencia intervenes, struggles with the now crazed Álvar and is fatally stabbed. Everyone, including Álvar himself, is stupefied. The killing is motiveless, accidental, and cannot be seen as an expression of Álvar's existential anguish, a spasm of metaphysical nausea. Martín Recuerda, keen to find a complete philosophical message similar to those he perceives in Sartre or in Alfonso Sastre's play *Escuadra hacia la muerte*, regards this absence of motive as the play's major structural weakness (1979: 88). The lack of logical motivation in Álvar's behaviour which undermines the Existentialist reading need not be seen as a dramatic weakness, however. He is deliberately made to remain an enigmatic figure, not an individualized protagonist but part of a dramatic structure designed to maintain a tension between determinism and historicism, in which the struggle that causes Valencia's death needs to emerge as senseless and motiveless.

Rodríguez Méndez concedes that at the time *Vagones de madera* was written, Existentialism was 'in the air', but insists that Álvar simply represents a Castilian archetype: 'Era seco y austero y tal, pero nada más' (interviewed in Thompson 1989: 442).[17] In an earlier interview he had declared that 'no hay influencia alguna de *Escuadra hacia la muerte*. Es otra cosa. No se parecen ambas obras, ni por el forro' (Isasi Ángulo 1974: 273).[18] There is an element of facetiousness in these remarks, but it is clear that his aims in *Vagones de madera* are very different from those of Sastre, despite superficial similarities between these plays. Sastre places his characters in a *situación límite* (extreme situation) in which they are totally isolated, physically and spiritually, surrounded by a world that is oppressive but vague and meaningless. The society from which they have come and the war in which they are engaged are undefined. Their past actions have already made them outcasts from society, and the drama centres on the struggle of each man to come to terms with the consequences of what he has done. Rodríguez Méndez's play, however, is firmly rooted in specific geographical and historical reality. The situation as a dramatic microcosm is superficially similar, but here it is the reasons for the existence of the situation (the social-historical dimension) that is important. These recruits are very ordinary representatives of the masses, with no past other than the collective *intrahistoria* of the Spanish people. The impact of the play depends upon the parallels between the particular situation and wider social and historical processes.

The third act shows how the remaining recruits – Luis, Pablo, Ferminillo and Estella – come to terms with what has happened. Pablo declares that Valencia has taught him what life is all about, but when called upon to explain what he has learnt, Pablo can only mumble vaguely: 'Pues... la vida es... sentirnos camaradas unos de otros, formar todos como una gran familia... En fin, no sé...' (*Vagones de madera* 1963: 54).[19] For it is the corporal who dominates this final act, controlling the men's behaviour and conditioning their view of events. His remarks parallel the dismissive words of the judge in Lorca's ballad: '¿Eso qué es? ¿Una riña más, qué? [...] Aquí no pasa nada. Se terminó el asunto' (51).[20] There is now a direct representative on stage of the powers that have forced the men into this situation and his domination is absolute. The corporal achieves this hegemony partly by threatening violence (as an agent of a Repressive State Apparatus), but what is more significant in this act is his manipulation of the men's attitudes (as an agent of an Ideological State Apparatus). Luis, Estella and Ferminillo are soon persuaded to abandon any consideration of the injustice of their position, as the corporal encourages brutal racial hatred of the Moroccans. The soldiers' enthusiasm becomes literally bloodthirsty:

> Luis – Yo, como pueda ensartar uno...
> Cabo – Podrás. Ya lo verás.
> Estella – Qué gustillo dará ver correr esa sucia sangre.
> Cabo – Dan ganas de bebérsela, chico (52).[21]

All their anger and aggression is focused on the 'other' designated as their enemy. They have been recruited into a nationalist ideology that replaces the vague discourse of spontaneous shared identity with a discourse of unity imposed by force. The corporal identifies himself with the other men, speaking the language of conventional *machismo* – war is a 'cosa de hombres' (a man's job) – and asserting that in a violent society one can only survive by using violence: 'La vida es eso: o pegas o te pegan' (55).[22] Ultimately, however, he represents a crude reflection of the official values that lie behind their oppression.

Although the social message of the play is clear enough, it nevertheless ends on a note of mystery and ambiguity. The train finally arrives at Algeciras and the sliding door is flung open unexpectedly. The closed, claustrophobic set suddenly opens out into a luminous panorama of a dawn sky and a shining sea (55). There has been repeated discussion of the sea during the journey, some of the men looking forward to seeing it for the first time. In the closing moments of the play, the actors stand with their backs to the audience, gazing ecstatically at the dawn. This luminous tableau, charged with symbolic resonance, is highly ambiguous. The dawn and the open space convey an impression of hope, liberation, perhaps a new beginning. The sea appears to represent an escape from the wagon and from the men's confined lives, but the question of what awaits them remains open. The positive associations of open space and light are juxtaposed here with a premonition of oblivion, a surprisingly gentle expression of the near certainty of violent death that the men face. The audience is left with an enigmatic gleam of hope in Pablo, who, inspired by Valencia's example, is the only character who has put up any resistance to the corporal's ideological hegemony. It is just possible that he – together with the audience, perhaps – is emerging from the experience with a greater understanding of his position in the world and a determination to bring about change.

The historical process played out in miniature in *Vagones de madera* is presented in a sense as a timeless one, part of the ongoing *intrahistoria* of a people repeatedly failing to articulate collective resistance to coercive ideologies and allowing the powerful to exploit their petty rivalries in order to perpetuate social injustices. However, there are aspects of the specific historical context which have particular resonance and set up significant parallels with the time and circumstances in which the play was written and first staged, locating the representation of collective identity firmly in historical processes.

Although the title page gives the time of the action as 'por los años de 1921' ('around 1921'), a curious form of imprecision that comes to be characteristic of Rodríguez Méndez's history plays, the graffiti on one wall of the set identify the year precisely as 1921 (39). The period between 1919 and 1923 in Spain was dominated by serious labour troubles and social unrest, fuelled by falling prices and wages, unemployment, and repression by government and employers. Workers' organizations and various republican and left-wing movements were gaining strength but were riven by bitter factionalism. One of the factors contributing to popular discontent throughout the country was conscription for colonial campaigns being waged sporadically in Morocco and the western Sahara, which became a class issue because of the provision allowing the rich to buy themselves out of military service on payment of a *cuota fijada*. Spain's involvement in northern Africa was driven by various uncoordinated forces – economic interests, military ambition, diplomatic manoeuvring, royal meddling and political calculation that attention could be distracted from internal dissent and the collapse of what remained of the empire by the pursuit of a new African empire.[23] Some popular support for these military adventures could be drummed up with jingoistic rhetoric in parliament and the press, yet in general the working classes that provided the cannon fodder were not convinced. Popular resentment against the *cuota* and against continuing casualties had flared up in 1909 and 1917, evasion of conscription was growing, and opposition to the war had begun to create a measure of temporary unity amongst anti-monarchist parties.

The year 1921 became painfully burned into the collective memory of the Spanish people because of a catastrophic military defeat at the hands of Moroccan forces under Abd-El-Krim, a tribal leader from the Rif region. A series of military and political miscalculations led to a large Spanish force, consisting mostly of conscripts, being cut off and massacred at Annual in July. Some 10,000 men were killed and several thousand captured. Gruesome accounts of the torture of prisoners stoked up popular panic and anti-Moroccan feeling in Spain (the corporal in *Vagones de madera* dwells calculatingly on the notorious detail of men being suffocated by their own severed testicles).[24] The demonization of Abd-El-Krim suppressed the fact that he had played a distinguished role in the Spanish administration of the region, and what Rodríguez Méndez's corporal characterizes as a kind of national crusade against an 'evil, degenerate race' (52) was essentially a mundane colonial skirmish over economic interests of limited value, turned by incompetence into the pointless sacrifice of thousands of lives.

The disaster was not only one of the worst military defeats Spain has ever suffered. Like Cuba, it was also the product of political failure, implicating the king, the government and the army in a national humiliation. An enquiry laid most of the blame on army officers, without pursuing political responsibilities. The army was offended, and politicians of the Left pressed for the culpability of the government and the king to be recognized. This pressure brought in a reformist Liberal government determined to re-assert civilian control and conduct a serious enquiry into the political and military failures exposed by Annual. It was this government – representing the Restoration's last chance to give the Spanish people responsible, progressive parliamentary rule – that was nipped in the bud by General Primo de Rivera's military coup of 1923, restoring the hegemony of the armed forces and bringing authoritarian nationalism back to the centre of Spanish politics.

The Moroccan war thus played a key role as one of the catalysts of the series of great upheavals of twentieth-century Spanish history: the dictatorship, the fall of the monarchy, the Second Republic, the civil war (set off by the army in Morocco) and the triumph of Francoism. The amount of historical knowledge required of an audience to appreciate the implications of the setting and action of *Vagones de madera* is no more than could be easily conveyed by brief programme notes, perhaps using selected newspaper headlines of the period. In any case, for many spectators in 1959, the resonances of the key elements of the play – the division of the people into *romanos* and *cartagineses*, the destruction of solidarity as a result of a pointless outbreak of fratricidal conflict, the re-imposition of control by means of crude ideological manipulation – were painfully immediate, as Martín Recuerda notes: 'Estaba latente, aun más reciente que en la actualidad, el millón de muertos de nuestra guerra civil, una de las llagas más incurables de la España de nuestros días' (1979: 80).[25]

The xenophobic jingoism of Rodríguez Méndez's corporal inevitably recalls elements of the propaganda used by both sides in the civil war. The Nationalists laid claim to the Catholic, Castilian tradition, dwelling on the Russian influences in communism and anarchism, linked with the old bogies of Judaism and Freemasonry, while the Republican government mobilized patriotic feeling by concentrating on the role of the Italian forces supporting the Nationalists and on the connections between Spanish Falangism, Italian Fascism and German Nazism.[26] A much cruder Republican ploy, prompted by the Nationalists' use of Moroccan troops, was to appeal to the old hatred and fear of the *moros* amongst a population with recent memories of losing friends and family in various Moroccan campaigns up to 1927 (Abella 1973: 294–95). Defenders of Madrid in 1936 were spurred on with slogans such as '¡Vamos a capar moros!' (Abella 1975: 147).[27] The grisly tales of torture and severing of testicles still circulated, and the threat of violence to women was played upon with particular insistence.[28]

The irony of the involvement of Moroccan troops in the Nationalists' patriotic 'Crusade' was not lost on the generals whose careers were forged in the Moroccan campaigns (including Franco himself). In an ingenious shift of thinking, they spoke of a common spirituality and a historical bond of *hispanidad*, in contrast to the materialism of their opponents.[29] The Moroccans were supposedly welcomed as brothers, 'con alegría y con impaciencia a reclamar un puesto de honor en la cruzada civilizadora que se emprendió el 17 de julio'.[30] However, the ancestral prejudices, nourished by Francoism's own mythology of Christian reconquest, were deeply rooted and remained strong for decades after the civil war. Maestre Alonso reports that even in the 1970s many families were terrified by the prospect of a son on military service being posted to Ceuta or Melilla (1975: 110).

Rodríguez Méndez himself was involved in a direct repetition of history shortly before writing *Vagones de madera*. At a loose end after returning from a trip to Argentina in 1955, he decided to re-enlist in the army. After postings to Valladolid, Zamora, Melilla and the Chafarinas Islands, he served briefly in the Spanish colony of Ifni during a minor war against local rebels. Although the outcome of the World War had put an end to Spain's imperial ambitions in northern Africa and independence had been ceded to Morocco in 1956, Spain remained in control of the small enclaves of Cabo Juby and Ifni in the south, the cities of Ceuta and Melilla in the north, and the large area of the Spanish Sahara. The Spanish authorities in Sidi-Ifni resorted to force several times to put down protests at Ifni's exclusion from independent Morocco. The violence escalated during 1957 until November, when the unofficial National Liberation Army and local tribes launched attacks on Ifni, Cabo Juby and various parts of the Saharan zone, supported by the Moroccan government. The Sahara and Cabo Juby were quickly pacified, but Spanish forces found themselves in difficulty in Ifni and were forced to fall back into the city of Sidi-Ifni. Cabo Juby was eventually abandoned, Sidi-Ifni remained in a state of virtual siege until ceded to Morocco in 1969, and the problem of the Sahara remained unresolved.[31] Neither Cabo Juby nor Ifni was of significant strategic or economic value to Spain, yet right-wing voices were raised in parliament and the press in protest at the surrender of what they regarded as integral parts of Spanish territory (Maestre Alonso 1975: 179).

Rodríguez Méndez had played a small part in one of the final episodes of Spain's inglorious colonial history. The following year, he put some of this military experience into *Vagones de madera*, which was staged by the Teatro Español Universitario in Barcelona in December 1959 (directed by José María Loperena). Although much of the immediate topicality may have been lost on the audiences in the Teatro Candilejas, since public opinion in Spain had not been fully informed about the events in Ifni (Maestre Alonso 1975: 166), the implications of the multiple historical resonances and the parallels with the chauvinistic discourse of Francoism were not lost on them. Martín Recuerda reports that the performances stimulated fierce debate, aroused strong feelings and excited young people attracted by the whiff of rebellion (1979: 33).

If the authorities in Barcelona also saw the play as rebellious or subversive, they were clearly prepared to take the risk of allowing a few student performances in a small independent venue.[32] However, applications for approval of productions in San Sebastián in 1960 and Madrid in 1962 were turned down. What is curious about the censorship file on *Vagones de madera*, though, is that of the seven censors who submitted reports on the text, only one unequivocally recommends prohibition. This is Miguel Ángel R. Arbeloa, the Provincial Delegate of the Ministerio de Información y Turismo in Guipúzcoa, forwarding the San Sebastián application to Madrid on 26 November 1960. He dismisses the literary and theatrical merits of the text as negligible and specifies the following political grounds for banning the play: 'Hay alusiones despectivas e injuriosas para S. M. el Rey Don Alfonso XIII. En el tercer acto un libelo contra el pueblo moro que no puede autorizarse en una representación pública, y alusiones más o menos directas contra el Ejército' (Ministerio de Información y Turismo 1960).[33] He also highlights the reference to priests organizing the battles between Romans and Carthaginians as an attack on religious education. Although the regime had little need to defend the reputation of Alfonso XIII, whom Francoists tended to see as a weak king who had presided over a decadent, factious system, supporters of the monarchy as an institution formed one of the influential political 'families' throughout the dictatorship, and Franco's negotiations with Juan de Borbón (Alfonso's son) over the possible restoration of the monarchy had frequently been high on the political agenda during the 1950s. What is really at stake is the principle of respect for traditional authority as embodied by the monarchy, the Church and the army, which the play clearly challenges through its dialogue and its action.

MINISTERIO DE INFORMACION Y TURISMO

DELEGACION PROVINCIAL DE GUIPUZCOA

AVENIDA DE ESPAÑA, 2-3.º - TELEFS. 13456-10558

Sección __C. y T.__

Núm. __2106/60__

EXPT.º N.º 311-60
3-12.60

Título: VAGONES DE MADERA.-

Autor: José María Rodriguez-Méndez.-

Género: Dramático.-

INFORME

Breve exposición del argumento:
Se trata del viaje de un grupo de soldados, a la campaña de Africa, durante el año 21. La acción se desarrolla en un vagón de mercancias que supone una unidad del tren militar. En el segundo acto se produce una reyerta con un muerto y un herido. La obra termina en el límite del viaje a través de la Peninsula ante el mar que se supone que se supone en Algeciras.

Valor literario:
Escaso y rayano casi constantemente en la chabacanería.

Valor teatral:
Escaso.

Matiz político:
Hay alusiones despectivas e injuriosas para S.M. el Rey Don Alfonso XIII. En el tercer acto un libelo contra el pueblo moro que no puede autorizarse en una representación pública y alusiones más o menos directas contra el Ejército.

Matiz religioso:
En algún pasaje de la obra se trata despectivamente a la educación y los educadores religiosos.

Juicio general que merece al informante:
No se trata de una obra susceptible de correcciones o tachaduras; creo que procede denegar la autorización en base a lo expuesto anteriormente. Todo lo que pudiera tener de contenido -que no lo tiene- sería destructivo.

San Sebastián a 26 de Noviembre de 1.960.-

EL INFORMANTE,

F/. Miguel Angel R. Arbeloa.-

Censor's report on *Vagones de madera*. Ministerio de Información y Turismo (1960), Expediente 311–60. *Reproduced with the permission of the Ministerio de Cultura (Spain) and the Archivo General de la Administración.*

José María Cano, on the other hand, is less inclined to make connections between the historical setting of the play and political issues in the present. His report refers to stylistic defects in the text but argues that the crudeness of the language is appropriate to the setting, the period and the characters (Ministerio de Información y Turismo 1960). He is also prepared to accept certain 'political' statements (such as Valencia's talk of wishing to smash a lamp on the king's head) as justifiable elements of the evocation of the period. The fact that the positive message of a desire for peace and harmony is expressed by a character who declares himself to be a Republican is acknowledged as a problem, but again excused as part of 'el ambiente de entonces' ('the ambience of the time'). He recommends authorization for audiences over the age of eighteen and identifies only two phrases to be cut, one mildly bawdy and the other jocularly disrespectful towards the Church.

Gumersindo Montes Agudo also recommends authorization for audiences over eighteen but sees much more need for trimming of objectionable material: 'La obra es amarga, tendenciosilla, con un antimilitarismo trasnochado. Pero nos parece descubrir en el autor condiciones de dramaturgo, por su pulso dramático acertado en tipos y diálogos' (Ministerio de Información y Turismo 1960).[34] He proposes fourteen cuts, some of them extensive. In seven cases, the problem is essentially political: he identifies expressions of antimonarchism (*Vagones de madera* 1963: 41, 43, 44) and of support for revolution and rejection of authority (43, 48, 49), as well as all the corporal's inflammatory remarks about the filthiness and treacherousness of the *moros* (for some of the censors, the protection of the regime's discourse of respect for Moroccans was clearly still a priority). Montes Agudo is also concerned about derogatory references to priests and certain indecorous expressions: 'mariconerías' (40) ('poncing about'), 'vente conmigo a la cama' (48) ('come to bed with me'), 'el único tío con todo puesto soy yo' (41) ('the only bloke with everything where it should be is me') and 'un marica' (53) ('a poof').

Despite the majority of two to one in favour of approval, the verdict issued on 13 February 1961 refused permission for the proposed production. The next two applications were also turned down, despite a report from a representative of the army, Juan Guerra y Romero, stating in April 1962 that he could see no serious problem with the work. When another application was made in 1964, one of the censors expressed surprise at the repeated banning of *Vagones de madera*. Marcelo Arroita-Jáuregui's report recommends authorizing the production for audiences over eighteen and comments:

> Sobre esta obra me parece que ha reinado una curiosa incomprensión (y, en general, sobre la obra dramática de este autor): *Vagones de madera* (igual que *El círculo de tiza de Cartagena*) se ha representado en Barcelona y, sin embargo, su representación en Madrid ha sido siempre prohibida (Ministerio de Información y Turismo 1960).[35]

Arroita-Jáuregui sees potential political implications in the text, but does not consider them relevant to present circumstances. He insists that the drama represents an 'episodio concreto y aislado, que no se puede considerar, ni histórica ni políticamente, como definitorio.'[36] He does not see the play as antimilitaristic, and concludes: 'En todo caso, desde 1964, cabría simplemente la cuestión de la supuesta inutilidad de la guerra de Marruecos; pero creo, sinceramente, que la obra no lo plantea.'[37] The authorization issued on 18 February 1964 is for a single performance open only to members of the Club Gesto over the age of eighteen, subject to inspection of the dress rehearsal, with the following lines removed (the same cuts were imposed on a production in Madrid in 1968):

> VALENCIA – ¿Abd-El-Krim? ¡Bah! Con mejor gusto lo estrellaría en otras cabezas. En otras. En la de Abd-El-Krim, no.
> ESTELLA – Pues en la cabeza coronada, si te parece. ¿Eso quieres decir? (*Vagones de madera* 1963: 39).[38]
> VALENCIA – Y ya que no podemos partirlo en la cabeza del tío de la corona, lo partíamos en uno de sus representantes, aunque sea un gañán de La Almunia (41).[39]
> VALENCIA – ¡Que se muera el tío de la Corona! (44).[40]
> VALENCIA – Por lo visto quiere hacer la competencia a Primo de Rivera (48).[41]
> PABLO – Eso es: en vez de degollar moros, que no nos han hecho nada, degollar romanos (49).[42]

Different censors came to very different conclusions about the degree of political risk allegedly posed by *Vagones de madera*. Such variability of interpretation was a constant feature of a system that operated according to well-recognized general assumptions but lacked a clear set of detailed guidelines. In some cases, lack of agreement led to plays being given the benefit of the doubt; more often, though, the censors' caution and fear of being caught out (for example, by approving a text subsequently judged by others to be unacceptable) tended to cause damaging delays, cuts or outright bans without any clear consensus having been established amongst them. Implicit in the division of opinion over *Vagones de madera* and other plays by Rodríguez Méndez is a debate about the interpretation of historical theatre. As long as a text did not make explicit critical parallels with the present, some censors (possibly looking for opportunities to exercise leniency) would argue that the historical material was self-contained and posed no threat, thus denying the drama any real significance, whilst others would seek out elements that could be taken as coded references to present circumstances, anxious to anticipate and close off dangerous responses by audiences. Both approaches meant a deadening oversimplification of the functioning of historical theatre, which made it extremely difficult for authors to judge how their work was likely to be received by the censors.

In the case of *Vagones de madera*, none of the censors argued that the play sets up a specific analogy with the Francoist present. It would be possible to interpret the struggle between the recruits as a metaphor for the civil war (pointless conflict destroying an attempt to create fraternity and equality), leading to dictatorship (the imposition of physical and ideological control by a brutal, chauvinistic military power). Even if any of the censors anticipated such a reading, they were probably reluctant to spell it out on paper, preferring to justify their rejection of the text on less dangerous grounds – attacks on the reputations of Alfonso XIII and General Primo de Rivera, and the uttering of racist sentiments (disregarding the fact that it is the representative of authority who incites them). Ultimately, the lines cut from the text in 1964 and 1968 are not crucial to the play's central opposition between two forms of collective identity or discourse: on the one hand, an instinctive sense of community and solidarity, and on the other, an ideology-driven, authoritarian nationalism.

En las esquinas, banderas (Put Out the Flags)
At first sight the setting of this play appears to be highly conventional: the opening stage direction briefly describes a drawing room in a modest country house. It turns out, however, that this is not the typical family home of bourgeois drama but a brothel in a village near Salamanca catering to local landowners and, later, to soldiers. The house is likened to a tomb and a convent, and gradually takes on a *Huis-clos* role similar to that of the freight car in *Vagones de madera* – a claustrophobic space functioning metonymically as a microcosm of larger social and historical processes. As in *Vagones de madera*, the personal conflicts within the confined group of characters are set against the background of a war. The time is specified more precisely in this case: 17 and 18 July 1936 (the days on which the military revolt broke out in Morocco and then took hold in mainland Spain, leading to civil war), and in the second part, 7 November 1936 (one of the crucial moments of the siege of Madrid).[43] Once again, though, the work does not offer detailed historical analysis or engage directly with the events of the war and the issues over which it was fought. The dates represent significant historical thresholds, but the emphasis remains on the small-scale action, on the impact of external events on the characters and how they define themselves in relation to a coercive ideology.

The protagonists here are female: Reyes (the proprietor) and the young women who work for her as prostitutes, Verónica, Soledad, Micaela and Alfonsa. It is not as clear in this play as it is in *Vagones de madera* that the interaction between the characters represents the acting-out of popular cultural identity, but I regard the joint rebellion against authoritarianism of Verónica and Micaela as a manifestation of the spirit of *machismo español* in the broad sense discussed in Chapter 2 – paradoxically, since part of what they rebel against is precisely *machismo* in the narrower sense of violent male domination. Like some of the men in the earlier play, they represent a search for a form of group identity which is not determined by ideology but grows out of shared experiences of work, hardship and everyday cultural practices.

The first part centres on the conflict between Verónica and Reyes, metaphorically reflected in an insistent opposition between light and dark. Reyes associates herself with the sunshine and vitality of her native Fez, while Verónica wants to shut out the sun and withdraw into herself, oppressed and depressed by Reyes's materialism and by the social conditions of the traditional community by which they are surrounded. The appearance of the mysterious stranger Vargas brings Verónica out of her sombre reticence, at the same time as introducing more direct references to the political situation. For her, Vargas represents freedom, political commitment and, above all, hope for escape from the oppressive environment of the house. She links her attraction towards Vargas with left-wing ideals: in Reyes's absence, she declares her admiration for the Republican leaders Largo Caballero, Azaña and La Pasionaria (*En las esquinas, banderas* 1964: 9, 12). The characters have not yet heard about the generals' insurrection, but the political crisis is on everyone's mind and the tensions driving the nation towards violence can be felt amongst them. Emotional and political motives converge as Verónica begs Vargas to take her away with him: 'Quiero dejar esto. Quiero ser libre. Llévame a la revolución, Vargas, llévame de aquí' (13).[44]

At the beginning of the second scene of the first part, Verónica's new-found optimism (and sudden liking for open windows and sunlight) is overshadowed by a sharpening of the emotional and ideological conflict with Reyes, and when Vargas fails to return as promised, her idealism is shattered.[45] She is repelled by the reactionary opinions of the visiting *ganaderos* (farmers) and by their status as unrepentant exploiters of labour, and it is later revealed that she leaves on her own, joins the Republican forces in the hills, and takes an active part in fighting and undercover espionage. When she reappears towards the end as a captive of the same men, who are now *requetés* in the Nationalist forces, she is beaten but defiant. She asserts her independence – both political and sexual – and declares that 'al fusilarme me hacéis libre' (38).[46]

The second part of *En las esquinas, banderas* concentrates on the effect of Verónica's rebellion on Micaela, who at first is presented as an unthinking supporter of the Nationalist cause. The war is in its fourth month, the battle lines are drawn, the territory and population of Spain are brutally divided. Micaela and Alfonsa, in a traditionally conservative community now within the Nationalist zone (somewhere near Salamanca), are subject to fierce wartime propaganda, as well as an intensification of the ideological influence of Reyes herself. The scene opens with the two women sewing sheets for soldiers and singing a Falangist anthem. They chat ingenuously about their contribution to the war effort and the heroism of the troops, and become excited at the apparently imminent fall of Madrid. Their vocabulary reflects the brutal ideological simplification of war, echoing the discourse of the corporal in *Vagones de madera*: Micaela comments about the Republicans that 'esos criminales no necesitan nada pa matar y saquear' (25).[47] Yet Micaela's awareness of the realities of war is superficial and naive. She is surprised to learn that soldiers' letters from the front are censored, and on hearing that the *requetés* plan to bring Verónica into the house in order to humiliate her in front of Reyes, she is horrified to find the violence suddenly brought much closer: 'Yo no quiero verla. Yo quiero divertirme' (35).[48]

Although there are early hints of tension between Micaela and Reyes, in the end it is the example of Verónica's courage and the brutal behaviour of the *requetés* that push Micaela into making a stand: 'Matarme con ella… porque con vosotros no quiero vivir. No quiero vivir con criminales' (37).[49] Another motive for her revolt comes out into the open: 'Siempre habéis dominado a las mujeres' (38).[50] Earlier, she had expressed excitement at the prospect of clients arriving and showed no shame at her profession. Now the *requetés*' contempt for the women (including Reyes) is very clear, and Micaela is repelled by their cruelty as both soldiers and males. Her final act of defiance is shockingly self-destructive: she rushes over to the brazier, scoops up a shovelful of hot embers and throws them into her own face. In practical terms, the gesture is utterly futile. She and Verónica are immediately taken out and executed. But she has registered her protest on her own body, refusing to allow the men to derive any further pleasure from her subjection: 'No pondréis vuestros labios en mi cara. Antes la destrozo' (39).[51]

At the end of the play Reyes's sense of security and righteousness has been broken down by the strength of Verónica and Micaela and the cruelty of the soldiers. She too is forced to drink the castor oil and to hear that the men have as much contempt for her as for the other women. At the end, she wants only to shut herself off from the violence. As the execution takes place outside, she closes the shutters and huddles together in terror with Alfonsa, wailing in despair. For their world is now dominated by men like the *ganaderos-requetés*. The hardening of the arrogance and self-interest of these men into hatred and brutality foreshadows the outcome of the civil war itself: idealism is crushed, principles of justice and humanity are swept aside. The play ends with the suggestion that the victors are men of bigotry, violence and vengeance. The victims include both those who attempt to stay out of trouble by conforming and those who make a futile stand in defence of humanity. Although the motivations of Verónica and Micaela are ambiguous, and our response to Reyes is likely to be mixed, this play contains a clearer opposition between positive and negative values than other, more sceptical works by Rodríguez Méndez. We shall see female characters represented more sympathetically than male characters in many of his plays, invested with qualities of empathy, compassion and sincere (if naive) idealism. Such qualities in other plays tend to be focused much more on family and community, and although the motivation here – in the ideologically polarized environment of the civil war – is clearly political, explicitly linked with violent gender conflict, the central problem is essentially the same as in *Vagones de madera*: the construction of a group identity based on shared humanity, in opposition to the coercive power of ideology.

En las esquinas, banderas has not been staged or published, and there is no record in the censorship files of an application for approval of a production. The topic of the civil war was virtually taboo throughout the dictatorship unless approached from an unequivocally pro-Nationalist angle, and it is inconceivable that Verónica's fervent republicanism, its effect on Micaela and the brutality of the *requetés* would have been tolerated. Most censors would also have found the topic of prostitution itself and the elements of violence unacceptable. A cynically pragmatic argument in favour of authorization might have been advanced along the lines of a point made by the military censor, Juan Guerra, about *Vagones de madera*: 'Los tipos que parecen jugar a una demagogia trasnochada, obtienen la oportuna contrarréplica dialéctica y circunstancial' (Ministerio de Información y Turismo 1960).[52] The 'comeuppance' administered by the *requetés* is certainly effective, eliminating the revolutionary and her disciple, and at the same time punishing the other women for their immoral profession. However, the censors tended to be very wary of any expressions of rebellion, and the mere presence or mention on stage of dangerous material would often be unacceptable regardless of the conclusions that might be drawn from the way in which it was represented.

La Mano Negra (The Black Hand)

Martín Recuerda quotes an account by Rodríguez Méndez of his military service in Cádiz (1950–51). He writes of comradeship, devotion to poetry and flamenco song and dance, and a lasting affection for Andalucía (1979: 26). As he points out, though, the picture of the region presented in La Mano Negra is far from idealized, in stark contrast to the comic sentimentality of plays by the Álvarez Quintero brothers and José María Pemán, or the mythic stylization of Federico García Lorca's tragedies:

> No hay en esta Andalucía de Rodríguez Méndez sentido del paisaje, de la luz, de la alegría. Es una Andalucía del hambre, de la emigración, del señoritismo parásito, de conspiradores, de caciques y de anarquistas que llegan a la libertad por medio del crimen (1979: 27).[53]

La Mano Negra is certainly a sombre work. The enclosed setting is gloomy and claustrophobic; the lives of the characters are hard; the language is subdued; there is little humour and no music, song or dance. In his classification of his works supplied to Martín Recuerda, the author's definition of the subject of this play is uncompromising: 'la esclavitud campesina' (1979: 222) ('peasant slavery'). The work provides a clearer, more detailed analysis than any of Rodríguez Méndez's other plays of the way of life of its characters, of the work they do, and of the methods used to intimidate and exploit them.[54] The setting is the gañanía (lodgings for agricultural labourers) of an estate between Córdoba and Jaén 'around 1911' (Teatro escogido 2005: 344).[55] The first act carefully builds up a picture of insecure seasonal employment demanding hard labour for low wages; spartan living conditions and strict discipline; minimal education, limited horizons and low expectations.[56] Unsentimental sympathy for the workers is evoked in the stage direction describing the entrance of farmhands returning from the fields: 'Rezuman miseria y ganas de vivir. Están curtidos por el sol y el viento, y tienen los movimientos ágiles y felinos de los labriegos del sur. Vienen cansados, sucios. Pero alegres por el trabajo y deseosos de un rato, por pequeño que sea, de libertad' (Teatro escogido 2005, vol. 1: 351).[57] Some of the men gather around some newspapers that one of them has brought in, but they are not interested in current affairs, even though the news is exciting and has local relevance. They insist that el Cojo (an old man with some education) read them a report of a bullfight, rather than news of crimes attributed to an anarchist organization, the Mano Negra, affecting a nearby estate. It is thus emphasized from the beginning that the political consciousness of the men and Cojo's ideological influence on them are minimal. Grateful for whatever work they can get and resigned to the status quo, these are not men with revolution on their minds.

The function of sexuality and religion as parts of a complete system of control are hinted at in this first act. It gradually becomes clear that one of the farmhands, Lebrija, is being forced to do sexual favours for the señorito (landlord) and Sole too owes her privileged position as housekeeper to her willingness to be the lover of Mariano, the aperador (estate manager), as well as his informer. Underlying the tensions between employers and employees are emotional ones, which explode in the climactic moments of the second act. There is an element of conventional rural melodrama in this clash of sultry passions, culminating in Lebrija's killing of Sole. The point, however, is to demonstrate how complete the exploitation of the workers is (sexual as well as economic), and to suggest a sordid private life behind the respectable façade of the landlord's regime. The required observance of religious rituals is shown to be a means of maintaining conformity and obedience in the workforce. Compulsory daily prayers are normally led by Mariano before anyone is allowed to eat dinner and go to bed. On this occasion, he charges Sole with ensuring that the men all pray as required by their master. A division then opens up between a group obediently praying with Sole and a band of 'segregationists' led by the foreman, Tobalo, who take advantage of the manager's absence to ignore the prayers and continue their discussion of the art of bullfighting. This rebellion is taken very seriously by Sole and duly reported to Mariano, who mentions it as a sign of subversion in his statement to the Civil Guard in act three (392).

The first act of the play thus establishes a set of emotional and social conflicts within the estate, while introducing a few passing references to violent events in the surrounding countryside and to the Mano Negra itself. The second and third acts intensify the internal conflicts and reinforce these suggestions of a wider pattern of oppression and discontent. Sole and Mariano repeatedly refer to the threat allegedly posed by the Mano Negra, as part of the *aperador*'s determination to stamp out unrest among his men by means of sackings, threats of violence, and constant vigilance. On a larger scale, the Civil Guard are carrying out a special drive against dissent. In the meantime, the workers are represented as simply trying to get on with their lives and with one another as best they can under hostile conditions. Their display of *machismo* and cultural creativity is even more constrained than that of the conscripts in *Vagones de madera*, their language dialectally authentic but sober, their instinctive sense of class solidarity undermined by the ideology of servitude and resignation.

It is interesting that Rodríguez Méndez chooses to set his play in 1911 rather than during one of the other periods in which anarchist-led attempts to mobilize agricultural workers in Andalucía provoked more high-profile conflict, such as 1903 to 1905 – when strikes were effective in many places – or 1918 and 1919 – when there was the greatest turmoil and the fiercest suppression. As Díaz del Moral (1969) makes clear, there was considerable organizational activity between 1910 and 1913, but there were few strikes and little violence. Public order and the interests of the landowners were not seriously threatened in the Córdoba area in March 1911: the agricultural workforce, although resentful, was not threatening serious revolt. While there was a violent, apocalyptic streak in the anarchist movements active in the Andalusian countryside, much of their activity consisted of relatively low-key syndicalist organization ultimately directed towards precipitating revolution by means of a general strike. The organized syndicates were based in workers' centres in the towns and villages, and spread their influence through oral and printed propaganda disseminated by *obreros conscientes* (politically conscious workers) who became tireless propagandists and educators, touring the estates, sharing the labourers' food and inspiring them with millenarian visions of a utopian society. The response of the landowners and the authorities varied considerably. Some sensible efforts were made to answer the workers' grievances, and improvements in wages and conditions were won in some cases. In other cases, panic and ruthlessness prevailed. The relatively moderate syndicates were persecuted, their leaders arrested indiscriminately, their meeting places closed down, their legitimate demands distorted and denounced as violent criminality. Public meetings were broken up, armed gangs guarded the estates, and workers were intimidated.

It is important, therefore, to realize that *La Mano Negra* is not the story of a great revolutionary crisis. Rodríguez Méndez deliberately selects not the most sensational moment of the period but a time characteristic of a gradually developing crisis, representative of the long-term, everyday subjection of the rural poor. Some signs of anarchist influence are evident, or at least feared by the authorities: Tobalo is something of an *obrero consciente* with potentially revolutionary ideas, although he is not actively subversive; Mariano sees the lack of interest in prayers as a warning sign, and keeps a close eye on what the men have read to them. However, the rebellion dramatized here is on a very small scale. There is no evidence that either Tobalo or Lebrija has anything to do with anarchist groups, nor that they have been actively plotting against their masters. The threat to the established order is a long-term one: it consists not of a terrorist conspiracy but of the resentment built up by continuing exploitation. Even Cojo, apparently in the classic mould of the wandering anarchist apostle, is probably nothing of the kind, and in any case seems to have little influence on the other men. The threat that he represents is education itself – giving the workers the ability to receive ideas from outside the carefully controlled world of the estate. The suppression carried out by Mariano and the Civil Guard sergeant is routine maintenance of order, exploiting the local crisis – the murder of Sole – as a pretext for a general purge of known and suspected troublemakers and a reimposition of control. This crackdown is evidently under way throughout the area, justified by deliberate exaggeration of the threat posed by anarchist influence and subversion. Mariano is anxious to attribute a political motive to the murder in order to cover up the murky sexual background involving the landlord. His statement carefully plays down the complex of emotional tensions, and insinuates a connection with the Mano Negra and Tobalo's defiant behaviour. The sergeant draws rapid conclusions about the case before even beginning to question the workers – 'Esto es cosa política. La Mano Negra' (392) – and warns Chispa off when he attempts to mention the master's involvement.[58]

The very existence of an organization called Mano Negra in Andalucía in 1911 is doubtful. A secret anarchist organization with this name had been active between 1879 and 1883, when strikes, demonstrations, riots and the burning of estates were met with tough measures by the authorities. A series of brutal political assassinations in Cádiz and Sevilla provinces in 1883 was attributed to the Mano Negra. Public outrage was quickly stirred up by the Press, portraying the Mano Negra and anarchist organizations in general as terrorists, murderers and arsonists, and the government used this climate of opinion to justify a massive drive to suppress all protest (Lida 1972: 250). Workers all over Andalucía were arrested on mere suspicion of membership of the Mano Negra, and the extent of the group's influence was wildly exaggerated, with estimates of its membership as high as 49,000. The witch-hunt resulted in fifteen executions and hundreds of prison and deportation sentences: 'La represión oficial demostró una vez más hasta qué punto las autoridades y los terratenientes abusaban de su poder, amparándose en acusaciones arbitrarias para silenciar cualquier forma de protesta entre los obreros del campo andaluz' (Lida 1972: 254).[59] Reference to the Mano Negra in a play set in 1911 is thus a deliberate anachronism: the organization was probably destroyed in 1883, although the idea of violent social struggle and *propaganda por el hecho* (propaganda by deed) survived alongside the syndicalism that became predominant in the anarchist movement after the turn of the century. The usefulness of the Mano Negra phenomenon to Rodríguez Méndez is its status as a folk myth, an awful legend to strike fear into the hearts of the bourgeoisie, and to be used by them to intimidate the more gullible peasants and labourers.

Martín Recuerda takes for granted the importance of the anarchist movement in this play. He sees Lebrija as the central character and suggests that the outcome is positive: 'El personaje, después de haberlo convertido la sociedad en asesino y anarquista, triunfa y encuentra la libertad por encima de todo' (1979: 219).[60] Lebrija does rebel and escape from the oppressive environment of the estate, but it is not clear that he has become an anarchist or gained real liberation. His murder of Sole does not constitute much of a triumph: she has been collaborating with Mariano's regime, but is more of a fellow victim than an oppressor. The motive for the murder is unclear, and seems to be more emotional than political. The killing is deliberately surrounded with ambiguity in order to emphasize the cynical manipulation of the circumstances by the *aperador* and the sergeant.

It is difficult to see Lebrija in a heroic light as the central figure of the play, since his role is a small one. He appears only four times, for short periods, saying very little, and until the murder, behaves submissively. The character who shows the greatest awareness and strength of personality, on the other hand, is Tobalo, and the emphasis of the play is on his self-sacrifice, not on Lebrija's escape. As foreman responsible to the *aperador*, Tobalo has a stake in the system, but unlike Sole, he clearly identifies himself with the ordinary labourers, treating them as equals. His rebellion is a quiet, gradual one. He wishes to avoid trouble, and does not actively encourage dissent (apart from leading the refusal to join in the prayers). He makes his final stand in the third act, making a heroic but futile gesture. He is the natural spokesman for the frightened group of men being interrogated by the Civil Guard. When the sergeant resorts to flogging the two young lads in order to put pressure on the older men, Tobalo is the one whose sense of humanity will not allow him to stand by while they are tortured. He takes the responsibility upon himself, first hoping that he can simply take the place of the sufferers, then accepting that only a full confession of all the crimes alleged to have been committed will save them. He desperately agrees to everything that the sergeant puts into his mouth: belonging to the Mano Negra, planning to murder Mariano, and plotting to burn down the house (401). As soon as Tobalo has capitulated, the sergeant reveals that he was already doomed, having been named in a confession extracted from Cojo the previous day. The sergeant has ruthlessly exploited Tobalo's humanity and integrity in order to obtain the corroborating confession, yet Tobalo retains his dignity. His defiance is crushed, but he has made a stand for fraternity and solidarity among the workers, defending their oppressed little community against the ideological manipulation and brute force wielded by the alliance of landowners and Civil Guard. If there is any sign of *machismo español* asserting itself in this play, it is in the quiet determination of Tobalo.

At the end, the system remains intact. The troublemakers have been carted off to prison or execution, the survivors are stunned and cowed. Only Antón has been influenced by Tobalo's courage, and he defiantly rejects Mariano's offer of continued employment and storms out, sickened by the *aperador's* smug triumphalism. In general, though, total control has been reimposed, and the dominant impression is of the renewed submissiveness and fatalism of the workers: 'Las cosas ya no tién remedio. [...] Tenemos que vivir' (403–4).[61] Mariano instructs them to shut up and get on with their work. The play draws to a melancholy close with a repetition of the communal prayers, emphasizing once again the function of religion in maintaining conformity. The gloomy circularity of the action has been lit up only briefly by the flare of Tobalo's rebellion and its effect on Antón.

La Mano Negra has never been performed and there is no record in the censorship files of an application for approval of a production. The subject matter is less obviously provocative than that of *En las esquinas, banderas*, and the censors would probably have been satisfied that there was little risk of dangerous parallels being drawn with present circumstances (as long as the insinuation of homosexuality was removed). In an interview of 1984, Rodríguez Méndez suggests that the relevance of the play – in the 1960s and also the 1980s – lies in the implication that life is still hard for the rural poor in the south: the text is based on 'historias que han pasado y que pasan todavía en Andalucía' (Thompson 1989: 431).[62] By limiting and manipulating the historical detail, and by concentrating the action into a confined microcosm, *La Mano Negra* is invested with a sense of timelessness and an emblematic significance, emphasized by these telling words near the end of the work: 'El Tobalo es inocente. El Tobalo es como nosotros. (*Pausa.*) El Tobalo es un hombre' (*Teatro escogido* 2005: 403).[63]

Although Francoism initially idealized rural life and agriculture, the regime did little to improve the lot of the Andalusian rural poor or to resolve the *latifundio* problem (large, inefficiently run estates offering unstable seasonal employment): 'Rural Spain remained the poor relation of the new industrial Spain. The sixties saw the mass exodus from the impoverished countryside with its high birth-rate to the cities of Spain and the factories of Europe' (Carr 1982: 752). Modernization in the more prosperous areas merely increased unemployment, adding to the pool of migrant labour (the Cordoban *campiña* is a notable example of this). Although Rodríguez Méndez's claim that conditions had still not improved significantly by the mid-1980s would be difficult to sustain objectively, the process dramatized in *La Mano Negra* has been echoed in recent years by the predicament of immigrant agricultural workers from northern Africa. Rodríguez Méndez argues that the political impact of the work lies in its exposure of continuing exploitation and underdevelopment in a supposedly advanced, prosperous, enlightened nation:

> Ha circulado poco porque era peligroso en aquellos tiempos, y todavía sigue siéndolo. La gente aquí en España queremos entrar en el Mercado Común (vamos, los que mandan, ¿no?), y quieren dar la impresión de que España ya es un país muy europeo. Y estas cosas no quedan elegantes, no quedan finas (Thompson 1989: 431).[64]

El vano ayer (Pointless Yesterday)

The treatment of history in *El vano ayer* is different in many respects from the approach followed in the other plays discussed in this chapter. The focus shifts from the collective towards the individual. After the helplessness of the conscripts in *Vagones de madera*, the women in *En las esquinas, banderas* and the farmhands in *La Mano Negra*, the protagonist of this work is a strong, alert, middle-class character with a clear understanding of the political and historical situation around her, whose private life is enmeshed with larger public events. Set in the north of Spain 'por los años de la Restauración' (*El vano ayer* 1963: title page) ('in the years of the Restoration'), the action centres on Jesuya, the idealistic wife of General Astarloa, exiled for his republican sympathies. She rashly decides to set off a planned anti-monarchist uprising before her husband arrives to lead it. The revolt is quickly suppressed by General Villacampa, who has had advance warning and proceeds in the third act to lure Astarloa into collaboration with the Government. The play is concerned primarily with Jesuya's political commitment, her decision to encourage the local people to start the uprising prematurely, and her response to its failure. History is thus represented as being shaped largely by the actions of individuals.

Beneath the surface of the drama played out between the active protagonists, however, lies Rodríguez Méndez's central preoccupation with *intrahistoria*: the position of the powerless masses in relation to the motive forces of history. Jesuya's relationship with the common people whose interests she claims to represent is not extensively developed, since much of the action focuses on the tension that builds up between her and the middle-class social environment that she rejects. Consequently, there is relatively little attention paid here to representing the culture of *machismo español*. The comfortable bourgeois home in which the drama is set has none of the oppressiveness of the spaces used in the other plays (and therefore less symbolic force), yet it comes to reinforce the suggestion that the protagonist is out of touch with the popular culture with which she identifies: inside the house ideas are debated, conspiracies are hatched and deals are done, while the people who suffer the consequences most directly and physically remain largely unseen outside.

The authenticity of Jesuya's commitment is first questioned by Josechu, one of the peasants who collaborates with her in the organization of the popular revolt. He stresses the contrast between the freezing squalor in which he is hiding out and the bourgeois comforts of Jesuya's house (*El vano ayer* 1963: 6). She is defensive, anxious to prove her credentials and those of her husband as members of the *pueblo*: 'Es pueblo como lo somos nosotros. [...] Es el general del pueblo' (9).[65] Nevertheless, her contempt for the smug complacency of respectable Restoration society (as represented by her sister's letter from Madrid and the tedious social gathering in the second act) is clear enough. She enjoys shocking her bourgeois friends with her declarations of revolutionary fervour when the revolt breaks out: 'Sí, me he vuelto loca. Pero de alegría... Esos disparos son de los nuestros. El pueblo que nos trae la libertad. Y con ese pueblo está mi casa y estoy yo' (30–31).[66]

Jesuya's standing in the eyes of the masses deteriorates drastically when the uprising is ruthlessly put down and the guerrilla leader is killed. The mob surrounds the house, accusing her of treachery. Jesuya becomes a pathetic figure, tortured by the idea that she has betrayed her people, her idealism made to look hollow, even melodramatic, her performance of popular cultural identity exposed as fake. She is denied even the possibility of heroic martyrdom, since Villacampa ignores her responsibility for setting off the revolt in order to trap her husband, who coolly compliments his opponents on having 'played well' as he accepts the Government's offer (44). Jesuya is defeated, humiliated and irrelevant. Meanwhile, the mob in the street is in an ugly mood. Villacampa calmly orders the street cleared with maximum use of force, and delights in the spectacle of the dragoons slashing at the crowd with their sabres. The ordinary townspeople too are ultimately powerless and irrelevant, pawns in a brief, arcane power struggle. Apart from the appearance of Josechu and Espinosa in the first act, the *pueblo* has been present only offstage, their exclusion from the stage symbolizing their exclusion from power.

The title of the play is another allusion to Antonio Machado's *Campos de Castilla*. The lines from which it is taken, from the poem 'El mañana efímero', are quoted at the beginning of the text: 'El vano ayer engendrará un mañana/ vacío y por ventura pasajero' (*El vano ayer* 1963: title page).[67] This poem, written in 1913, is one of a series in which Machado reflects on the political and moral stagnation of Spain and on the ineffectuality of intellectual initiatives for change which prove to be out of touch with ordinary people. Rodríguez Méndez uses the phrase 'el vano ayer' to suggest a judgement on the whole period of the Restoration (from the restoration of the Borbón monarchy in 1875 to Primo de Rivera's coup in 1923, or to the declaration of the Second Republic in 1931). He sums up his view of the period in *Comentarios impertinentes sobre el teatro español*: 'La Restauración puso en marcha una política de apariencia liberal que resultaba fiel heredera del "despotismo ilustrado", es decir, que preconizaba un Gobierno para el pueblo, aunque sin el pueblo' (1972b: 16).[68]

At a time when the social consciousness and political organization of the masses were growing rapidly, an oligarchy of capitalists, landowners, bishops and generals attempted to keep revolution at bay through a corrupt constitutional system, protecting traditional interests behind a façade of progressive liberalism. Like leading members of the Generation of 1898, Rodríguez Méndez condemns the fraudulence of the Restoration and the gulf between the rulers and the ruled, and it is these concerns that are brought out by *El vano ayer*. The dialogue of the first two acts reveals the essence of a range of middle-class attitudes that help to sustain the system: suspicion of 'la dichosa política' ('damned politics', a phrase used by several characters) fuelled by memories of the disorder of the Republic of 1873; insistence on the value of political stability and economic progress; religious conservatism embodied in the sanctimonious *coronela* (Colonel's wife); mildly anti-clerical liberalism that shies away from real social change, falling back on the Hobbesian cliché 'libertad sin orden no es libertad, es libertinaje' (20).[69] It is Villacampa who embodies the brutal reality lying behind the civilized façade of the Restoration. With the complicity of the liberal middle class, the status quo is maintained by the use of conspiracy, blackmail and, ultimately, brute force. Villacampa, clearly under the direct orders of the Government, is cynical and contemptuous of the 'plebe' – an ignorant mass to be manipulated and ruthlessly controlled (41). *El vano ayer* represents Restoration Spain as a sophisticated constitutional system that is ultimately founded upon violent repression.

The episode dramatized in the play does not correspond to any particular event of the late nineteenth century. No date is specified, and detailed historical knowledge is required to pick up the references in the text which pin the action down to late 1895: to José Martí and renewed insurrection in Cuba, to General Martínez Campos (commander-in-chief of the Spanish forces in Cuba from 1895 to 1896), and to Cánovas as prime minister (his last period of office was from March 1895 to August 1896, and he was assassinated in 1897). There is an author's disclaimer after the cast list insisting on his interest in the general character of the period rather than the details:

> El autor advierte que los acontecimientos de tipo político y social que sirven de fondo al drama son intencionadamente imprecisos, por cuanto interesa más al autor dar conocimiento del estado anímico de unos personajes en una época precisa – la Restauración borbónica – que el reproducir exactamente la Historia (*El vano ayer* 1963: title page).[70]

Indeed, the play contains some details which actually confuse the correspondence with recorded historical events. For example, Villacampa (here the loyal general who suppresses the revolt) was the name of a general who led an unsuccessful republican *pronunciamiento* in Madrid in 1886. Sagasta arranged a pardon for Villacampa for political reasons, just as the rebel general Astarloa is forced to accept political rehabilitation at the end of *El vano ayer*. This minor confusion provoked by the use of the name Villacampa may be deliberate sabotage of historical accuracy, a mischievous red herring offered to anyone attempting to tie down the drama to verifiable details.

The title of the play implies that the progeny of the *vano ayer* of the Restoration is the *mañana vacío* of Francoism. Rodríguez Méndez confirms in an interview of 1977 that he sees the Restoration as 'el "precedente" del aprisionador período dictatorial franquista, y como una época de ambigüedades propia para cometer cantidad de impostura y mistificaciones' (interview in Pérez-Stansfield 1983: 245).[71] Both Martha Halsey (1980: 30) and José Monleón emphasize this link and use the lines from Machado as a general description of Rodríguez Méndez's treatment of Spanish history, since several of his plays are set in the Restoration. Indeed, Monleón argues that the main point of *El vano ayer* is to construct an elaborate parallel between the late nineteenth century and the Francoism of the early 1960s: 'La obra es, de comienzo a fin, un drama en clave transparente' (1968a: 49).[72]

The most important connection between the two periods is the claim that each regime continues to be the guarantor of peace, stability and prosperity two decades after the turmoil of a divisive republic. Josefa, a character in the play who is not an unconditional supporter of the Restoration, nevertheless sees it as preferable to the 'savagery' of the First Republic. Franco made much of his claim to have established a definitive, lasting peace, not only by winning the war but also by finding the final solution to the factiousness of democratic politics. During the 1960s, the political apathy engendered by this diminishing *ansia del vivir* (desire to get on with life) was reinforced by improvements in the standard of living and an encouragement of consumerism and self-interest: 'Franco himself believed that with "decent clothes", football matches and TV [...] the working class would have no cause for complaint' (Carr 1982: 725). Although the Spanish economy suffered a downturn in the 1890s, it had enjoyed a relative boom during the early years of the Restoration. In *El vano ayer*, it is the *coronela* who particularly emphasizes the material benefits of political stability, and she asks in genuine puzzlement when the revolt breaks out: 'Pero, ¿qué quieren ahora? ¿Qué más quieren si lo tienen todo?' (30).[73]

However, the desire for order and the enjoyment of prosperity were not enough. Franco's regime tightened its political grip as it loosened its control over the economy in the 1960s. Opposition amongst workers and students was growing, and was fiercely suppressed. There was no major uprising (and certainly no liberal general to lead a *pronunciamiento*), but one instance of the Government's ruthlessness became particularly notorious and prompted well-publicized protests from artists and intellectuals in 1963–64: the violent suppression of the Asturian miners' strikes. The execution of Julián Grimau in April 1963, on charges relating to his activities during the civil war, also brought forth a chorus of protest in Spain and abroad. In 1962 there were still 468 political prisoners held in Burgos, and in 1963 two more executions followed that of Grimau.[74] The system that claimed to have transcended class war and given the people what they wanted was still very obviously relying on force to maintain the illusion of consensus.

Rodríguez Méndez's *coronela* also represents the religious conservatism that lay at the heart of Francoism, here presented as a conventional, slightly ridiculous sanctimoniousness. The references to a 'progressive' Church, to Pope Leo XIII and his encyclical of 1891 entitled *Rerum Novarum* reflect developments in the Catholic Church of the early 1960s. The Second Vatican Council of 1962–63 gave the Catholic Church a more liberal, socially conscious face, and John XXIII issued an important reformist encyclical, *Pacem in Terris*, in 1963. The play presents an ironic picture of the *cura progresista* (progressive priest) in the character Don Augusto, who claims to identify himself with moderate liberal politics yet is perturbed by the increasingly progressive encyclicals issuing from the Vatican and is reluctant to put the new principles of social responsibility into practice. *El vano ayer* implicitly questions the depth and sincerity of the social awareness of the new Catholicism, and this scepticism is also extended to other ineffectual sectors of the opposition: the ambivalent, opportunistic liberals and the ingenuously idealistic revolutionaries, neither group in touch with the real *pueblo*. *El vano ayer* hints at a tacit understanding between conspirators and government, a mutual acceptance of the 'game'. Even the references to Europe have topical relevance to 1962, the year in which Spain first applied to join the European Economic Community and several opposition parties met in Munich to protest against this possibility. Rodríguez Méndez's *profesor francés* conveys an impression of a self-indulgent opposition enjoying stimulating debate and a comfortable life in the glamorous capitals of Europe, while in Spain, as Jesuya bitterly reminds him, nothing changes. Rodríguez Méndez's implicit condemnation is directed both at those who sneer at Spanish reality from a distance and at those who sentimentalize or idealize it.

Other details in *El vano ayer* complete the careful historical analogy. Monleón concludes that such detailed parallelism is counterproductive, obscuring the dramatic situation, and relates that, on attending the first performance of the work (at the Festival de Teatro Nuevo in Valladolid in 1966), he and others felt that the analogy was not only too overt, but also too simplistic – although he goes on to express his disappointment at the fact that many younger members of the audience did not understand the political message, or at least did not think it important, criticizing the play solely in terms of its formal conventionality (1968a: 49–50).

The Valladolid production (directed by Rodríguez Méndez himself) was authorized by the Junta de Censura on 18 October 1966 for audiences over the age of eighteen, subject to the usual condition of an inspection of the dress rehearsal. The censors' reports show that, as usual, they were on the lookout for political 'intentions', alert to the possibility of unauthorized readings of history or subversive connections with the present. The text caused a degree of concern and two jocular phrases from the second act were cut, both implying mild disrespect towards the armed forces. The consensus of the reports, however, is that neither the historical references nor the parallels with the present are sufficiently concrete to pose a significant threat.

The religious censor, Father Blajot, argues that 'dado que no hay identificación de personajes históricos, aparte de las referencias a Cánovas, etc., creo que puede autorizarse esta fantasía' (Ministerio de Información y Turismo 1966).[75] His only concern is about how the priest will come across in performance. Florencio Martínez Ruiz firmly declares that the work cannot possibly refer to current circumstances, and Víctor Auz Castro feels that 'la tesis política, si la pretendió el autor, se desdibuja bajo el drama personal de la esposa del general'.[76] Bartolomé Mostaza even suggests that the text's sceptical treatment of the liberal opposition to the Restoration can be read as favourable to the current regime: 'Trata de la inanidad de toda oposición de los exiliados del poder que se niegan a colaborar y, al fin, fracasan del peor modo: aceptando una cartera. Es el caso del General Astarloa.'[77] He maintains that unless the challenge is too blatant to ignore, it is advisable to avoid drawing unwelcome attention to a work by banning it, an argument that emerges increasingly frequently in censors' reports towards the end of the dictatorship (and an accurate calculation in the case of *El vano ayer*, judging by Monleón's comments on the reception of the play in Valladolid): 'Si la vetásemos, sería confesar que lo que pasa en *El vano ayer* es lo que pasa hoy. Sería impolítico, a mi juicio.'[78]

The most interesting report on *El vano ayer* is by Sebastián Bautista de la Torre. His suspicions, ironically, are alerted by the author's disclaimer about historical accuracy, which he suspects may be a device to distract attention from politically sensitive analogies. If so, the tactic proves counterproductive:

> De no existir esta advertencia, podría examinarse la obra con la natural objetividad; pero, después del aviso queda la duda de si realmente el autor habrá tratado de operar con clave. Y ya se hace un tanto sospechoso el juego de los exiliados, de los generales del pueblo, de las rebeldías, de los generales gobernantes, etc..., aunque todo ello se sitúe en tiempos de la restauración borbónica... Es lo malo de los avisos previos, que te ponen en guardia sobre intenciones que a lo mejor no existen siquiera.[79]

There is no reason now not to take at face value Rodríguez Méndez's declaration that he is more interested in the general atmosphere of the period than in reproducing History. *El vano ayer* is based much more upon the psychological development of a single character than any other Rodríguez Méndez text, exploring a social and ideological environment through the personal crisis of its protagonist. It certainly suggests connections with the period in which it was written, but not simply in order to make a coded protest against specific features of the regime in power at the time. Monleón's contention that the play is an obviously coded text is, ironically, undermined by the readings of the censors – and not because they were too obtuse to spot the clues. The main point is a general one about long-term historical processes. Both the Restoration and Francoism (in its evolved, post-authoritarian form) are identified as hegemonic systems claiming to represent the will and the interests of the people and to offer stability and prosperity, but in reality denying the masses any control over their destiny, absorbing organized political opposition into themselves, and ultimately sustaining themselves by force when the complicity of their victims breaks down. The implication of *El vano ayer* is that Rodríguez Méndez's critique of the Restoration as a period in which the interests of mass of the population were ignored by the ruling oligarchy also applies to the Franco period. The core of the play is the revelation of the gulf between Jesuya's idealist (and essentially ideological) claim to represent the common people and the reality of the everyday lives of those people.

El vano ayer provides a thematically interesting contrast to the other texts discussed in this chapter in that it underlines the marginalization of the *pueblo* by largely excluding them from the stage. It adopts an appropriate form, deliberately following conventions of space, action, dialogue and character reminiscent of nineteenth-century bourgeois drama. If this ends up being one of Rodríguez Méndez's weakest plays, it is perhaps because those conventions are followed too unselfconsciously (unlike the blatant caricature of *El círculo de tiza de Cartagena* and, later, *Flor de Otoño*, which provides more effective ways of representing the bourgeoisie).[80] In contrast, the constraints of a single, claustrophobic set, a conventional three-act structure and straightforwardly realistic dialogue are exploited to powerful effect in the grittier environments and more down-to-earth voices of *Vagones de madera*, *En las esquinas, banderas* and *La Mano Negra* to represent popular *machismo* under pressure.

Notes

1. Buero's other history plays adopt different approaches: in *Historia de una escalera* the historical contexts of the first two acts and the momentous events of the 1930s impinge only implicitly on the *intrahistoria* of the staircase; *El concierto de San Ovidio* is set in France and its protagonists are not well-known historical figures. The protagonists of *Misión al pueblo desierto* are not identifiable figures either, but are sufficiently engaged in public events to qualify as 'world-historical individuals'.
2. Buero was attacked by both left-wing and right-wing critics for this apparent dismissal of the traditional *pueblo* as a brutish rabble (discussed in detail in Thompson 1994).
3. 'Spain as tragedy: this is my constant theme, which of course turns out to be the theme of man and society as tragedy as well.'
4. Halsey takes the phrase from Lindenberger (1975).
5. 'Fundamental structuring principles used by playwrights in the Franco period.'
6. 'All those ideas about the emptiness, nausea, tedium and so on of human existence, which had such a revolutionary impact amongst young people in Europe in the 1940s.'
7. 'We've left everything behind us, our troubles and our joys. It's as if we were all someone else now, someone new. As if we'd just been born. [...] And you only need to look at the life of any one of us, any young bloke from anywhere in Spain, to feel a kind of consolation, to see that we're all brothers.'
8. 'So what if we're heading for the slaughterhouse? So what if they crate us up like fighting bulls? We're young and we know how to have a good time! Come on then, let's have a drink and cheer up a bit!'
9. 'TORERO – In every village there's always two or three geezers who set themselves up as bosses and they're never off your back... ESTELLA – It's our destiny, isn't it? We've always got to be someone's slave.'
10. 'TORERO – We've got no chance of getting on together, there's always somebody who doesn't want to be part of the collectivity. THE OTHERS – (*In unison, sarcastically.*) Woow! VALENCIA – Jesus, Torero, you can really talk. You should be a politician. What a word: collectivity.'
11. 'The Romans were the good guys and the Carthaginians were the bad guys. I was always a Carthaginian. We'd always be worst off in class, but as soon as we got out of school we'd lay into them with stones and stuff, and it was always us who came out on top, the Carthaginians.'
12. 'What has happened here is what always happens: four Romans and five Carthaginians have died.'
13. 'What makes you think any of us, you, me, anyone, can ever win?'
14. The town of Albacete has for centuries been known as a centre of knife-making. The classic *navaja albaceteña* is a folding clasp knife with a broad, curved blade.
15. 'He's a mysterious and slightly sombre character. It's how I see Castilla: a region that's rather sombre, tormented, depressed, antiquated and decadent.'
16. 'But sometimes you feel like you're dragging a lot of baggage behind you... And it's impossible to... You can't... What I'm trying to say is you can't forget the truth. It's like a kind of agony.'
17. 'He was arid, austere and so on, but that's all.'
18. 'There's no influence whatsoever of *Escuadra hacia la muerte*. It's totally different. The two plays have nothing in common.'
19. 'Well, I suppose... life is... feeling that we're comrades, like we're all one big family. Something like that, I don't really know.'
20. 'So what does it amount to, eh? Just another argument. Who cares? [...] There's nothing going on here. That's it, case closed.'
21. 'LUIS – If I could just get the chance to skewer one of them... CORPORAL – You will, don't worry. You'll see. ESTELLA – I can't wait to see some of that filthy blood flowing. CORPORAL – It makes you want to drink it.'

22. 'That's what life's all about: hit them before they hit you.'
23. See Maestre Alonso (1975: 68–69) or Madariaga (2000) for a discussion of the interests involved.
24. For further details of the defeat, its causes and its consequences, see Maestre Alonso (1975), Carr (1982: 516–23) or Balfour (2002).
25. 'Lying in the background was the still relatively recent memory of the million victims of our civil war, one of the most unhealable wounds afflicting present-day Spain.'
26. These priorities come across vividly in Republican propaganda posters, collections of which are accessible online: Vergara (1998) and Brandeis Libraries (2003).
27. 'Let's castrate some Moors!'
28. Dolores Ibárruri spoke of 'la morisma salvaje, borracha de sensualidad, que se vierte en horrendas violaciones de nuestras muchachas' (quoted in Maestre Alonso 1975: 143).
29. 'La raza mora es una raza escogida, una raza de privilegio' ('The Moors are a select race, a privileged race'). From a radio broadcast by General Queipo de Llano in November 1936, quoted in Cabanellas (1977: 268).
30. 'With joy and impatience to claim a place of honour in the civilizing crusade launched on the 17th of July.' From a book of the early 1940s by Tomás García Figueras, quoted by Maestre Alonso (1975: 114, 117).
31. See Maestre Alonso (1975) for further details of this uncomfortable episode, or Bárbulo (2002) for a recent overview of Spain's involvement in the Sahara.
32. The production may have been authorized by the local delegation of the Ministerio de Información y Turismo, as there are no documents relating to it in the censorship file for Vagones de madera held at Alcalá.
33. 'There are deprecating and insulting allusions to H. M. King Alfonso XIII. In the third act, a libel against the Moorish people which cannot be permitted in a public performance, and references of varying directness hostile to the Army.' All quotations from documents contained in theatre censorship files are referenced as Ministerio de Información y Turismo. Each bibliography entry gives the number of the expediente (file) and of the caja (box) in which it is stored, as well as the topográfico code indicating the physical location of the box in the archive. The date given is the year in which the file was set up, although many expedientes cover various applications over several years.
34. 'The play is bitter in tone and makes a rather trite political point based on outdated antimilitarism. But it does provide evidence of the author's potential as a playwright, in the dramatic effectiveness of some of the characters and dialogue.'
35. 'It seems to me that a curious failure of comprehension has afflicted this play (and the dramatic work of this author in general): Vagones de madera has been staged in Barcelona (as has El círculo de tiza de Cartagena), and yet it has always been banned in Madrid.'
36. 'A specific, isolated episode, which cannot be considered representative in either historical or political terms.'
37. 'In any case, from the point of view of 1964, the only issue that might be of significance is the supposed futility of the Moroccan war; but I sincerely believe that the play does not take it up.'
38. 'VALENCIA – Abd-El-Krim? Hah! I'd rather smash it [the lamp] on somebody else's head. No, not Abd-El-Krim's. Somebody else's. ESTELLA – A head with a crown on it, eh? Is that what you mean?'
39. 'Since we can't get the chance to whack the geezer with the crown over the head, we could at least do it to one of his representatives, even if he's only a yokel from somewhere out in the sticks.'
40. 'Death to the geezer with the crown!'
41. 'Looks like he's trying to compete with Primo de Rivera.'
42. 'Yeah, that's it. We shouldn't be cutting Moors' throats, they haven't done us any harm. We should be cutting Romans' throats instead.'

43. The notes beneath the list of characters mention only two days, but in fact the two *momentos* of the first part cover two consecutive evenings.
44. 'I want to get away from this. I want to be free. Take me to the revolution, Vargas, get me out of here.'
45. There is a suggestion that he has been killed as a result of betrayal by Reyes, who cryptically remarks that 'se dejó matar' (33) ('he let himself be killed').
46. 'By shooting me you're setting me free.' The *Tercios Requetés* were the traditionalist Carlist regiments of the Nationalist army, recruited mainly from Navarra and the Basque Country; their uniform featured a distinctive red beret with a tassel.
47. 'Those criminals don't need any excuse for killing and looting.'
48. 'I don't want to see her. I just want to have fun.'
49. 'Go on, kill me alongside her. I don't want to live with you. I don't want to live with criminals.'
50. 'You've always dominated women.'
51. 'You won't touch my face with your lips. I'll destroy it first.'
52. 'Those characters who play an outdated role as demagogues get their comeuppance in dialectical and practical terms.'
53. 'In Rodríguez Méndez's Andalucía, there is none of that sense of landscape, light and joyfulness. It is a land of hunger and emigration, of idle, parasitic landowners, conspirators, *caciques*, and anarchists achieving liberation by means of criminality.'
54. Rodríguez Méndez obtained much of his background information from a classic study originally published in 1929: Díaz del Moral (1969).
55. The date 27 March 1911 is specified in the dialogue during the first act (*La Mano Negra* 1965: 16). The third act takes place the following day.
56. For general analysis of the historical context, see Carr (1982: 15–17, 417–19), and for details of wage levels, food prices, rents and working conditions, Malefakis (1970). These conditions affected enormous numbers of people, as landless labourers constituted by far the largest social class in southern Spain: as late as 1956, they still made up 43.3 per cent of the active rural population.
57. 'The hardship they have experienced and their thirst for life are clearly evident. They have been weathered in the sun and wind, and move with the catlike agility of the country folk of the south. They are tired and dirty. But they are glad to have work and are looking forward to a moment, however brief, of freedom.'
58. 'This is political. The Black Hand gang.'
59. 'The official repression showed once again the extent to which the authorities and the landowners were abusing their power, using arbitrary accusations to silence all forms of protest amongst the agricultural workers of Andalucía.'
60. 'The character, having been turned by society into a killer and an anarchist, triumphs and finds freedom in spite of everything.'
61. 'There's nothing we can do. [...] We've got to live, haven't we?'
62. 'Stories that have happened and still happen in Andalucía.'
63. 'Tobalo's innocent. Tobalo's just like us. (*Pause.*) Tobalo's a man.'
64. 'The play hasn't received much attention because it was dangerous at that time, and it still is. People here in Spain want to join the Common Market (well, the people in charge, anyway), so they want to give the impression that Spain's already a very European country. And things like this don't look good, not civilized enough.'
65. 'He's one of the people just as we are. [...] He's the people's general.'
66. 'Yes, that's right, I've gone crazy. But with happiness... The shots out there are being fired by our side. It's the people bringing us liberty. I'm with them and so is my household.'
67. 'Yesterday was pointless, tomorrow will be vacuous and possibly fleeting.'
68. The Restoration put in place a political structure that appeared to be liberal but was in fact a faithful inheritor of 'enlightened despotism'; that is, it offered government *for* the people but *without* the people.

69. 'Liberty without order is not liberty, it is unbridled licence.'
70. 'The author wishes to point out that the political and social events forming the background of the drama are intentionally imprecise, since he is more interested in conveying the state of mind of a group of characters in a particular period – the Bourbon Restoration – than in reproducing History accurately.'
71. 'The precursor of the stifling period of the Franco dictatorship, and a time full of ambiguity, providing plenty of opportunities for deception and mystification.'
72. 'From start to finish, the work is a transparent *comédie à clef.'*
73. 'But what do they want now? What more can they ask when they've got everything already?'
74. These figures, together with other evidence of the continuing repressiveness of the Franco regime in the 1960s, are given in Blanco Aguinaga et al. (1983: 175–77).
75. 'Since historical personages are not identified, apart from references to Cánovas, etc., I believe that this fantasy can be authorized.'
76. 'The political message, if one was intended by the author, is obscured by the personal drama of the general's wife.'
77. 'It is about the pointlessness of the opposition of those who are exiled from power and refuse to collaborate, ending up by failing in the worst possible way: by accepting a post in government. That is what happens to Astarloa.'
78. 'Banning this play would be tantamount to acknowledging that what happens in *El vano ayer* is what happens today. It would be inadvisable, in my view.'
79. 'If this declaration had not been added, the play could be examined with the usual objectivity; but the presence of the disclaimer makes one wonder if the author may have attempted to work in code. And then the whole business with the exiles, the generals of the people, the rebellions, the ruling generals, etc., begins to look rather suspicious, even though it is all set in the Bourbon Restoration… That is the trouble with these authors' notes: they alert you to intentions that may not even exist.'
80. The practical circumstances of a commission influenced the form and style of the work: 'Se hizo así para un grupo que quería esto' (Roderíguez Méndez interviewed in Thompson 1989: 448) ('It was done like that for a theatre group that wanted this type of play').

4

HISTORY FROM BELOW (2): OPEN SPACES

The first model of historical theatre 'from below' developed by Rodríguez Méndez, based on intense conflicts in confined spaces, represents Spain as a stifling historical and ideological space in which popular cultural identity is allowed little room for expression and creativity. The Aristotelian organization of the dramatic action in three acts, combined with elements of repetition or premonition, tends to give the representation of history a sense of circularity, inevitability or immobility. The second model, analysed in this chapter, reduces this emphasis by opening up the physical spaces in which the action takes place, by deploying more episodic dramatic structures, and by making room for less inhibited performances of versions of *machismo español* within the urban communities that generate them. With larger casts and more flexible staging, these plays offer more comprehensive views of cultural environments and suggest a more evenly balanced tension between human action and historical determinism. This is still 'history from below', but with a broader, more varied perspective.

El círculo de tiza de Cartagena (written in 1961, staged in 1963) marks a kind of transition in Rodríguez Méndez's theatre, designed to apply the idiom of independent popular theatre being developed by Pipironda to a larger project. This 'comedia popular' treats history as farce, celebrating a moment of popular rebellion but at the same time subjecting both the bourgeoisie and the turbulent *pueblo* to caustic satire. *Bodas que fueron famosas del Pingajo y la Fandanga* (written in 1965, first staged in 1976) is labelled 'tragicomedia popular', and while it maintains an element of comedy and affectionately celebrates the popular culture and language of Madrid, the overall effect is darker and more emotionally complex. In *Historia de unos cuantos* (written in 1971, first staged in 1975), classified simply as a 'drama', comedy is largely abandoned while the homage to the popular culture of Madrid is made explicit in self-conscious references to the *género chico*. This is the only play in which Rodríguez Méndez uses a chronicle-like episodic structure covering an extended period of popular history, which gives an unprecedented sense of ordinary people's involvement in historical change but ultimately emphasizes the continuity of *intrahistoria*. Although the tone of *La Chispa* (written in 1983), an 'aguafuerte dramático madrileño' (dramatic engraving from Madrid) with echoes of Goya and Ramón de la Cruz, is reminiscent of the satire of *El círculo de tiza de Cartagena*, the popular uprising of 1808 against the French is treated more straightforwardly as a manifestation of collective heroism. All four of these texts use the stage in flexible and imaginative ways to construct lively, linguistically rich representations of the culture of *machismo español* at key moments in its development – and all five show women to be as central to that culture as men.

El círculo de tiza de Cartagena

On the title page of *El círculo de tiza de Cartagena*, Rodríguez Méndez makes even more of a point than usual of minimizing the importance of historical detail in his dramatization. The time of the action is indicated teasingly as 'durante la revolución cantonal de 187...' ('during the cantonalist revolution of 187...'), while two disclaimers assert that the author has not intended to create an accurate historical reconstruction of the events or the ambience of the period (*El círculo de tiza de Cartagena* 1964: 11). In a sense, this play clearly contains more recognizable History (public events corresponding to historiographical records) than any of the texts discussed in the previous chapter. As we shall see, though, the rejection of historical 'reconstruction' signalled by these declarations is carried through in every aspect of the text – in the vagueness or trivialization of detail, in the reduction of the scale of events and in the farcical treatment of characters and action. When accused in an interview by Isasi Ángulo of failing to carry out an adequate historical critique of cantonalism, Rodríguez Méndez makes an important distinction between historical material (identifiable events, persons and environments) and a historicist approach (essentially, using historical material to exemplify general patterns or processes): 'En esa obra no hay "crítica histórica" alguna. La historia se refiere exclusivamente al "ambiente", a la "localización". [...] No confundamos el "historicismo" con lo "histórico"' (Isasi Ángulo 1974: 274).[1]

The playwright also acknowledges on the title page that some elements of Bertolt Brecht's dramatization of the chalk circle legend have found their way into *El círculo de tiza de Cartagena*. Like *The Caucasian Chalk Circle*, Rodríguez Méndez's text employs the device of a test of motherhood by means of a chalk circle as part of a tale of an honest maidservant finding her way through the convulsions of revolution and tyranny. Although this play opens with what looks for a moment like a Brechtian narrative device (an actor appears on stage before the curtain rises and addresses the audience), there are significant differences of detail and overall effect between these two versions. Rodríguez Méndez's nod towards Brecht turns out to seem more like an ironic sneer at the beginnings of a Brechtian trend in Spanish theatre than a serious adoption of his techniques.[2]

The lively opening scene dramatizes the build-up to the revolts of 1873 in Cartagena as farce. The opening stage direction evokes a panorama of the city with an ironic lyricism that unmistakably echoes Valle-Inclán: 'A lo lejos, las rejas del famoso Penal lagrimean sobre el agua e inspiran reformas penales a oscuros y románticos regeneradores del pueblo' (14).[3] The conspirators' political discussion is a confused, comical blend of idealism, mundane preoccupation with the launch of a new boat and with the cost of fireworks, and healthy appetites for food and wine. The gathering divides into two factions: *progresistas* (Currito the lamplighter, Julio the poet, José Antonio and the waiter) and *moderados* (don Antonio the politician, Torquemada the bar owner and don Pedro the journalist). The conservatism of the moderates, indicated by an attachment to traditional ideas of order, private property and religion, conflicts increasingly sharply with the angry radicalism of the younger men. These positions correspond roughly to a series of political conflicts which tore apart the First Republic of 1873, between moderate *benévolos* and radical *intransigentes*, federalists and centralists, intellectuals and popular activists. The cantonalist revolts were the explosive result of a long accumulation of political tension, fed by widespread popular disillusion and discontent. An *intransigente* faction in Parliament had staged an abortive coup in Madrid in mid-June 1873 and planned a network of coordinated local uprisings for July. In the case of Cartagena, the uprising was set off prematurely on 12 July by the man sent from Madrid (Gálvez Arce), creating a complex four-sided struggle between the moderate national leadership, the power-seeking leaders of the *Comité de Salud Pública* (Committee of Public Safety – a reference to the French Revolution) in Madrid, their independently minded envoy, and the local activists in Cartagena, who were unsure about following Gálvez Arce's lead.[4] Rodríguez Méndez, however, simplifies the political situation, largely cutting out the national perspective and reducing the conflict to two clear components: conservatism and revolution. Don Antonio is the fictional counterpart of Gálvez Arce, but his reactionary instincts come to the fore when the local hotheads push the situation out of his control. Although the clash of attitudes in the play is based on serious political issues, the tone remains comical, the stage directions and language suggesting an atmosphere of farce and sardonic irony reminiscent of Valle-Inclán's *esperpentos* (expressionist black comedies written in the 1920s).[5]

In the play it is Julio and the progressives who decide that the time for rhetoric is past and take direct action, storming the prison and taking over the city. The violence, however, is presented as grotesque comedy, the dead jailers described in an esperpentic stage direction as 'monigotes' (puppets) (23). Meanwhile, as the revolution overtakes them, the moderates move swiftly onto the side of order and established authority, wasting no time in offering to save the governor's wife and baby from the mob. Once again, the seriousness of the action is undermined by don Antonio's inflated rhetoric and other comic business involving the improvised baptism and the obsession of the Governor's wife (doña Charito) with attempting to take with her as many of her possessions as she can.

In the same way as the political process is simplified, reduced to a local scale and turned into grotesque satire, the representation of the cantonalist regime in the second *estampa* transforms the professional defence of a heavily armed city besieged for five months by government forces into a brief, comically amateur episode featuring a shack on the beach serving as the headquarters of the High Command of the cantonalist forces, a few drunken ex-convicts armed with shotguns, and a fishing boat. The revolutionary 'army' is led by Julio the poet, whose concern now seems to be limited to his verses and the charms of Rosita, the serving-girl who has taken care of doña Charito's baby. The men on guard duty express vague attachment to notions of freedom, anti-clericalism, revolution and the integrity of the common people, but that is as far as the political content goes, since their principal motive seems to be a simple desire for revenge against their former oppressors (27).

The anarchic triumph of the revolutionaries is short-lived. In the third scene, the city is badly damaged by bombardment and the canton has crumbled. Doña Charito returns to power with military backing, the rebels are in chains, and the three moderates are fervent supporters of her regime. The judge appointed to oversee the restoration of order turns out to be the drunken ex-convict Bulería, who gleefully turns the victors' concept of justice on its head by his idiosyncratic use of what he calls 'the judgement of God' (45): the legendary chalk circle, representing a deliberate trivialization of what was in reality a period of severe retribution and repression. Amidst much hilarity, don Antonio is almost executed, the rebels are set free and doña Charito is humiliated. In the short epilogue, doña Charito is definitely in command once again. She orders Bulería to be hanged, rejecting all democratic processes and the support of the politicians, who now become irrelevant: 'Apartaos de mí, no he de caer de nuevo en vuestra ignorancia… He de implantar la dictadura en Cartagena. En ausencia de mi esposo, mando la ciudad' (52).[6] The volte-face of the moderates and the return to power of doña Charito reproduces in satirical, localized form the historical process of the national Republican leadership's lurch into authoritarianism in response to the cantonalist crisis. The Salmerón and Castelar governments brought the generals back into Spanish politics in order to crush the revolts and sought the support of Conservatives and the Church, precipitating a crisis in the republican movement which ultimately led to the military coup that restored the monarchy at the end of 1874.

The ideological conflict, the treachery of the moderates, the death of Currito in the second scene, the failure of the popular uprising and the reimposition of authoritarian government are all potentially grave subjects. And yet, apart from one or two sombre moments, the treatment is relentlessly comical. The details of the historical record are evidently distorted, yet the overall effect is a truthful – if exaggerated – reflection of the absurdity of the real events. The cantonalist movement had authentic popular roots and some serious political objectives, but turned out to be naive, confused, and doomed to accelerate the demolition of the whole republican project.

The impression of cynicism and pessimism left at the end of Rodríguez Méndez's play is what differentiates it most clearly from Brecht's *The Caucasian Chalk Circle*. There are obvious similarities of plot: the violent seizure of power; the situation in which the wife of the deposed governor is so concerned with rescuing her material possessions that she flees without her baby; the predicament of the maid who is left holding the baby; the reversal of political fortunes; the accidental appointment of a subversive judge with a liking for alcohol, and the resolution of the dispute over the child through the chalk circle's exposure of the real mother's selfishness. Brecht also treats his 'historical' material with a degree of black humour and satirical detachment, but ultimately makes a constructive political point about the capacity of working people to take control of their fortunes, which is made clear by means of the narrative frame. The story told by the singer offers no resolution of the problem of social injustice within the world of the main dramatic action, apart from the confidence that the tyranny of the great cannot last forever. However, the present-day frame shows this same Caucasian world much later as an egalitarian society rebuilding itself after beating off the German invasion. The principle they establish is illustrated by the chalk circle episode, and forms the major theme of Brecht's play, clearly declared at the end:

> That what there is shall belong to those who are good for it, thus
> The children to the maternal, that they thrive;
> The carriages to good drivers, that they are driven well;
> And the valley to the waterers, that it shall bear fruit (Brecht 1963: 96).

In contrast, the political situation in *El círculo de tiza de Cartagena* is less straightforward and there is no positive solution whatsoever. Rodríguez Méndez dramatizes the failure of political action, the betrayal of egalitarian ideals, the inertia of the masses. Although his play shows traditional authority temporarily humiliated, it ultimately points less to the inevitability of the downfall of tyrants than to the inevitability of the return of tyranny. Rosita plays a smaller part in the action of *El círculo de tiza de Cartagena* than Grusha does in *The Caucasian Chalk Circle*, and the chalk circle itself is of less central importance in Rodríguez Méndez's version. The link between the two principles of earning the right to motherhood and determining the just ownership of property or resources is not clearly established by means of a narrator or framing device, nor does it seem to be implicit in the action, for the work does not deal seriously with the question of rights of ownership, except in so far as these may be seen to be part of a general concept of social justice. The chalk circle test is used twice in *El círculo de tiza de Cartagena* – both don Antonio and doña Charito are humiliated. The first contest in the circle consists of a simple test of physical strength, yet a kind of natural justice is done, as don Antonio's duplicity is revealed. The second trial matches – with some changes of detail – the test of maternity in Brecht's version: the biological mother's selfishness is exposed by her willingness to take advantage of the surrogate mother's concern for the child, and the judge enrages the governor's wife by awarding the child to the servingwoman. So the chalk circle device is used in *El círculo de tiza de Cartagena* for two purposes: to condemn the behaviour of don Antonio and doña Charito, and to praise that of Rosita.

Oliva has described the primary theme of this work as 'la exaltación de las virtudes del pueblo llano' (1978: 90) ('the exaltation of the virtues of the common people'), but this is to go too far. Rosita does embody qualities of simplicity, honesty, courage and humanity; she is committed to the cause of the revolution but is not prepared to abandon the governor's wife in the midst of giving birth, and her instinct to look after the abandoned baby is stronger than her sense of duty towards her class. However, it is difficult to see the play as a whole as a straightforward paean to popular virtue. Indeed, false sentimentalization of the *pueblo* is one of the traits of romantic republicanism that is satirized here. Rosita's rejection of ideology in favour of instinctive humaneness is not shared by the other working-class characters, who are generally represented as opportunistic and egotistical. Just as the bourgeois characters manipulate ideology for their own benefit (Charito exploits the rhetoric of charity and justice, while Antonio speaks of revolution at one moment and constitutional legality at another as it suits his purposes), the representatives of the people disingenuously misinterpret it to excuse venal or selfish behaviour. Julio's role as leader of the cantonalists is undermined by the comic business about avoiding unsavoury rhymes in his verses and by the interest he takes in Rosita, and the commitment of his men to principles of equality and fraternity is shaky:

> J. ANTONIO – Niño, acerca el frasco.
> EL MOZO – Ya no soy mozo de taberna.
> J. ANTONIO (*A Filigranas.*) – Me parece que llevabas razón antes, cuando hablabas de calentar a este niño… Tendremos que volver a los antiguos sistemas… (28).[7]

In view of the satirical treatment of the ideals of both popular revolution and liberal reform, together with the blurring of the political message 'that what there is shall belong to those who are good for it', it might have been expected that this play would have little trouble with the censors. A reading that drew parallels between the anarchic collapse of the First Republic of 1873 and 1874 and the demise of the Second Republic of 1931 to 1939 (encouraged by the reference to establishing a dictatorship) might even have regarded the restoration of order, authority and Catholic morality at the end of the play as commendable. However, the first application for approval of a production in Madrid by the group Teatro del Candil was turned down in May 1962 despite having the prestigious backing of José Tamayo (director of the Lope de Vega company). Although concerned that the author's intention was not clear, José Luis Pelegrín recommended authorization for audiences over the age of eighteen (Ministerio de Información y Turismo 1962). Adolfo Carril, on the other hand, was not in favour of authorizing the production. His report complains that having a hysterical woman (Charito) as the mouthpiece of order and decency devalues 'la reacción natural ante unas ideas comunistoides'.[8] Two further reports were commissioned, and again there was disagreement. José María Cano recommended approval with six cuts in addition to those identified by Pelegrín (three of them mildly irreverent references to priests). His report insists that the situation and characters 'deben tomarse como ya pasados y cualquier suspicacia, sugerencia o similitud con situaciones y personajes posteriores supondría, a mi juicio, una interpretación desorbitada y nada inteligente'.[9] Father Manuel Villares, on the other hand, considers the play irredeemably plagued with vulgarity and crude 'revolutionism'.

The director of Teatro del Candil, Luis Balaguer, submitted an appeal in October 1962 requesting a review of the decision, arguing that the piece is merely a situation comedy 'sin otra idea que la de caricaturizar un "patriotismo" mal entendido, egocentrista y sensiblero'.[10] Two more censors were brought in. While Bartolomé Mostaza dismisses the play as a dramatic failure but does not consider it dangerous, Gumersindo Montes Agudo takes a surprisingly hostile and simplistic view:

> Toda la historia tiene una línea demagógica, una inclinación izquierdista manifiesta. Es como un canto libertario, una apología revolucionaria. Pasada de moda, injusta y resentida. No existe ninguna razón que justifique la puesta en escena de esta pieza, políticamente peligrosa y teatralmente absurda.[11]

Authorization was finally given in November, but the Madrid production never took place. In the meantime, Dora Santacreu and Carlos Lucena had applied for approval of a production in Barcelona, which was given on 4 December subject to the following cuts (page references are to El círculo de tiza de Cartagena 1964):

> FILIGRANAS – Iba bien disfrazado el tío [el fraile]... Yo le tomé por una vieja.
> JOSÉ ANTONIO – Porque se me ocurrió tirarle del moño.
> EL MOZO – Me gusta ver a los tíos dando patadas en el aire (28).[12]
> FILIGRANAS – El Jefe estaba muy solo. La poesía no le bastaba. De pronto se ha encontrado padre putativo.
> JOSÉ ANTONIO – Como San José (32).[13]
> BULERÍA – La República... ¡puah! (Escupe.) Un servidor es tradicionalista. Tradicionalista! (36).[14]
> JULIO – Si quieres morir conmigo escupe a la cara de esa mujer cuando tengas que descubrir la tuya... Yo moriré blasfemando (41).[15]

What seems to matter most in the end, therefore, is superficial evidence of the irreligious attitudes of the rebels, regardless of whether these characters are presented favourably or unfavourably: the audience is not trusted to come to its own conclusions. The removal of Bulería's claim to be tradicionalista appears more puzzling. The motive may have been to avoid associating a character who turns out to be subversive with traditionalist (that is, monarchist and Catholic) values in a general sense, or with Tradicionalismo in a specific political sense. On the other hand, the problem with this line may have had more to do with the internal politics of Francoism. The Carlist party Comunión Tradicionalista had been subsumed into the Falange in 1937, which since the late 1940s had been increasingly sidelined by other forces in the regime and by the beginnings of modernization: radical Falangism and old-fashioned Traditionalism were awkward topics to which the Francoist establishment simply preferred not to draw attention.

The inability of the censors to agree on whether El círculo de tiza de Cartagena posed a political or moral threat is partly the result of the text's own ambiguities – its frivolous treatment of weighty historical events, its satirization of both revolution and conservatism, its ironic attitude towards both the bourgeoisie and the masses. There is, however, one clearly positive, hopeful element in the play: the independence of spirit shown by Rosita, who decides to place her maternal instincts above the pressures of authority and the interests of self and community. Against the background of opportunistic egotism on the one hand and the passivity of the masses on the other, Rosita displays compassion and a down-to-earth scepticism about ideology: 'Yo soy revolucionaria como la que más. Pero hay cosas y cosas. El corazón es lo primero' (17).[16] Her unassuming courage, humanity and sense of solidarity make Rosita the representative in this play of the positive spirit of *machismo español*, which in a sense is what she is defending when she claims that doña Charito's baby is her own: 'Puedo andar sobre leños encendidos para probar la legitimidad de mi linaje' (48).[17]

The child Rosita cares for may represent some kind of hope for the future, but the uncertainty of that future is emphasized by the quotation from Antonio Machado's *Campos de Castilla* that heads the play:

Ya hay un español que quiere
vivir y a vivir empieza
entre una España que muere
y otra España que bosteza.
Españolito, que vienes
al mundo: te guarde Dios.
Una de las dos Españas
ha de helarte el corazón (10).[18]

This poem and others in the collection refer to the emergence of a new, enlightened Spain demanding change with regenerative zeal, while the old Spain, decaying and introspective, obstructs such change. In *El círculo de tiza de Cartagena*, the new dawn of the idealists is a false one (just as the boat dedicated to the canton with the name Nueva Aurora is hastily rechristened Charito de Cartagena). Rodríguez Méndez rejects the notion of a regeneration led by an enlightened elite and suggests that the possibilities for salvation already exist within the *pueblo* itself. It is Rosita and the *españolito* she will bring up who represent the only positive element here, not the middle-class revolutionaries or the irresponsible working men who follow them.

Bodas que fueron famosas del Pingajo y la Fandanga (The Great Day Pingajo and Fandanga Got Wed)

Bodas que fueron famosas del Pingajo y la Fandanga (1965) inaugurates an impressive series of mature works that combine the austere bleakness of the early dramas with the popular, festive character of the Pipironda pieces, adding more sophisticated, imaginative staging to produce ambitious tragicomedies of powerful theatrical effect. *Bodas, Los quinquis de Madriz* (1967), *Historia de unos cuantos* (1971) and *Flor de Otoño* (1972) break out of the suffocating spaces of the *Huis-clos* plays and construct more varied, dynamic and spectacular representations of social environments and historical moments. To some extent the technical innovations evident in these plays (fluid, episodic plot structure; schematic, flexible staging; silent action, fantasy sequences and projections; greater use of music and sound effects) are the product of a period characterized by a general preoccupation

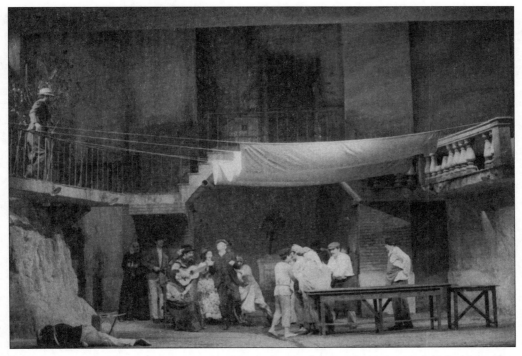

Bodas que fueron famosas del Pingajo y la Fandanga, Teatro Bellas Artes (Madrid), November 1978. *Photograph by Manuel Martínez Muñoz.*

in all the arts with the re-examination of aesthetic forms, moving away from the social realism of the 1950s. However, these plays represent an enrichment of Rodríguez Méndez's realism rather than a change of direction, a synthesis of previous lines of development designed to represent collective cultural identities more completely and more vividly.

Moreover, there were other factors motivating the evolution of his style. *Bodas, Los quinquis de Madriz* and *Historia de unos cuantos* represent a rediscovery of the author's own cultural roots in a traditional working-class district of Madrid (around the Plaza de Cascorro). His family had moved from Madrid to Barcelona in 1939, and he had lived in Madrid again between 1952 and 1956. Back in Barcelona in the 1960s after serving in the army, he was, according to Martín Recuerda (1979: 160), deepening his knowledge of the Spanish classics, of popular theatrical traditions based on Madrid (the comic *sainetes* and *zarzuelas* of Ramón de la Cruz and of the late nineteenth-century *género chico*), and of the historical contexts from which they emerged. The investigations that gave rise to the essays of the early 1970s also fed into these plays, most obviously in the case of *Historia de unos cuantos*, which is closely linked to *Ensayo sobre el machismo español*. In addition to this intensification of the author's interest in cultural history, the increasing marginalization imposed on him by censorship and by the conservatism of the theatrical establishment paradoxically conferred a degree of creative freedom by removing the constraints of writing for particular companies or venues. The requirement for large casts and fairly elaborate technical resources was to some extent a response to the assumption that the plays were unlikely to be staged under the prevailing conditions in any case: 'Lo que yo escribo no está destinado directamente a los escenarios en uso y abuso' (Rodríguez Méndez 1968b: 17).[19]

The structure of these plays is based not on tightly focused microcosms but on the accumulation of loosely connected situations, using short scenes as vivid snapshots. The result is an approximation to epic theatre, though without any conspicuous Brechtian devices, emphasising open-endedness instead of the closed, fatalistic structure of a unified three-act development, producing a degree of distancing inherent in the need for schematic staging and frequent changes of setting, and suggesting to some extent an effect similar to that of narrative (a sequence of past events, rather than a continuous present re-enactment). The fluid structures allow greater scope for visual qualities and overall theatricality, including the integration of music, song and dance. Rodríguez Méndez now devotes less attention than in some of the early dramas to the motivation of individual characters. The emphasis is on the collective character of communities (or in the case of *Flor de Otoño*, on the ways in which the protagonist parodically responds to the characteristics of various social groups) and on the language they use, which is lively and richly colloquial, authentically recreating dialect and period features. It becomes increasingly evident that dialogue is being presented much more as an affective performance of identity than as a rational exchange of views, that the act of speaking is often more significant than the meanings of the words. These plays show Rodríguez Méndez's concept of theatrical realism becoming more flexible and imaginative, an evolution in which dramatic form is not taken for granted but explored, extended and used self-consciously, showing awareness of the fact that theatrical representation does not reproduce reality but mediate it.

The central theme of *Bodas*, according to the classification supplied by the author to Martín Recuerda, is 'la desintegración del pueblo' (1979: 124) ('the disintegration of the people'). Put like this, the idea may sound grossly simplistic, but what is dramatized in all Rodríguez Méndez's plays is a complicated process of social and cultural change: the erosion of the people's vitality, cultural identity and sense of solidarity, set off against an affirmation of what survives – gestures of defiance, solidarity and compassion. In *Bodas*, the picture becomes particularly complex, representing the *pueblo* both as a grotesque reflection of a corrupt social order and as a repository of individuality and collective creativity. The community featured in the play is both subject to the hegemonic discourse of Restoration Spain and at the same time satirically challenging it.

This time, Rodríguez Méndez has chosen a conventional landmark of Spanish history at which to place the action of the drama: 1898, in the midst of the 'Disaster' of the loss of Cuba, Puerto Rico and the Philippines, which finally destroyed the declining credibility of the Restoration's political system and exposed the emptiness of the pride of this debilitated imperial power.[20] However, *Bodas* is not a rigorous analysis of the causes and effects of the 1898 crisis as such. It presents a wider, richer panorama of Restoration society than the earlier works, but political and military events remain in the background while the dramatic action focuses on small-scale incidents and the cultural practices of a marginal yet emblematic community. In a series of vivid scenes, the principal characters move between various locations in Madrid and social contexts, from their own infra-urban slums to the corrupt hierarchy of the military barracks, the fringes of respectable society in the park, the rich (but rotten) core of that society in the Casino, and finally to the no-man's-land of the place of execution. Along the way we catch glimpses of a parade of peripheral characters: children playing, soldiers and officers, passers-by and sweet sellers in the park, policemen, casino cashiers, hangers-on at the wedding.

For his 1978 production, José Luis Gómez attempted to flesh out what he saw as an incomplete social portrait. He added extra stage business and peripheral characters, especially at the beginning of the play and in the fourth scene. Some of these characters were merely noisy onlookers and elements of local colour, while others – such as a political agitator dragged away by the police – were introduced in order to point up the implicit social tensions. Gómez's programme notes carefully specify that 'la clase social que aparece como protagonista no es *el pueblo*, sino *el lumpen* de la época, un grupo de marginados y delincuentes, desprovistos de toda oportunidad de salir de su situación, presos en el círculo vicioso de la miseria y el delito' (Gómez 1978).[21] It is true that the main characters of *Bodas* belong to a relatively small sector of the population, but they are more representative of the people as a whole than Gómez suggests. The social focus of the play is deliberately restricted. The society of Restoration Spain is seen from the perspective of the people at the bottom of the social heap. The world of Pingajo is cut off from – but dominated by – the official society in which the hegemonic moral and cultural values are defined, and where the economic and political power lies. Large numbers of people in Spain at the end of the nineteenth century inhabited a kind of underworld: the movement of population from the countryside into the towns was accelerating, especially into the great cities, where the poor lived precariously in conditions of extreme deprivation. The colonial defeats of 1898 added a considerable number of repatriated soldiers to the existing population of marginalized groups scratching a sordid living on the fringes of the prosperous cities. As used by Marx with reference to Louis Bonaparte's seizure of power in France in 1851, the term *lumpenproletariat* refers not to a specific social class but to the flotsam and jetsam of a changing, fragmenting society: a shifting, more or less classless mass. Pingajo and his companions are easily recognizable in Marx's description (though not portrayed with the contempt expressed by Marx):

> Alongside decayed roués with dubious means of subsistence and of dubious origin, alongside ruined and adventurous offshoots of the bourgeoisie, were vagabonds, discharged soldiers, discharged jailbirds, escaped galley slaves, swindlers, mountebanks, lazzaroni, pickpockets, tricksters, gamblers, *maquereaux*, brothel keepers, porters, literati, organ grinders, ragpickers, knife

grinders, tinkers, beggars – in short, the whole indefinite, disintegrated mass, thrown hither and thither, which the French call *la bohème* (Marx 1999: V).

There is a linguistic link between this description and Rodríguez Méndez's anti-heroic protagonist (a conscript recently returned from the defeat of Spanish forces in Cuba). The German word *Lumpen* has the same meaning as the Spanish *pingajo* or *pingo* (rag, tattered cloth), and *Lump* is a rogue or beggar. Pingajo's nickname is not only a description of his physical appearance (and of his alleged role as a kind of battlefield scarecrow in Cuba), but an expression of his social status. The main significance of the term *lumpenproletariat* lies in

> drawing attention to the fact that in extreme conditions of crisis and social disintegration in a capitalist society large numbers of people may become separated from their class and come to form a 'free floating' mass which is particularly vulnerable to reactionary ideologies and movements (Bottomore 1983: 292–93).

Rodríguez Méndez does not deal with the vulnerability of such people to particular political movements. However, *Bodas* is concerned with two aspects of the phenomenon: firstly, the existence of this 'disintegrated' lumpen mass as a direct product and reflection of an unstable, degenerating capitalist society; and secondly, the political apathy of this mass and its acceptance of elements of authoritarian and nationalistic ideologies. Thus, *Bodas*, while not concentrating on the most numerically significant social group of the period, nor presenting a comprehensive cross section of classes, portrays a community which ironically reflects an entire corrupt nation.

In his contribution to the programme for the 1978 production, Monleón praises Gómez's efforts to give life to the setting and the secondary characters, but effectively argues that the insistence on getting a 'complete fresco' onto the stage is unnecessary. He insists that *el lumpen*, although it does not include those engaged in industrial labour or workers' organizations, is also *pueblo*, and makes the point that the existence and influence of other social forces is implicit in the condition and behaviour of the characters who appear on stage: 'Las desventuradas bodas del Pingajo y la Fandanga se alzan como un suceso minúsculo que nos permite, sin embargo, vislumbrar el fondo de una época' (Monleón 1978a).[22]

What the portrait of this particular community of marginalized *machos* brings out very clearly is the performative nature of their cultural identity. The play is made up of a series of short *estampas* (prints), a term that suggests static images in a picturesque or *costumbrista* style. The storyline is simple, with one significant development in each *estampa*: Pingajo wins Fandanga's hand in the first, then he and the girl's father overcome the opposition of the mother in the second; in the third, Pingajo is forced to agree to deliver his fiancée to the lascivious lieutenant, but in the fourth he decides not to do so; having deserted and stolen the officer's uniform, Pingajo plans a robbery with his friends in the fifth, which they carry out in the sixth; as they use the proceeds of the robbery in the seventh to celebrate Pingajo's wedding, the thieves are arrested; and in a sombre epilogue, a group of women witnesses the execution of Pingajo by firing squad. Each scene, however, consists mostly of animated, slightly ritualized, often competitive acts of self-expression, and each pair of scenes comprises an episode that could almost stand on its own as a popular *sainete*. The effect is to highlight a series of verbal and visual gestures, enacted by individuals within a collective idiom. In the end, though, these gestures are not static and certainly not merely picturesque: they are related to historical change and invested with brutal tragicomic irony.

The play opens with a silent enactment of a ritual of the cult of *machismo*: a game of *la rana* (consisting of tossing coins into the mouth of a frog-shaped receptacle) in which each man's standing in the eyes of the others – as well as a valuable prize – is at stake. When Pingajo scores his five hits, his skill begins to be elevated to an almost mythical level. The others look at him 'como si ante ellos estuviera el mismo maestro Lagartijo en persona, tal es su admiración' (*Bodas que fueron famosas del Pingajo y la Fandanga* 1979: 59, stage direction).[23] A kind of ironic nobility is conferred upon the scruffy *sorche repatriado* (demobilized soldier), who is praised as a 'hero' for having successfully avoided the nasty business of combat in Cuba (59).[24] At this point, therefore, the men carry out a deliberate comic inversion of Establishment discourses concerned with national honour, the glory of military conflict, and pride in duty and self-sacrifice.

The language in which these men express their *machismo* is vividly colloquial, frequently exclamatory. As usual, Rodríguez Méndez indicates in the text the elisions and contractions of dialectal speech: 'Pos esto no es na. Hubián tenío que verme ustés hace un año pa San Isidro' (59).[25] The lexis is rich in slang and in expressive metaphors and metonyms: a rifle is a 'chopo' (59) (apparently referring to a poplar tree but in fact derived from Italian *schioppo*, a loud bang or the firearm producing it); the innkeeper announces the need to 'regar estos esponsales' (60) ('irrigate the betrothal'); Fandanga is a 'gustoso bocao' (62) ('tasty morsel'); and a pickpocket's fingers are 'dátiles' (63) ('dates'). These characters 'se emborrachan tanto con palabras como con vino, hablan más para sentirse vivos que para dialogar, hablan porque es la única manera de apuntalar su inútil existencia, una manera de espantar el miedo y la profunda soledad' Capmany 1968: 57).[26] At times they become incongruously pompous in speech and manner, acting out comically formal rituals. Ironic references to the traditions of chivalry appear several times in the dialogue:

> PINGAJO – ¿Me se adjudica o no me se adjudica la doncella?
> PETATE – Te se adjudica. Testigos son estos caballeros (59).[27]

Petate becomes particularly solemn, striking a patriarchal pose and delivering a sententious discourse: his daughter has been won 'con fuero de nobleza' ('by right of nobility'); the girl is 'el tesoro más grande de este mundo' ('the greatest treasure in the world'); he and Salamanca were 'los reyes del Hacho Ceuta cuando la flor y la nata de la majeza española estaba confiná en aquellos amenes' (60–64).[28] There is a series of ritualistic gestures to mark this important occasion: embraces, histrionic weeping, toasts, raising of arms as if casting a spell, slapping on the back, bowing in honour of Lagartijo and the innkeeper's wine. They declare that the wedding is to be a demonstration of their collective *majeza*, which in this context (as argued in *Ensayo sobre el machismo español*) is equivalent to *machismo*: 'Pa que vea el mundo entero que en nuestra España no falta alegría ni majeza' (62).[29]

This alternative society is at once cut off from and deeply influenced by the official Establishment. The *machos* of *Bodas*, while viewing the Restoration with ironic detachment, nevertheless build their own social relationships around notions of honour, patriotism, ceremony and status which are derived – in a distorted fashion – from the respectable models handed down to them. Capmany observes how Pingajo, driven by fear and ignorance, regurgitates 'las fórmulas éticas que ese orden establecido le enseñó' (1968: 58).[30] This response is similar to that of the earlier *machos* exemplified by Escarramán, summed up in *Ensayo sobre el machismo* as rejection and imitation at the same time (Rodríguez Méndez 1971a: 45). They cannot avoid being recruited to some extent into the dominant ideology, but at the same time they challenge it through parody.

For the moment, the characters' confident, cocky mood is reminiscent of Manolo, Rodríguez Méndez's second archetype of *machismo español*, and there are clear echoes of Ramón de la Cruz's play: the mock-heroic language, the cheerful delinquency, the importance of the tavern as the focus of the action.[31] El Petate is the counterpart of the ridiculously sententious patriarch in *Manolo* (tío Matute) who marries off his daughter to the returning hero. The so-called campaign from which Manolo returns has been waged in the prisons of North Africa, a route also followed by Petate and Salamanca. The name Pingajo itself appears in another *sainete* by De la Cruz, *El mal casado*. The Madrid *castizo* setting is more than just a common location. *Ensayo sobre el machismo* argues that works such as *Manolo* made a significant contribution to the cultural environment that still characterized the area at the beginning of the twentieth century. The link between Pingajo and Manolo is therefore not a purely literary reference, but an expression of this blending of popular culture and social reality.

Pingajo and his friends share some of Manolo's swagger and contempt for both the upper classes and the notion of working for a living. The men of *Bodas* also display the instinctive localized patriotism of Manolo, a patriotism centred on their *patria chica* rather than the nation. They have little respect for the conventional ideals of military glory and national honour, yet they are not totally impervious to the jingoism of the time. The toast '¡Y viva España y que se mueran los yanquis!' (*Bodas* 1979: 62) ('Long live Spain and death to the Yankees!') seems to be more or less straight-faced. Petate appears to take seriously the idea of national disgrace, and it is presumably the military humiliations of 1898 to which Tuerto refers with the phrase 'nuestras esgracias' (62) ('our misfortunes'). But then mocking irreverence comes through again at the end of the scene: when the men drink a toast to Spain, it is 'con mucha sorna' (68) ('full of sarcasm') and a great deal of laughter.

So it is that the ambiguity is maintained. The ideas, behaviour and language of Restoration society are imperfectly reflected in the *pueblo* alienated by it. This distortion is in part a consciously ironic exaggeration of the grotesqueness of the system, in part an indication of the ignorance and subjection of the people. In the first *estampa*, the cheerful self-confidence predominates. The grim reality of slum life is forgotten; the dirty, inglorious war treated as a joke. The play begins with many of the elements of a light-hearted *sainete*, but it will prove to be a *sainete para llorar* (a comedy to make you weep).

The immediate link between the first and second scenes is the intervention of Madre Martina, the local *beata* (sanctimonious lay sister) and gossip. She scurries off to let Carmela know of the match that her husband has so casually arranged for their thirteen-year-old daughter. This carries the plot forward to the conflict between Petate and his wife, but also introduces additional thematic elements. Madre Martina herself represents a hypocritical, degraded form of religion – her piety is empty, her rituals mere routine, her evangelism simply a way of making a living. Her sales pitch switches in an instant from holy scapularies to pictures of bullfighters when she catches sight of Petate and his friends (66). The men take none of this seriously, but Carmela does not appear to be so confidently cynical. Her view of the world and standards of behaviour are clearly conditioned by the kind of superstitious Catholicism peddled by the *beata*. She expects some measure of consolation from religion, but gets very little. Petate's casual giving away of Fandanga adds to Carmela's despair, and she ends up repeating obsessively '¡No hay Dios!... ¡No hay Dios!' (73).[32] Her faith provides no spiritual or practical aid, and she bitterly repudiates it in her anger and desperation. Martina's answer to everything is apocalyptic fatalism. She propagates the message of Madre Rafols: that the world is in a state of antireligious barbarism soon to be brought to an end by the Second Coming.[33] All social and personal misfortune or disruption is thus merely part of the general decadence of the times. This moralizing message is linked to a reactionary nationalist discourse: '¡Ay tiempo de desgracias y bien de desgracias, que por un lao cañonean nuestros barcos y por otro nuestra honra!' (72).[34]

The presence of the witch-like granny in this scene comically undermines Martina's sanctimoniousness, and the *beata* continues to be ridiculed at other moments in the play. Religion is therefore presented as something largely irrelevant to the real needs of the people, and antipathetic to their more spontaneous community culture of *machismo*. It is part of an ideology demanding conformity and passivity, closely associated with reactionary political forces. Like the other components of the Establishment's system of values, it is debased and distorted as it is handed down to the *pueblo* and reproduced in grotesque figures such as Madre Martina. To some extent, the people are dependent upon it, yet the fact that they are also able cheerfully to reject it is a sign of strength and independence. At one stage, even Salamanca and Petate go through the motions of crossing themselves and praying for divine assistance, but ironically they do this as they set off for the raid on the Casino at the end of the fifth scene (98).

The other major topic developed in this second scene is the effect of *machismo* on the women in this community. Petate clearly feels that his daughter can be treated as a sexual object to be given away as a prize, though he dresses this sordid fact up in trappings of chivalry. Carmela is not even consulted: the patriarch decides. Carmela protests passionately at the abuse of a girl of only thirteen, at his failure to consult her about such an important matter, and at his general neglect of the responsibilities of a husband and father. Petate expects to be the uncontested master of his household and, infuriatingly for Carmela, receives greater affection from Fandanga than she does. In this respect, the men of *Bodas* aspire to characteristics of both of their models of *machismo* – the crude domination practised by Escarramán and the cavalier seduction of Manolo. They do not fill either role very impressively. As the *Ensayo* suggests, the desire to dominate is at bottom a sign of weakness and insecurity. Nevertheless, the scene ends with reconciliation all round – and more drinking. Carmela may be a victim of *machismo* in many ways, but ultimately the second scene shows that she is nevertheless a proud member of this community in her own right, happy to share a drink with the men in celebration. Later, the wedding scene expresses a joyful sense of festive harmony in which the women are fully involved.

The family conflict set up in the first *estampa* is resolved in the second with Carmela's acceptance of the marriage. The third introduces a new complication and source of tension: Pingajo's craven promise to hand his fiancée over to the lecherous lieutenant. The portrait of *machismo* becomes more unpleasant, now in an ugly military setting. The scene begins with some rough-and-tumble comedy, as Pingajo returns to the barracks and his fellow soldiers join in his drunken parody of military formalities (78). The core of the scene is a lengthy dialogue between Pingajo and the lieutenant, which, blending crude comedy with violence and pathos, brings out Pingajo's grovelling cowardice in the face of the officer's egotistical bullying, as well as suggesting the corruption and degradation of the military establishment. A kind of sado-masochistic game is played out between the two men in which Pingajo, afraid of the physical violence constantly threatened by the lieutenant and of the possibility of losing his relatively comfortable position as the officer's crony, cringes abjectly and makes facetious jokes while the lieutenant boasts and beats him, and both of them drool lewdly over the prospect of Fandanga's young flesh. Part of the reality of *machismo*, therefore, is far from the confident merriment of the Manolo archetype. The way in which the two men discuss Fandanga, although occasionally humorous in the colourfulness of its language, is unpleasantly salacious. The girl is seen as merely an object, to be used and cast aside.

The image of the army conveyed by this third *estampa* is an important component of the historical analysis. The idle, debauched lieutenant represents a set of social values idealized by Restoration society. Although Cánovas and other political leaders had succeeded in establishing civilian control of government after 1874, breaking the cycle of military *pronunciamientos* for nearly half a century, the interests of the armed forces were a powerful factor conditioning the politics of the Restoration.[35] Its cumbersome bureaucracy, inflated and underpaid officer corps, and lack of equipment and professionalism were constant obstacles to efficiency. The generals still considered themselves guardians of the nation's honour and integrity, and were a powerful force in the defence of their material interests and dignity, as well as of the conservative political status quo. The critique implicit in *Bodas* is not so much of the political power of the army in itself as on its social influence, on the myth of the army as a pillar of respectability, patriotism and virtue. The lieutenant's laziness, corruption, vulgarity and brutality parodically demolish this myth. The whip with which he sadistically enforces discipline is ironically known as the Code of Military Justice, a masterly comic touch that sums up the degradation of the military ideal.

After this vision of institutionalized corruption, the military theme re-emerges in *estampas* five and six, which provide brief glimpses of the undeserved respect evoked by the lieutenant's uniform when it is worn by Pingajo. Since the episode in the barracks, he has begun the rebellion which culminates in the robbery by refusing to deliver Fandanga to the lieutenant and deserting. He now turns up to the rendezvous with Petate and Salamanca strutting proudly in the splendid stolen uniform and playfully pretends to arrest them. His companions may pour scorn on military institutions and values, but they are still impressed by the trappings:

> PINGAJO – Me han saludao toos los quintos. Y en el tranvía me han cedío el asiento. Me han tomao por un héroe glorioso.
> PETATE – Y héroe glorioso eres (97).[36]

They are aware of what this reveals about the hypocrisy and superficiality of respectable attitudes, yet they themselves begin to take such illusions seriously. Pingajo is seduced by the prestige lent to him by the uniform, and at the same time enjoys mocking the attitudes that he imitates. When he leads the raid on the Casino, he plays his role as an officer with panache, building up to a deliberate, highly amusing, travesty of military values and rhetoric. Announcing that a military coup has broken out, he and his accomplices fill their pockets. He continues his satirical speech with great relish while stashing away the money: 'Habrá que poner una dictadura, pero una dictadura fetén y ya habrá quien la imponga pa acabar con tanto ratero, tanto desaprensivo como circula por estos madriles' (100).[37] Pingajo's claim that the robbery is morally justified – since the army has been chronically underfunded while the idle bourgeoisie has been living it up back home – is a deliberate parody of the classic military *pronunciamiento*, and conscious comic irony on his part is essential to this scene. It seems to escape the notice of Antonio Fernández Insuela, however, who takes Pingajo's words at face value as a serious criticism of 'la situación de España' (Fernández Insuela 1981–82: 295). In a sense, Pingajo does express a criticism of the state of the nation, but he is simply not equipped to make a coherent political statement. What is happening is more interesting: the ideas that he expresses are derived from the prevailing reactionary rhetoric, but mischievously inverted by the delinquent *majo*.

Let us now turn our attention back to the *estampa cuarta*. Despite an apparent slowing of the action as Pingajo strolls through the park with his fiancée, this scene marks a major turning point in the play. Underlying the tranquil, cheerful atmosphere of a spring afternoon in the Retiro, considerable tension is built up around the situation initiated in the previous scene: Pingajo has agreed to deliver Fandanga to the lieutenant, but her innocence and vulnerability begin to trouble his conscience. There is a studied picturesqueness about the setting – the *zarzuela* music; the parade of soldiers and young ladies; the boats on the lake and the sweet seller. Fandanga is dressed up in pretty flounces and ribbons, looking like an officer's daughter being escorted by her father's subordinate. Martín Recuerda describes this scene as deliberately *costumbrista*, with 'ráfagas del género chico' (1979: 135) ('flashes of the *género chico*'). There are one or two specific references. The tune played by the violinist is the popular 'Marcha de Cádiz'. The *zarzuela* of that name is about an indigent *cesante* (a civil servant who has been made redundant by a change of government) and here Rodríguez Méndez provides a pair of them sitting on a bench, commenting comically on the state of the nation and the behaviour of Pingajo.[38] Although these elements do not strictly constitute a violation of verisimilitude, the *zarzuela* atmosphere does seem to be intentionally exaggerated. The effect is of deliberate artificiality: a rose-tinted image to contrast incongruously with the sordidness of scene three, and against which to set the tense struggle of Pingajo with his conscience.

The scene in the park begins playfully, but the mood gradually changes. At first, Pingajo wishes merely to delay the betrayal for as long as possible, and attempts to entertain the girl with a toy windmill and chatter about the wedding. Little by little, her childish enthusiasm brings home to him the enormity of what he is planning to do: '¿A jugar?... ¡Ja...!, menúo juego' (92).[39] He ends up forbidding her to go to the barracks and dragging her home by force. It is on the bench in the Retiro that Pingajo makes his real rebellion. The scene is slow, understated and tinged with gentle humour, but marks the crucial transition in the construction of the central character. He has been presented up to this point as something of a shallow caricature. Indeed, part of this portrayal has been his own deliberate (and largely unsuccessful) attempt to project an image of himself as a confident *manolo* figure. The evidence of Pingajo's real weakness and the inauthenticity of this pose has been clear. Now he shows great strength by making the positive decision to defy the lieutenant, and thus reject the callous egotism which lay behind the plan to abuse Fandanga.

Both Martín Recuerda and Fernández Insuela feel that the motivation for Pingajo's decision is insufficiently clear. They are looking for evidence that he has genuinely begun to love Fandanga, for a properly formed relationship. Fernández Insuela argues that Pingajo appears to treat the girl purely as a child and that 'Rodríguez Méndez no explica con claridad los mecanismos psicológicos que llevan al Pingajo a enamorarse de la Fandanga y a no entregarla al teniente' (1981–82: 294).[40] Martín Recuerda also considers the relationship too schematic, inadequately dramatized. He describes the characterization of Pingajo and Fandanga in terms of 'naturalism', suggesting that their behaviour is conditioned purely by natural (animal) instincts. Pingajo is seen as a chaotic, elemental creature, following his most brutal instincts, and yet essentially good and innocent (1979: 133–34). Martín Recuerda insists on seeing both of these characters as slightly mentally retarded, and then finds himself surprised by both the conversion in the park and Pingajo's self-assurance in the fifth and sixth scenes.

I feel that these critics give the characters less credit than they deserve. There is little justification for dismissing Pingajo as mentally retarded. He is certainly uneducated, desperate and humiliated, yet from the beginning he displays a certain expressiveness and cunning. He is not a failure in the terms of his own community: he has some of the stylishness required to perform the role of *macho*, and some of the intelligence vital to the struggle for survival in a hostile world. It is also true that he and the other characters are driven to a large extent by primal urges. Crude appetites for sex, food and alcohol are much in evidence. In the absence of a social framework of morality which is genuinely relevant and based upon consensus, there is little respect for the law, for property or for propriety. These characteristics, moreover, are not confined to socially marginalized groups. They are also displayed by the lieutenant – the figure who is closest to being a representative of the ruling classes of the Restoration. So the 'naturalism' of the characterization involves both innate impulses and a large measure of social conditioning, which is produced not only by an absence of relevant moral standards, but also by the active degradation of the people through oppressive social organization and the operation of ideological apparatuses.

Consequently, Pingajo's motives can be seen as more complicated – and more coherent – than Martín Recuerda and Fernández Insuela argue. His change of mind does not need to be justified in terms of love, since it is explicable as a manifestation of compassion and self-respect. Pingajo says very little in this scene to reveal his thoughts, but it is clear that he recognizes two things: his own cowardice in making the agreement, and his responsibility for protecting a fellow human being even more vulnerable than himself. Some complexity may also be seen in the figure of Fandanga, who need not be played entirely as the innocent, wilful little girl. She is a more interesting character if we see her mischievous childishness as to some extent affected. Pingajo seems to be unsure whether to treat her as a child or as a sexual object, and she – perhaps unconsciously – plays upon this ambiguity. She cannot suspect what really awaits her at the barracks, but it is not just the promise of sweeties that makes her so keen to go: she enjoys men's interest in her, without yet being fully aware of the possible consequences.

So the episode in the park is a key moment. Pingajo rejects the inhumanity of the lieutenant, knowing that this will cost him dearly. He recognizes Fandanga as an individual towards whom he must feel some sense of responsibility, and with whom he has more in common than with the lieutenant. As a result of this decision, he regains some dignity and independence – a kind of redemption. His action is, in its small way, a political statement, a gesture of rebellion, for he renounces collaboration and immediate self-interest, and shows solidarity with one of his own kind. This episode represents the same kind of affirmation of fundamental human values that emerges from the other plays – the values defended by Valencia, Rosita, Micaela and Tobalo. In the midst of poverty, oppression and depravity, some basic human respect and vitality can survive.

Pingajo and his companions then complete their rebellion with the spectacular robbery. This is the ultimate expression of their *machismo*, a public display of skill, daring and sheer cheek; an exultant rejection and mockery of authority and respectability. *Ensayo sobre el machismo español* discusses the importance of criminality in the culture of *machismo*. For Escarramán, there is little choice: to submit to honest labour would be to capitulate, and he either survives by cunning and strength or he does not survive. Manolo may collect a wage from time to time, but in general he disdains work because it is beneath his dignity. He is never a full-time, professional thief, merely 'un pillo de vida desenvuelta y espontánea' (Rodríguez Méndez 1971a: 86).[41] It is this carefree, insolent delinquency to which the men of *Bodas* aspire. Petate talks with pride of their stay in the Hacho prison in Ceuta, and Salamanca seems to be renowned for the nimbleness of his 'dátiles' (*Bodas* 1979: 63). The emphasis in scenes 5 and 6 is on the audacity of the robbery, the skill of the robbers and the pure thrill of the adventure. On the other hand, the three *compadres* are too stupid to avoid being caught. Pingajo continues to strut around in the stolen uniform; money and gifts are liberally distributed to family and friends; plain-clothes detectives are even pressed to join the wedding celebrations. The felons are easily picked up and ruthlessly punished. The rebellion is short-lived and, ultimately, futile – repeating the pattern perceived in all of the earlier works.

Before the final destruction of Pingajo, the wedding celebration takes place. Part of the purpose of this seventh scene is the creation of dramatic suspense, sharpened by elements of comedy, building up to the arrest at the height of the banquet. *Estampa* 7 has another important function, though. It is a well-developed example of the festive interlude before disaster that features in all of Rodríguez Méndez's works in one form or another. These episodes tend to involve the consumption of wine and demonstrate two things: the need for some momentary escape from hostile circumstances; and the possibility of collective understanding, of sympathetic communal relationships on a very basic level. *Ensayo sobre el machismo español* highlights these brief 'epicurean' interludes of escape and companionship shared by the *escarramanes* of the seventeenth century as an affirmation of vitality and concrete reality (Rodríguez Méndez 1971a: 33). In the next historical phase of *machismo*, the capacity for carefree hedonism is an essential accomplishment of the successful *manolo*.

The scene is genuinely and joyfully festive. The stage directions specify a jubilant spring morning, tables loaded with food and wine, snatches of *zarzuela* tunes and *pasodobles*, dazzling costumes, and a general atmosphere of excited celebration. In the first scene Salamanca had declared that the marriage would have to be as good as the *pueblo* deserves (63), so the wedding feast is not merely a fleeting opportunity to drown sorrows and fill empty bellies but a celebration of the community and its spirit of *majeza*. There is a strong emphasis on the collective nature of the occasion, and specifically on the generous distribution of gifts, food and drink. Petate insists on including the entire community: 'Que no se quede naide del barrio sin comer hoy' (110).[42] The traditional dance into which the guests launch themselves involves forming a circle, in the middle of which individuals take turns to dance on their own, improvising flamboyant movements while the others clap and sing. Apart from its value as pure spectacle, the form of this extended song-and-dance sequence is a vivid expression of both collective harmony and individual virtuosity.

Fernández Insuela sees this scene as an important part of a process of 'degradación hacia la tragedia' ('degradation towards tragedy'), making a great deal of the link with the Camacho episode in *Don Quixote* prompted by the opening stage direction of the scene. He draws several interesting but tenuous parallels between the two celebrations in order to show that Pingajo's wedding feast represents a negative, degraded reflection of its classical model (1981–82: 298). Clearly, the wedding scene in the play ends in disaster and many of its features are considerably less idealized than in its Cervantine counterpart. To view it as a negative image of degradation, though, is to diminish its value as an affirmation of human vitality and its function as a genuinely joyful communal interlude before the catastrophe. Although Rodríguez Méndez is not interested in mere *costumbrismo*, some moments of celebration expressed through elements of folklore are an integral part of the world of his characters.

Finally, the epilogue provides the grim dénouement: 'El Orden borrará la inútil molestia que es el "Pingajo", vencido, apaleado, miserable, delincuente' (Capmany 1968: 59).[43] And yet this final scene is far from perfunctory. The execution is preceded by an extended discussion among the group of women who have come to witness it, and the climax itself is a powerful blend of pathos and grotesque black comedy. Most critical attention has focused on the tragicomic nature of the execution; it is also useful to observe what emerges from the moments leading up to it.

The women are revealed at the beginning of the epilogue grouped around Mother Martina, just finishing a rosary. Martina repeatedly attempts to impose a religious emphasis, but this is almost completely ignored by the other women, who leave her to pray on her own. Her empty piety has become irrelevant, displaced by more immediate communal concerns. In contrast to the passive fatalism of Martina, some of the other women express anger and defiance, producing the only coherent statement of protest to be articulated by any of the characters in this work:

> OTRA MUJER – Porque en esta España nunca ha habío justicia con el pueblo. Ni justicia, ni vergüenza, ni na.
> UNA MUJER – Lo que yo digo es que no somos mujeres y que ya no quean riñones en los Madriles, sino que habíamos tenío que tirarnos a ellos y hacerles trizas la piel, que pa eso Dios nos dio las uñas (114).[44]

The appeal is to the collective sense of *machismo*, in which the women feel they have as much stake as the men. Pingajo and Petate have begun to acquire the status of folk heroes – the latter for dying bravely, while Pingajo is described as a prince who looked after his own (112). The women reaffirm their community spirit, and underline the contrast between this humanity and the ruthlessness and indifference of the system.

So the pride and defiance of the *pueblo* is – albeit briefly and futilely – embodied in these grieving women. However, the overall effect of their conversation is complicated by continuing ambiguity. There is a pathetic attachment to the same ideals of military honour and patriotism sustaining the system that oppresses these people. They recognize that the military law under which Pingajo has been sentenced is brutal and unjust, yet still see this as conferring some kind of prestige upon him:

> UNA MUJER – A él lo afusilan por el aquel del fuero melitar.
> UNA MUCHACHA – En eso sale ganando, porque dicen que es muerte de honra.
> UNA MUJER – Habrá que verlo morir. Como un húsar (113).[45]

This ambiguity is most powerfully and ironically expressed through the symbolic device of the flag. The women plan to bury Pingajo's body in the national colours as if he had been killed heroically in combat. The lieutenant in charge of the firing squad stumbles over the ragged flag and contemptuously kicks it aside. One of the women retrieves it and clutches it to her breast. It is with this dirty, tattered rag that at the end the women reverentially cover the body – a national emblem abused by the soldier who is supposed to defend it but, perversely, treasured by the people whose victimization it is used to legitimize.

At the centre of the closing moments of the play is the pathetic, ridiculous figure of Pingajo. The staging carefully isolates him by moving the women to one side and keeping the firing squad itself off the stage altogether.[46] The officer pours some brandy into him, pushes a cigarette into his mouth, slaps him on the back and disappears. 'El Pingajo se queda solo como un auténtico pingajo, medio escoreado hacia un lado, con la cabeza colgando y el cigarrillo colgando del labio' (119).[47] This distressing scene is given a further twist towards the grotesque as the victim – out of his senses with terror and alcohol – collapses prematurely at the sound of the rifles merely being loaded. The lieutenant, becoming irritated and impatient, picks him up, revives him and scolds him. The touches of black comedy are masterful:

> ¡Será gilí este tío!... ¿Pos no se ha desmayao? [...] (*Le agitan entre los dos. Le dan cachetillos en la cara. El Pingajo abre los ojos asombrado y les mira como si ya estuviera en el otro mundo.*) [...] Hasta que no oigas el disparo no te tiés que mover... Quieto ahora. (*Le deja bien colocado, como si fueran a hacerle una fotografía, y vuelve de prisa a desaparecer.*) (120).[48]

This time, the procedure is brisker and the salvo hits Pingajo before he reaches the ground. In figurative terms, he has lived much of his life on his knees. Now he dies literally on his knees, abject and ridiculous. The lieutenant, business-like, gives him a quick *coup de grâce* and marches his troop away. His 'honourable death' has been wretched and grotesque, a ghastly parody of the dignity of military ritual. He is eliminated and discarded.

Machismo has been reduced to the shattered scrap of flesh that was Pingajo, but the women are still there. Slowly, they get up, drape the flag over the body and kneel round it. The curtain falls on this silent tableau of grief. It is essential that this final image convey some sense of strength and solidarity. Despite everything that has happened, the women are united and claim Pingajo as their own hero. The covering of the body with the flag is a small but significant act of defiance. The symbol of the flag has been loaded with irony, and they now make it their own, suggesting that they are the real Spain, however beaten and ragged. This community, and by extension the *pueblo* as a whole, have been defined primarily in terms of the men. Yet it is the women who survive and maintain some human dignity, offering the only positive note in this bitterly tragicomic ending. Ultimately, the men's arrogant display of *machismo* is revealed as shallow and fragile; they are crushed by the state, leaving the less ostentatious but more durable women to represent the underlying spirit of their community.

The dignity and emotional directness of the closing moment, together with the delicacy of Pingajo's crisis of conscience in the park and the candid communal celebration of the wedding scene, all counterbalance the elements of grotesqueness and black comedy which most commentators on *Bodas* have emphasized, usually linking the style of the play to Valle-Inclán's *esperpentos*.[49] The settings, the tone of the language and the apparent sketchiness of the characterization may at times echo the *esperpento*, and Pingajo inevitably calls to mind Valle's *sorche repatriado* in *Las galas del difunto*, Juanito Ventolera. However, Rodríguez Méndez never creates caricature as extreme as Valle's dehumanization of ridiculous, manipulated figures. While *El círculo de tiza de Cartagena* acknowledges its debt to Valle, *Bodas* is more emotionally complex and more sincerely humanist. Both writers draw on the *género chico*, but as I have argued earlier, Rodríguez Méndez takes it more seriously as a manifestation of popular culture. Rodríguez Méndez views his characters face to face, not from the puppet-master's position raised above them. José Luis Gómez's programme notes for the 1978 production are in tune with the playwright's vision in this respect: 'El esperpento está ahí, a la vuelta de la esquina. Si se llega a él, sólo será a través de la humanidad de los personajes, no de una idea apriorística y literaria del mismo' (1978).[50]

Perhaps the most significant departure from the text in Gómez's production was to omit the flag from the epilogue, leaving the grieving women grouped loosely around the body. Martín Recuerda reports that the use of the flag had been prohibited by censorship in 1970, when a production had been planned in Barcelona but had never taken place (1979: 140).[51] However, no such ban affected Gómez in 1978 at the Teatro Bellas Artes. Instead, according to Rodríguez Méndez, a kind of reverse self-censorship operated: 'No se atrevieron a sacar la bandera "nacional" por miedo a resultar "reaccionarios"' (private correspondence with me, February

1986).[52] The flag is an essential component of the powerful irony of the last scene, bringing together the symbolic associations of the term *pingajo* (linking the people as ragged *lumpen* with the image of a tattered nation). Its conventional nationalistic value is negated, reappropriated by the women to honour the antiheroic Pingajo and to stand not for a state, a monarch or a patriotic ideal, but for a battered people.

A full picture of what the censors found objectionable in this text cannot be reconstructed, since most of the material relating to *Bodas* is missing from the theatre censorship archive. There appears to have been an application for approval of a production before 1970, but the file is untraceable. As noted above, the documentation from 1970 is missing, as is that from 1974: file number 205–74 contains only a handwritten note of November 1975 saying that the archive copy of the text is in the possession of the Director General. This application was presumably for the production by the Assemblea d'Actors i Directors de Barcelona which turned out to be the premiere. Approval seems to have been given in April 1974, but the production did not take place until August 1976, as part of the first Festival Grec. I have not yet been able to find out whether the delay was due to censorship, nor what cuts were imposed.

Some evidence of the regime's hostile response to this play can, however, be found in the records relating to censorship of publications. José Monleón had planned to publish the play in the Taurus volume of 1968 containing *La tabernera y las tinajas* and *Los inocentes de la Moncloa*. When the edition was submitted for the process of 'voluntary consultation' introduced by the 1966 Press Law, one of the readers made no objections while the other recommended a large number of cuts. At first, the decision was to impose all but one of these cuts, but the head of department subsequently amended the document to the effect that *Bodas que fueron famosas del Pingajo y la Fandanga* be removed from the volume altogether. The hostile censor's report is specifically concerned about perceived political parallels with present circumstances:

> Aunque el autor desarrolla la acción en el año 1898, ha puesto una serie de frases, unas de carácter político y otras de tipo militar, que por su analogía podrían tener encaje en la actualidad y que son críticas al Régimen actual. Así en la página 182, al hablar unos carteristas dicen: 'después de pasar veinticinco años de paz en la trena.' Tal condena no puede admitirse en un tipo de delincuente como el de carterista; y, sin embargo, dice veinticinco años de paz en la cárcel, periodo igual al que ahora se ha tenido de paz. Así se puede deducir de otras frases que atañen a la milicia y a la Justicia (Ministerio de Información y Turismo 1968).[53]

The censor's suspicions are initially alerted by the apparently gratuitous mention of twenty-five years of peace, which he takes to be a satirical reference to the official celebrations held in 1964.[54] The topicality would have been more evident when the play was written in 1965, but the censor clearly felt that the phrase signalled a subversive intention. Apart from the phrase 'de paz', almost all the cuts recommended are concerned with the representation of the army: references to the lieutenant as a 'señorito' (*Bodas* 1979: 64–65); the jocular use of the titles 'coronel' and 'general' by Pingajo and a fellow soldier (78); and stage directions specifying the dishevelled appearance of the sergeant and the fact that he thrashes the conscripts with a belt (79–80).[55] The entire conversation between Pingajo and the officer about the prospect of deflowering Fandanga and their debauched life in Cuba, including the use of the 'Code of Military Justice' and the comic business with the bottle of brandy (81–86), is judged unacceptable. Also marked for suppression are: the *cesante*'s comical remark about army officers letting their batmen look after their children (93); Pingajo's declarations about the army during the robbery (99–100); a reference in the epilogue to the fact that Pingajo is being executed under military law (113); the women's protests about the absence of justice for the people (114); and the statement 'bien merece el pobre que lo envolvamos en la bandera, como a los soldaítos que mueren en campaña' (115).[56]

The main concern of the censors, therefore, was to avoid having the army satirized or associated with corruption, indiscipline, abuse of rank or debauchery, and to remove any suggestion that military law might be brutal or unjust. Although the reference to twenty-five years of peace was perhaps unwise, since it unnecessarily drew attention to a specific link with the time in which the text was written, the general resonance of the text's disrespectful treatment of military institutions and values was enough to trouble the censors. If the generals had enjoyed disproportionate influence on the politics and social values of the Restoration, military hegemony was the defining feature of the Franco regime: 'Those who had fought in the Civil War remained the most consistent bearers of the mystique of the Crusade' (Carr 1982: 698). The Nationalists' victory of 1939 had supposedly saved Spain from communism, godlessness and ruin, and the armed forces continued throughout the dictatorship to play a large part in government at national and provincial level. Compulsory military service was used to inculcate traditionalist, nationalist values in the male population, and the army retained a crucial role in the preservation of civil order.[57] The summary martial law under which Pingajo is executed was still being used to condemn terrorists in the 1970s. Even more than it had been during the Restoration, the army was held to be the bastion of traditionalism, historical continuity and moral rectitude.

The army was still a force to be reckoned with in the politics of the transition to democracy, as demonstrated by the attempted coup of 1981, but the Madrid premiere of *Bodas* in November 1978 was not subject to political censorship. The Comisión de Calificación decided upon an age restriction of fourteen years, although Francisco Martínez's report proposes eighteen years in view of the generally violent nature of the work (Ministerio de Cultura 1978). Ironically, Gómez's emphasis on realism and period detail, like his decision to do away with the flag, risked reproducing the effect so often sought by Franco's censors with respect to history plays: to discourage analogies with the present by making the representation of the past as complete and self-contained as possible. Whereas Rodríguez Méndez tends, as we have seen in several plays, to introduce elements that deliberately obscure or disrupt historical detail and coherence, Gómez set out to create a more complete social 'fresco', using Pío Baroja's descriptions of social deprivation in Madrid as his primary model of cultural reference rather than the *género chico*, and including a selection of texts and images from the period in the programme. He states a desire to 'crear una realidad analógica, no documental' ('create an analogous rather than documentary reality'), but gives no indication of where the analogies might lead other than the suggestion that the point is to present social history as collective memory: 'La realidad imaginada como memoria' ('reality imagined as memory') (Gómez 1978).

The links between the world of *Bodas* and the Spain of the late 1970s made by some reviewers of Gómez's production focus on the social environment rather than the military dimension. Pérez Fernández observes that 'esos bajos fondos madrileños [...] están todavía vivos, a un paso de la Puerta del Sol, sumidos muchos en el mismo clima de abandono y de desesperanza' (1978: 53).[58] The uncontrolled growth of shanty towns around Madrid and Barcelona (already under way in 1898) as emigration from the countryside accelerated had been one of the major social problems of the 1960s. The rough world of the *chabolas* features in novels such as Ferres's *La piqueta* (1959) and short stories by Ignacio Aldecoa, as well as in Rodríguez Méndez's plays *La batalla del Verdún* (set in Barcelona) and *Los quinquis de Madriz*, which is an obvious contemporary counterpart of *Bodas*. In November 1978, many people were acutely aware of how far Spain still was from the consolidation of the principles enshrined in the new Constitution, which had been approved by the Cortes in October and was about to be put to a referendum. It promised to guarantee democratic *convivencia* (coexistence, living together in harmony) and the rule of law, to defend human rights and to 'asegurar a todos una digna calidad de vida' (Centro de Información Administrativa 2003: 'Preámbulo').[59]

José Monleón's review praises Gómez for placing everyday human experience at the centre of broader historical and political processes and offers the following conclusion:

> La obra, situada en el 98, se inserta en los albores de ese no resuelto todavía discurso político de España. Cuando a la 'pérdida' de las colonias sucedió el enfrentamiento entre el espíritu de la Restauración y el deseo de partir de la realidad encarnada por esa pobre sociedad popular que llega ahora – entre la estridencia minoritaria – para decirnos, una vez más, que también existe. Aunque ya no viva en la misma cueva ni vayan por las calles soldados mendicantes vestidos de rayadillo (1978b: 74).[60]

This is why he and others saw the 1978 production (subsidized by the Government, inaugurating the Centro Dramático Nacional) as an episode of great political and cultural importance in Spain's transition to democracy.

Historia de unos cuantos (Anyone's History)
In *Historia de unos cuantos*, the everyday lives of the characters are connected much more directly with public history than was the case with *Bodas que fueron famosas*

del Pingajo y la Fandanga. The setting is again the *barrios bajos* of Madrid at the beginning of the twentieth century, but the community in this play is part of the established proletariat rather than the drifting lumpenproletariat. The individuals are placed much more centrally and consciously in their historical, social and political context. Although they still have little control over their collective destiny, these people are seen to be directly affected by major events, becoming actively involved in the upheavals of the Second Republic and the civil war. They show understanding of these situations and some independence of thought — far from the almost total alienation of the characters in *Bodas*. Julián is an unprecedented figure in Rodríguez Méndez's work: someone capable of exploiting the circumstances that make victims of other members of his class, transforming himself into one of the exploiters. Mari Pepa, Felipe and Pichi are less active characters, yet none of them is completely passive or ignorant.

This play therefore offers the clearest presentation so far of the constant tension in Rodríguez Méndez's work between change and immobility. The *pueblo* is placed more concretely and actively in the movement of history, and becomes more diverse and changeable. The people are at times mute victims of forces outside their control, or bystanders to events; but they can also be idealistic rebels and unscrupulous manipulators. The extended timescale means that this work is the only one to portray significant change taking place in the lives of its characters. The ten *momentos* of *Historia* cover more than forty years of turbulent history, from some point soon after the colonial disasters of 1898, through the assassination attempt at the royal wedding of 1906, the 1920s during the Moroccan war, the decline of the Primo de Rivera dictatorship, the Second Republic and the outbreak of the civil war, to some time in the grim 1940s. Through this period, changes in the political system, in economic relationships, class positions, social behaviour, language, attitudes and cultural practices are observed from the point of view of a traditional working-class community in old Madrid.

The phrase with which Rodríguez Méndez sums up the subject of this play is 'la destrucción de la fe' (Martín Recuerda 1979: 222). In general terms, 'the destruction of faith' is a useful summary of the principal sequence of events in *Historia de unos cuantos*: the long-awaited, euphoric establishment of the Republic, embodying the hopes of the ordinary people, followed soon after by its destruction. However, as always, the idea of faith is an ambiguous, sceptical one. Mari Pepa will end up declaring that 'lo que es a mí la República m'ha traío más desgracias que toas las monarquías juntas' (*Historia de unos cuantos* 1982: 191).[61] The progression of the drama consists less of the erection of positive ideals which are then frustrated, than of a questioning of idealism itself. The *fe* that is to be destroyed is not a single, unequivocal value, but a range of human attitudes. The figures of Julián, Mari Pepa, Felipe and Pichi represent four different responses to the world — four different kinds of *fe* which are as much strategies for survival as hopeful ideals.

The first scene provides a light-hearted opening. The time is 'años de 1898' (117) ('around 1898'), but there are only the slightest of references to the political upheavals and social turbulence of the period. The prime function of this first scene is to evoke an atmosphere (geographical, social and cultural) and to introduce the main characters. The long opening stage direction establishes a physical setting and a social situation: workman's clothes, topical photographs and posters, the typical street sounds of Madrid filtering in from outside. Then specific references to the *género chico* begin to be insinuated: tunes from *La verbena de la Paloma* (1894), together with characters and lines from Ricardo de la Vega's most famous *zarzuela*: Señá Rita's catchphrase 'ique tiees madreeee! (118) ('you've got a mother, you know!'); and Julián's description of himself as 'un honrao cajista que gana cuatro pesetas' (125) ('an honest typesetter on four pesetas'). To this world of *La verbena de la Paloma*, Rodríguez Méndez adds Mari Pepa and Felipe from *La Revoltosa* (by López Silva and Fernández Shaw), as well as one or two other secondary figures from popular theatre of the period. The plots of the original works are recalled as episodes in the recent past of the characters, who are now placed much more firmly within a historical context.

The borrowing is respectful, but not without a certain affectionate irony. Julián's response to the barrel organ tunes which disturb his *siesta* is irritation, and it is he who introduces Rita's famous catchphrase, said to himself 'en tono de burla' (118) ('in a mocking tone'). Mari Pepa has changed from the flighty Revoltosa into a fearsome, henpecking wife. Julián, too, has begun to change. The proud boast of being 'an honest typesetter on four pesetas who owes nothing to anyone' is modified, as he repeatedly complains about 'cuatro cochinas pesetas' ('four miserable pesetas') and admits that he has received some help from his stepfather (125–26). He dismisses the fuss he made over Susana as a temporary fit of festival madness (124), from which he has recovered by learning to control his passions as advised by the tavern-keeper.

The interpretation of *La verbena de la Paloma* dramatized in *Historia de unos cuantos* is expounded in detail in *Ensayo sobre el machismo español*, which presents Julián as the archetypal *macho* of the late nineteenth century, reproducing some of the arrogant flamboyance of Manolo but with a social consciousness that is entirely new (as discussed in Chapter 2). Julián's trajectory from commonsensical socialism to unscrupulous opportunism mapped out in the *Ensayo* makes up the main storyline of the play, contrasted with the destruction of Felipe and Pichi and the dogged stoicism of Mari Pepa. The first scene of the play hints at the evolution to come. He makes it clear that the head is already outweighing the heart, and draws a sententious parallel between his personal situation and the national crisis: 'Porque el pecao de los españoles es ése: la falta e raciocinio' (125).[62] As for his involvement with the Socialist Party, it is mentioned only briefly in this first scene. Julián simply includes political rallies in the list of activities that define his way of life as a normal working-class male, along with the occasional drink, the occasional fiesta and going to bullfights (126).

Julián retreats into the background in the second scene so that the relationship between Felipe and Mari Pepa (some seven years later) can be developed. Once again, there is an elaborate evocation of atmosphere before the action gets under way: children's songs and games, bright May weather in the park, festive picnicking, the inevitable organ-grinders and hawkers. Much of the scene is then devoted to a mildly comical presentation of Mari Pepa's bullying of the long-suffering Felipe. Her concerns are everyday, domestic ones: the care of the baby, the preparation of food, keeping an eye on the older child. This fierce concentration on family and community relationships will prove to be the main driving force within Mari Pepa.

Underneath the surface of the light-hearted evocation of the *género chico*, tension is gradually built up and the impact of external events begins to intrude into the lives of the characters. They are enjoying a public holiday to celebrate the wedding of Alfonso XIII in 1906. A spectator with some knowledge of history will expect some link with the assassination attempt which took place on this day: this expectation is not disappointed, but the incident is used in an indirect way. More important than the bombing itself are the feelings that emerge around it. Juan José guesses that something big may be about to happen and protests at the money being squandered on the royal wedding while the people go hungry and unemployment grows (134).[63] His antagonist is Señor Candelas, the classic self-important *guardia municipal* (municipal policeman) of the *género chico*, now retired but still scolding Juan José for his seditious talk. His message is one of submission and acceptance: 'Por mucho que digáis u dejéis que icir, el mundo sigue p'alante y unos comen y otros miran' (134).[64] Although the discussion is brief and inconclusive, its dramatic function is to underline the link between public events and the lives of ordinary people.

The scene comes to a climax not with a direct dramatization of the bombing itself, but with the reaction to it of the crowds surrounding the wedding. The situation is full of confusion, panic and a hint of euphoria at the possibility of the royal couple having been assassinated. Mari Pepa's priorities, however, are clear: 'Cállese señor Juan José y deje la política a un lao... Vaya a ver si saben aónde está el Felipe y el José Luis' (140).[65] There is a brief discussion about Julián which is incidental to this scene but serves to anticipate the situation presented in the third. Mari Pepa reveals that he has married Susana, set up his own printing works, begun to prosper, and they 'want nothing to do with the poor' (138). His evolution is well under way.

So the third scene (set in 1920) finds a prosperous *don* Julián well established in his own substantial printing works. The scene reiterates elements of the first *momento*. Both begin with a wordless, static tableau featuring the figure of Julián in a room that contains clues to his way of life. The working man's cap and clothes hanging up at the beginning of the play have been replaced by a gentleman's jacket and boater. The young man we first saw on a bed in his underwear now sits behind a desk wearing a neat white shirt and a waistcoat with a gold watch chain, looking prosperous. There are still posters related to the Socialist Party and bullfighting on the wall, but these have evidently been printed by Julián himself. In both scenes, after a short exchange between Julián and a third person, Felipe is introduced, unemployed, desperate and asking for help. Once again, Julián is affable but condescending, and offers no real help. He complains again about working hard to earn four pesetas, the sum now more figurative than ever, since he has just handed his employee twenty-five pesetas to buy beer, prawns and cigars. Finally, each scene is brought to a close with the entrance of two women: in the first instance, Mari Pepa and a boisterous, pleasantly vulgar Rita; now it is Susana and a more sedate Rita, both of them expensively attired. This overt parallelism between the first and third scenes highlights the transformation of Julián, the continuing decline of Felipe, and the misplaced trust of the latter in his opportunistic friend.

The dialogue between the two men is full of telling, ironic details revealing the changes that have been taking place. Julián has acquired a way of talking about 'los pobres obreros' ('the poor workers') in the first-person plural while at the same time considering their problems in a detached, theoretical manner. He insists on discussing Felipe's predicament in terms of party politics and personalities, an outlook meaningless to Felipe. With amazing insensitivity, he comments on the conscription of José Luis for the ill-fated Moroccan campaign as if it were something in which neither of them was personally involved. His commitment to the Socialist Party remains firm, but his conception of politics is becoming increasingly divorced from everyday concerns and he refuses even to acknowledge Felipe's timid request for financial help to buy his son out of military service.

The tension established by the prospect of José Luis being sent to Africa makes the link with scene four. The stage direction informs the reader that the time is the winter of 1921, in a Madrid saddened by the military defeats in Morocco (153), and this background is soon made clear in the dialogue. A cold, grieving Mari Pepa is convinced that her son is dead (and this is confirmed in the next scene). Now that she feels personally the direct consequences of political decisions, she becomes angry and rebellious, railing at 'ese mameluco que tenemos por Rey' (154) ('that idiot we've got as our king') for having taken her son away. She instinctively holds the king responsible, as the most visible representative of political power, but her notion of possible action is ingenuous, to say the least.[66] In an echo of *Vagones de madera*, the war is seen here as an alien, meaningless affair, arranged by those in power for their own purposes, making use of the sons of the peasantry and the proletariat as cannon fodder.

At this point, when the simple pathos of this scene seems firmly established, Rodríguez Méndez introduces a pair of characters who bring about a crucial change of tone: the facetious organ-grinder and the lottery-ticket seller who ingratiates herself with Mari Pepa and Serafín by pretending to have two sons of her own in Morocco. Serafín, moved and foolishly hopeful all of a sudden, buys a ticket, but the emptiness of this apparent spark of hope is brutally exposed as soon as he and Mari Pepa leave and the audience learn that the lottery-ticket seller is not the helpless, lonely widow she claims to be and has sold Serafín a fake ticket. The fourth scene marks an emotional low point in the action of *Historia de unos cuantos*, as the tone of the drama takes on something of the bitterly tragicomic quality of parts of *Bodas que fueron famosas del Pingajo y la Fandanga*. The pathos of Mari Pepa's loss is shot through with the painfully black comedy of the impudent confidence trick.

After the gloom of the fourth scene, the fifth *momento* seems to offer a fresh start, the beginning of an upward movement. The opening stage direction is a particularly lengthy evocation of atmosphere and historical background. It emphasizes the modernity of the late 1920s, the political agitation and excitement of the slide towards a republic, and the sunlit beauty of a spring morning in Madrid. The pace of events is accelerating, but this scene still deals primarily with personal relationships, turning our attention back to the friendship between Felipe and Julián. However, before Julián appears, we are introduced to another character who is to play a larger role in subsequent scenes: el Pichi, Felipe's second son. He intervenes only briefly here, and seems to be unassuming, anxious not to jeopardize his position at the Palace Hotel, deferential towards Julián. The most important feature of his presence here is his father's idolization of him. Felipe now seems to be living through others, enjoying a vicarious *machismo* through his son's attractiveness while still mourning the loss of his other son, a fact he does not hesitate to point out to Julián.

There is a detail in the dialogue between Felipe and his son which serves as a reminder that the pride of the *macho* in his family and community can at times manifest itself as a much less attractive bigotry or chauvinism. Pichi mentions that the Palace Hotel has employed a black doorman, to which Felipe retorts scornfully: '¿Y van a compararte a ti con un negro? ¡Amos, calla chaval! ¡Un negro! Si los negros sólo sirven pa vender lotería y aún' (162).[67] As *Ensayo sobre el machismo español* makes clear, *machismo* in all its forms is an essentially egotistical approach to life. It involves a valuable affirmation of liberty, creativity and community spirit, but its perspectives are often narrow.

The scene is mostly concerned with the relationship between Felipe and Julián, furthering the evolution begun in the first *momento* and continued in the third. Julián is evidently wealthier and becoming influential in the Socialist Party, although he still insists on denying this and claiming to be just a man of the *pueblo*. Now, Felipe's dependence on Julián has been formalized as overt patronage. Julián delegates routine party work to him, and praises him patronizingly for his dedication. He regularly cleans Julián's shoes, and even stands in the queue to obtain bullfight tickets for him. Nevertheless, Felipe is not entirely self-abasing. The relationship is not primarily a commercial one, since he repeatedly refuses to accept payment for the shoe-cleaning. The dependence is personal, rather than financial. Felipe has submerged his own individuality in the *machismo* of his son, and in the prestige and authority of Julián. It could be argued that Julián is taking advantage of him, exploiting his trust in order to advance his own position in the party and to feed his own sense of importance – Mari Pepa later makes precisely this accusation (192). On the other hand, Julián cannot be seen exclusively as an unscrupulous opportunist. His affection for Felipe is genuine and he values his friendship, if only as a means of maintaining an emotional link with his working-class roots. Most important is his vigorous defence of Felipe against the interference of the hussar who automatically assumes that the scruffy bootblack must be molesting the elegant gentleman. His sentimental attachment to his class is still strong and, after all, as a socialist he is not yet a natural member of the Establishment.

The hussar's function in this scene is that of a representative of the military dictatorship established by Primo de Rivera in 1923. By 1929, Primo's Military Directory had been replaced by largely civilian government, but military involvement at national and local levels was still substantial, and the dictator exercised direct control through the Union Patriótica party. The Iron Surgeon's simplistic view of the world – based on instinctive patriotism, a hatred of liberal parliamentary politics, and a belief in national unity and individual obedience – was the dominant ideology still being pressed upon the nation, and the dignity and privileges of the armed forces were protected more zealously than ever. Infuriated by Felipe's impudence, the swaggering hussar is able to summon a policeman and order him to arrest Felipe. This brief military intervention is a mild satire of military power compared to the detailed portrait of corruption and depravity given in *Bodas que fueron famosas del Pingajo y la Fandanga*. The stage directions indicate that the martial swagger should be slightly ridiculous: the hussar in his flamboyant uniform 'parece una máscara' (168) ('looks like a masked caricature'). His appearance and his trite remark recall the *género chico* – the phrase 'los tiempos adelantan que es una barbaridá' (168) ('Isn't it shocking how fast things are changing?') is from a song in *La verbena de la Paloma*. Felipe emerges with greater dignity in the eyes of the audience by challenging him and what he stands for, and this small rebellion provides an important, upbeat climax at this point. It is an illustration of a general observation made in this scene's opening stage direction: 'El antimilitarismo cunde, etc., etc., pero en el "pueblo de Madrid" todo esto se traduce confusamente, en ráfagas de apasionamiento, de alegría incontrolables' (161).[68] It is a premonition of a greater rebellion, but is rash and impetuous. The republic anticipated by this incident has just been declared when the next scene begins, and this impression of confusion and *apasionamiento* is continued and expanded.

The sixth scene is full of euphoric, communal celebration.[69] The tension of the preceding years has come to a head and produced a republic which the masses, at last, can feel represents their interests. This scene is an example of the festive interlude always present in Rodríguez Méndez's work, here on a national level. In the other plays, the joyous scene is always an interlude preceding disaster; in *Historia de unos cuantos*, the catastrophe too will be a national one. As well as simple jubilation, the scene is intended (initially, at least) to convey an idea of cooperation, of people working together willingly and responsibly in a common cause. The action begins with Felipe and some friends working together on the decoration of the *patio*, and they comment on how unusual and satisfying this sense of involvement in communal action is (174). However, the tone is not uniformly positive. Underlying the rejoicing and harmony is an ambivalent view of the Republic. This lively scene is punctuated by remarks which reveal naive over-optimism, misunderstandings and deliberate distortion of the aims of the new regime. Two sardonic female onlookers malevolently ridicule expectations of social revolution:

VECINA – Pues yo he tenío mucha suerte, porque llevaba tres meses atrasá en el pago el alquiler y supongo que ahora como no pagaremos casa...

LA OTRA – Sí, sí,…. que se cree usted eso. ¿Se va a creer que éstos atarán los perros con longanizas? ¡Lo va a ver usté!

VECINA – (*Muy maligna.*) Pues, mujer… ¿no va a ser verdá eso del reparto social? (174–75)[70]

The attitudes of most of the other characters are enthusiastic and ingenuous. A policeman lurches tipsily in, celebrating the transfer of his loyalty to the people and trying to tear the royal insignia from his uniform. His main reason for republican enthusiasm, however, seems to be the prospect of the legalization of divorce. Also proclaiming a change of allegiance is Pichi, exultantly tearing off his waiter's uniform and calling for a boiler suit. He has been involved in a popular takeover of the Palace Hotel, and assumes that the revolution is all but complete. Two other touches complete the impression of comic irony. The general exhilaration over the arrival of Julián, now a city councillor, causes a portrait of the allegorical figure of the Republic (based on the French Marianne) to be dislodged and fall on the heads of some of the celebrants. Then, amid the joyful hubbub of the end of the scene, just as everyone is gathering around their councillor for a group photograph, the notorious lottery-ticket seller bursts in brandishing a figurine of the republican icon: '¡Se rifa la República!… ¡A diez el número!… ¡Vaya República que rifo hoy!' (183).[71]

This scene is at the centre of the play's structure. The political developments lying in the background of the first five scenes culminate in this popular triumph, which already begins to crumble from this point onwards. It also marks the apotheosis of Julián as a combination of prosperous businessman and ambitious socialist politician, and is an emotional peak after which the tone becomes increasingly sour. It contains genuine celebration of change, hope for the fulfilment of egalitarian ideals, and simple human warmth in abundance, but it is fraught with ambiguity. Some of the expectations are so high as to be foolish; some so low as to allow only cynical passivity. There is a general tone of frivolity and an affectionate caricaturing of popular attitudes. Despite this ambiguity, however, there is one feature of all this that is of unquestionable value. The people at last feel that they are actively involved in the shaping of their history, and that the society in which they live is beginning to reflect their sense of identity rather than an alien set of bourgeois values. It is as if their traditional *machismo* were being given official recognition. This feeling is best expressed by a man who vigorously rebuts a negative remark by Felipe:

HOMBRE 1 – Lo dicho, las flores son cosa de muerto…

FELIPE – ¡Y bien muertos están los pobres!

HOMBRE 3 – Eso sí que no. ¡Más vivos que nunca y más gloriosos! (175)[72]

The end of the scene of celebration brings Felipe's son Pichi briefly to our attention again, and he becomes the central figure of the seventh *momento*. He has marked the triumph of the people by rejecting a position as a servant of the bourgeoisie and proudly taking up manual labour. The scene is set a few years after 1931, under a republic taken for granted by Pichi but showing signs of violent conflict. He now represents the characteristic *machismo* of the period, the next step on from Julián as chronicled in *Ensayo sobre el machismo español* (see Chapter 2). Pichi's hedonism and political enthusiasm are attractive but irresponsible, his *casticismo* is contaminated by a taste for consumer products, and his moment of euphoria is destined to be brief.

The action of this brief scene concentrates on Pichi's carefree sexual attractiveness, yet there are signs in the background that the carnival is breaking down into violence – signs that Pichi is determined to ignore. If it becomes necessary, he will be among the first to defend the ideals of the Republic, but until then, the most important thing is to enjoy oneself and not be bothered with 'politics'. Pichi soon finds out that everyone is affected by politics in a broad sense. It turns out here that his father is among a group of workers battling with the Guardia de Asalto, which Pichi refuses to believe until it is too late. He does eventually dash out to help, but it emerges in the next scene that Felipe has been killed. The Republic that seemed to begin as a victory for the people is degenerating into conflict. Felipe becomes one of the first victims of the collapse, and Pichi's irresponsibility is cruelly exposed. Rodríguez Méndez does not analyse the causes of the failure of the Republic. Whoever is responsible, people like Felipe are always the innocent victims, and the author concentrates his attention on them.

The last three scenes of the play are short, creating a quickening rhythm as war approaches. Mari Pepa has not played a significant part in the action since the fourth scene. Now she stands at the centre of the climax and dénouement, still passive, yet increasingly angry. It is she who comes to embody the ultimate significance of the work. Scene 8 is set in July 1936, just before the outbreak of war. The mood is already grim, for Mari Pepa is mourning Felipe's death and condemning Pichi's irresponsibility. She holds the Republic responsible for the death by pneumonia of old Serafín after the celebrations, for the murder of Felipe, and for the delinquency of Pichi, who had been so well behaved when he worked in the Palace Hotel. These may not be entirely rational accusations, but it is of primary dramatic importance that Mari Pepa, the archetypal suffering bystander, can recognize no real benefit from the five years of Republican government. She was sceptical about its idealistic promises in the first place, has found few signs of their fulfilment, and is still struggling to survive while her men are taken from her and the same few opportunists prosper. She aims the accusation directly at Julián: 'A mí me mataron un hijo en Melilla y vosotros me habéis matao al marío, ¿que quieres que yo ahora te dé las gracias por tu ayuda? ¿Mientras vosotros estáis hechos unos señorones?' (193).[73]

In the midst of this angry despair, the real strength of Mari Pepa begins to emerge. She has little hope, yet she is not defeatist. We see here the first evidence of a tremendous pride and durability as she rejects Julián's offer of help. She is determined to hold onto the sense of class, community and place which she feels Julián has long ago betrayed. This stubborn pride lies at the core of *machismo*, but in Mari Pepa it is without the conceitedness and pomposity of the men. As always, it is domestic responsibilities and human relationships that are important to her. What she resents most strongly in Pichi is the abandonment of his child, for which she disowns him, taking responsibility for the baby herself. To Mari Pepa, the care of a single child (within the culture to which she and he belong) is more important than all the rises and falls of successive republics and monarchies.

The ninth *momento* takes the action forward a few more days, to the 18th of July itself, showing Mari Pepa again in the same *patio* on the Calle de Ministriles, while around her the historical events approach their explosive climax. She does not appear especially worried by the bombs, gunshots and food shortages, but is angered and saddened by the news of mobs burning churches, assuming that Pichi is among them. Mari Pepa has not been conspicuously pious at any point in the play; she is no *beata*. What is important to her, though, is that the local church forms part of the life of the community, and is bound up in her family history: 'Pero ¿serán capaces de hacer esa barbaridá? Madre mía, pensar que una está bautizá y casá en esa iglesia. ¡Bárbaros!' (p.196).[74] At this point Pichi dashes in, on his way to the fighting with a revolutionary *comité*. Mari Pepa is stunned by her son's unexpected arrival and rapid departure, yet she ultimately gives him a kind of support, turning on the *vecina* who makes a mordant remark about church-burning (198). Mari Pepa may just have condemned him as a shameless atheist but she instinctively defends him when he is attacked by another. This tremendous humanity and capacity for forgiveness is demonstrated even more powerfully a moment later when a hunted Julián slips into the *patio*. The contradiction between his material ambitions and his socialist commitment has become irreconcilable: his business has been confiscated and he begs for refuge. Mari Pepa does not hesitate. She takes him in without question. Pichi and Julián have ended up on different sides of the conflict, but she accepts both of them regardless of political categories.

Martín Recuerda warmly celebrates these qualities of Mari Pepa. He sees her as an example of Iberian individualism and a symbol of 'un pueblo que sabe perdonar' (1979: 178–80) ('a people that knows how to forgive'). The character of Mari Pepa seems to strike a powerful emotional chord in this critic, which leads him to describe her with an admiration that may not be unreservedly shared by all readers or spectators. The play does not demand that we necessarily sympathise wholeheartedly with Mari Pepa, nor does it lead us to condemn Julián. Her political indifference could be seen as defeatist, a symptom of alienation and ignorance. Her attitudes may seem overcautious, even reactionary, in comparison with the progressive ideals of some of the other characters. Nevertheless, she clearly becomes the central figure of these final scenes, embodying values of humanity, decency and resistance to ideology with which Rodríguez Méndez's female characters are frequently endowed. Rosita of *El círculo de tiza de Cartagena* had declared that for her the heart comes before the revolution (*El círculo de tiza de Cartagena* 1964: 17). For Mari Pepa, *corazón* means, as well as love for her own family and compassion towards anyone in need, a deep loyalty towards her community and its traditions. She clings to these simple values, distrusting all else.

The war itself is briefly represented by a cacophony of sounds in the dark – a clash of remote, unseen forces, out of which Mari Pepa emerges older, more bitter, but undaunted. She is scratching a precarious living on the margins of a new society founded on fear and corruption, in a cold, dismal Madrid. It is Julián who steps out of an impressive limousine, plumper and wealthier than ever, and hoping to buy reconciliation with Mari Pepa. His opportunism has run its full trajectory, leaving socialism far behind in order to emerge from the cataclysm on the winning side, as foretold in *Ensayo sobre el machismo español*. The scene offers only a sketchy view of this post-war world, with no clear details of political and economic structures, nor of Julián's position in it. Perhaps the car with its uniformed chauffeur is a hint that Julián holds some official post. In any case, one must assume that he is now part of the Establishment, one of the victors. In the tightly controlled, autarkic economy of the *años del hambre* ('years of hunger') it was impossible to prosper in business without political influence. Moreover, in such a rigid and stagnant official economy, the only substantial profits to be gained were from the black market, kept going by widespread official corruption.[75] We may assume, then, that Julián has influence as well as money, and that he is one of the few who control the black economy, at the lowest level of which Mari Pepa struggles to survive.

The Madrid production of *Historia* provoked controversy over the development of Julián, seen by some commentators as conveying a contradictory or reactionary (anti-socialist) message. Monleón regrets the fact that the social structure of post-war Spain is not made clearer in the final scene, but argues that there is no contradiction: 'Porque, en última instancia, y contemplado desde la vida popular, Julián es un hombre que se aprovecha toda la vida de aquellos a quienes defiende en sus discursos' (1976: 47).[76] From Mari Pepa's point of view, all politicians, whatever the flavour of their rhetoric and the shape of the institutions they invent, have always betrayed the *pueblo*, which remains in the same position while they pursue their own ends. Julián is simply an opportunist, whose transformation into one of the *vencedores* is thus consistent with the earlier development of the play, with the ideas expressed in *Ensayo sobre el machismo*, and with Rodríguez Méndez's other work. Despite his defence of this outcome, Monleón considers the political analysis oversimplified and regrets the absence of some more positive character with a well-informed commitment to the real transformation of Spanish society (1976: 49). The author himself vigorously resists attempts to tie his characters to particular political identities. In 1977, complaining about excessive politicization of his work, he referred to the debate over the implications of *Historia de unos cuantos*:

> Una obra que había sido prohibida durante algunos años y que había sido amnistiada con el recorte de sus vuelos, fue denunciada como políticamente reaccionaria – por los críticos pedantes, desde luego – sólo porque no se determinaba claramente a qué partido político, o a qué doctrina determinada pertenecían algunos de sus personajes, personajes a los que el autor sólo quiso dar el testimonio del sufrimiento padecido precisamente por los avatares políticos que tuvieron que soportar (Rodríguez Méndez 1977: 94).[77]

While Julián manages to take advantage of the twists and turns of politics, Mari Pepa tries to ignore them and remains their eternal victim. The moving final scene expresses her bitterness, but also her strength and independence. In her view, Julián has betrayed what she clings to (family, community, class identity) in his rise to affluence, allowing others to suffer. She repeats her accusation that he has actively exploited his own kind in order to prosper, an accusation implicitly directed against all *aprovechaos* who climb to prosperity by trampling on others. To Mari Pepa it seems obvious that those who profit from war and exploitation must be the same people who arrange for such things to happen. Her men have died; Julián has survived and prospered. Therefore he shares the responsibility.

Mari Pepa's final act of defiance is to reject the help that Julián now offers her. She recognizes that she should not prevent José Luis from accepting Julián's patronage, but for herself, integrity is everything: 'Contigo, con vosotros... Ni a la puerta e la calle. Yo aquí, en mi barrio, en mi casa. En lo mío, en lo que me queda, en lo que nos queda' (202).[78] She has declared her identity in those few words – 'mi barrio', 'mi casa', 'lo mío'. The final emphasis on 'nos' eloquently links her destiny with that of her entire class (from which she implicitly excludes Julián). Mari Pepa is the most powerful embodiment of this sense of place and community, so that the desolate ending becomes a lament for its passing.[79] The final image is one of sadness, hardship and utter solitude, skilfully dramatized to suggest both defiant independence and pathetic defencelessness. As in *Bodas que fueron famosas del Pingajo y la Fandanga*, the men are destroyed, along with the *machismo* they display, while the women remain, beaten and grieving but strong. Much of the colourful distinctiveness of their way of life disappears with the men, while the feeling at the heart of both works survives in the women.

In the figures of Julián, Felipe, Mari Pepa and Pichi, the play presents four contrasting facets of the *pueblo*. Each has pursued a different kind of *fe* – an understanding of the relationship between self and society. Julián has relied upon his ability to take advantage of circumstances in order to improve his own position, pragmatically adapting, and finally abandoning, his professed commitment to a collectivist, altruistic ideal. Felipe ingenuously places his trust in the talents, authority and good faith of others, principally Julián and Pichi. The Republic briefly gives him a greater degree of self-esteem, but ultimately destroys him. Pichi blithely takes political commitment for granted – a fashionable attitude with little sense of responsibility. When the crisis comes, he throws himself into it impetuously and dies for ideals about which he has not thought in any depth. At the centre of things stands Mari Pepa, observing the turmoil around her with steady scepticism. Her kind of *fe* rests upon what is closest to her: her family, the local community with its cultural traditions and its loyalties, respect for human life, and a simple desire to be allowed to make a living and bring up one's children in peace. There is a gradual convergence of the national historical events and the individual lives of the characters, from the vague references to Cuba at the beginning to the direct involvement of everyone in the war. In the final scene, the movement seems to have burnt itself out and Mari Pepa remains, a symbol of the people's unchanging *intrahistoria*. Many changes have taken place around her, but her story suggests that they have been largely superficial. Under the surface of social and political history, life remains much the same, if not worse.

Thanks to this quadruple character structure and the sense of progression afforded by the extended timescale, *Historia* amounts to a more complex historical and social observation than the earlier works. The two principal portraits of *machismo español* reflect different historical circumstances; evolution of character is seen to arise from changing situations; personal and national affairs interact; and there is movement between classes and between political standpoints. The conspicuous metatheatricality inherent in the intertextual references to the *género chico* makes the performativity of cultural and gender identities explicit, while at the same time the evolution of the characters in response to historical change makes it clear that the performances do not constitute fixed stereotypes but complex, ambiguous mixtures of social scripting and individual improvisation.

Another result of the chronological structure of *Historia* is that the work becomes a bridge between the past and the period in which it was written. The birth and death of the Republic is the collective equivalent of the individual rebellions in the other plays: motivated by the same experience of hardship, equally futile in the end. The play is an account of the making of the present, a story of *vencedores* and *vencidos* (victors and vanquished), but without Manichaeism. The characters emerge as winners or losers (in the war and in society) as a result of complex circumstances and motivations, not because of inherent goodness or evil. Julián comes out on top as an influential member of the new regime by following his own self-interest, not through any belief in the rightness of the cause. The play therefore implies a rejection of the Francoist mythology of the Crusade, the legitimacy of total victory, the Manichaean vision of Catholic good and Communist evil. By 1971, the regime was no longer driven exclusively by this obsession, but it remained an important factor in official discourse and in the personality of the *Caudillo*. Indeed, the early 1970s – after the relative 'opening-up' of the 1960s – saw a resurgence of authoritarianism in government in response to growing opposition. The Nationalists' claim to have fought the Crusade on behalf of all Spaniards is undermined by Rodríguez Méndez's picture of the *vencedores* as men like Julián, siding with the rebels in order to protect their own interests and quickly cashing in on the victory while the masses starve.

Any play dealing with the origins of the Franco regime – the Restoration, the Republic and the civil war – was bound to be examined very carefully by the censors. The passage of *Historia de unos cuantos* through the censorship system turned out to be longer and more tortuous than that of any other works by Rodríguez Méndez, since the ambiguity of its treatment of the political issues and its mixing of lightweight popular comedy with hard-edged social realism unsettled many of the official readers and revealed an extraordinary degree of divergence in their evaluations of the text. There are no reports in the files at Alcalá to explain the banning of a Barcelona production planned by Ricard Salvat for 1972, but the documentation relating to further attempts to stage the play in 1973 to 1975 is particularly extensive and revealing.[80] The first application was for a production in Valencia to be directed by Antonio Díaz Zamora. During May-June 1973, eight censors produced reports, six in favour of authorization (with cuts in most cases) and two against; despite the majority in favour, no decision was made and the production never took place. An

ARGUMENTO

INFORME

Esos "cuantos" que indica el título son, nada menos, que Mari Pepa, Felipe, Susana, Julián, Juan José, Serafín el Enturero, la señá Rita y el Tabernero. El autor de este engendro ha pretendido, sin encomendarse a Diní al diablo, continuar la vida de estas personas desde 1898 al invierno de 1939, tras el término de nuestra guerra, pasando por el derrumbamiento de la Comandancia de Melilla (1921), la bomba de la boda del rey (1906), los alegres años 20, las vísperas de la caída de la Dictadura, el 14 de abril de 1931, las luchas callejeras de la República y el 18 de julio de 1936.

Todo eso ha pretendido el autor reflejar en esta larga obra, en diez cuadros, donde la aviesa intención es manifiesta. Tanto Felipe como Julián son antiguos socialistas (sin permiso de Ricardo de la Vega ni de López Silva), pero mientras el primero fracasa siempre, el otro triunfa en todos los regímenes, incluido el actual.

Las supresiones serían tan copiosas que desnaturalizarían la obra; por eso la prohibo.

SUPRESIONES

PROLOGO págs. —————————————————————————————————

ACTO 1.º págs. —————————————————————————————————

ACTO 2.º págs. —————————————————————————————————

ACTO 3.º págs. —————————————————————————————————

EPILOGO págs. —————————————————————————————————

Vocal —————————————
(Firma)

Censor's report on *Historia de unos cuantos*. Ministerio de Información y Turismo (1973), Expediente 251–73. Reproduced with the permission of the Ministerio de Cultura (Spain) and the Archivo General de la Administración.

application in 1974, for a Madrid production to be directed by José Luis Alonso, produced two more reports, both recommending approval, but by March 1975 the case remained unresolved and this project was also eventually abandoned. In the meantime, José Martín Recuerda had requested permission for a student production at Salamanca in April 1975. Approval was given, subject to a number of cuts and a stipulation that performances could only be given in the studio theatre run by Martín Recuerda's Cátedra Juan del Enzina at the University. This was the play's first performance. The commercial premiere in Madrid (directed by Ángel García Moreno) was authorized quickly, though with more cuts than those imposed on the student production, and took place on 28 November 1975 in an atmosphere of anxiety and excitement generated by the death of Franco on 20 November. A last-minute crisis provoked by the official who inspected the dress rehearsal threatening to close the show was averted by Rodríguez Méndez himself, who telephoned the Director General.

Some of the censors perceived a clear political 'intention' in the work, even if they did not all regard it as dangerous enough to merit prohibition. Their reports use phrases such as 'tendenciosidad evidente' ('obvious tendentiousness'), 'un mitin político de "rojillos" desengañados y derrotados' ('a political rally of disillusioned, defeated reds'), and 'aviesa intención' ('a malicious intention') (Ministerio de Información y Turismo 1973). By December 1974, the nervousness occasioned by the imminence of political change is evident in Vicente Ruiz Martínez's recommendation that 'esta obra debería ser considerada por la superioridad, en estos momentos [en] que se prepara el devenir de un nuevo rey, por conllevar en su contexto la justificación del fracaso de una República – la II Española, precisamente'.[81]

In contrast, several censors did not find the play dangerous at all. Father Cea, for example, declares it to be permissible and even positive. José María García Cernuda's report is surprisingly candid in its assumption that audiences will derive a simplistic moral from the dramatic action: 'Resulta ejemplar en su conjunto: los republicanos (del pueblo bajo) idealistas e ingenuos llevan siempre la peor parte, mientras el vividor sobrenada en todas las circunstancias y se adapta a todo con tal de seguir prosperando.'[82] Antonio Albizu is confident that the text appears to contain no political intentions, but is concerned that particular details (especially Republican emblems) might be given undue emphasis in performance. Fray Mauricio de Begoña is the only one to mention possible 'paralelismos con la actualidad' ('parallels with the present'), but does not specify what these might be and, in any case, does not regard them as serious.

The divergence of opinions with respect to the overall acceptability of the play is matched by the variety of recommendations for particular lines to be cut. Certain preoccupations are shared by several censors, but there is no single cut on which all can agree. Some seem to be concerned about indecorous language, but such suppressions are not included in the definitive decisions. Some (perhaps with monarchist sympathies or an eye to the imminent post-Franco future) are worried about expressions of disrespect towards the royal family, while others highlight elements of anti-clericalism. One of the lines marked most frequently for suppression is Mari Pepa's outburst at the end of scene 8: '¡Hipócritas toos, jesuitas, que sus parecéis al Pae Laburu!' (*Historia de unos cuantos* 1982: 194).[83] Presumably, the objection is to the association of Jesuits with hypocrisy (and the fact that the speaker directs the accusation at people she accuses of church-burning). The degree of concern about the specific reference to an obscure Jesuit appears puzzling, but may be explained by the fact that Father Laburu became a film censor after the civil war.

Many of the cuts proposed – and most of those confirmed in the final verdicts – are on political grounds. Some of the censors recognized that in a scene set in April 1931 it was historically appropriate to have Republican flags and portraits of Fermín Galán y García Hernández on stage, with characters shouting '¡Viva la República!', as long as the overall impact of the play was not favourable to the Republic. Others, however, felt that such details would simply be inflammatory regardless of the context surrounding them, and these elements were consequently suppressed as a condition of the permit issued in May 1975. The certificate issued in November for the Madrid premiere does not specifically ban the flags, posters and slogans, but it was precisely these things to which the inspector at the dress rehearsal objected, holding the production to the conditions imposed earlier. Apart from these obvious emblems of proscribed political institutions, there was also a more general concern about expressions of rebellion against authority, antimilitarism or lack of patriotism. The line that attracted most attention (and was banned in all three certificates issued) was Julián's remark that 'si los pobres soldaos no fueran tan borregos lo que tenían que hacer es disparar contra sus jefes y no contra los moros' (*Historia de unos cuantos* 1982: 147).[84] Even if the censors appreciated the irony inherent in the way Julián says this to the helpless Felipe, the simple fact of having these words uttered on stage – especially at a time when the authorities were increasingly afraid of losing control – was clearly unthinkable. The moment at which Felipe himself challenges military authority also provoked some unease: his declaration that he has no respect for those who sent his son to die in Morocco was cut in the May 1975 verdict, and in November the whole argument with the hussar was removed, suggesting that the authorities had become even more nervous about a scene that might appear to be encouraging social unrest.

I observed in the introduction to this book that the censors saw their role as the maintenance of an order that was not only moral and political but also aesthetic, 'saving' dramatists from their own misjudgements and protecting the public from 'bad' plays. Some of the most interesting comments in the reports on *Historia de unos cuantos* are those that define the problem posed by the text in terms of the intersection of genre expectations and politics. The 1973 and 1974 applications classify the work as *comedia de costumbres* (a comedy of popular customs) and *sainete* respectively, and Luis Tejedor seems happy to read it on this level: 'Estampas madrileñas, llenas de color y vida. Confieso mi entusiasmo al leerlas' (Ministerio de Información y Turismo 1973).[85] Alfredo Mampaso's report, on the other hand, argues for prohibition on political grounds despite the fact that the *sainete*-like character of the piece 'le quita peligrosidad' ('makes it less dangerous'). Florencio Martínez Ruiz, more subtly, suggests that the rooting of the play in popular culture exacerbates what would otherwise be a tolerable degree of political dissidence: 'El populacherismo y el costumbrismo documental de *Historia de unos cuantos* más complica que salva esta sarta de pequeñas inconveniencias, en último término, políticas que la hacen obra difícil.'[86] José Luis Vázquez Dodero, meanwhile, is indignant at what he regards as malicious distortion of the perceived intentions of the *género chico* sources: 'El autor de este engendro ha pretendido, sin encomendarse a Dios ni al diablo, continuar la vida de estas personas desde 1898 al invierno de 1939 […]. La aviesa intención es manifiesta.'[87]

In a sense, these readings are the most perceptive, since they at least recognize the centrality of Rodríguez Méndez's preoccupation with popular culture and the representation of cultural identity. Vázquez Dodero's report concludes that the production should be banned altogether because the cuts required to make it acceptable would be so numerous that 'desnaturalizarían la obra' ('they would completely change the nature of the play'), implicitly acknowledging that the real challenge posed by the work lies in the way in which it destabilizes conventional genre expectations by relocating the *género chico* in a realistic historical context, thereby problematizing cultural forms that the Establishment wishes to preserve as apolitical *costumbrismo*.

La Chispa (The Spark)

I have repeatedly argued that one of the key factors in Rodríguez Méndez's representation of collective identity is the avoidance of idealization or sentimentalization. The *pueblo* is associated with cultural authenticity, creative energy and compassion, but is not consistently invested with heroism, moral integrity, social solidarity or coherent political awareness. The dramatic impact of the characters who form the collective protagonists of *Bodas* and *Historia de unos cuantos* depends to a considerable degree on the moral, political and emotional ambiguity of the responses they are designed to elicit from audiences. *La Chispa*, in contrast, is disappointingly uncomplicated in its treatment of popular resistance to the French occupation of Madrid in May 1808. The author explains the genesis of the play in terms of a reaction against the emerging social-democratic orthodoxy of the post-Franco transition, especially as represented by the liberalizing populism of Enrique Tierno Galván (Socialist Mayor of Madrid from 1979 to 1986). The play was written in 1983 for a competition associated with the establishment of the *Fiesta de la Comunidad de Madrid*, held on 2 May each year to mark the uprising of 1808. The author, assuming that the organizers of the Festival would be more interested in celebrating the new spirit of liberal democracy than the traditional patriotism associated with the 2nd and 3rd of May (inevitably focused on Goya's paintings of the events), was determined to go against the grain:

Así, temiendo lo peor, lo que yo hice fue exaltar la gloriosa jornada frente a los afrancesados, ésos que creían que Napoleón iba a traernos las luces, el buen gobierno, etc. Los loores del gran siglo de la *Igualdad, Fraternidad y Libertad*. Por eso, yo quise poner de protagonistas a los que lo fueron auténticamente. Es decir, a los *chisperos* y *Manolos* de los barrios de Maravillas y El Rastro, es decir a mis paisanos, mirados con tan malos ojos por los universalistas afrancesados y bonapartistas de los nuevos tiempos de la transición.[88] Volví, pues, los ojos a aquella siempre sagrada página de heroísmo y resistencia que mostró a la historia el pueblo al que yo pertenezco (Rodríguez Méndez 1999: 43–44).[89]

The author was not surprised that the prize was not awarded to *La Chispa*. The language he uses here deliberately echoes the simplistic, chauvinistic mythology of traditional right-wing nationalism, which condemns the influence of the French Enlightenment for having diverted Spain from its true (Catholic) destiny and suggests direct links between liberal secularization in the eighteenth and nineteenth centuries and the threat of communism in the twentieth, both supposedly resisted by the Spanish people. One school history book from the Franco period recounts how 'todos los de España' ('every single Spaniard') swore to defend country, king and flag in 1808: 'Se lanzaron como leones al combate y salvaron a la Patria de las garras napoleónicas. En nuestros días, los héroes de la Cruzada de Liberación con igual valor la han salvado también de las garras comunistas' (Edelvives 1958: 118).[90]

In contrast, one of the interesting features of the culture of the late 1970s and 1980s was the recuperation of the historical memory of republicanism, stimulated by the return and honouring of prominent exiles, notably Dolores Ibárruri and Rafael Alberti. Central to that historical memory was the sustained defence of Madrid, which was characterized as heroic popular resistance – supported by the solidarity of fellow workers in other countries – to the reimposition of the hegemony of traditional interest groups backed by authoritarian regimes in Germany and Italy. Some of the Republican wartime propaganda celebrating the defence of the capital drew specifically on the mythology of 1808.[91] This, for a moment, is what Rodríguez Méndez's account of the historical resonance of *La Chispa* appears to refer to: 'Porque yo viví también un terrible asedio de Madrid, por los años de 1936 y 1939, y pude comprobar las grandes virtudes de un pueblo perdedor, pero consciente de lo que es someterse a una potencia extranjera' (1999: 44).[92] The point, however, is to turn the recovery of Republican history on its head:

En aquella ocasión la potencia soviética. Y yo recuerdo un Madrid poblado de banderas rojas con la hoz y el martillo y viví aquellos otros fusilamientos a orillas del Manzanares, que no tuvieron nada que envidiar a los de la montaña del Príncipe Pío de 1808. Así, *La Chispa* viene a ser un aguafuerte muy madrileño donde se transparentan las dos épocas en que Madrid supo ser una ciudad tan sufrida y generosa como lo ha sido siempre (1999: 44).[93]

Further recollections of the civil war in the same conference paper are similarly revisionist, emphasizing church-burning, huge portraits of Lenin and Stalin dominating Madrid, and his father's escape from a communist death squad. 'Y aquella época siniestra [...] veo que ahora quieren señalarla como una época de no sé qué signos esperanzadores. Pero la liberación de todo aquello nos vino en la primavera de 1939 con las tropas del general Franco' (1999: 46).[94]

La Chispa has some of the strong points of earlier works such as *Bodas* and *Historia de unos cuantos*: a lively evocation of the language and cultural practices of a particular community at a particular point in its historical development; a strong sense of the importance of popular culture in defining collective identity (in opposition to the values of the elite); and an affirmative emphasis on the role of women in making individualistic *machismo* more cooperative and compassionate. Like *Historia de unos cuantos*, it acquires a metatheatrical dimension by recreating one of the archetypes from *Ensayo sobre el machismo español*, turning Ramón de la Cruz's carefree Manolo (almost forty years later) into a leader of the resistance against the Napoleonic occupation. This development of the figure of Manolo is prefigured in the *Ensayo*, but there a clearer distinction is made between the local patriotism inspired by the popular culture of his *barrio* and a protonationalist patriotism predicated on the legitimacy of the Bourbon dynasty and a supposed national unity of purpose in opposing the French. The transformation of the popular explosion of faith and enthusiasm of 1808 into 'una nueva servidumbre' (Rodríguez Méndez 1971a: 78–79) ('a new servitude') described in the *Ensayo* is not hinted at in *La Chispa*. Instead, the pride of these characters in their community is fused with apparently unquestioning support for king and country. '¡Viva Madriz!' is shouted alongside '¡Viva España!' and 'Viva la reina María Luisa' (*La Chispa* 1999: 116, 121, 133). Manolo himself has been serving the empire in North Africa, and he does not seem to be joking when he recounts his exploits 'defendiendo a la patria contra infieles' (112) ('defending the homeland against unbelievers'). In the second part of the play, on 3 May after the French reprisals, the women set up a shrine to 'los héroes que dieron su sangre por Madrí' ('the heroes who gave their blood for Madrid') topped by the national flag (134). Clearly, the historical situation is very different from that of *Bodas que fueron famosas del Pingajo y la Fandanga*, but such echoes of the earlier play make the absence of irony in these elements of *La Chispa* all the more striking.

Where an ironic or satirical intention is signalled is in the text's subtitle, 'Aguafuerte dramático madrileño' ('Dramatic etching of Madrid'). The term *aguafuerte* refers to a mordant or corrosive technique of representation and suggests an oblique tribute to Goya, who perfected the aquatint method of etching in this period (his satirical *Caprichos* were published in 1799). The painter himself does not appear in Rodríguez Méndez's play, nor are the scenes depicted in his famous paintings of the events of 2 and 3 May reproduced on stage or described. Instead, a second-rate, slightly effeminate painter (*El Pintamonas*) becomes the focus of some rather weak pieces of comic business: he is thrown out of the hairdressers' house for asking them to pose for a picturesque portrait in the style of Goya's paintings of *majas*, and at the end is intimidated again by an aggressive group of women when he sets about painting them as heroes of the resistance, producing his own image of 'El Dos de Mayo glorioso' (*La Chispa* 1999: 141) ('the glorious Second of May'). This character is a Gallicized *petimetre* (of the type ridiculed in Ramón de la Cruz's *sainetes*) who at first deplores the common people's lack of cultural refinement and later seeks to ingratiate himself with them, jumping on the bandwagon of popular patriotism. Goya is therefore invoked more in terms of social satire than of the heroic emotionalism of *La carga de los mamelucos* and *Los fusilamientos del 3 de mayo*, but the satire is based on little more than facile chauvinism.

The painter is also associated with Don Homobono, a pompous *petimetre* who represents the supposedly unpatriotic inclination of the enlightened intelligentsia towards the reformist policies introduced by the French. He appears briefly with another gentleman, Don Santos (who is never seen again), in order to complain about the reactionary fanaticism of a 'pueblo atrasado' ('backward people') that refuses to accept the benefits of reason (109). A little later, when he reappears with the *pintamonas*, the playwright seems to forget that this character has already been on; the stage direction introduces him as a new character and the conversation in which Boliche asks for alms but is told he deserves his punishment is repeated (114–15). Don Homobono turns up again, even more briefly, in the second part of the play, but his dismay at the violence is not developed dramatically. He is simply a stock figure designed to lampoon the 'universalistas afrancesados y bonapartistas de los nuevos tiempos de la transición' in contrast with the sound instincts of the common people. A certain degree of simplification of issues and historical circumstances has been observed in earlier plays by Rodríguez Méndez, yet this has always been redeemed by elements of ambiguity or complexity in the action and characterization. In this case, compounded by careless construction and a failure to build up any real dramatic tension or engagement with characters, the result is structural and conceptual oversimplification.

Although the contrast between affected *afrancesados* and down-to-earth, patriotic *chisperos* remains simplistic, there is nevertheless one aspect of the play that is developed in an interesting way. To an even greater extent than in the earlier works, the representation of communal *machismo* focuses primarily on the female characters. Superficially, the hero of the piece is Manolo, the swaggering *majo* who becomes one of the leaders of the resistance. However, most of the dramatic action and stage space is devoted to the women of the district, who play a crucial role in convincing Lieutenant Ruiz to release arms to the people at the end of Part 1 and in reconstructing a sense of community in Part 2. While the men's displays of bravado tend to be largely individual gestures, the courage shown by the women is more collective and cooperative, and they turn conventionally feminine activities into expressions of communal defiance. María and Antonia continue to provide hairdressing services in the ruins of their house, and all the women work together to prepare food while dancing and singing anti-French songs – 'pa que vean que no nos asustamos por na' ('to show 'em we're not afraid of nothing'), as Manolo puts it (132).

The dramatic impact of *Bodas que fueron famosas del Pingajo y la Fandanga* and *Historia de unos cuantos*, and to some extent of *El círculo de tiza de Cartagena*, is essentially tragicomic. In the archetypal terms used by Hayden White (based on Northrop Frye), they represent history as a mixture of Comedy, Tragedy and Satire, whilst avoiding the Romantic mode of emplotment, which is essentially heroic, 'a drama of the triumph of good over evil' (1973: 9). They celebrate the centrality and vitality of popular culture at the same time as recognizing the forces that bring about its gradual destruction and taking an ironic view of its moral value and ideological function. White argues that 'Romance and Satire would appear to be *mutually exclusive* ways of emplotting the processes of reality', and that whereas the Ironic vision articulated by Satire can coexist with Tragedy and Comedy, it tends to negate the naïve idealism of Romance (1973: 9–10). Perhaps this is the trouble with *La Chispa*. Its more simplistic treatment of popular patriotism constitutes an element of Romance that displaces both the comic and the tragic, and sits uneasily with the satirical approach. Rosita, Mari Pepa and the women in *Bodas* build resistance to ideological control out of their sense of community; there is little sign of the women in *La Chispa* doing the same.

Notes

1. 'There's no "historical critique" in that play at all. History is used in it to provide an ambience, a physical setting. [...] Let's not confuse a "historicist" approach with "historical" material.'

2. Picking up on the impact of performances by the Berliner Ensemble in Paris in the mid-1950s, some independent theatre groups (especially in Barcelona) had by the late 1950s begun to perform plays by Brecht and experiment with the techniques of 'epic' theatre. See Cornago Bernal (2000: 375-484) for a comprehensive analysis of the influence of Brecht on Spanish theatre in the 1960s.

3. 'In the distance, the bars of the famous prison shed tears onto the water and inspire notions of penal reform in obscure, Romantic regenerators of the people.'

4. See Hennessy (1962) for a detailed account of the political complexities of the First Republic and cantonalism.

5. Monleón (1968a: 33, 42) emphasises the influence of Valle – rightly with respect to this play but less convincingly in the case of *Bodas que fueron famosas del Pingajo y la Fandanga*, as I shall argue in the next section. Lyon (1983) remains the best full-length study of Valle's theatre.

6. 'Stay away from me. I won't be led astray again by your ignorance... I must establish a dictatorship in Cartagena. In the absence of my husband, I rule the city.'

7. 'J. ANTONIO – Hey, kid, bring us the bottle. TAVERN BOY – I don't have to wait on you any more. J. ANTONIO – (*To Filigranas.*) I think you were right earlier, you know, when you were talking about giving this lad a thrashing... We're going to have to go back to the old systems.'

8. 'The natural reaction against communistic ideas.'

9. 'Should be understood as situated in the past, and any suspicion or suggestion of similarity to more recent situations and personages would, in my view, constitute a distorted and far from intelligent interpretation.'

10. 'With no intention other than to caricature a kind of "patriotism" that is misguided, egocentric and sentimental.'

11. 'The whole story follows a rabble-rousing line, a clear leftist tendency. It is like a libertarian anthem, a defence of revolution. Out of date, unjust and resentful. There can be no reason to justify the staging of this play, which is politically dangerous and theatrically absurd.'

12. 'FILIGRANAS – That friar was well disguised, wasn't he? I thought he was an old woman. JOSÉ ANTONIO – We only caught him because I happened to give his hair a tug. TAVERN BOY – I like watching them kicking in the air.'

13. 'FILIGRANAS – The boss was very lonely. Poetry wasn't enough for him. And now he's suddenly found he's going to be a surrogate father. JOSÉ ANTONIO – Like Saint Joseph.'

14. 'BULERÍA – The Republic... bah! (*He spits.*) Me, I'm a Traditionalist. A Traditionalist!'

15. 'JULIO – If you want to die with me, spit in that woman's face when they make you show yours. I'll die blaspheming.'

16. 'I'm as revolutionary as anybody. But you've got to know what's what. The heart comes first.'

17. 'I'd walk over hot coals to prove the legitimacy of my lineage.'
18. 'There is a Spaniard wanting to live and just beginning to live, between a Spain that is dying and another Spain yawning. Little Spaniard coming into the world, may God protect you. One of those two Spains will freeze your heart.'
19. 'What I write is not designed for the stages currently used and abused in Spain.'
20. It should be noted, though, that the time is indicated with the usual imprecision: 'por los años de desgracia de 1898' (*Bodas que fueron famosas del Pingajo y la Fandanga* 1979: 56) ('in the unfortunate years around 1898').
21. 'The social class that appears as protagonist is not really the *pueblo*, but the *lumpenproletariat* of the time, a marginalized and delinquent group deprived of any opportunity to escape from their situation, trapped in a vicious circle of poverty and crime.'
22. 'The ill-fated marriage of Pingajo and Fandanga emerges as an event that, although minuscule, allows us nevertheless to glimpse the background of the period.'
23. 'As if the famous bullfighter Lagartijo were there in person, such is their admiration.'
24. References to the Cuban war in this text bring in an interesting selection of period slang. *Manigua* is an indigenous Caribbean word referring to tropical scrub or rainforest. *Sorche* is a corruption of English 'soldier', used especially to refer to a low-ranking, inexperienced recruit. *Mambís* (or *mambí*) was the name given to those who fought against Spain in the wars of independence in Santo Domingo and Cuba.
25. 'Tha's nothin'. Ya should've seen me las' year at San Isidro fair.'
26. 'Become as drunk with words as with wine, speak more to feel that they are alive than to communicate, talk because it is the only way they have of propping up their pointless existence, a way of banishing fear and profound solitude.'
27. 'PINGAJO – Is the maiden assigned to me or not? PETATE – She is indeed. These gentlemen are witnesses.'
28. 'The kings of the Hacho jail in Ceuta, when Madrid's finest were banged up there.'
29. 'So the entire world can see there's no shortage of joy and pizazz in Spain.' The adjective *majo* has come to mean 'nice, attractive, likeable' in modern Spanish, but the notion of *majeza* is historically associated with the figure of the *majo* (and female *maja*) as representatives of the popular culture of Madrid in the eighteenth and nineteenth centuries, as portrayed dramatically by Ramón de la Cruz and pictorially by Goya.
30. 'The codes of behaviour that the established order has taught him.'
31. Rodríguez Méndez confirms that, as well as the popular song 'De bellotas y cascajo' and his own knowledge of Madrid, Ramón de la Cruz's *Manolo* had an influence on the composition of *Bodas* (interviewed in Thompson 1989: 430).
32. 'There's no God! There's no God!'
33. Madre Rafols was an apocalyptic Catalan prophet who made a name for herself in the 1890s by warning of the imminent end of the world.
34. 'Oh, age of misfortune heaped on misfortune! Our ships and our honour under bombardment!'
35. See Carr (1982: 558-59) and Boyd (1979: 3-25) on the influence of the military on Restoration governments.
36. 'PINGAJO – All the squaddies have been salutin' me. And a bloke gave me his seat on the tram. They've been treatin' me like a hero. PETATE – That's what you are, mate. A glorious hero.'
37. 'We'll have to set up a dictatorship, a really good dictatorship. And don't worry, somebody'll step in to do it soon enough and clear up all the thieving, delinquent trash loitering around the streets of Madrid.'
38. *La marcha de Cádiz*, by Valverde and Lucio y García-Álvarez, was first performed in 1896.
39. 'To play?... Yeah, sure, but not the kind of games you're thinkin' of, love.'
40. 'Rodríguez Méndez does not provide a clear explanation of the psychological mechanisms that lead Pingajo to fall in love with Fandanga and decide not to hand her over to the lieutenant.'

41. 'A light-fingered trickster taking whatever chances come his way.'
42. 'Make sure no-one in the neighbourhood goes without food today.'
43. 'The established order will wipe away the hapless irritant that is Pingajo, defeated, battered, wretched, delinquent.'
44. 'ANOTHER WOMAN – Ordinary people have never had justice in this country. No justice, nor respect, nor nothing. A WOMAN – I reckon we're just not real women and nobody in Madrid's got any guts any more, 'cos we should've jumped 'em and torn 'em to pieces, that's what God gave us fingernails for.'
45. 'A WOMAN – It's that martial law they've sentenced him with. A GIRL – He's lucky, then, isn't he? They say it's an honourable death. A WOMAN – I bet he'll die well. Like a hussar.'
46. José Luis Gómez's 1978 production placed the firing squad onstage, as part of a general tendency to show the repressiveness of the state more explicitly.
47. 'Pingajo is left alone like a real rag, tilting to one side, his head bowed and the cigarette dangling from his lip.'
48. 'What a prat! He's only gone and fainted on us. [...] (*The two men shake him and slap his face. Pingajo opens his eyes in astonishment and stares at them as if he was already in the other world.*) [...] You're not allowed to move 'til you hear the shots, all right? Now, keep still. (*He puts him in position, as if posed for a photograph, and rapidly disappears again.*)'
49. For example, Monleón (1968a: 52), Oliva (1978: 97-103) and Pérez-Stansfield (1983: 237).
50. 'The *esperpento* is there, just around the corner. If we get there, it will be by way of the humanity of the characters, not out of some preconceived idea of what the *esperpento* is supposed be.'
51. The *expediente* numbered 0/3-70 refers to this proposed production, but unfortunately contains only a typewritten copy of the text, without any of the censors' reports. Parts of scene 3 (in which Pingajo and the lieutenant discuss their experiences in Cuba), Pingajo's ironic remarks about the army at the end of scene 6, and references to the flag in the epilogue do not appear in this version of the text (Ministerio de Información y Turismo 1970a).
52. 'They didn't dare to put the flag on stage for fear of looking "reactionary".'
53. 'Although the author sets the action in 1898, he has included a series of references, some political and others military, which by analogy could be taken to be relevant to the present and critical of the current administration. For example, on page 182, in a conversation between pickpockets someone says: "after twenty-five years of peace in the clink." Such a long sentence would not be imposed on a minor offender such as a pickpocket, and yet he refers to twenty-five years of peace in prison, the same period of peace that we have had in this country. Other phrases alluding to the armed forces and the justice system have similar implications.'
54. In both the 1978 production and the Cátedra edition, the phrase 'de paz' is omitted (*Bodas* 1979: 63).
55. Some of these details in stage directions are also omitted in the 1979 edition.
56. 'The poor fellow deserves to be wrapped in the flag, like the boys who die in battle.'
57. Rodríguez Méndez's accounts of his own military career (as a conscript and later as a volunteer) are ambivalent. On the one hand, he valued the comradeship and the opportunity to get to know his country and its people better. On the other hand, army life is portrayed as tedious and vicious, and he is particularly troubled by the gulf between the privileged officer class and the demoralized mass of the ranks. See Martín Recuerda (1979: 31-32), Jiménez Sánchez (1998: 90-91) and Rodríguez Méndez (1999: 47-48); and in a fictionalized form, the novel *El cisne de Cisneros* (Rodríguez Méndez 1981) and the flashback to Trueno's military service in *Los quinquis de Madriz*.
58. 'Those Madrid slums [...] are still there, a stone's throw from the Puerta del Sol, many of them steeped in the same atmosphere of neglect and despair.'
59. 'To ensure a decent quality of life for all.'
60. 'The play, set in 1898, deals with the beginnings of a political debate in and about Spain that is still unresolved. It was a time when the loss of the colonies was followed by the confrontation

between the spirit of the Restoration and a desire to build from the bottom up, paying attention to the social reality embodied in the masses, in the society that is now coming forward – amongst the strident demands of various minorities – to remind us once again that it exists too. Even if people no longer live in caves and ex-soldiers in tropical uniforms can no longer be seen begging on the streets.'

61. 'As far as I'm concerned, the Republic's brought me more grief than all the monarchies put together.'

62. 'That's the typical sin of the Spaniard: not thinking things through.'

63. Juan José is a re-creation of the eponymous hero of Joaquín Dicenta's play of 1895. He too has an interesting past to which Serafín the policeman refers obliquely, but which he does not want to discuss (137). Serafín ('the painter') is another figure from the *género chico*: the strutting *chulo* in Arniches's *El amigo Melquíades* (1914).

64. Whatever you lot say or don't say, the world goes on the same way, with some people eating and others just watching.

65. 'Now you be quiet, Juan José, and stop going on about politics… Go and find out where Felipe and little José Luis are, will you?'

66. Although the generals and politicians exercised more direct control over the Moroccan campaigns, King Alfonso's influence was an important factor in the willingness to pursue the war and in the miscalculations that led to the disasters of 1921.

67. 'And they're comparing you to a negro? Come off it, lad! A negro! Blacks are only good for selling lottery tickets, and even that's pushing it.'

68. 'Antimilitarism is spreading, and so on, but amongst the ordinary people of Madrid all this is interpreted in a rather confused way, producing waves of uncontrolled fervour and exhilaration.'

69. The 14th of April 1931 is one of the author's own earliest memories. Aged five, he witnessed a spontaneous ceremony in Madrid in which the Republican tricolour was placed in the hand of the statue of Eloy Gonzalo Cascorro, a popular hero of the Cuban war (Monleón 1974b: 11). He also remembers a film about Galán, the executed leader of the Jaca uprising of 1930, in which the hero's body is covered with the flag by a woman representing the Republic: 'Los chiquillos aplaudíamos y vitoreábamos a Fermín Galán' (quoted in Martín Recuerda 1979: 13-14) ('All of us children applauded and cheered Fermín Galán').

70. 'NEIGHBOUR – Well, I've been lucky. I was three months behind with the rent, and I expect we won't have to pay rent no more… ANOTHER NEIGHBOUR – Oh, yeah, very likely. You really think they'll be paving the streets with gold all of a sudden, do you? NEIGHBOUR – (*Very maliciously.*) So you mean it's not true, all that stuff about redistributing wealth?'

71. 'I'm raffling the Republic! Tickets only ten each! Win this lovely Republic today!'

72. 'FIRST MAN – Like I said, flowers are for when someone's died. FELIPE – Well, the poor *are* pretty much dead. THIRD MAN – No, they're not! More alive than ever and more glorious!'

73. 'They killed one of my sons in Melilla and you lot have killed my husband. And now you expect me to thank you for helping me? While you and your family have turned into a bunch of toffs?'

74. 'Can they really be capable of such an atrocity? Mother of God, when I think that I was baptized and married in that church! Savages!'

75. On the pervasiveness of the black market in the post-war, see Carr (1982: 740-42), Abella (1985), and particularly Richards (1998: 108-109, 134-40, 165-69), who shows how participation in the black market could function as a form of popular resistance.

76. 'Because ultimately, from the point of view of the everyday life of the people, Julián is a man who throughout his life has taken advantage of the people he defends in his speeches.'

77. 'A play that had been banned for years, and then amnestied with some of its sting removed, was denounced as politically reactionary – by pedantic critics, of course – merely because it did not make clear to which political party or specific doctrine some of its characters owed allegiance. The point of these characters was precisely to bear witness to the suffering caused by the political changes by which they were affected.'

78. 'I'm not going anywhere with you, you and your kind. Me, I'm staying here, in my neighbourhood, in my home. Where I belong, with what I've got left, what *we*'ve got left.'

79. The feeling is clearly of great importance to Rodríguez Méndez himself. The setting of *Historia de unos cuantos* is his own *patria chica*. The work portrays his people and his cultural roots (see Martín Recuerda 1979: 15, 162-63).

80. For detailed analysis of this documentation, see Thompson (2004a).

81. 'At a time when preparations are being made for the accession of a new king, this work should be considered by a higher authority, since its background deals with the justification for the failure of a Republic – the Second Spanish Republic, specifically.'

82. 'Overall, the play is exemplary: the idealist, ingenuous Republicans (from the lower classes) always come off worst, whilst the survivor manages to come out on top and adapts to any situation so as to continue to prosper.'

83. 'You're a bunch of hypocrites, Jesuits! As bad as Father Laburu!'

84. 'If only those poor soldiers weren't such chickens, what they ought to be doing is shooting at their commanding officers, not at the Moors.'

85. 'Typical scenes of Madrid life, full of colour and vitality. I must confess that I have read them with enthusiasm.'

86. 'The crude populism and documentary picturesqueness of *Historia de unos cuantos* complicate rather than compensate for the assortment of relatively minor (ultimately political) inconveniences that make it a troublesome play.'

87. 'The author of this monstrosity has, without seeking leave from either God or the Devil, set out to continue the lives of these characters from 1898 up to the winter of 1939 [...]. The malicious intentions are obvious.'

88. *Chispero*: a blacksmith; or a man from the district of Maravillas in Madrid, whose inhabitants were known as *chisperos* on account of the large number of smithies in the area (from the definition in Real Academia Española 1992: 650).

89. 'So, fearing the worst, what I did was to celebrate the glorious opposition to those who collaborated with the French believing that Napoleon was going to bring us enlightenment, good government, etc. – the myth of the great age of Equality, Fraternity and Liberty. Consequently, I decided that the protagonists of my play would be the people who were the real protagonists of the events. That is, the *chisperos* and *Manolos* of the Maravillas and El Rastro districts, my countrymen, who are looked down on by the Frenchified, Bonapartist universalists of the new age of the transition. So it was that I turned my eyes towards that eternally sacred page of heroism and resistance revealed to history by the people to which I belong.'

90. 'Like lions they threw themselves into the fight and saved the Fatherland from the talons of Napoleon. In our own time, the heroes of the Crusade of Liberation, with equal valour, have also saved the Fatherland from the talons of communism.'

91. For example, a poster bearing the slogan '¡Fuera el invasor!' ('Out with the invader!') juxtaposes an image of a Republican infantryman with one of an early nineteenth-century *majo* (Bardasano 1937).

92. 'Because I too lived through a terrible assault on Madrid, between 1936 and 1939, and I was able to see at first hand the great virtues displayed by a beaten people, conscious of what it means to be subject to a foreign power.'

93. 'On that occasion the foreign power was the Soviet Union. I remember a Madrid filled with red flags with the hammer and sickle, and I experienced those other executions on the banks of the Manzanares, every bit as brutal as the ones on the hill at Príncipe Pío in 1808. So *La Chispa* is a kind of etching infused with the true spirit of Madrid, revealing the two periods in which the city showed most powerfully its essential resilience and generosity.'

94. 'And now it turns out that people are looking back to that sinister period as a positive one offering hopeful signs of some kind. But we were liberated from all that in the spring of 1939 with the arrival of Franco's troops.'

5

LEADING ROLES IN HISTORY

Historia de unos cuantos marks the high point of the evolution of Rodríguez Méndez's theatre of collective 'history from below', after which the emphasis of his work shifts to plays centred on more prominent, active protagonists, some of them well-known historical figures. These characters are closer to the model of the 'world-historical individual' in the Lukácsian (originally Hegelian) sense referred to at the beginning of Chapter 3: an individual engaged in work of social significance, at the centre of a dramatic conflict that represents the essential dynamic of the collision of underlying social forces in a particular period (Lukács 1969: 119). Rodríguez Méndez succinctly sums up the point of using prominent figures from history as the focus of historical drama: 'Son individuos que han llegado a encarnar su época de manera única. Al dramatizar su vida, se dramatiza su época; al dramatizar su época, se entiende mejor la nuestra' (quoted in Gabriele 1997: 81).[1] What each of the figures used by Rodríguez Méndez as protagonists represents about his or her period, however, is not necessarily what is conventionally identified as its most significant feature. The analysis of plays in this chapter aims to show that popular cultural identity remains at the centre of the dramatist's historical vision. His protagonists are not invested with the kind of transcendental awareness and moral authority that Buero Vallejo gives to his historical protagonists Esquilache, Velázquez and Larra. They are all in some sense at odds with the dominant ideology of their time, but their dissidence is articulated more in terms of their relationship with the culture of the ordinary people around them than of their engagement in key events or decisions. The 'collision' of forces remains essentially the same as in the 'history from below' plays, between official (ideologically hegemonic) culture and popular (dissident) culture, and as always, each force influences the other. The dramatic and historical importance of these leading players, therefore, lies primarily in their connection to and performance of versions of *machismo español*.

Lluiset in *Flor de Otoño* (1972, first staged in 1982) is a lawyer from a prominent bourgeois family, but plunges into the multiple subcultures of Barcelona at the end of the 1920s and radically redefines *machismo español* as anarchist, gay and bilingual. In *El pájaro solitario* (1974, first staged in 1998), San Juan de la Cruz is both a solitary mystic and a stubborn rebel whose poetry and presence connect most powerfully with the humblest and most disreputable of the common people. In *Literatura española* (1978, first staged in 1996 as *Puesto ya el pie en el estribo*), Miguel de Cervantes is a prestigious figure treated with respect by illustrious contemporaries but defined primarily by his relationships with the *pueblo* (as represented by characters from his own works) and his participation in its culture. Since it takes the form of a monologue, *Teresa de Ávila* (written and performed in 1981) does not show its protagonist in direct relation to the people, yet it emphasizes the rebelliousness and humble background of a saint often appropriated by religious and political conservatism. *Isabelita tiene ángel* (1976, first staged in 1993) offers a quirky view of Queen Isabel I, portraying her as a pragmatic, down-to-earth woman who remains sceptical about the ambitions and ideological fanaticism of those around her. King Alfonso VI, as recreated in the parodic *Reconquista* (1981), is a kind of medieval Flor de Otoño who casts aside his official role as leader of the Crusade, embracing Islamic culture and flaunting his bisexuality. *Soy madrileño* (1987) is the most straightforwardly popular of these plays, celebrating the ingenuity and boldness of the nineteenth-century folk hero Luis Candelas and satirizing the political confusion of the regency of María Cristina.

Flor de Otoño (Autumn Flower)

Set in Barcelona in early 1930, *Flor de Otoño* marks a striking departure from the preceding works in its cultural environment, its tone and its theatrical techniques. The urban setting here is sleazy, dangerous and multicultural. The dialogue is a disorderly mixture of Catalan and Castilian, with a sprinkling of dialectal influences imported from all over Spain. The protagonist, Lluiset, gleefully plays three contradictory roles as lawyer, cabaret singer and terrorist, switching between the stuffy hypocrisy of his bourgeois family, the sordid glamour of the Barrio Chino (red-light district) and the amateur militancy of an anarchist group. The *pueblo* here is remarkably heterogeneous, including manual labourers, soldiers, vagrants, criminals, entertainers, students and policemen. As in the 'history from below' plays, though, it is still celebrated for its creative energy and linguistic inventiveness in the face of hardship and official oppression. Lluiset's performances are partly an individual response to his personal and social circumstances, but are also inspired by and dedicated to the hybrid popular culture surrounding him.

This colourful protagonist is therefore a very useful dramatic device, moving between the two principal opposing sectors of Restoration society: on the one hand, the ruling industrial bourgeoisie, and on the other, the various fragments of the proletariat and lumpenproletariat. In a piece written to accompany the first publication of *Flor de Otoño*, Rodríguez Méndez sums up the social situation and what it means to him:

> Lluiset era la Barcelona que yo tengo vivida y que tiene un misterio casi indescifrable, una poesía sórdida curiosa, una rebeldía soterrada, procedente de la delincuencia portuaria, aplastada por el peso de una burguesía puritana, insufrible... Yo quería expresar ese conflicto compuesto por varias clases sociales

Flor de Otoño, Teatro Español (Madrid), December 1982. *Photograph by Manuel Martínez Muñoz.*

en lucha sorda, que sólo se dan en Barcelona y no creo que en ninguna otra parte del mundo: una clase burguesa repugnante, una clase proletaria aburguesada, una clase inmigratoria balbuceante en la diáspora, una clase encanallada y delincuente, como hay en Nápoles, que convive con las otras y se transforma camaleónicamente según épocas (1974a: 15–16).[2]

In order to convey the confusion and cultural hybridity of the setting, the dramatic structure is unusually flexible and dynamic, its two parts divided into a number of short scenes set in various locations and punctuated by inventive linking devices. The first scene is designed to indicate 'el «qué», el «cómo» y el «porqué»' ('the what, the how and the why') of the wealthy Serracant family's way of life, initially by means of a lengthy stage direction describing the set (*Flor de Otoño* 1979: 123). Several commentators have remarked upon the descriptive, narrative quality of the stage directions in this play, even more elaborate than those used in *Bodas* and *Historia de unos cuantos*.[3] In addition to providing practical instructions for staging, they generate impressionistic evocations of atmosphere, highlight details in ways difficult to realize on stage, and at times become commentaries in which an ironic authorial voice intrudes. The opening stage direction is a lingering enumeration of the ornate details of doña Nuria's sitting room, but also makes clear how we are to interpret these details: 'Clase burguesa entre las burguesas anunciada por aquella chimenea de mármol blanco' (124).[4] The author playfully imitates the language and attitudes of this smug, comfortable class: '¿Cómo es posible que a semejantes horas alguien se atreva a llamar de este modo a una casa decente y además lo haga por la puerta principal y no por la de servicio?' (124–25).[5]

The technique can therefore be considered novelistic not only in the extensiveness of the description but also in the imposition of a tone and a point of view. It may also be seen, however, as filmic. The narrative voice is reminiscent of cinematic voice-over, and tiny details are picked out as if in close-up, some of them apparently animated: there are pictures of ladies emerging from the Liceo opera house; a signed photograph of Alfonso XIII seems to shudder as coarse drunken singing is heard in the street, but the presence alongside of a figure of the baby Jesus surrounded by paper flowers 'hace mantener la compostura al monarca' (124).[6] It is impossible to realize directly on stage all the suggestions thrown up by the opening stage direction, especially as this is just one of a number of settings required, yet they are crucial indicators of several factors that need to be built into the conversion of verbal signs into visual and acoustic ones: a tone of irreverent caricature, together with markers of class, taste, period and national identity. The stage language is further enriched with verbal and visual references to cinema (titles of films and allusions to Pola Negri, Rudolph Valentino, Mae West and Marlene Dietrich), as well as various intertextual references to theatre, cabaret and opera, explicitly emphasizing forms of live performance. Doña Nuria is associated with mainstream bourgeois drama, posing histrionically in a way reminiscent of the famous actress María Guerrero, and her conversation later on with Lluiset's friend Ricard is described in the stage direction as 'benaventina' (168). In a different style, the ceremony with which the Serracants bring their family meeting to an end is likened to a grotesque puppet show. Lluiset himself is the main focus of this metatheatricality, performing multiple roles in Castilian and Catalan with conscious irony and a playful mastery of pastiche. He mimics Valentino, Mae West and Dietrich, but also refers to operatic heroines (157–62), Parisian cabaret (148–49) and La verbena de la Paloma (149). As a result, the notion of identity (cultural, gender, national and class identities) as performance is given greater complexity in this play, involving a wider range of performative genres. However, it becomes clear that Lluiset's performance is ultimately directed towards a search for a kind of authenticity through popular culture.

Lluiset himself does not appear on stage until the second scene, after the social environment in which his family moves has been visually and linguistically sketched out in the first scene. The projection of a newspaper page linking the two scenes performs several functions (131–32). It provides economical plot exposition (explaining why the police have raided doña Nuria's house in the middle of the night), evokes a bourgeois discourse of moral outrage, refers to the cinema (both in the advertisement for La Madona de los coches camas and in the nature of the technique itself), and introduces a tantalizing announcement of a cabaret performance by Flor de Otoño. The projection is supposed to disappear as if ripped away by an angry female hand (133), a striking device that works like a cinematic cut to the scene in which Nuria demands to see the Civil Governor, accompanied by her son in his role as the timid, respectable lawyer don Lluis de Serracant.

The third scene – the family conference – continues the satirical treatment of the class and culture represented by the Serracant family by means of a kind of pastiche of bourgeois melodrama, now moving decisively into grotesque, ritualized caricature, featuring characters identified only as 'the fat gentleman', 'the thin gentleman', 'the hunchbacked gentleman', 'the plump lady' and 'the blonde lady'.[7] At the beginning of the scene, they sit in stiff silence apart from the peculiar 'gorgoritos de ópera' ('operatic gurgling') they make as they sip their coffee (135). When they do speak, they utter comical expressions of indignation and meaningless clichés. Comedy is not the only point of the scene, however, since it also makes clear the extent of the Serracants' economic interests and the lengths to which they are prepared to go to defend them, while dropping ironic hints that at least one of them has more to do with 'la gent del hampa' (136) ('the riff-raff') than he would like to admit.

The expressionistic caricature culminates in a lengthy ritual of leave-taking, in which the characters' gestures are exaggerated and their voices can no longer be heard – an 'escena de marionetas tenebrosas' (140) ('a shadowy puppet show'). In the meantime, the focus is shifting to Lluiset, an image of subversive vitality sharply contrasted with the lifeless conventionality of his family. The stage at this point is split (suggesting cinematic cross-cutting), showing Lluiset in his apartment in the Barrio Chino in the process of transforming himself into the outrageously camp Flor de Otoño, while the family ritual is still being played out on the other side of the stage. The Flor de Otoño persona is thus shown to be deliberately created by Lluiset as a gesture of rebellion against the culture of bourgeois respectability.[8] His clothes are the conventional evening dress of a wealthy gentleman-about-town, but worn with an exaggeratedly effeminate bearing and ostentatious make-up. The only changes he makes for the cabaret performance are to replace the black jacket with a sequinned tailcoat, to add a coloured plume to the top hat and to elaborate the make-up. He does not create an entirely different, original persona but an adaptation of what he already has and is, impudently creating his own conscious caricature of the conventional image of the *hijo de buena familia* to set against the unconscious caricature played out by his family. He does not dress as a woman, and his performance is not strictly a drag act. Although Flor de Otoño is coquettishly effeminate, the image is androgynous, modelled on Mae West (who performed in the 1920s as a male impersonator as well as on stage and screen as a wisecracking vamp) and on Marlene Dietrich (most memorably photographed in a masculine suit and top hat).[9]

The scene ends with a masterly twist that decisively confirms the idea that Lluiset is making a gesture of mischievous rebellion directed at his family, exposing the absurdity of their conventions and the corruption that lies beneath. The illusion of two separate actions in different places is shattered when Lluiset takes out a handkerchief and waves it at his departing relatives. They cannot see him, but from the audience's point of view he is mocking them directly. This development introduces the possibility that the caricatured representation of the family is not so much a creation of the author as Lluiset's own vision, which he playfully shares with the audience, to the soundtrack of the song that he is about to perform in the Bataclán nightclub (anticipating the transformation of the real audience into the intradiegetic audience attending Flor de Otoño's show).

The clientele of the Bataclán mixes gangsters and prostitutes with members of the middle and upper classes: a microcosm of a colourful, corrupt city which exposes the falseness of the myth of bourgeois respectability. Lluiset's uncle demands to be allowed in but is thrown into the street by a doorman unimpressed by his status. Flor de Otoño's performance on stage is playfully anti-Establishment in its references to cocaine, its teasing of a gentleman with the look of an American financier accompanied by two elegant ladies, and the cheeky irreverence of 'el otro día me metieron en un cartucho de papel y me llevaron ante Su Majestad, que había pedido que le llevaran la flor más bonita de la Rambla' (151).[10] There is, moreover, an ironic reference to the culture of popular *machismo español*: 'Así me gustan los hombres a mí..., con coraje... Con lo que hay que tener, como en *La verbena de la Paloma*' (149).[11] Flor de Otoño, in a paradoxical way, can be seen as another representative of *machismo*, in the tradition of the casual, comical criminality of Manolo and the arrogant, irresponsible sensuality of Pichi, drawing on and transforming popular culture and the language of the streets. Of course, Flor de Otoño is far from macho in the conventional sense of the term, and does not have the same *castizo* character as Pingajo or Pichi: the flavour of this version, responding to its particular time and place, is deliberately camp, cosmopolitan and bilingual, with echoes of Parisian cabaret, US cinema and orientalism. Nevertheless, Flor proudly claims to be 'flamencona', and expresses a local loyalty akin to the pride of the other *machos* in their *patria chica*: 'París, oh París... Pero donde esté Barcelona que se quite tot' (149).[12]

In true cabaret style, Flor de Otoño involves members of the Bataclán audience in the act, playing up to a local, familiar clientele. Consequently, the whole scene offers opportunities for extending the performance out into the auditorium, fusing the real and fictional audiences as admirers of Flor de Otoño.[13] Lluiset's performance as Flor de Otoño continues after he leaves the cabaret stage amidst adoring applause, and in the following scene, when he is taken by Ricard and Surroca to the army barracks with a stab wound in his neck, he cannot resist the opportunity for further role playing, romanticizing the situation comically but charmingly: he claims to be the Marqués de la Marina and evokes Marguerite Gautier, la Traviata, Jimena to the lieutenant's Cid, and Don Quijote's Dulcinea.

The representation of the soldiers as sleepy incompetents who do not notice that their armoury is being is emptied by Lluiset's companions as he creates a diversion is reminiscent of parts of *Bodas que fueron famosas del Pingajo y la Fandanga*, although the lieutenant in this case is much less vicious and debauched. Flor's mock idealization of the army as the 'flower of chivalry' is rounded off with '¡Viva el ejército español!' (164) ('Long live the Spanish army!') as the three revellers make off into the night with armfuls of rifles. No malice towards the soldiers themselves is suggested, however, for these men are more of the ordinary people who survive as best they can in the lower levels of the system, like the policemen in the first scene and the door staff at the Bataclán, trying to stay out of trouble and watching the turbulence of the world around them with a wary, jaundiced eye. Lluiset's relationship with the masses is ambiguous. He evidently feels an affinity with people outside the privileged circles of the family and class that he rejects, yet he is ostentatiously different from ordinary working men and women, not for a moment claiming to be one of them. There is some degree of genuine commitment to the interests of the *pueblo* in his attitude, but to a large extent his actions are those of a bored *señorito* rebelling against his asphyxiating upbringing.

The second part of the play begins with another newspaper projection, which picks up elements from the first part: the naming of Flor de Otoño as the alleged murderer of la Asturianita, Flor's connection with the Bataclán, a retraction of the implication of a member of a respectable family, and a report on the theft of arms from the Atarazanas barracks. The family has successfully made use of its influence to rescue its reputation, and the Press once again faithfully reflects the ideology of the ruling class. Yet the personality of Flor never seems far away. An advertisement for the film *El desfile del Amor* recalls Surroca's sarcastic remark to Flor at the end of the first part, and another for a performance of *La Traviata* reminds us of the romantic fantasy about dying like Verdi's heroine.

The projection simultaneously summarizes part one and launches us into part two, directly into another family meeting, for the action begins with doña Nuria triumphantly reading out the newspaper's retraction. This second family scene essentially serves the same function as the first: caricature of bourgeois respectability. The cast is the same, the setting and actions identical, with the same feeling of stiff, vacuous ritual, and once again, the scene closes with a family ritual of solidarity as they stand up together and sing the *Virolai*.[14] For the reader or spectator, the most enjoyable aspect of this scene is the dramatic irony generated by the family's belief in the lie they have helped to perpetuate – that Lluiset is not Flor de Otoño. One of them even proposes that Lluiset himself act as the family's lawyer in their claim for damages. The subsequent conversation between doña Nuria and Lluiset's lover Ricard serves to complicate this dramatic irony by suggesting the possibility that Lluiset's mother is more aware of the reality of the situation than she shows. The indication in the stage direction opening the scene that it is 'benaventina' (168) implies well-mannered artificiality; if Ricard is acting out a socially prescribed role, as if he were in an urbane drawing-room comedy by Jacinto Benavente, the possibility emerges that Nuria too is doing so consciously, in an attempt to elicit more information about what Lluiset is really up to. In the previous scene, she seemed to be playing down the urgency of taking further action and using Lluiset as their lawyer, despite the fact that she had earlier been the one most committed to decisive action.

The stealing of the rifles at the end of the first part anticipated Lluiset's third incarnation as the anarchist revolutionary, which is developed in the third scene of the second part, set in the Cooperativa Obrera del Poble Nou. There is still something of Flor de Otoño's frivolity and effeminacy in his manner, but he slips only occasionally into the full role for comic effect: 'Ácrata, una es ácrata. Pero también tiene corazón' (174).[15] None of the other characters uses feminine forms to address him in this scene, and there are no sniggering remarks about homosexuality. In contrast to the camp overacting of the scene in the barracks, he is now more restrained, dealing more straightforwardly with the barmaid, the market porters and the other activists, at times deliberately echoing their vocabulary: 'Una tunda, una buena tunda, una panadera, sí señor... pero de chipén, de órdago, de padre y muy señor mío' (176).[16]

Although Lluiset is in charge of a planning a potentially devastating act of terrorism, its seriousness is undermined by the amateurishness of the conspirators, his gestures of frivolity, and moments of slapstick comedy. The bomb produced by the students – apparently a spherical comic-strip device, wrapped in newspaper – is tossed from one character to another until one of the Civil Guards says 'se acabó ya el cachondeo' ('enough pissing about') and throws it out of the window, producing a massive explosion (182). The spectacular battle scene that follows brings the reality of violence closer, as the workers' co-operative is progressively demolished by gunfire and some of the comrades are badly wounded. However, elements of comedy are still noticeable in the slogans shouted by the fighters, the way in which Lluiset turns the gunfight into another camp performance, and the stage direction specifying that an anarchist slogan on the wall reading 'La propiedad es un robo' ('Property is theft') has been partly shot away leaving 'La propi es un robo' ('Tipping is theft') (182).

One element of this scene we are meant to take seriously, though, is Lluiset's genuine concern for the terrified barmaid. She has been introduced in lyrical terms in an earlier stage direction: 'Como flor en el fango, [...] abre la corola de sus dieciséis años como una esperanza de paz y felicidad en el siniestro rostro del surburbio ácrata e industrial' (173).[17] When Lluiset comforts the girl, he seems to see in her a pure representative of the *pueblo*. It is here that he comes closest to articulating a sincere political commitment: 'No tinguis por, nena. ¿Que no veus que lluitem per tú y per las noias com tú? ¿Que no veus que lluitem perque no hagi mes sang, ni mes violacións, ni mes fam? [...] ¿Que no veus, nena, que lluitem perque tots, tots sigueu felisus?' (185).[18] This should be accepted as a genuine, if simplistic, statement of Lluiset's allegiance to the oppressed, of the fact that he repudiates his own class not merely because they are stuffy hypocrites, but because they are responsible for an unjust society that can be changed.

There is a danger that this sense of social commitment may not impress itself with sufficient clarity on the reader or spectator. Lázaro Carreter sees Lluiset as weak and manipulated, simply degenerate: 'Sus vicios, completados con el de la droga, lo han conducido al crimen; y sus amistades lo mezclan en actividades ácratas' (1974: 17).[19] This is to diminish him drastically, in the same way as the accusing journalist's voice of the trial scene dismisses Lluiset as 'voluntariamente cegado por las cadenas del vicio' (*Flor de Otoño* 1979: 188).[20] Reviewers tended to think that Lluiset's motivation was not well conveyed by the 1982 production. Fernández Torres (1983) regrets the psychological superficiality of the character, while López Sancho feels that the play is ultimately reactionary since it suggests that 'todo lo que Lluiset hace de malo y de criminal es porque es homosexual y drogadicto' (1982: 59).[21] A production could, however, convey a greater sense of distance between Lluiset and his degeneracy, suggesting that he deliberately adopts these 'vices' in order to express his rejection of his upbringing and his reidentification with popular culture in all its vulgarity and degradation. García's 2005 production emphasized the deliberateness of Lluiset's involvement in anarchism by showing him as a revolutionary activist right at the beginning.

The trajectory towards seriousness accelerates as the defiant voices of the comrades shouting wildly through the spectacular demolition of the co-operative give way to the sombre, disturbing atmosphere of the 'trial' scene. The stage is mostly in darkness, with menacing hints of shapes, shadows and reflections. The offstage voices are harsh, impersonal and garbled. In the midst of this unsettling gloom and confusion, Lluiset, Ricard and Surroca sit together, impassively enduring the assault of the voices under harsh spotlights. The contrast is a severe jolt. The faces of Lluiset's accusers and judges are never seen: the disembodied voices are totally dehumanized representatives of the Establishment, conducting a form of show trial, a public purging of noxious elements from the body of society. There is an element of caricature in this which verges on absurdity and recalls the grotesqueness of the family meetings earlier in the play, but the starkness of the setting would inhibit any but the blackest sense of comedy here. From amongst the babble of voices of concerned citizens interrupting the official declarations, one voice emerges saying 'tranquilitat i bons aliments' (188) ('tranquillity and good food'), the phrase repeated meaninglessly by the blonde lady during the first family conference: a mischievous touch of parody, and more important, a clear link between these condemnations and the Serracant family. These are the voices of Lluiset's family and class, disowning him and closing ranks in indignant self-defence, now completely dehumanized, existing only as a disembodied discourse of power masquerading as morality.

Throughout this torrent of indignant abuse, the three prisoners sit totally still, oblivious of the rhetoric, beyond caring. The opening stage direction specifies that they should stare straight ahead, and the direction at the end of the scene makes clear that 'siguen desafiando al público a través de su mirada enloquecida' (189).[22] This device forges a direct link between the stage and the auditorium, putting the spectators in the position of the accusers, as suggested by Martín Recuerda (1979: 201). The audience's attitude towards Lluiset is likely to have been ambivalent so far. He has ingratiated himself with us by his vitality and iconoclastic sense of mischief, but his behaviour may be seen by some spectators as distasteful. He can be regarded as a spoilt, irresponsible señorito. Whatever our attitude may be, we are now brought face to face with Lluiset in a direct confrontation that is designed to be an unsettling experience.

The final scene is set in the prison in Montjuïc castle shortly before the inevitable execution. The atmosphere is gloomy, yet Lluiset lights it up with a renewed sense of theatricality and the scene turns out to be an amazing blend of levity, gravity and pathos – quintessential tragicomedy, in which the tragic is painfully funny and the comical is frighteningly serious. The comedy is centred on the frantic efforts of the priest to extract some sign of repentance from the condemned men. Lluiset cannot resist the opportunity for subversive frivolity, undermining the priest's parable of the centurion who cared for his slave with sexual innuendo, facetiousness and an insistence on replying in Catalan to the Castilian-speaking chaplain. Later, at the moment of maximum tension when the first light of dawn begins to seep in and footsteps are heard approaching, Lluiset continues to tease the priest, who makes his final appeal. Not only does he tease him; he begins to feel sorry for him and makes a remark that, although irreverent, is intended to appease his confessor, offering him something that can be interpreted as the sign he is so anxious to see:

> LLUISET – (*Desasiéndose.*) ¡Quina calandria, aquest home! (*Mirando fijamente al sacerdote.*) Si existe Dios, lo veré muy prontito y le saludaré de tu parte, chato… (*Y le da un puñetazo cariñoso en la barriga.*)
> SACERDOTE – (*Radiante.*) ¡Aleluia, aleluia, santo, santo, santo, santo! (192)[23]

Lluiset's clowning is acquiring a tragic dimension. Maintaining his sardonic defiance in the face of death, he still finds it in his heart to humour the tiresome clergyman, allowing him to feel that he has succeeded in saving a soul. Solemnity returns and the tension rises again as the prison commandant arrives and the prisoners are offered the traditional last request, then Lluiset comes up with another astonishing tragicomic gesture: with great aplomb, he asks to be allowed to put on some lipstick (192). This fusion of light and dark tones, with repeated building up and shattering of tension, is powerfully theatrical. Lluiset dominates the scene, turning this terrible moment before death into another performance, another game.

The commandant, after a moment of consternation and embarrassment, prepares to lead the prisoners out to the firing squad, but there is still one major surprise in store. Doña Nuria has been allowed a few minutes to bid her son farewell, and they are left alone with a single silent guard. She is surprisingly calm, having invented the pathetic fiction of Lluiset's voyage to Mexico in a desperate attempt to protect herself from the full emotional impact of what is happening. Lluiset, surprised and moved, plays along with her fantasy. While this conversation and the final monologue teeter on the verge of oversentimentality, they provide a fascinating revelation of the extent of Nuria's understanding of her son and of what he has done.[24] As part of the fiction of the trip to Mexico, she has brought Lluiset a small suitcase containing a few things for the voyage: his pyjamas, cologne, perfume and lipstick. The low-key, almost casual way in which doña Nuria acknowledges the truth suggests that she has known or suspected it for some time. At this point we know that she is consciously acting out a pretence, deliberately deluding herself as a form of self-defence. This forces a reappraisal of all her earlier appearances, reinforcing the suspicion that her 'Benaventine' role playing was as conscious as Ricard's; that she was fighting the battle over the newspaper reports in the knowledge that they were true; that she has been deceiving herself and her family, torn between her social position and her love for her son. Doña Nuria is thus transformed from a shallow, puppet-like caricature into a genuinely tragic figure who sympathizes with Lluiset's rebellion. The emotional impact of these closing moments is highly ambiguous: intense pathos mixed uncomfortably with a hint of comedy. Also perceptible is an assertion of the simple human dignity that tends to be the only positive value to survive disaster in Rodríguez Méndez's theatre. The temptation to regard Nuria as a pitiful, almost contemptible figure is offset by the stage directions indicating that she should display some strength and resolve at the end. When the shots are heard, 'se tambalea' ('she totters'), but then 'se yergue' ('she straightens herself up') (195).

Rodríguez Méndez's determination to avoid simplistic moral categorization of his characters has been most clearly evident in his refusal to idealize the oppressed poor. Although his *pueblo* is not represented entirely favourably, some of the works written before *Flor de Otoño* may be in danger of oversimplifying the negative representation of the oppressors (army officers, landowners, capitalists). *Flor de Otoño* begins by presenting a hostile, dehumanized portrait of the Serracant family – albeit in a parodic, expressionistic manner. By the end, though, this apparently simplistic stereotyping has given way to ambiguity, and the characters of Lluiset and his mother have become increasingly complex. What this reveals is that the system – the economic and political power structures, the social conventions, the ideology – is to be seen as the oppressor, rather than the individuals. Thus, the accusers at the trial have no human identity – they are simply voices articulating a rigid discourse. Those who defend their privileged positions within the system lose their humanity, forcing themselves into grotesque rituals of social conformity and celebrating the empty myth of a free and virtuous society. From the beginning, Lluiset rejects and parodies this pretence through his own pretence; matches their corruption and grotesqueness with his own decadence and absurdity, until the system destroys him. And, ultimately, Nuria too becomes a victim and acknowledges the falseness of her world.

The position of the *pueblo* as more spectator than protagonist in this social drama has been noticeable at various points, and a representative of the ordinary people is present in this final scene: an anonymous sentry stands silently in the corner. He plays no part in the action, but the author does not allow us to forget that he is there: 'Al fondo la silueta del centinela que la mira con los ojos muy abiertos' (195).[25] Although its effect is more or less that of a soliloquy, Nuria's final speech is explicitly directed at him, in Castilian. The drama that revolves round the exceptional personalities of Lluiset and Nuria has, from the beginning, been played out against the background of a real world of everyday work and basic survival – the *intrahistoria* of the mass of the people, with which Rodríguez Méndez's other plays make us familiar.

The sense of community and collective strength that features strongly in the other works is less prominent in this one. The *pueblo*, in this place, at this time (before the popular enthusiasm of the Republic), is represented as fragmented. Most of the ordinary people encountered in this play (policemen, soldiers, nightclub door staff, market porters, a barmaid) are conducting their own small struggles for survival.

They are unobtrusive bystanders who observe the excesses of the gangsters and the bourgeoisie with detachment. The only example of collective action is the battle in the *Cooperativa obrera* – a brave but futile effort. Lluiset is an exceptional, active figure, yet ultimately his impact on history is no more significant than theirs. His dramatic importance lies not in the actions of a 'world-historical individual' but in the acting that subverts an official cultural identity and adopts a popular one – his own distinctive version of the culture of *machismo español*.

The protagonist of *Flor de Otoño*, unlike those of the other plays discussed so far, is based on a real historical figure. At the time of the Madrid premiere in 1982, Rodríguez Méndez explained that he based the character on journalistic sources of the early 1930s:

> Era un personaje del barrio chino, que trabajaba como travestí en un cabaret, con otras estrellas también rutilantes, como 'La Cubanita', 'La Asturianita', y que tenía afinidades anarquistas hasta el punto de participar en el asalto al cuartel de Atarazanas. Pero todo lo demás es invención mía: que fuera abogado laboralista por las mañanas, que perteneciera a la alta burguesía de Barcelona, que tuviera un trágico final (quoted in Pérez Coterillo 1982).[26]

A sample of such source material is reproduced in *Primer Acto* 173 with the text of the play: an article by José María Aguirre, a journalist writing in 1933 about the Barrio Chino and the real-life Flor de Otoño, accompanied by photographs.[27] Aguirre, clearly showing his distaste for the sordid underworld he is exploring, evokes Flor de Otoño's 'afeminadas contorsiones' ('effeminate contortions') in the back room of a notorious Barrio Chino club, and describes him as 'un peligrosísimo individuo, asiduo concurrente a los medios extremistas y pistoleros de acción' (1974: 21).[28] Thus the two dimensions of decadent transvestite and anarchist activist already coexisted in the historical model, to which Rodríguez Méndez adds the crucial link with the bourgeoisie, injecting a powerful dose of sardonic humour that holds the three incarnations of Lluiset together and creating a protean character who can move between the various levels of a volatile, heterogeneous society.

While the colourful figure of Flor de Otoño and the Barrio Chino atmosphere are recreated faithfully in the play, Rodríguez Méndez has made some significant changes to the material taken from Aguirre's account, notably in the time at which the action is set. The indication given in the opening stage direction is unusually precise: 'Nuestra historia empieza en un mes de enero del año de gracia de 1930' (*Flor de Otoño* 1979: 122–23).[29] The dictator Miguel Primo de Rivera was forced to resign on 28 January 1930, and doña Nuria's reference in the first scene of the play to the end of the dictatorship (128) situates the action around the end of that month. The decadent nightlife of Barcelona, on which Aguirre reported in the context of well-meaning efforts by the government of the Republic to clean up areas like the Barrio Chino, is represented by Rodríguez Méndez as a product of the social tensions and cultural hybridity of the 1920s, and as a symbol of the crumbling of the hypocritical bourgeois status quo of the Restoration. The anarchist insurrections which took place in 1932 and 1933 in various parts of Catalonia (including the theft of weapons from the Atarazanas barracks, mentioned by Aguirre) are not only moved back in time in the play so that they are directed against the monarchy and its social structures rather than the Republic, but are also dramatized in such a way as to diminish the scale of the events and present them as relatively improvised and amateurish.[30]

The years of the Republic offer a more complex and ambiguous picture, aspects of which are dramatized in *Historia de unos cuantos*: popular triumph followed by disillusion; conflict between various republican and left-wing factions; the outright opposition of anarchists to the Azaña government; the contradiction of a liberal civilian regime using force against dissent as ruthlessly as the preceding military one. January 1930 provides a clearer, simpler context against which Lluiset's rejection of his upbringing can be played out: the death throes of a social order based on monarchy, tradition, capitalism and military authority. The moral, political and economic corruption of the Establishment is reflected in the underworld that feeds from it, and in Lluiset's deliberate parody. The self-righteous posturing of the ruling groups is shown to be utterly hollow, their social conventions empty rituals disguising ruthless self-interest. Furthermore, the transformation of doña Nuria implies a secret recognition by even the firmest pillars of the regime of the falseness of their world view, and becomes a metaphor for the breakdown of confidence in military and monarchical rule.

The sense of social decay and of the imminence of the collapse of a political regime which is evoked by *Flor de Otoño* was particularly resonant at the time the play was written. In the early 1970s, the regime was entering a phase that Carr describes as 'the agony of Francoism': 'A process of decomposition that seemed to find a parallel in the physical decay of the Caudillo, stricken with Parkinson's disease' (1982: 732–33). Between 1969 and 1973, Admiral Carrero Blanco attempted a return to ideological orthodoxy and authoritarianism after the relative *apertura* (opening-up) of the late 1960s. Student protests, industrial strikes and ETA terrorism escalated, while Basque and Catalan nationalism gained strength. Even the support of the Catholic Church for the regime was gradually draining away. The government responded with states of emergency (in 1969–70 and 1970–71) and military trials. Executions continued right up to the time of the Caudillo's death: the anarchist Salvador Puig Antich in 1974, five Basque nationalists in September 1975. Economic development, the tourist boom and increased contact with Europe were breaking the grip of conservative National-Catholicism on the minds of the people, while the Francoist reactionaries railed from their 'bunker' against the immorality and criminality supposedly encouraged by liberalism.

In view of the attitudes shown by Franco's censors in response to other texts by Rodríguez Méndez, there is no doubt that a number of elements of *Flor de Otoño* would have been judged unacceptable before 1976: the political implications of possible parallels between military regimes, including Nuria's line thanking God for the end of the dictatorship (*Flor de Otoño* 1979: 128); various expressions of support for communism, anarchism and Catalanism; the general mocking of bourgeois family values; the light-hearted treatment of criminality and debauchery; Lluiset's flamboyant homosexuality and his mother's acceptance of it at the end. Unfortunately, however, most of the evidence of the censors' reaction to the work appears to be missing from the files archived at Alcalá. The publication of the work in *Primer Acto* in 1974 (without cuts) was made possible by a brief period of liberalization under Pío Cabanillas as Minister of Information and Tourism, and there are indications in the theatre censorship files that a production was at least provisionally authorized in the same year: 'Calificación de 1974, para mayores de 18 años' ('Approved for audiences over 18 in 1974') is written on the certification documents for the 1982 production (Ministerio de Cultura 1982).[31] It is clear, however, that attempts to stage *Flor de Otoño* in the 1970s were frustrated by the combined effects of censorship, caution on the part of potential producers and the ambitious theatrical demands of the text itself.[32]

There is a censorship file on *Flor de Otoño* in the Alcalá archive, set up in 1974 (number 115–74), but all it contains is a copy of the typescript. Proposed cuts are identified with the marks '< ... >', some of which appear to have been confirmed, since the lines are crossed out, with the word 'Sí' ('Yes') written in the margin, presumably by the secretary of the Junta. The censor wielding a red crayon is concerned about left-wing and separatist political slogans. The three cuts confirmed are: '¡Visca el comunismo llibertari!' (*Flor de Otoño* 1979: 183) and '¡Arriba el comunismo llibertari!' (185), shouted by the militants during the battle in the *cooperativa*; and 'Viva el comunismo libertario' (192), Ricard's last words before the execution.[33] The censor using a blue ballpoint is, more mysteriously, worried by some of the indignant phrases uttered by the disembodied military voice in the trial scene (187–88), but none of these cuts is confirmed. Evidently, an application for authorization was considered in 1974, and if it was initially approved by at least some of the censors, the production in question did not take place. It is likely that other members of the Junta de Censura evaluated the text and found much more to object to than the specific cuts identified above.

Another challenge posed by *Flor de Otoño* to Francoist orthodoxy lies in its Catalan dimension. While it is far from articulating any kind of nationalist manifesto, the play celebrates the cultural richness and cosmopolitanism of Barcelona, and the Catalan language itself, in a way that unavoidably challenges the determined centralism of the regime. The use of Catalan on stage would not in itself have been sufficient cause for censorship in the early 1970s. The absolute prohibition of publications and performances in languages other than Castilian had been eased in 1946, and by the late 1960s permission was frequently being given for theatrical productions in Catalan, albeit mostly non-commercial productions in small venues. What would have caused the censors some concern, however, is the way in which Catalan is conspicuously used by characters in the play as a marker of identity and an expression of opposition to an authoritarian political regime run from Madrid and attempting to impose the use of Castilian. The suppression of Catalan autonomy was one of the primary objectives of both Primo de Rivera's coup of 1923 and the 1936 uprising that brought Franco to power, and both dictators made a determined effort to discourage the use of the Catalan language. By the time Primo's dictatorship collapsed in January 1930, however, the repressive measures introduced against the Catalan language and other cultural activities had provoked widespread resentment: 'Its late phase demonstrated in embryonic form what would be the result of anti-Catalan policies under Franco. [...] With the return of democracy, the language was already experiencing a comeback and the new freedom found a fertile ground for its further diffusion' (Conversi 1997: 37).

The Catalan spoken in the play by both middle-class and working-class characters, as the author makes clear, is not intended to be lexically or syntactically pure:

> Los personajes de *Flor de Otoño* no hablan precisamente en catalán, sino en barcelonés. No hay que confundir esa especie de lunfardo castellano-catalán, con ciertas incrustaciones de 'lingua franca' portuaria que se habla en Barcelona, con la movible e imprecisa lengua catalana. [...] Es un catalán mío (1974a: 16).[34]

Yáñez offers a more precise analysis of the uneven Catalan spoken in this play: 'Un catalán transcrito según su pronunciación y plagado de castellanismos tanto léxicos como sintácticos' (1993: 258).[35] This liminal form of Catalan is mixed in the text with various dialects of Castilian, reflecting the linguistic diversity of a cosmopolitan city home to a growing nationalist movement but at the same time absorbing immigrants from all parts of Spain (the surge of immigration into Catalonia of the late 1920s was repeated on a larger scale in the 1960s).[36] One of the objectives of the play is simply to celebrate this diversity in both periods. Each of the lower-class characters uses his or her patois with pride and relish, brandishing it as a sign of cultural *machismo* in the same way as the characters do in *Bodas que fueron famosas del Pingajo y la Fandanga* or *Historia de unos cuantos*. They enjoy mixing Catalan and Castilian, they savour resonant turns of phrase and delight in ironic shifts of register, as in the response of the policemen to Nuria's protests in the first scene: 'Uno ya tiene el 'cul pelat', que dicen ustedes los catalanes, en estos menesteres, dicho sea con perdón, para sentirse ofendido y elevar un parte por desacato' (*Flor de Otoño* 1979: 129).[37]

The most varied collection of accents is heard in the *Cooperativa obrera*. Ricard begins briefing the four dockers in straightforward Castilian, but elements of other dialects soon intrude:

> RICARD – Se trata de suministrar un correctivo a un tipo, vamos, quiere decirse, de dar una paliza a un gachó.
> CAMÁLIC CATALÁ – Sí, señor, una panadera que diem en catalá...
> CAMÁLIC ANDALUZ – Amoo, una capuana que llaman en mi tierra...
> CAMÁLIC GALLEGO – Una güena soba...
> CAMÁLIC MURCIANO – (*Orondo y efusivo como buen levantino.*) Soba, tunda, zurra, panaera, curra, vaselina... (*Tienen que cortarle los otros.*) (175–76).[38]

Lluiset also uses a vigorous blend of the two languages, sometimes mixing them within the same sentence. His cabaret song and accompanying commentary are principally in Castilian but enlivened by phrases in Catalan. He adapts his speech according to his mood and according to whom he is with: sarcastically lyrical at the barracks, rivalling the colloquial verve of the dockers on the subject of the planned beating.

Castilian is clearly the official language of the regime, used in relations with the police, the Civil Guard, the governor's secretary, the army, and the priest in the prison. However, the Serracant family use Catalan amongst themselves with pride and sing the *Virolai* as a ritual of family solidarity. *Flor de Otoño* shows the Catalan bourgeoisie asserting their Catalan identity (historically bound up, for them, with the protection of the region's prosperity) against both the political centralism of Primo de Rivera's recently departed government and the cultural contamination being brought by immigration. Doña Nuria insists on addressing the Castilian-speaking secretary partly in Catalan, and proudly describes her son as 'un modelo de catalán' (134) ('a model Catalan'). She is surprised at the end of her interview with Ricard that he has spoken Castilian throughout, and one of the uncles complains about the number of undesirable 'murcianus' (a general term embracing immigrants from Murcia and other parts of the south of Spain) flooding into the city and threatening to 'ensorrarnos a tots' (139) ('bring us all down'). Strict linguistic nationalism is the preserve of the middle-class characters in the play, who are in the process of creating their own regional version of the hegemony maintained by central government. The lower classes, on the other hand, show a delight in linguistic flexibility and hybridity which is shared by Lluiset, who tries out various dialectal identities with the same subversive relish as he gains from playing with gender, cultural and class identities. Language is therefore being used as a marker of identity in different ways by various social groups.

By the time this play was staged in 1982 (in Valencia and Madrid), the author considered the new hegemony of official Catalanism as oppressive as the Spanish nationalism of the old regime and the new forms of censorship by means of selective, politically motivated public subsidy as damaging as the old. The linguistic nationalism that has conditioned the cultural policy of the Generalitat de Catalunya since the early 1980s has certainly meant the almost complete exclusion from Barcelona stages of the work of dramatists born or resident in Catalonia but writing in Castilian.[39] Costa's 2003 production of *Flor de Otoño*, which expanded and regularized the text's use of Catalan, made a small but important contribution to counteracting that tendency. Some critics celebrated the show's bilingualism and deplored the fact that it had taken more than thirty years for this emblematic work to be staged in the city in which it is rooted: 'Josep Costa ha corregido la anomalía objetiva que suponía ignorar por tanto tiempo una espléndida tragicomedia genuinamente barcelonesa, con personajes y pasajes vinculados sustancialmente a Barcelona y de la que sus ciudadanos estábamos in albis' (Benach 2003).[40] The celebration of cultural and linguistic diversity in 1930s Barcelona is an integral part of Rodríguez Méndez's general critique of processes of cultural homogenization. Lluiset's sexual and political rebellion is partly an individual gesture but also participates in the wider cultural resistance to ideology of the community surrounding him. García's otherwise excellent production at the Centro Dramático Nacional in 2005 completely devalued this crucial dimension of the play by translating all lines in Catalan into Castilian; the physical setting was still Barcelona but the linguistic environment was drained of authenticity and diversity.[41]

Flor de Otoño is above all a gesture of defiance and a demand for freedom, personal and collective. At the time of the premiere in 1982, the author recognized that individuals now enjoyed greater freedom to give expression to their sexual and social identities, but suggested that the issues raised by *Flor de Otoño* had still not been resolved: 'Las contradicciones del individuo con su entorno en la búsqueda de la libertad son hoy más fáciles de expresar, pero difíciles de vivir' (Rodríguez Méndez quoted in *El País* 1982).[42]

El pájaro solitario (The Solitary Bird)

The three plays that pay homage to writers of the Golden Age (Saint John of the Cross in *El pájaro solitario* and Cervantes in *Literatura española*, followed by *Teresa de Ávila*) trace a geographical, literary and spiritual journey back to the centre – to Castilla, to a key period in the evolution of the Spanish language and a Spanish national culture, and to an ideal of the writer in contact with the common people in a fertile relationship of reciprocal influence. The author's prologue to *Literatura española* reaffirms the centrality of these three writers to his vision of Spanish culture: 'Cervantes, en fin, es – junto con Teresa, con Juan, con Fray Luis, con… – la literatura española. La literatura española del pueblo, la literatura española para el pueblo' (Rodríguez Méndez 1989: 18).[43] All three are presented as rebels in some sense, renouncing social status, resisting ideological conformity, and combining popular and learned elements in their writing. As an antidote to the prevailing *incultura* that neglects or distorts the classics, the canonical status and cultural significance of these writers is reaffirmed. Rodríguez Méndez displays a profound knowledge of and respect for their work. At the same time, though, their legacy is distanced from the conservative national-Catholic tradition and represented as an organic part of popular culture.

There are risks inherent in the use of well-known historical figures, especially iconic ones, as dramatic characters. A workable balance needs to be struck between the demands of the historiographical record, accumulated myth and fictional invention. *El pájaro solitario* minimizes these risks by focusing on a single crucial episode in Juan's life, without exploring its causes or consequences in detail, and by making him a mysterious, reticent character. The emphasis of the play is much more on the effect that the protagonist spontaneously has on the people around him than on his actions or ideas, and he is not presented either as an inspired preacher or as a heroic social reformer. The process leading up to his imprisonment in Toledo in December 1577 could have provided fascinating material for historical drama, tracing the doctrinal and political struggle within the Carmelite order between the Discalced (*descalzos*) reformers and official orthodoxy, with interventions by the king and the Pope. The order's backlash against the dissidents decreed at Piacenza in 1575, challenged by the *descalzos* holding their own unofficial chapter in 1576, giving rise to Juan's first arrest, could similarly have been turned into powerful drama, while the second arrest of 1577 could have featured the invasion of the convent by armed men followed by Juan's astute and spirited defence of the legitimacy of his position.[44] Instead, Rodríguez Méndez's play opens in the monastery at Toledo, with a short introductory scene in which Juan is denounced by Prior Maldonado before being scourged and trampled on by the Calced brothers. His mute humility contrasts starkly with the sneering of the friars and the merciless diatribe of the prior, and the visual impact is vividly envisaged in the stage directions, perhaps reflecting the fact that the play was first produced for television:[45]

> Sombras zurbaranescas levemente traspasadas por lanzas de luz. [...] El frailecillo se baja el hábito y deja desnudas sus esqueléticas espaldas, a la vez se inclina hasta tocar con la frente en el suelo formando un arco con su cuerpo, blanco y lívido entre la luz agria del refectorio (*El pájaro solitario* 1993: 11–13).[46]

The remainder of the first part of the play is set in Juan's cell in the sweltering August days leading up to his escape, many of the details based on the first biography of San Juan, *Historia del Venerable Padre Fray Juan de la Cruz* by Jerónimo de San José (Madrid, 1641).[47] He is shown to be meek, chastened and contemplative, immersed in prayer and in the composition of verses that will become the *Cántico espiritual*. More important than the protagonist himself, however, is the relationship that develops between him and his young jailer, and what is emphasized about the verses is that they are inspired by popular love songs being sung outside in the street (as recounted by Jerónimo de San José). The unnamed jailer, an illiterate lay brother from a peasant family, is initially suspicious, unsure whether to believe that what he has caught the poet writing – the third stanza of the *Cántico espiritual* – is simply a transcription of *coplas de mozo* (popular love songs):

> Buscando mis amores,
> iré por esos montes y riberas,
> ni cogeré las flores,
> ni temeré las fieras,
> y pasaré los fuertes y fronteras (*El pájaro solitario* 1993: 16).[48]

Declaring that he has never been able to memorize verses, the jailer nevertheless makes Juan repeat the lines several times and subjects them to a rudimentary kind of critical analysis or exegesis (in a sense anticipating Juan's own prose commentary on the *Cántico espiritual*), asking why the flowers should not be picked: 'Las flores, que son la presencia de Dios y de la Virgen en el mundo. ¿No habíais de coger?' (17).[49] At the end of the conversation, he discovers to his surprise that he has memorized the complete stanza. Later, sharing his wine with the poet, he quickly learns another stanza: 'En la interior bodega/ de mi amado bebí...' (31–33).[50] The simplicity and intimacy of this response to literature is contrasted with the scholastic aridity of the discussion between the two visiting friars about the nuances of their translation of Saint Anselm. At the end of the first part, when it is discovered that Juan has escaped, the submissive jailer is transformed into a wild-eyed rebel, defying

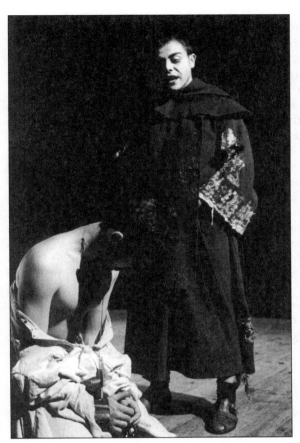

El pájaro solitario, CEU San Pablo (Valencia), 1998. *Photograph courtesy of J.M. Rodríguez Méndez.*

the authorities and bellowing out the poetry he has learnt as if it were a battle cry. The poet draws the language of love from popular culture, infuses it with spirituality and returns it to the *pueblo*, as a result awakening in them a heightened sense of cultural and social awareness.

The other key episode in the first part is Juan's nocturnal vision (or dream) in which Saint Teresa of Ávila urges him to escape. Jerónimo de San José's account of the imprisonment of San Juan includes a vision of the Virgin Mary, who assures him that he will soon leave the prison (Brenan 1973: 33). Rodríguez Méndez turns this into an encounter (fantastical or imagined) with a very down-to-earth Mother Teresa who chides him for his fatalism and tells him to take a more practical approach. It is she who makes the link with Juan's own image of the mystic as a solitary bird perched on a rooftop (anachronistically, since the prose commentary on the *Cántico espiritual* in which the image appears was not written until around 1582), encouraging him to fly out of his prison like the ecstatic soul from the body. As the vision of Teresa fades, the jailer finds Juan reciting lines from the *Cántico* in his sleep, creating the suggestion that his own poetry brought the apparition into being.

Juan does effectively fly out of his prison, like a bird, as the jailer says (*El pájaro solitario* 1993: 43), by leaping out of a window holding onto a rope of knotted sheets, leaving behind what is left of his tattered habit snagged on the bars, and dropping into the river Tajo.[51] The setting and tone of the second part of the play are strikingly different from the lugubriousness of the monastery: in the Plaza de Zocodover, there is a cheerful, noisy bustle as market stalls are dismantled and a motley crowd of traders, tarts, ruffians, vagabonds and servants loiter for a drink and a dance and a song. Some time goes by before Juan reappears, as apparently inconsequential episodes are played out. Cañamar, a ruffian pretending to be a soldier just returned from heroic imperial campaigns, attempts to get away with not paying for generous rounds of drinks, and there is excited talk about the infamous Escarramán, who it is said has recently escaped from prison. When a filthy, dishevelled, naked figure scurries out of the darkness and hides amongst the market produce, the comical expressions of alarm and confusion from the crowd are again drawn out more lengthily than one might think the main dramatic action requires. The point of both the initial scene-setting and the exaggerated reaction to Juan's appearance, though, is to build up a popular cultural and linguistic environment into which the protagonist is thrust, drawing on various literary sources of the period: Cervantes, Quevedo and various popular dramatic and poetic forms (*entremeses*, *jácaras* and *romances*). The references to Escarramán are crucial in cementing the link to the desperate, aggressive but creative form of *machismo español* seen by Rodríguez Méndez as characteristic of the late sixteenth and early seventeenth centuries. As explained in Chapter 2, *Ensayo sobre el machismo español* relates Escarramán and his kind both to the antiheroes of the Picaresque tradition and to the mystic poets, arguing that the most authentic character of the period lay not in the aristocratic and ecclesiastical elites but in the dissidence of these groups, each marginalized but together representative of the people as a whole:

> La realidad estaba en aquel Carmelo, en aquellos sopistas de las universidades, en aquellos pícaros sirviendo a muchos amos y engañándoles a todos, en los corrales de la jacarandina y la gurullada, poblados de mujeres enclaustradas y jaques agresivos. En el pueblo esclavo y obediente sólo por el terror y la desmoralización (Rodríguez Méndez 1971a: 29).[52]

The challenge posed to the empty, baroque discourse of the empire by the mystics lies in the simplicity of their language and their uncompromising dismissal of earthly authority:

> El movimiento místico [...] forma un conglomerado de células vivas, que se oponen fundamentalmente a la retórica oficial, al propugnar un reino celestial frente al imperio terrestre (Rodríguez Méndez 1971a: 27).[53]

The rebellion of Escarramán and his kind is more aggressive and more flamboyant. The roots of their subculture have significant Judaic and Islamic components. They act out a parody of baroque pomposity, including a colourful and elaborate argot that incorporates elements of Arabic, French, Italian and Flemish. These groups form ghettos in the imperial cities with their own dialects, social structures and cultural traditions.

This, then, is the vulgar but vital milieu in which the solitary bird comes to earth. The mock formality of the language used by Cañamar (one of Escarramán's sidekicks) in his attempt to pass himself off as a *miles gloriosus* contrasts comically with the richly colloquial argot of the other characters, full of exotic vocabulary: *garlar* (to chatter), *envesar* (to flog), *rufo* (pimp), *en coritate vivo* (naked), *el Coime de las Clareas* (God), *gurapas* (galleys), *finibusterre* (gallows). At first, Juan's dishevelled appearance, nakedness and silence terrify the crowd, the more superstitious of whom take him for a demon; others wonder if he might be Escarramán himself on the run. The initial response of the rabble to the saint is therefore decidedly unreverential. They warm to him when they discover that he is a fugitive from justice, and the women seem to be impressed by the manly attributes initially thought to be a demonic tail. Moved by Juan's humility and ravaged beauty, the people at the bottom of the social hierarchy take pity on him and save him from arrest: the young jailer from the monastery pretends not to recognize him, and two of the prostitutes drag him through the streets until he is finally taken in by Discalced Carmelite nuns.

As the women struggle to revive the delirious Juan, a miraculous linguistic connection is established, echoing the jailer's absorption of the saint's poetry in the first part of the play. Juan begins to mutter lines from the *Cántico espiritual*, which la Coscolina and la Méndez initially find unintelligible. When la Méndez goes off to seek help from the Carmelites, Coscolina kneels next to Juan and mysteriously, extremely slowly, paraphrases extracts from the *Cántico* (different from the verses mumbled earlier by the poet), speaking the words that the soul addresses to the Beloved: 'Ay, herida me dejaste como el ciervo en el monte, y ya no pienso cosa, no hablo otro lenguaje. Amar es mi ejercicio. [...] Las montañas, los valles nemorosos, las ínsulas extrañas, los ríos sonorosos (76–77).[54] Juan's language of love and self-surrender appears to have been transferred into her by some kind of osmosis, turning her sexual desire into a spiritual awakening: 'Ese lenguaje, ese canto suave del pájaro, transforma el interior de la Coscolina, va llenando el vacío interior de su guardesa, convirtiendo sus palabras en palabras nuevas, liberando' (Muñoz Quirós 1993: xvii).[55] The pure language of mysticism is radically different from the promiscuous argot of the social underworld, but a mysterious connection has been established between them. As before, the poetry that came from the streets is returned to the streets, awakening compassion and self-awareness in those it touches.

Jiménez Sánchez (1998: 150) proposes that *El pájaro solitario* is the first clear sign of an evolution in Rodríguez Méndez's work towards the affirmative representation of Christianity. He recognizes the condemnation in several earlier plays of religious institutions and of the hypocrisy inherent in the alliance of Church and secular power throughout history, but seeks to show that the promotion of general ideas of tolerance, compassion and solidarity becomes associated more and more explicitly with religiosity. He suggests that Rodríguez Méndez has grown closer to the Church, although the recent unpublished autobiographical document that he cites in support of this assertion – an account of an intuition of the existence of God experienced by the playwright in 1955 – adds 'sin que ello supusiera la práctica de la religión católica, que sigo sin practicar aún' (Rodríguez Méndez cited in Jiménez Sánchez 1998: 148).[56] Whatever the truth about the author's personal convictions, Jiménez Sánchez argues that religious belief is expressed directly in plays written since the late 1970s.[57] *El pájaro solitario* is therefore seen as the product of a search for a return to traditional Catholic values and for 'modelos arquetípicos que sirvan de propuesta o de contravisión a la sociedad del bienestar' (1998: 150).[58]

Jiménez Sánchez highlights the implied links in the play between San Juan and Christ and describes the effect he has on Coscolina in terms of a religious conversion: 'En el fondo es un modo de testimonianza de la presencia de Dios en el hombre, que forzosamente irradia a otros' (1998: 155–56).[59] However, this reading ignores both the sexual and social dimensions of the encounter, highlighting only the religious. Coscolina is initially attracted to Juan as a man, for his body and his voice, which is described in a stage direction as soft and deep, 'enormemente viril' (*El pájaro solitario* 1993: 64) ('enormously virile'). La Méndez at first takes Juan to be not Christ but her former lover, Escarramán, and her response to him is earthy and physical. The love expressed by Coscolina through the language of the *Cántico* is both erotic and spiritual. There is little in the text (apart from her absorption of Juan's language) to confirm the notion of her being irradiated by the presence of God, whereas what is clear is that she is inspired, like the jailer earlier, to defy the ecclesiastical authorities in ferocious defence of Juan. The scene ends with her spitting in the prior's face and declaiming more or less the same words from the *Cántico* as those bellowed by the jailer. The ordinary members of the *pueblo* in this play are not merely passive beneficiaries of the saint's special relationship with God; what he receives from them is equally important. What is most significant is not the protagonist's function as an archetypal model of religiosity but his relationship with the people around him: his participation in the culture of *machismo* (which, as always, is defined as much by women as by men). In the final scene of the play, as he recovers in the care of the nuns, he emphasizes both his relationship with God and with the people: 'Es el pueblo el que ha de salvarnos, hijas mías' (79).[60]

Literatura española (Spanish Literature)

If the 'reality' of Spain in the sixteenth and seventeenth centuries lay – according to *Ensayo sobre el machismo español* – in the everyday dissidence of people like Escarramán and the mystics, the literature of the period most highly valued by Rodríguez Méndez is that which responds to the creativity and vitality of these countercultures: 'El realismo de los grandes autores españoles, con Cervantes a la cabeza, es la réplica más hermosa, la contestación más clara a los falsos valores de una época' (1971a: 30).[61] Miguel de Cervantes, therefore, although more integrated than San Juan de la Cruz into the cultural establishment (and ideological state apparatuses) of the time, also represents the ideal of the writer truly in touch with the popular culture surrounding him. While San Juan's poetry responds indirectly to that cultural influence, transforming it *a lo divino* (in a spiritual mode), Cervantes's prose and dramatic works represent and reproduce it more directly: in parts of *Don Quijote* and the *Novelas ejemplares*, and especially in the *entremeses*.[62] In *Literatura española*, Rodríguez Méndez's *homenaje escénico a Cervantes y la lengua española* (dramatic homage to Cervantes and the Spanish language), Cervantes is represented as being in more immediate and regular contact with the everyday life of the people than was the case with San Juan.[63]

Literatura española has a simple structure: an aged Cervantes sits at the window of his house in Madrid observing the little dramas played out around him. Two of the passers-by are other writers: the playwright Lope de Vega is arrogant and pompous, while the poet Luis de Góngora is surprisingly down-to-earth. The rest are fictional characters taken from various works by Cervantes and brought together into a single community around the writer's house, representing various sectors of the *pueblo*. Their stories are interwoven and developed with affectionate wit. Tomás Rodaja, the eponymous protagonist of the story *El licenciado Vidriera*, still suffers from the delusion that he is made of glass, but has found a technical solution to the problem. Thanks to Cervantes's interventions, Preciosilla the gypsy ends up marrying Rinconete (both characters from stories in the *Novelas ejemplares*), who has escaped from the criminal underworld of Sevilla and makes a new life as Agustinillo the water seller – the story as narrated in *La gitanilla* about the little gypsy girl who turns out to be a nobleman's daughter is explained as a fantasy made up to entertain her. Cristinica, the maidservant from the play *La guarda cuidadosa*, is still being fought over by Pasillas the sacristan and the soldier, who is still preventing the lad asking for alms for Señora Santa Lucía's oil lamp from going about his business. There is a wife who entertains a barber and a sacristan in the absence of her husband (as in the play *La cueva de Salamanca*), who is fooled on his premature return by the absurd pretence that the two men are demons haunting his house, although no student is available to perform the exorcism.

As in *Historia de unos cuantos*, the extension of the lives of fictional characters beyond the temporal and spatial bounds of the works in which they first appear has the effect of emphasizing the performative nature of the culture they inhabit, and at the same time suggesting that these figures pre-exist both this text and the original ones – as if Cervantes were drawing his stories and language directly from the community around him, writing about real people whose lives and speech are in turn influenced by his recreation of them. Not only does the writer observe the culture of this community, though: he participates actively in it, helping to create incidents and develop situations that form narrative and dramatic plots. Hearing of the wife's plan to invite the barber and the sacristan to her house, he comments with relish: 'Paréceme que empieza aquí otro buen entremés' (*Literatura española* 1989: 57).[64] It is he who intervenes to save her from the ire of her returning husband, persuading Góngora to act as exorcist and feeding appropriate lines to the various players. He engages the poet's interest by drawing mock-classical literary parallels, but what is important to Cervantes is the spontaneous connection of literature to everyday popular life thanks to the privilege of having 'todo el teatro delante de sus narices' (30) ('the whole theatre right under your nose'), as the character known as 'Santa Lucía' puts it.

In the final scene of the play, Cervantes becomes immersed in a totally unforeseen storyline: as he dozes by his window, someone reaches through the bars and leaves a newborn baby in his lap. This development, based on a situation in one of the lesser-known *novelas ejemplares* (*La señora Cornelia*), serves as a convenient plot device to tie up loose ends – Cervantes helps Preciosa and Rinconete to marry and persuades them to care for the child – and to bring all the characters together in the street for a communal celebration. It is also given an intriguing metafictional significance. Cervantes initially hides the baby in the chest in which he keeps his manuscripts (including the *Novelas ejemplares*), and wonders sardonically if some of the literature might rub off on the child. Rinconete, denying that he and Preciosa are the parents, suggests that the child must have come out of the stones of the city, an idea that appeals to Cervantes: 'La piedra es el padre, la calle es la madre' (81).[65] The child is the offspring of the city itself and of the community inhabiting it: 'El hijo del pueblo. Vuestro hijo, vecinos' (84).[66] Furthermore, since the baby has been linked to the manuscripts, so Cervantes's stories too are the offspring of that city and that *pueblo*. Rodríguez Méndez makes this implication explicit in his prologue: '*Literatura Española* llamo a la comedia. Porque así siento yo a nuestra literatura. Nacida del arroyo, como "el hijo de la piedra", bautizada bajo las estrellas nocturnas por un hombre de bien, cantada y bailada por el barrio o la aldea' (1989: 20).[67] The integration of the writer into the community and into the culture of *machismo español* is emphasized towards the end of the scene by the disappearance of the window grille that separates Cervantes's house from the street, as he joins in the singing and dancing.

However, this is 23 April 1616, the day of Cervantes's death. The fiesta fades, the community and the houses disappear, and he is finally alone in the moonlight, 'con el pie en el estribo' (86) ('with his foot in the stirrup'). Cervantes's most famous characters have so far been absent from Rodríguez Méndez's homage; now Sancho Panza appears and talks to his creator as if he were Don Quijote. Cervantes is absorbed into his own fictional world, wandering off into the early morning mist with Sancho, the intellectual and the man of the *pueblo* forever travelling side by side in conversation: 'Y anímese, mi señor, que aún habemos de alcanzar juntos muchas jornadas y largo habemos de coloquiar en nuestra lengua romance. Vos con vuestra sabiduría y yo con los refranes de mi pueblo' (86–87).[68]

In many ways, *Literatura española* is a relatively unchallenging piece of theatre, with little of the ironic edge or theatrical impact of *Flor de Otoño* or *El pájaro solitario*. The homage to a canonical writer is sincere, even sentimental, and most of the action is little more than a genial reworking of episodes from the *entremeses* and *Novelas ejemplares*. If the text had been written ten years earlier, the Francoist censors would have approved it with enthusiasm, but in 1978 its very traditionalism becomes an anti-Establishment protest against the various social and cultural forces that the author regards as mounting 'una constante, implacable y demoledora ofensiva desde todos los estamentos contra mi lengua y mi literatura' (Rodríguez Méndez 1989: 19).[69] Above all, the play represents his own longing for the kind of integration of literature and popular culture which he attributes to Cervantes – but recognizes as unachievable in the modern world: 'Tal vez no he conseguido lo que también deseaba: que esta *Literatura Española* fuera un poco la expresión de mi dramaturgia, una dramaturgia [...] que ha crecido junto al pueblo que me vio nacer, en la madrileña calle de la Ruda' (1989: 20).[70]

Teresa de Ávila

Another aspect of Rodríguez Méndez's return to the Castilian core of Spanishness was the move from Barcelona to Ávila (in 1978 to El Barco de Ávila, then to the provincial capital in 1980). He immersed himself not only in the work of Cervantes, San Juan de la Cruz and Santa Teresa de Ávila, but also in the traditional folk culture of Castilla. The Grupo de Teatro Barcense de Castilla la Vieja, which he founded in El Barco with Francisco Galán Álvarez and Fidencio Prieto, toured the region (including a Madrid premiere at the Centro Cultural de la Villa in 1979) with *Castilla, pequeño rincón*, a show combining texts by Rodríguez Méndez with poetry from the Golden Age and folk music and dance.[71] The 'oratorio dramático' *Teresa de Ávila*, written in 1981 to mark the fourth centenary of the saint's death, is a homage to the city as well as to Santa Teresa, and was first performed in the Santo Tomás monastery in Ávila by Mari Paz Ballesteros.[72]

The text is composed largely of selections from the saint's own writings (extracts from her autobiography and from *El libro de las Fundaciones*, and the poem 'Vivo sin vivir en mí'), performed as a monologue by a single actress, together with stanzas from the *Cántico espiritual* spoken by an offstage voice supposed to be that of San Juan. The five *momentos* covering Teresa's life from the age of fifteen to her death are linked and briefly contextualized by an offstage or recorded narrative and, at one point, other voices evoking popular controversy in Ávila about Teresa's reforms. Dramatic structure and staging are therefore as simple as possible, designed for performance with minimal resources in churches and similar spaces, and reflecting the traditional form of the oratorio. No scenery is required, and lighting is of crucial importance in evoking settings and moods. All the emphasis is on the solitary, frail but indomitable figure of Teresa and on her voice. The passages selected by Rodríguez Méndez highlight her physical suffering from illness, moments of self-doubt and her struggles against the conservatism of the Calced hierarchy, yet her faith is unshakable and she remains refreshingly candid, plain-speaking and unaffected.

Jiménez Sánchez suggests that in this work Rodríguez Méndez sets out to show a spiritual path based on the development of a personal relationship with God, as part of his growing preoccupation with a search for 'valores tradicionales' ('traditional values') embodied in archetypal models of sanctity (1998: 163). In this case, Jiménez Sánchez's reading is more convincing: *Teresa de Ávila* is a more straightforwardly religious play than *El pájaro solitario*, and its spiritual sincerity is evident. Moreover, the social dimension here is less prominent. Although her role as a dissident is emphasized, Teresa is not shown in direct contact with the people as San Juan is in *El pájaro solitario*, and the kind of connection between reformist mysticism and popular *machismo* proposed by the author in *Ensayo sobre el machismo español* is not made in this work.

What does come across strongly, however, is the simplicity and idiomatic warmth of Teresa's language. Studies of her writings, starting with those written by her contemporaries, have frequently drawn attention to the colloquial quality of her style: 'A light, almost conversational, often elliptic and oral style with great individual syntactic liberties' (Hatzfeld 1969: 23).[73] She writes plainly and candidly about her emotional and spiritual experiences in a way that appears to establish a dialogue with her readers, and it is this communicative directness that puts her on the side of dissident realism in opposition to the hegemonic, mystifying rhetoric of the imperial elite. While Rodríguez Méndez's dramatization finds effective ways of enlivening the recitation of Teresa's texts through movement, changes of mood and direct address to the audience, it does not attempt to obscure their status as written discourse. In the first scene, a subtle distancing device draws attention to the recited nature of the monologue: Teresa pauses, repeats a phrase, then the stage direction indicates that 'vuelve al discurso' (*Teresa de Ávila* 1982: 206) ('she returns to her speech'). During the final scene she reads out letters that she is writing while she seems to hear the voice of San Juan de la Cruz reciting lines from the *Cántico espiritual*. At the end, she stops writing and her account of an experience of mystical ecstasy blends with San Juan's poetry. She dies with his lines on her lips: 'Apártalos, amado,/ que voy de vuelo' (226).[74] Spiritual transcendence is thus generated partly by language – a language that once again represents the ideal of the interconnectedness of popular speech and literature.

Isabelita tiene ángel (Isabelita Touched by an Angel)

If Santa Teresa can to some extent be plausibly represented as a rebel against the imperial-ecclesiastical Establishment, it is less easy to do so in the case of the other great female icon of National-Catholicism, Queen Isabel I *la Católica*.[75] Traditionally associated with strict religious orthodoxy, with the suppression of dissenting voices and with racial intolerance, she would not appear to be a suitable candidate for identification with the culture of popular *machismo* (especially in view of Rodríguez Méndez's sympathetic view of the Islamic and Jewish dimensions of the Iberian cultural heritage). She was a favourite subject of triumphalist historical dramas and films after the civil war, appropriated by the Nationalists as a key component of their mythology of the restoration by force of national and religious unity, her femininity representing a humanization of the virile Crusade by association with the Virgin Mary.[76] Cereceda's textbook on the history of the empire, for example, marvels at the combination in Isabel of astonishing perseverance, untiring dynamism and uncommon valour with 'la ternura, el cariño profundo, la delicadeza exquisita, las dotes todas de corazón y de espíritu, con perfiles que serán siempre el encanto y atractivo mayor de la feminidad' (1940: 34).[77] As in the case of Teresa, Isabel's reputation for resoluteness and independence of mind has also lent itself to reassessments of a more critical kind along feminist lines, as in Concha Romero's plays *Las bodas de una princesa* (1988) and *Juego de reinas* (1990), which represent her as an intelligent, strong-willed woman who challenges patriarchal assumptions and finds her own balance between her personal independence, her responsibilities as queen and her emotional needs.

Originally composed in 1976, *Isabelita tiene ángel* was revised in 1992 for publication in the journal *Estreno* with the subtitle 'Homenaje dramático a Isabel la Católica en el quinto centenario del Descubrimiento' ('Dramatic Homage to Isabel the Catholic on the Fifth Centenary of the Discovery [of America]'). The reference to the quincentenary of 1992 appears, however, to be either opportunistic or ironic, since Isabel's role in making Columbus's voyages possible is dealt with only briefly, and even then in a satirical tone: Isabel refers disparagingly to the explorer and ridicules the idea of sailing westwards to Asia and the possibility of finding the money to fund his absurd plan (*Isabelita tiene ángel* 1994: 23). This is the first of Rodríguez Méndez's plays in which the protagonist is undeniably a 'world-historical individual' directly involved in the major political events of the period, yet it is far from a straightforward celebration either of the queen herself or of what might traditionally be regarded as the glories of her reign. The dramatization focuses insistently on the private point of view and emotional development of a character who is presented as ordinary, down-to-earth and self-effacing, pushed against her will into a decisive role in history. While public events are referred to obliquely, as the product of external pressures Isabel attempts in vain to resist, the dramatic action, set at various moments of her life from the age of sixteen to her death, is predominantly private, consisting mostly of intimate dialogues in which Isabel reveals her thoughts and feelings to an angel.[78]

The figure of the angel is fantastical: he flies, he claims to be a messenger from God, and while Isabel ages his appearance does not change. Yet he is a surprisingly scruffy, worldly angel whose fondness for wine has a deleterious effect on his flying skills, and his relationship with Isabel at times seems more amorous than spiritual. The sixteen-year-old princess waits anxiously for him to come to her bedchamber at night as if he were a lover, singing a traditional *romance de amigo* (love song) and exchanging a kiss with him when he arrives. Once Isabel has dragged the angel in through the window, it is clear that he is tipsy and rather the worse for wear: 'Las alas hermosas pero sucias de barrio y con la punta de una de ellas doblada y medio rota' (11).[79] The ironic representation of the angel as a human, fallible, almost ridiculous figure is built up through comically mundane details (such as Isabel repairing his damaged wing with a needle and thread) and down-to-earth colloquial dialogue. Although the text contains some elements of period language, the conversations between the queen and her angel are conducted in the kind of relaxed, modern popular language used in so many of Rodríguez Méndez's other plays (with elements of Madrid dialect). Certain expressions belong unmistakably to the twentieth century, such as '¡Anda que te ondulen, guapo!' (23) ('Go and get yourself a perm, handsome!'), an exclamation used in *Historia de unos cuantos* as an indicator of slang in vogue in the 1920s and 1930s. Fernández Insuela feels that these conspicuously modern elements are incongruous, arguing that while they may bring Isabel closer to a modern spectator the device risks trivializing the character (1994: 9). Clearly, part of the point of this strategy is to facilitate identification by making both Isabel and the angel ordinary, personable and familiar. However, the deliberate anachronism also has the crucial effect of making the angel's role an extrahistorical (or metahistorical) one: he stands outside the historical process as a commentator, making predictions about what is yet to happen, and enabling Isabel to step momentarily out of her historical role in order to reflect upon it from a subjective point of view.

The angel is therefore not merely a comic device but has an important function in the creation of a sense of historical perspective. While his visits seem to be valued by Isabel as private moments of escape from her responsibilities, he in fact devotes much of his energies to persuading her to face up to those responsibilities and accept what he presents as her historical destiny. In a sense, he represents the voice of official history and political imperatives, speaking the rhetoric of nationalist ideology. It is he who converts Isabel's mystical notion of the thread she is constantly spinning as a link between people's hearts and God into a political symbol: 'El hilo que ha de unir los corazones, las tierras, los reinos, porque así ha de ser para gloria y provecho de...' (*Isabelita tiene ángel* 1994: 13).[80] She cuts him off impatiently: 'No empieces con lo de siempre que no va por ahí la cosa' (13).[81] Horrified at the human cost of the war she has reluctantly waged to secure the throne, she questions the angel's credentials as a divine representative and effectively accuses him of being part of a political conspiracy by vested interests legitimizing itself as God's will. She covers her ears when the angel's rhetoric becomes particularly overheated at the prospect of empire ('la mayor hazaña de la Historia', 23) ('the greatest achievement in History'), and even the ideal of a unified national language is deflated:

> ÁNGEL – Hay que mantener los reinos. Unir las tierras nuevas y las tierras viejas. Y extender esa lengua, nuestra lengua...
> ISABELITA – ¿Qué lengua? (25).[82]

On her deathbed in the final scene, Isabel appears to have come to terms with her place in history, accepting it as God's plan. Yet the newly serious tone does not last. Prompted by the angel, she concludes that it was being surrounded by madmen that made her what she was, which the angel triumphantly declares to be 'el enigma de tu destino' ('the enigma of your destiny'), reassuring her that she has a place in heaven because all the angels are mad too (28). The odd tone of mundane whimsicality that has characterized their whole relationship tips right over into preposterous kitsch at the end, as the angel pulls on Isabel's emblematic thread, she floats across the room towards him, and the two of them soar off into the blue accompanied by the warbling of a celestial choir. It is difficult to imagine all this being played entirely straight, as a serious homage to the heroine of National-Catholicism.

Jiménez Sánchez, however, does take *Isabelita tiene ángel* seriously as another expression of the author's search for national salvation through traditional Catholic values: 'Ahora busca en la historia una figura que represente los grandes valores tradicionales que deben configurar también hoy a nuestro pueblo español' (1998: 159). This critic does not acknowledge the element of comedy in the play and, more alarmingly, appears to be determined to justify the persecution of Muslims and Jews which characterized Isabel's reign (1998: 158). I would not argue that the representation of Isabel is hostile or satirical, or that it questions her religious convictions. She emerges as a sympathetic, well-meaning character, inspiring sympathy as an ordinary person who feels weighed down by a divinely ordained mission yet resigns herself to God's will. However, the quirky, antiheroic character of the text is not consistent with the degree of religious and political seriousness attributed to it by Jiménez Sánchez. What is emphasized is not the evangelizing, nation-building mission in itself but the ordinariness of the person called upon to undertake it and the colloquial, down-to-earth nature of the language she speaks, which links her to San Juan, Cervantes, Santa Teresa and the *pueblo*. The diminutive suffix of 'Isabelita' is not only an indicator of intimacy but also a marker of oral language. Although she is not exactly a representative of popular resistance or *machismo español*, since she is unavoidably part of the Establishment and remains an isolated figure able to talk freely only with her angel, she nevertheless speaks the language of ordinary people and shares their scepticism about ideology and the discourses of power. This is where her dramatic importance – and her significance within the context of Rodríguez Méndez's work as a whole – is primarily situated.

Reconquista (Reconquest)
While the key element of irony may be implicit or partly concealed in *Isabelita tiene ángel*, it thrusts itself into the open in another play about a medieval monarch reluctant to wield power and to conform to religious, cultural and political expectations. *Reconquista*, bearing the subtitle *guiñol histórico* ('historical grand guignol'), is a grotesque satire that hilariously debunks various myths of Spanish nationalism: the forging by Alfonso VI of the core of a Spanish nation centred on Castilla; the Reconquest as a sacred Crusade of Christians united under the banner of St James; the centrality of Catholicism and virility to that struggle and to the formation of a national identity; and the heroic, stoical integrity of El Cid. For once, instead of offering an alternative, popular perspective on the conventional historical record, Rodríguez Méndez subjects it here to blatant caricature. While I have argued, with reference to all the plays except *El círculo de tiza de Cartagena*, against the temptation to make comparisons with Valle-Inclán's theatre, the carnivalesque demythologization carried out in *Reconquista* is clearly reminiscent of the *esperpento*, and now it is the playwright himself who makes the link. The parody is explicitly aimed at the tendency of traditional historiography to transform untidy, anarchic historical reality into ideologically coherent myths, revealing the distortion inherent in the writing of history by means of exaggeration and inversion:

> Pero otras veces el dramaturgo, más que reescribir la Historia lo que hace es presentarla según las fuentes y documentos oficiales, es decir la Historia escrita por los sesudos historiadores, pero con cierto distorsionamiento, después de pasarla por aquel *callejón del gato* de nuestro maestro. Porque también la historia puede manipularse hasta convertirla en un guiñol esperpéntico, o en antruejo de carnestolendas, sin que pierda su carácter histórico. Éste pudiera ser tal vez el caso de mi obra titulada *Reconquista* (Rodríguez Méndez 1999: 42).[83]

Starting from a hagiographical account of the reign of Alfonso VI written in the twelfth century by a monk, and playing it off against a debate between historians over whether Alfonso married his sister Urraca, Rodríguez Méndez sets out to show that 'tras los grandes fastos se encierra siempre la caricatura de ellos' (1999: 43).[84] So the conquering emperor of the chronicle is imagined as effete and indecisive in contrast to 'la varonil Urraca' (1999: 43) ('the manly Urraca'); the Reconquest is represented as an essentially political and economic process masterminded by the Vatican; and the establishment of Santiago de Compostela as a site of pilgrimage is based on a hoax orchestrated by Cluniac monks.

Introduced by a prologue set immediately after the king's death, the nine main scenes of the play focus on decisive moments in his reign: his sister lamenting the division of their father's kingdom;[85] the siege of Zamora;[86] Alfonso's coronation as King of Castilla; the occupation of Toledo;[87] the conquest of Valencia by Rodrigo Díaz de Vivar, *El Cid*;[88] the consolidation of Santiago de Compostela as a major site of pilgrimage; the replacement of Mozarabic liturgy by the Roman forms promoted by Pope Gregory and the order of Cluny; the defeat of Alfonso's army by the *Almorávides*;[89] and finally, the probably apocryphal marriage of Alfonso and Urraca.[90]

Alfonso the Brave's reputation for uniting the Christian kingdoms and leading a phase of decisive advances in the Reconquest is deflated by making the protagonist of *Reconquista* comically unwarlike, completely uninterested in power, sensitive and camp, with a very un-Christian fondness for Islamic culture. It is his ruthless and ambitious sister who has Sancho murdered, drags Alfonso back from exile in Toledo, installs him as King of Castilla, pressures him into taking Toledo, and forces him to sign up to Pope Gregory's reforms and pursue the Crusade against Islam. The culture of the Muslims is generally represented as more civilized, refined and humane than the uncouth, aggressive culture of the Christians. Alfonso wishes he was back in Toledo with his beloved al-Mamún and complains of having to live amongst savages (*Reconquista* 1999: 66). The Cid, one of the key icons of the National-Catholic vision of history, features in the Zamora scene as an arrogant, foul-mouthed bully in charge of a loutish rabble.[91] The Church is ridiculed in a way that would have horrified Franco's censors a few years earlier: the bishop at Zamora (who later becomes the Archbishop of Toledo) is a craven drunkard, the sanctity of pilgrimage to Santiago is trivialized, and Urraca is clearly seen to be using religion purely to further her own political ambitions.

The debunking of the traditional myths of Spanish nationalism is not the only, or even the primary, objective, though. Some of the new ideals of the post-Franco period – integration into Europe and the value of the monarchy as guarantor of national cohesion – are also implicitly subverted. Moreover, at the time the text was written (1981), historiography in Spain was regaining credibility as an objective discipline free from political control. The authority of established historians was being challenged, including that of Menéndez Pidal, whose prestige as the expert on the age of the Cid had been unassailable for decades. During and immediately after the dictatorship, when history was unavoidably distorted by ideology, Rodríguez Méndez had usually dramatized alternative points of view centred on everyday life, rarely resorting to facile parody of well-known events and world-historical characters. Now that professional historians were themselves reclaiming objectivity and historicism and challenging traditional versions, he went against the grain in the opposite direction by writing a play that deals with big public events and prominent personalities but treats them in a cavalier manner and appears to mock the whole notion of historical accuracy.

An element of ironic metahistorical comment is introduced in the opening scene, which sets up a frame conditioning the audience's reception of the remaining scenes.

After an episcopal voice intones an official funeral eulogy to Alfonso in Latin, a Jewish scribe is seen on stage; the scholarly voice that reads out what he is writing – a translation into modern Spanish of the preceding Latin text – gradually sounds more and more like the first voice. The scholarly chronicle of Alfonso's life and reign is thus seen to be merely a reproduction of (or to be displaced by) the official discourse, and the historian becomes indistinguishable from the Church propagandist: a moment later he takes off his cap and dons the mitre and vestments of a Christian priest. Urraca's ghost appears and chides him for not telling the whole story. He has mentioned Alfonso's five wives and two concubines, but not Urraca, who claims to have been the king's first and only true wife. There follows a discussion of what necessarily gets left out of official, written history: she suggests that History could not be written without certain 'olvidos' ('things forgotten'), and they agree that her role will never be written (53). Nevertheless, since Urraca remains on stage at the end of this scene and moves immediately into the monologue set in 1065 after the death of her father, the impression is given that the re-enactment now being presented to the audience is her version. Though she cannot control the official historical record, her spirit presides over the alternative version offered by theatre. She is the dominant figure throughout the play, and in the final scene carries out some obvious reimagining (if not rewriting) of history, insisting to the bewilderment of the archbishop that the disastrous battle of Sagrajas has been a great victory for Castilla and León, to be celebrated by her marriage to her brother.

Along the way, this apparent appropriation of history by the woman marginalized in the official record is matched by a number of blatant liberties taken by the author with the historical record, particularly with respect to the sequence of events dramatized. The date of Alfonso's death, agreed by all sources to be 1109, is given in the eulogies at the beginning of the play as 1147. In the scene showing Alfonso preparing for his coronation as King of Castilla (in 1072) he already has a Burgundian queen, but he did not marry Constanza of Burgundy until 1079. It is made clear in the play that Alfonso and al-Mamún were lovers during the former's exile in Toledo, which is consistent with Rodríguez Méndez's reinterpretation of the king as a sensitive soul rebelling against the aggressively masculine culture of the crusading Christians. The text departs from the historical evidence, however, by having al-Mamún, who died in 1075, still in place as king of Toledo when Alfonso occupies it ten years later, so as to centre the dramatization of the conquest on Alfonso's anguish at being forced to betray his personal promise to a friend (comically contrasted with the cynicism and greed of his troops). The scene immediately following the occupation of Toledo centres on the arrival of Minaya, Rodrigo Díaz's lieutenant, announcing that the Cid has conquered Valencia and offers it as a gift to Alfonso. This is loosely based on episodes in the second *cantar* of the *Poema de mío Cid*, in which after conquering Valencia, the Cid sends Minaya Álvar Fáñez to Alfonso with gifts, as a result of which the king pardons him and agrees to the marriage of his daughters to the *infantes* of Carrión. Rodríguez Méndez's satirical version exaggerates the generosity of the gifts, shifts the focus onto Urraca, and brings forward the Cid's capture of Valencia by several years.

Several scenes of the play deal with religious developments during the reign of Alfonso VI, which are also drastically condensed and simplified. The scene entitled 'El misterio de Roma' ('the mystery of Rome') seems to conflate three separate events: the promotion by Alfonso of Santiago de Compostela as a site of pilgrimage, the original discovery of the apostle's tomb in 813, and the construction of the first basilica in 896. And for good measure, the hermit who has just been visited by the Cid and is fooled by the Burgundian knights into thinking that he has had a vision of Joseph of Arimathea, is identified as Pero Abad, presumably the scribe who was to produce a copy of the *Cantar del Cid* (but not until the fourteenth century!). The careful compromises reached in reality with the Muslim and Mozarabic communities of Toledo, together with the complex negotiations engaged in by Alfonso with the Pope and Cluny regarding the adoption of Roman liturgy and other ecclesiastical matters, are all condensed into a scene in which the king is forced by Urraca to order the destruction of mosques and the prohibition of the Mozarabic liturgy.[92]

As for the marriage between Alfonso and Urraca that brings the play to a climax, the author was probably familiar with an article on the subject published by Menéndez Pidal and Lévi-Provençal in 1948. Reilly is prepared to accept that Alfonso's relationship with his sister was close and that she had some influence at his court, but does not find the evidence of incest convincing:

> A thirteenth-century Muslim source, whose sources in turn have been alleged to be eleventh-century ones, accuses Alfonso of carnal relations with his sister, but Alfonso, as the arch-enemy of Islam, was generally blackened in character by those sources. The thirteenth-century chronicler Gil de Zamora reports the fact, incredible in the strictest sense of that term, that Alfonso actually married Urraca in order to persuade her to surrender Zamora to him in the fall of 1072 (1988: 74).

Rodríguez Méndez is not content merely to pick up this contentious titbit and move it to a later moment. By having Alfonso and Urraca exchange clothes and roles, fulfilling her lifelong fantasy of being king and giving Alfonso his perfect part as her queen, he brings the development of the relationship between these characters to a surprising and suitably bizarre culmination.

Having carefully weighed up all the available evidence, Reilly stresses Alfonso's considerable strategic and political skills and his 'personal preference for the active life of the camp rather than the indulgences of the court' (1988: 369), concluding that 'what matters most is the public record. By any measure of it Alfonso VI of León-Castilla was a great king' (1988: 379). Rodríguez Méndez's esperpentic reinterpretation (turning the 'life of the camp' into a life of camp) transforms Alfonso into a ridiculous figure to some extent, but at the same time makes him a sympathetic dramatic character, thanks to his opposition to the corrupt, ruthless political forces surrounding him and his defence of religious and intercultural tolerance. Liberated from his function as an icon of crusading nationalism, the figure of Alfonso becomes a representative of an alternative Spanish identity that values the cultural hybridity of medieval Iberia and resists the project of ideological and cultural homogenization being imposed at the instigation of Rome. Although he does not have direct contact with the common people as most of the other protagonists discussed in this chapter have been, his resistance to the dominant ideology of his time means that he too can be linked to *machismo español*. Both he and his sister show the talent for colourful, down-to-earth popular language that is essential to the culture of *machismo*. Urraca does so more frequently and more forcefully, but Alfonso occasionally puts on an impressive display to show his frustration at the incompetence and bigotry of his followers: '¡Me cagüen en la madre que os parió a todos ya de una vez...! Que ya me estáis tocando los... [...] ¡Que soy capaz de ir yo por delante y llevar a mi amigo vuestras cabezas después de cocidas y peladas...! ¡Pero coño, ya, coño...!' (*Reconquista* 1999: 73).[93] They collaborate at the end of the play to stage a burlesque wedding ceremony that celebrates their rejection of conformity and mocks the solemnity of Crown and Church.

Soy madrileño: Crónica del tiempo de Luis Candelas (I'm from Madrid: Chronicle of the Life and Times of Luis Candelas)

It is no accident that the title of this *folletín teatral* (dramatic *feuilleton*) sounds like a personal declaration of identity by its author. Written in 1987, it is, like *La Chispa*, a celebratory product of Rodríguez Méndez's return to residence in the heart of Madrid (in 1983) and to his cultural roots in the most *castizo* districts of the capital. Ever since his execution in 1837, Luis Candelas has been the heroic subject of popular legends and songs, novels and plays, films, television series and even a comic strip, all of which identify him closely with Madrid and its folk culture.[94] Theatrical treatments include a *juguete cómico* by Ramón de Valladares (*Por amor y por dinero, o Una aventura de Luis Candelas*, 1849), a *drama histórico* in verse by José Conde (*Luis Candelas, o El bandido popular*, 1893), an *aventura legendario-popular* in verse by José Silva Aramburu (*Luis Candelas*, 1927), and Lauro Olmo's *Luis Candelas: El ladrón de Madrid* (Olmo 1997), written in the same year as *Soy madrileño*. Candelas is one of Spain's archetypal *bandoleros*, a dashing, Robin Hood–like character robbing the rich to give to the poor, famous for the ingenuity of his heists, the generosity with which he distributed his booty amongst his community, and his eschewal of violence. Morales y Marín traces a long tradition of such figures before and after Candelas, all embodying an uneasy mixture of nobility and criminality, popularly regarded as morally superior to the injustice and corruption of the respectable society that condemns them. Candelas's famous last words, as reported in the newspaper *El Español* on the day after his garrotting, lay claim not only to this moral superiority but also to piety and patriotism: 'He sido pecador como hombre, pero nunca se mancharon mis manos con la sangre de mis semejantes. Digo esto, porque me oye el que va a recibirme en sus brazos. Adiós, patria mía, sé feliz' (*Enciclonet* 2004).[95]

These features therefore appear to make Luis Candelas an ideal representative of Rodríguez Méndez's notion of *machismo español*, in the confident, flamboyant mode of Ramón de la Cruz's Manolo. Rooted in a traditional working-class community, he embodies the impudent subversiveness and linguistic flamboyance with which popular culture challenges the corruption, hypocrisy and artificiality of the

Establishment. As in the time of Manolo fifty years earlier, that Establishment is characterized as out of touch with Spanish popular identity: the first scene emphasizes the foreignness of Queen María Cristina (regent after the death of Fernando VII in 1833), while the constitutional concerns of liberal politicians are shown as largely opportunistic and irrelevant to ordinary people. Candelas is therefore presented as the authentic representative of Spanishness; as usual, though, Rodríguez Méndez emphasizes local rather than national patriotism. At the end his Candelas addresses himself not to his *patria* but to Madrid and its people, and is acknowledged by them as their hero:

> CANDELAS – Al fin voy a salir y ver de nuevo [...], aunque sea por última vez, sí, el cielo de mi Madrí, la gente de mi Madrí, las calles hermosas de mi Madrí... (*Vacila, la emoción le vence y acuden los Hermanos de la paz y la caridad.*)
> HERMANO 1° – Y Madrí no te olvidará...
> HERMANO 2° – Tú eres Madrí... (*Soy madrileño* 1998: 172)[96]

The play also exploits other interesting aspects of the part-factual, part-mythical biography of Candelas: his relatively high level of education, his other life posing as a wealthy man about town, and his connections with freemasons and liberal politicians. However, Rodríguez Méndez does not make much of this bourgeois dimension of the character, preferring to emphasize his identification with life in the streets and taverns of Lavapiés and ignoring such details as his government post as a customs officer.[97] The tenth scene, subtitled 'Un hogar burgués de 1830' ('a bourgeois home in 1830'), briefly shows him in an elegant setting playing his role as the nobleman don Luis de Zambrano, but he soon scandalizes his wife by slipping back into more everyday language and behaviour.

The fourteen instalments of the chronicle build up a lively sketch of Candelas and the cultural and political environment surrounding him. The first scene satirizes the queen's infatuation with Agustín Muñoz, the former commander of her guard with whom she has secretly contracted a morganatic marriage; he warns her that she cannot afford to pardon Candelas, since this would lead to the secret of their marriage being made public. Interestingly, Muñoz is presented fairly favourably, as a plain-speaking man of the people who sympathizes with Candelas but is prepared to let him be sacrificed for political expediency. The remaining scenes focus primarily on Candelas himself: in prison confidently awaiting the queen's pardon in response to his letter, then in flashbacks to his wayward childhood, the growth of his reputation as a bandit, his most celebrated robberies and the closing of the police net around him, culminating in a heroic final scene in which he goes nobly to his death amidst the acclamation of the crowd.

The theatrical and thematic weakness of this play, in my view, is that it portrays Luis Candelas too sympathetically and straightforwardly, without the ironies, ambiguities and failings that give Rodríguez Méndez's most interesting protagonists their significance and theatrical impact. Lluiset is an extravagant mixture of bravery, vulnerability, frivolity and sordidness; San Juan's ascetic purity is set off against his grotesque appearance in the square and his intimacy with the women who save him; Queen Isabel is presented as surprisingly down-to-earth and unassuming; King Alfonso is simultaneously ridiculous and appealing. The characterization of Luis Candelas, in contrast, presents no surprises and generates little dramatic tension, constructing a version of *machismo español*, and therefore a vision of the historical moment, that are relatively simplistic and one-sided. At the end of the previous chapter, I suggested – with reference to Hayden White's categories of historical 'emplotment' – that the elements of Romance in *La Chispa* work against the effectiveness of its satirical and tragic dimensions. In *Soy madrileño*, the presence of Romance is made explicit in the choice of period and in the conceit of structuring the work according to a genre appropriate to that period – a sensationalist *folletín*.[98] The doomed figure of Candelas has tragic potential and his relationship to the society in which he lives generates promising satirical material, yet the simplistic idealization of him as a popular hero means that neither of these possibilities is adequately realized and the historical vision lacks depth.

In the plays discussed in this chapter the notion of history as the evolving performance of cultural identity has been given an additional dimension by shifting the focus from communities to prominent individuals. Nevertheless, the emphasis remains essentially the same as in the 'history from below' works. Each of these protagonists is firmly placed within a popular cultural (and especially linguistic) environment, and the primary point of interest of each play is the relationship between the distinctive personality of the individual and the collective identity surrounding him or her. Both the collective and individual performances are characterized by a tension between what is scripted or directed (sedimented cultural patterns and political and economic factors outside the control of the individual) and what is improvised (self-expression and resistance to ideological conformity). The improvisation is never a purely individual act, though: it is rooted in popular cultural traditions and imbued with the collective spirit of *machismo español*.

Notes

1. 'They are individuals who have come to embody their period in a unique way. When you dramatize their lives, you dramatize their period; when you dramatize their period, you gain a better understanding of our time.'
2. 'Lluiset represented the Barcelona that I have known. It has an almost unfathomable mystery about it, a strange and sordid poetry, a hidden rebelliousness, all coming out of the underworld of the docklands, stifled by the weight of a puritanical, insufferable bourgeoisie... I wanted to express this conflict between several warring social classes, which exists in Barcelona in a form that I don't think is found anywhere else in the world: a repugnant bourgeois class, a gentrified proletariat, an emerging class of immigrants from various parts of Spain, and a corrupt criminal class, like in Naples, coexisting with the others and adapting chameleon-like from one period to another.'
3. See Halsey (1980: 38), Martín Recuerda (1979: 186) and Oliva (1978: 111).
4. 'This is the cream of the haute bourgeoisie, as indicated by that white marble fireplace.'
5. 'How can anyone possibly be calling at a respectable home at this hour? At the front door, too, rather than the tradesmen's entrance!'
6. 'Helps the monarch to maintain his composure.'
7. This caricature is reminiscent of Valle-Inclán's parody of Echegaray, especially in *Los cuernos de don Friolera*.

8. Ignacio García's production in 2005 did not bring out this point. Instead of making Lluiset visible at the same time as the family gathering, he was placed in one of the boxes at the side of the stage during the first scene: with his mother on stage, he was shown scattering anarchist leaflets over the audience and shouting revolutionary slogans. This was appropriately metatheatrical, but shifted the focus from Lluiset's relationship with his social context to the more personal one with his mother.

9. Pedro's Olea's film adaptation, *Un hombre llamado Flor de Otoño* (1978), does not take up the cinematic references and changes the emphasis by making Lluiset a transvestite, whose transformation into Flor de Otoño is not a gesture of subversion but an anguished expression of a suppressed 'true' homosexual self.

10. 'The other day they wrapped me up in paper and presented me to His Majesty, who'd sent out for the prettiest flower on the Rambla.'

11. 'That's the kind of man I like... With courage. With what a man's gotta have, like the girl in *La verbena de la Paloma* says.'

12. 'Paris, oh, Paris... But there's nothing quite like Barcelona.'

13. Antonio Díaz Zamora's 1982 production drew spectators into the performance from the moment they entered the theatre, greeting them with 'un ambiente de cabaret de barrio chino, con todos los actores disfrazados de travestis haciendo números de sala de fiestas cutre' (Fernández Torres 1983: 14) ('the atmosphere of a red-light district nightclub, with the whole cast dressed up in drag performing numbers from a tacky cabaret show').

14. A hymn devoted to the Black Madonna of Montserrat, with something of the status of a Catalan nationalist anthem (with words by Jacinto Verdaguer).

15. 'Well, of course I'm an anarchist. But a girl's got a heart too.'

16. 'A thrashing, a real thrashing, a bloody good kicking... So he won't know what's hit him, the mother of all kickings.'

17. 'Like a flower in the mud [...], she opens up the petals of her sixteen years and projects a promise of peace and happiness onto the sinister face of the anarchist, industrial suburb.'

18. 'Don't be afraid, sweetheart. Can't you see we're fighting for you and all the girls like you? So there'll be no more blood and rape and hunger. Can't you see we're fighting so that everyone, *everyone*, can just be happy?'

19. 'His vices, including drug abuse, have led him into crime; and his friendships get him involved in anarchist activities.'

20. 'Voluntarily blinded by the chains of vice.'

21. 'Everything bad and criminal that Lluiset does is caused by his drug addiction and his homosexuality.'

22. 'They continue to challenge the audience with their crazed stare.'

23. 'LLUISET – (*Pulling away.*) What a pain this chap is! (*Staring at the priest.*) If God does exist, I'll be seeing him soon, so I'll say hello from you, shall I, mate? (*And he gives him an affectionate little punch in the belly.*) PRIEST – (*Radiant.*) Hallelujah! Hallelujah! Sanctus, sanctus, sanctus!'

24. According to Rodríguez Méndez, Díaz Zamora's 1982 production succumbed to the temptation of overplaying the pathos of the closing speech, allowing the actress to turn it into a tragic *tour de force* (private conversation, 1986). According to Massip (2003), Costa's 2003 production in Barcelona achieved a better balance, as did García's in 2005 with a very well-judged performance by Jeannine Mestre.

25. 'In the background, the silhouette of the sentry watching her with eyes wide open.'

26. 'He was a well-known figure in the red-light district of Barcelona who worked as a drag artist in a cabaret, alongside other equally sparkling stars such as "La Cubanita" and "La Asturianita", and had anarchist connections to the extent that he took part in the raid on the Atarazanas barracks. But all the rest is my creation: that he was a labour lawyer in the mornings, that he belonged to the haute bourgeoisie of Barcelona, that he came to a tragic end.'

27. This issue of *Primer Acto* contains the first published text of *Flor de Otoño*, together with Aguirre's article and other useful supporting material: biographical notes, 'Conmigo mismo'

by Rodríguez Méndez, 'Sobre *Flor de Otoño*' by Fernando Lázaro Carreter, and an article by Sebastián Gasch on the Barrio Chino.

28. 'An exceedingly dangerous individual, an assiduous companion of extremists and gunmen.'
29. 'Our story begins in January of the year of our Lord 1930.'
30. There were major uprisings in 1930 following the fall of Primo de Rivera, but not in Catalonia. It was not until 1931 that Catalan anarchist organizations gained strength and became dominated by extremists with a violent agenda: see Tuñón de Lara (1981: 127), Carr (1982: 623) and Jutglar (1982b: 139).
31. Three former members of the Junta de Censura – Antonio de Zubiaurre, Padre Jesús Cea and José Luis Guerra – all agreed on a classification of sixteen years in 1982. None offered any comments on the work.
32. See Monleón's lament about the impossibility of either *Flor de Otoño* or Martín Recuerda's *Las arrecogías del beaterio de Santa María Egipcíaca* reaching a stage during the dictatorship (1974a: 78), and press comments at the time of the Madrid premiere about censorship and other difficulties in the past (*El País* 1982 and Millás 1982).
33. 'Long live libertarian communism!'
34. 'The characters in *Flor de Otoño* do not exactly speak Catalan, but rather the language of Barcelona. This mixture of Castilian and Catalan spoken in Barcelona, with elements of a docklands lingua franca stirred in (rather like the *lunfardo* of Buenos Aires), shouldn't be confused with the shifting, imprecise Catalan language. [...] It's my own version of Catalan.'
35. 'A Catalan transcribed according to its pronunciation and infested with Castilianisms in both its lexis and its syntax.'
36. On immigration to Catalonia since the early twentieth century, see Jutglar (1982a: 28-43).
37. 'I've had this kind of pain in the arse often enough [literally, 'my arse shaved, as you Catalans say'], if you'll pardon the expression, so as not to take offence and charge you with disrespect for authority.'
38. 'RICARD – The job's to teach someone a lesson, you know, beat a bloke up. CATALAN DOCKER – Right, boss, we'll give him a kneading, as we say in Catalan... ANDALUSIAN DOCKER – Yeah, a hiding, that's what we call it where I come from... GALICIAN DOCKER – A bloody good drubbing... MURCIAN DOCKER – (*Effusive and grandiloquent, as a man from the east coast should be.*) A drubbing, a thrashing, a whacking, a kneading, a hammering, a whipping... (*The others have to shut him up.*)'
39. This process is comprehensively documented in an unpublished doctoral thesis by Lourdes Orozco (2004).
40. 'Josep Costa has corrected the blatant anomaly of the longstanding neglect of a fine, genuinely Barcelonian tragicomedy with characters and settings unmistakably rooted in Barcelona, of which the citizens of the city were in ignorance.'
41. Olea's film *Un hombre llamado Flor de Otoño* also dispenses with Catalan dialogue and three of the Barcelona settings that have particular significance in the play: the modernist Eixample district, the Atarazanas barracks by the docks, and the bar in the immigrants' suburb of Poble Nou. The result is a disappointing flattening of the complex cultural perspectives explored by Rodríguez Méndez's text.
42. 'The contradictions between individuals and their surroundings which arise in the quest for liberty are easier to express nowadays but still difficult to live with.'
43. 'In the end, Cervantes – together with Teresa, Juan, Fray Luis – is Spanish literature. The literature of the Spanish people, Spanish literature for the people.'
44. A clear account of these events is given in Kavanaugh (1991).
45. According to Jiménez Sánchez (1998: 150), it was first conceived as a film script in 1975. This was adapted for television and shown on Televisión Española 2 in 1976. The text was then revised in the early 1990s for publication as a stage play (1993).
46. 'Shadows reminiscent of a Zurbarán painting, faintly pierced by shafts of light. [...] The humble friar pulls his habit down off his skeletal shoulders and bends over so that his forehead touches the floor, forming an arc with his body, pale and livid in the harsh light of the refectory.'

47. Gerald Brenan reproduces the key details of Jerónimo de San José's account (1973: 29–38).
48. 'Seeking my Love/I will head for the mountains and for watersides,/I will not gather flowers,/nor fear wild beasts;/I will go beyond strong men and frontiers' (Kavanaugh & Rodríguez's translation in Juan de la Cruz 1991).
49. 'Flowers are the presence of God and the Virgin in the world. Shouldn't you pick them?'
50. 'In the inner wine cellar/ I drank of my Beloved' (Juan de la Cruz 1991: stanza 26).
51. Other accounts of the escape are less spectacular. According to Kavanaugh (1991), the saint lowered himself onto the top of a wall and followed it round to where he could climb down into the garden of a neighbouring convent.
52. 'Real life was there amongst the Carmelites, the lower-class students getting through university on charity, the picaresque rogues serving many masters and deceiving all of them, and in the dens of the criminal underworld, inhabited by cloistered women and blustering braggarts. In the ordinary people, enslaved and obedient only out of terror and demoralization.'
53. 'The mystic movement [...] forms a network of live cells which poses a fundamental challenge to official rhetoric by insisting on a celestial kingdom in opposition to the terrestrial empire.'
54. 'Oh, you left me wounded like the stag in the forest, and now I can think no more, I can speak no other language. Love is my only occupation. [...] The mountains, the wooded valleys, the strange islands and sonorous rivers.'
55. 'That language, the soft song of the bird, transforms Coscolina internally, filling the emptiness inside his protector, turning her words into new words, liberating her.'
56. 'Without the experience leading me to the practice of the Catholic religion, which I still do not practise.'
57. The other plays in which Jiménez Sánchez sees this most strongly are *Isabelita tiene ángel* and *Leyenda Áurea* (discussed briefly in the final chapter).
58. 'Archetypal models that can offer an alternative vision to that of the modern welfare state.'
59. 'Fundamentally, it is a way of bearing witness to the presence of God in man, which necessarily radiates out to others.'
60. 'It is the people who shall save us, my daughters.'
61. 'The realism of the great Spanish authors, with Cervantes at their head, is the finest retort, the clearest challenge to the false values of an epoch.'
62. Escarramán himself appears in the *Entremés del rufián viudo llamado Trampagos* by Cervantes. He turns up at Trampagos's wedding celebration, tells a story of service in the galleys and escape from the Turks, hears how he has become a legend in his homeland and performs several sprightly dances.
63. The text was performed in Melilla in 1996 as *Puesto ya el pie en el estribo* (the title of Cervantes's last piece of writing), and published in the *Teatro escogido* (2005) as *El rincón de don Miguelito*.
64. 'I have the feeling that another nice little comedy is getting under way.'
65. 'The stone is the father, the street is the mother.'
66. 'The child of the people. Your child, neighbours.'
67. 'I call the play *Spanish Literature*. Because this is how I feel about our literature. Born in the gutter, like the "child of the stone", baptized under the stars by a good man, sung and danced around the neighbourhood or the village.'
68. 'Come, good master, stir yourself. We've a long way to go together, and a lot of talking to do in this old Romance tongue of ours. You with your wisdom and me with the sayings of my village.'
69. 'Constant, implacable and devastating attacks from all quarters on my language and my literature.'
70. 'Perhaps I haven't achieved another thing that I desired: that this play should be a kind of summing-up of my dramatic work, which [...] has been formed alongside the people amongst whom I was born, in the Calle de la Ruda in Madrid.' When the play was performed in Melilla, the author himself played the role of Cervantes in the final scene, giving him the opportunity to act out his self-identification with his hero.

71. Details are given in a special issue of *El Diario de Ávila* published as part of the Ayuntamiento de Ávila's tribute to the playwright (González 2001).

72. Rodríguez Méndez also collaborated on Josefina Molina's television series based on the life of Santa Teresa.

73. García de la Concha (1978: 91–133) makes clear the extent to which Teresa's 'estilo de ermitaños' ('hermit's style') is a deliberately cultivated literary style rather than the product of naïve spontaneity.

74. 'Withdraw them [your eyes], Beloved,/I am taking flight!'

75. See Graham & Labanyi (1995: 184–85) on Francoist manipulation of both Teresa (the patron saint of the Falange's Sección Femenina) and Isabel as Catholic models of femininity.

76. See my discussion of some representative plays in Perriam et al. (2000: 36–38).

77. 'Tenderness, deep fondness, exquisite delicacy, all gifts of the heart and the spirit, combined in a way that will always constitute the greatest charm and attraction of femininity.'

78. The title is a play on words: *ángel* used with the verb *tener* (to have) means wit or amiability.

79. 'His wings are beautiful but covered in dirt, the tip of one of them bent and almost broken off.'

80. 'The thread that is to unite hearts, lands, kingdoms, because that is how it must be for the greater glory and good of...'

81. 'Don't start all that again. It's nothing to do with it.'

82. 'ANGEL – We must keep the kingdoms together. Unite the new lands with the old. And spread the language, our language. ISABEL – Which language?'

83. 'But on other occasions, rather than rewriting history what the dramatist does is to present it more or less as it appears in official sources and documents – that is, History as written by the wise historians – but with a degree of distortion, having taken it through the Callejón del Gato [Cat Alley, a street in Madrid with distorting mirrors cited by Valle-Inclán as a metaphor for his expressionist approach to theatre, the *esperpento*]. Because history can also be manipulated to the point at which it is turned into an esperpentic *guignol* or carnival show, without losing its historical character. This is perhaps the case with my play *Reconquista*.'

84. 'Caricature always lurks behind the façade of great events.'

85. On the death of Fernando I in 1065, his realms were divided between his sons: León to Alfonso, Castilla to Sancho, and Galicia to García (annexed by Alfonso in 1073). See Reilly (1988) for information on Alfonso's reign.

86. Alfonso was deposed by Sancho in 1072 but, thanks to the intercession of his sister, took refuge with al-Mamún, ruler of Toledo. Sancho was murdered while besieging Zamora, with the result that Alfonso became King of Castilla as well as León.

87. Alfonso exercised control over several of the Muslim *taifas* (kingdoms) in the 1070s and 1080s, and Toledo under al-Mamún was a useful buffer zone. When al-Mamún was succeeded by al-Qadir in 1075, the balance of power maintained by Alfonso broke down and he began to pursue a more aggressive campaign against the *taifas*, culminating in the occupation of Toledo in 1085.

88. After being banished from Castilla by Alfonso in 1081, the Cid operated as a kind of freelance warlord, largely in the service of the Muslim ruler of Zaragoza. He was pardoned by Alfonso in 1086 and carried out expeditions on his behalf, but they fell out again in 1088, by which time he was in control of Valencia.

89. Under pressure from Castilla-León, the *taifas* sought help in 1086 from the North African Mûrabit (*Almorávid*) emir Yusuf ibn-Tashufin, who defeated Alfonso's army at Sagrajas. The *Almorávides* withdrew, but returned in 1088 and again in 1090, when they took control of the whole of Al-Ándalus.

90. Urraca Fernández never married. She lived at the court of Alfonso, where she exercised considerable political influence until her death in 1101. She consistently supported Alfonso in his rivalry with their brothers, and is accused by some sources of ordering the murder of Sancho at Zamora.

91. See Abós Santabárbara (2003: 125–28 and 327–30) on Francoist mythologization of the Cid, who was exalted for his dedication to the project of a united Christian Spain.
92. Alfonso acceded to the implementation of Gregorian reforms, the growth of Cistercian influence and papal control of the appointment of bishops, but resisted Rome's assertion of sovereignty and allowed the Mozarabic community in Toledo to continue to practise its Visigothic forms of Christian ritual.
93. 'For Christ's sake get on with it, you bunch of wankers! Stop messing me about. [...] If you don't get a bloody grip I'll get there first and bring my mate your heads, peeled and stewed! I mean now, damn it, now!'
94. The best-known account of Candelas's exploits is Espina (1929). Films about him were made in 1926, 1936 and 1947. The comic strip *Luis Candelas* by El Cubri appeared in the magazine *Madriz* during the mid-1980s and was published in book form in 2001 (Barcelona: Ponent).
95. 'As a man I have been a sinner, but my hands have never been stained with the blood of my fellow men. I say this because He who is going to receive me in His arms is listening. Farewell, my fatherland, be happy.'
96. 'CANDELAS – At last I'm going to get out and see once more [...], even if it is for the last time, the sky of my Madrid, the people of my Madrid, the beautiful streets of my Madrid... (*He hesitates, is overcome by emotion, and is supported by the monks.*) 1ST BROTHER – And Madrid won't forget you. 2ND BROTHER – You *are* Madrid.'
97. According to Reverte Coma (2003), Candelas's mother found him a respectable job as an 'Agente del Fisco', responsible for combating smuggling.
98. The *folletín* emerged in the 1830s. Originally the term referred to stories published in instalments in newspapers, characterized by 'una intriga emocionante y a veces poco verosímil, pero de gran efecto para lectores ingenuos, en el que se enfrentan personajes perversos y bondadosos, sin apenas elaboración psicológica y artística' (Real Academia Española (1992: 981) ('plots that tend to be exciting and lacking in verisimilitude but appealing to ingenuous readers, in which wicked and virtuous characters are opposed to one another, with very little psychological or stylistic development'). Later it was also applied to theatrical or cinematic works of a similar nature.

6

FADING ECHOES OF THE PAST IN CONTEMPORARY SPAIN

Chapters 3, 4 and 5 have focused on the core of Rodríguez Méndez's theatre, the history plays, in which his vision of the evolution of cultural identities in Spain is dramatized most colourfully and most powerfully. Set in various periods from the Middle Ages to the 1930s, and in various locations around Spain, these texts offer a fascinating variety of approaches to the key challenges of historical theatre identified at the end of Chapter 2: the management of the balance between the coherence of the overall story and the incoherence – or incompleteness – of the succession of events as seen from the particular points of view of characters and spectators; and the tension between a determinist or cyclical view of history and a contingent, changeable, open-ended one. We have seen a constant set of social and cultural preoccupations being reworked in diverse ways: a distrust of all forms of power and promises of progress; a search for versions of collective identity based on the cultural practices of ordinary people rather than on ideology; an unequal clash between official (hegemonic) culture and popular (dissident) culture.

This chapter will take a briefer look at plays that are set at or just before the time in which they were written, representing communities and individuals in the second half of the Franco dictatorship and since 1975. While a sense of historical perspective is discernible in most of these texts, their primary focus is on the representation of social and cultural environments recognizable to contemporary audiences as their own (or at least as existing contemporaneously somewhere contiguous to their own social space). The image of the *pueblo* and the concept of Spanishness that emerge here are much more diffuse, lacking the distinctiveness and dynamism that characterize the dramatization of earlier periods, and this impression corresponds to the analysis presented by Rodríguez Méndez in *Ensayo sobre el machismo español* and other writings, as was noted in Chapter 2. In the essay and the plays with contemporary settings, *machismo español* has been beaten into submission and then seduced by consumerism into conformity, so that the masses are represented as passive recipients of culture rather than active producers of it, and the theatrical forms used to represent them tend to be correspondingly less dynamic.

Última batalla en El Pardo (Last Battle at El Pardo)

The text known originally as *Las veladas del Pardo*, then *Escucha, España* and finally *Última batalla en El Pardo* was completed in 1976 and first staged in 2001. It can certainly be regarded as a history play both in the obvious sense of being set in a period that is past, albeit recently (from the early 1950s to the late 1960s), and in the more analytical sense of constituting an examination of historical processes. Discussion of this play has nevertheless been left until this final chapter for two reasons. The first is that it represents an exception within the author's work in that it focuses exclusively on 'world-historical individuals' whose relationship stands for the significant collision of social forces of their time. The two generals – a *vencedor* (victor) clearly identified as Franco, and a *vencido* (loser) based primarily upon Segismundo Casado, the Republican general who attempted to negotiate with Franco at the end of the civil war – have played crucial roles in national history but are represented as cut off from ordinary people, popular communities and the culture of *machismo español*. While the defeated general wearily recognizes the extinction of his own significance and of the cause he defended, the victor claims to have taken complete control of the historical process. Ultimately, though, both are revealed in the context of Rodríguez Méndez's work as a whole to be irrelevant to the real long-term story of the people and their culture. The second reason is that *Última batalla en El Pardo* serves very effectively as a link between the past explored in the plays analysed so far and the present dramatized in those to be discussed in this chapter. The text consists of a series of dialogues taking place between about 1953 (around the time of the regime's pact with the USA) and 1968 (the year of Casado's death), in which the two protagonists reminisce about the civil war of 1936 to 1939 and reflect on its relevance to the present – as that present becomes successively more remote from the seminal events that defined one man as the victor and the other as the vanquished. The dramatic action therefore goes back to the time at which Rodríguez Méndez was taking his first tentative steps as a dramatist and ends at a point more or less contemporaneous with the composition of the play.

The ailing dictator's declaration in the final scene that he is determined to remain in power could have corresponded to the current political situation for a reader or spectator in the early 1970s, but by the time the text was completed at some point in 1976, it was already history: Franco had died on 20 November 1975, and the king's appointment of Adolfo Suárez as prime minister in July 1976 confirmed that profound political and social change would be unstoppable. Ironically, the play proved at that time to be unacceptable to those who might have staged it because the subject was both too recent (a critical portrait of Franco when his regime was still largely in place) and too remote (an unhelpful preoccupation with the painful memories of the civil war when the nation needed to look to the future): 'Noté a la hora de darlo a leer a la poquísima gente que lo leyó una buena dosis de turbación. Siempre se me decía lo mismo: "Hay que olvidar la Guerra Civil", "Son cosas que están demasiado cerca y aún es pronto", etcétera, etcétera' (Rodríguez Méndez 1991: 24).[1]

When *Última batalla en El Pardo* was finally staged in 2001, memories of the civil war and the dictatorship were still alive and contentious for many people. The premiere in Ávila (as part of the city's homage to the playwright) was held on the day before the twentieth anniversary of the failed military coup of 1981.[2] The attempt by Colonel Tejero and other high-ranking officers to turn back the clock and reimpose military rule was being extensively analysed in the media, and the author, the director, the actors and many of the audience were amongst those recalling where they were on the night of 23 February 1981 and how they had felt at the prospect of a return to dictatorship, repression and possibly even civil war. One of the impressions that emerges most strongly from the play is the arrogance with which the *general vencedor* asserts his God-given right to decide the destiny of the nation, together with his chilling contempt for the masses and for all those whom he regards as weaker than himself, lacking the military virtues of discipline, single-mindedness and ruthlessness. The *tejerazo* of 1981 threatened for a moment to return attitudes such as these to power in Spain.

Effective though *Última batalla en El Pardo* is as a critique of past military hegemony, its importance to audiences in the twenty-first century does not necessarily depend upon an appeal to first-hand memories of the civil war or the events of *23–F*, nor upon an understanding of the ideological legacies of Francoism and republicanism. In his programme note, Rodríguez Méndez characterizes the play in general terms as an unresolved contest between 'el poder sin la gloria y la razón sin la fuerza' ('power without glory and reason without force'), played out through an unequal struggle in a confined space between two men increasingly conscious of their mortality (Rodríguez Méndez 2001). He was delighted to find in Ávila that a preview audience of secondary school students with a very limited knowledge of the historical background responded enthusiastically and intelligently to the dramatic situation and the relationship between the two characters.

Over the course of six encounters in a room in Franco's palace at El Pardo, a fascinating dynamic slowly develops out of the subtle shifts and variations in what is essentially a repetitive structure that might at first sight appear to have limited theatrical potential. On each occasion, the two men meet in a slightly different manner, the stage business focuses on a different prop or sound effect, the conversation develops in a different way, and above all, time has passed.[3] Although the *general vencedor* attempts to immobilize time within the space of the dramatic action, its passing is demonstrated by references to events in the world outside, by the bell of a nearby clock and by the physical aging of the characters. If the victor initially comes across as cold, arrogant and manipulative but slightly ridiculous, while the general who commanded the defence of Madrid for the Republic is more likely to gain the sympathy of the audience as a dignified representative of liberal, humane values, the contrast does not remain so straightforward. The author has described how his sympathies lay initially with the defeated general, whom he imagined as the central character to be developed in contrast with a relatively stylized figure of power, but the personality of the victor, fed by intriguing details of things reported or rumoured to have been said and done by Franco, took over the drama:

> Desde que empecé a escribir el drama la figura de Franco fue imponiéndose, fue arrollándolo todo, como si volviera a ganar otra guerra y decidí que Franco surgiera con todas sus realidades. Sin embargo, en lo que respecta al perdedor, me fue imposible concretarle demasiado y menos darle un vigor que no reclamaba (Rodríguez Méndez 1991: 23).[4]

As the defeated general fades into self-pity, the victor grows into a complex and energetic, if not quite likeable, protagonist. He is repeatedly characterized in stage directions as catlike and predatory despite his plumpness: 'Es gordo. De formas redondas y gatunas, nariz aguileña y ojos vivarachos. Entra casi de un salto, como el gato que se lanza contra el ratón. Lleva la gorra en la mano y se mueve con una enorme soltura' (*Última batalla en El Pardo* 1991: 31–32).[5] Even in scene 5, when the dictator is around seventy years of age, he still hops about like a bird and twirls like a ballerina (78–79), wearing down the morale of his decrepit opponent by his physical energy as much as by his unanswerable assertion of martial and moral superiority, relishing the opportunities he awards himself of toying with his prey. He turns his own longevity into the ultimate proof of the legitimacy and permanence of the victory that is as much his own as it is that of his political class, and equates the other man's exhaustion and defeatism with the definitive obliteration of the values he once defended. He has even been fantasizing about the possibility of cryogenics allowing him the ultimate victory of returning rejuvenated to power after a period of hibernation. In the final scene, the *general vencido* has died and the *vencedor* cannot resist the temptation to have the last word in a simulated telephone conversation (recalling once again the moment at which the defeated general surrendered Madrid by telephone at the end of the war): while the deceased always displayed an 'espíritu meramente defensivo' ('a purely defensive spirit'), the victor declares that 'la rendición nunca entró en mis planes de campaña' (94) ('surrender was never part of my plan of campaign').

History is therefore represented in this play not as the lived experience of ordinary people but as an ideological weapon appropriated and manipulated by a powerful individual as part of a military strategy of 'aprovechamiento de la victoria' (Rodríguez Méndez 1991: 22–23) ('exploitation of victory'). The dictator, not content with absolute political power, aspires to control not only the present but also the past by imposing and constantly re-enacting his version of history (and, more fancifully, the future, by living for ever): 'Si pudiera uno, de la misma manera que dirigir los ejércitos encauzar la Historia y aún reparar sus errores pasados. Algo he hecho yo sobre eso, pero desgraciadamente la Historia, muchas veces, va por caminos diversos' (*Última batalla en El Pardo* 1991: 60).[6] He acknowledges that he cannot convince everyone and that some historians are outside his control: he refers resentfully to 'errors' propagated by an English writer in the pay of Freemasonry (88), presumably a reference to Hugh Thomas's *The Spanish Civil War*, first published in 1961. The defeated general's own half-hearted attempts to contest the victor's hegemony on the grounds of rationality and human rights are brushed aside.

Instead of the spontaneous, evolving collective performance of cultural identity evoked in Rodríguez Méndez's other history plays, therefore, this text comprises a very different kind of performance. In a closed, claustrophobic space constructed by the dictator as a refuge from public life and a nostalgic recreation of the simpler life of wartime, he directs and stars in private re-enactments of a history immobilized into mythology, obliging the reluctant loser to relive the battle for Madrid, the surrender by telephone and the humiliation of defeat. He reveals near the end that he has recorded their conversations, so that he can replay them endlessly even when his antagonist has left the stage for ever. Although each of the participants in this sterile, repetitive performance claims to stand for a set of shared values and a version of national identity, neither of them represents a collective cultural identity in the complex, creative, subversive way exemplified by the *machismo español* of Pingajo, Lluiset, Mari Pepa, Pichi, San Juan de la Cruz and Alfonso VI.

The *general vencedor* controls the dramatic space and the performance carried out within it, and easily wins his personal contest against his antagonist. However, the audience's perception of him is coloured by increasing signs of fanaticism, fallibility and gullibility. He appears to believe that he is assisted by both divine and demonic powers (*Última batalla en El Pardo* 1991: 66–71); he breaks into a hysterical rant about communist and masonic conspiracies (74); he has been led to believe reports of the invention of a motor run on water (82) and of the mass conversion of Japan to Christianity (81); and, having declared his enthusiasm for cutting-edge technology, he fumbles ineptly with a simple tape recorder (89–90). Above all, the spectator's or reader's historical and cultural knowledge generates dramatic irony: the dictator was soon incapacitated by Parkinson's disease and died as his regime crumbled in the face of overwhelming evidence that he had not won the hearts and minds of the Spanish people. The reconstructed wartime bunker in which *Última batalla en El Pardo* takes place recalls the metaphorical *búnker* of reactionary authoritarianism into which the Franco regime was frequently described as retreating in its final years. Outside it, though, alternative visions of the past and the present were already being narrated, debated, dramatized and negotiated. The victorious general's discourse is contested not just by the passage of time but by the perspectives created by Rodríguez Méndez's other works.

Contemporary Spain: the decline of *machismo español*

As in his historical theatre, Rodríguez Méndez's primary focus in plays with contemporary settings is on everyday life outside the refuges constructed for themselves by the powerful. Between the mid-1950s and the early 1990s, texts set in the present explore the same fundamental concerns we have identified in the history plays, but now *machismo* is a spent force. As noted in Chapter 2, Rodríguez Méndez's *Ensayo sobre el machismo español* describes the final disintegration of the cultural energy and sense of community that were still alive before the civil war. Under first the pressures of authoritarianism and austerity, then the homogenizing influence of industrialization and globalization, Rodríguez Méndez sees the Spanish people becoming merely a 'masa consumidora' (1971a: 166) ('a consuming mass'). Communities are represented in these plays as fragmented and lacking cultural

Los inocentes de la Moncloa, Teatro Cómico (Madrid), January 1964. *Photograph by Manuel Martínez Muñoz.*

creativity, and individuals as isolated and alienated; the spirit of rebellion that used to grow from communal identities is defused and dissipated.

Rodríguez Méndez's first play, *El milagro del pan y de los peces* (*The Miracle of the Loaves and the Fishes*, written in 1953 and first staged in 1960) matches the claustrophobic intensity and suppressed violence of the *Huis-clos* plays discussed in Chapter 3. The set – a convent used as a women's prison – and dramatic structure – a tense build-up to a revolt provoked by a shortage of food – clearly suggest the repressiveness, economic austerity and ideological confinement of post-war Spain. The all-female cast consists of the nuns who have been turned into jailers, seeing their traditional culture of asceticism and obedience degraded into an oppressive penal regime, while being denied the resources to carry out the task properly. Although it is not clear whether the women in their charge are political prisoners, one of the nuns compares them to the mob that attacked the convent during the war and remarks that 'estamos en una época en que las cárceles se pueblan' (*El milagro del pan y de los peces* 1953: 9–10).[7] The drama focuses not on the plight of the inmates themselves, who can only be heard offstage protesting and rioting, but on the conflict between two factions amongst the nuns: one (led by the pragmatic Mother Superior) determined to maintain order and the other (led by the brooding, ambitious Dulce Nombre) prepared to provoke chaos in the name of liberty. What is on one level a theological debate and spiritual crisis is also a fascinating political struggle between the authoritarian but ultimately humane Mother Superior and the apparently mystical Dulce Nombre, who turns out to be cynically manipulative. Like *En las esquinas, banderas*, this play focuses on women under pressure within a confined space, forced into conflict with one another by political and natural forces beyond their control. However, the preoccupation with colloquial language and popular cultural identities that was to become the defining characteristic of Rodríguez Méndez's work is not yet evident here. These women tear one another apart in an atmosphere of gloom and fatalism, speaking a hard-edged, starkly poetic language with none of the colloquial exuberance of the speech of the popular characters seen in other plays. There is no rebellion like that of Verónica and Micaela in the civil war play, and the *pueblo* that might have played such a role is significantly kept out of sight.

The plays written by Rodríguez Méndez in the early 1960s for La Pipironda are less emotionally intense than *El milagro del pan y de los peces*, since they were designed for performance in relatively informal circumstances, using simple resources and unconventional venues in working-class suburbs of Barcelona. Most of these pieces are short, with contemporary working-class settings. *La tabernera y las tinajas* (*The Tavern Landlady and the Earthernware Jars*), also known as *Auto de la donosa tabernera* (written in 1959 and first performed in 1960), is set in the present, in a village in the south or east of Spain. However, apart from a few references to football, the action of this light-hearted traditional farce might just as well take place in any period in the last two hundred years or so. In its satire of the local oligarchy (the mayor, the secretary of the town council and the wealthy landowner) in contrast with the down-to-earth honesty of the *tabernera*, it anticipates *El círculo de tiza de Cartagena* in a highly simplified form, without the political complications and ambiguities of the later play. The *tabernera*'s exposure of the hypocrisy of the powerful links her to Rosita from *El círculo de tiza de Cartagena* and to the strong, long-suffering women who make up the heart and soul of *machismo* in other history plays. Thanks in part to its political and moral innocuousness (and the positive representation of the priest), *La tabernera y las tinajas* was Rodríguez Méndez's most frequently performed text in the 1960s and 1970s; but even so, an age limit of eighteen was imposed by the censors as late as 1974. The only significant concern expressed by a censor was a warning that 'debe cuidarse en la escena final no confunda la actitud del sacerdote' (Ministerio de Información y Turismo 1971b).[8]

In parallel with his work for La Pipironda, Rodríguez Méndez achieved his first major success with *Los inocentes de la Moncloa* (*The Innocents of La Moncloa*, written in 1960 and first performed in Barcelona in 1961). The production in Madrid in 1964 was enthusiastically received by predominantly young audiences who identified strongly with the frustration of the characters undergoing the demoralizing tribulation of *oposiciones* (examinations for entry to public service), based on the author's own experiences a few years earlier, and listened eagerly for hints of political dissidence in the dialogue.[9] However, although the characters express bitter dissatisfaction with the society in which they live, the play deliberately disappoints any expectations of a decisive political statement. Prompted by the plight of the nameless, undernourished young man from Córdoba who dies in the third act, its principal characters edge towards an articulation of social consciousness and rebellion, but this quickly fades into fatalistic passivity and they make the compromises that allow them to be absorbed into the system:

> Tienen que pasar estas cosas..., ¿comprendes? Estas pequeñas cosas, para que nos demos cuenta de algo. De que somos unos pobres inocentes que no saben dónde van; de que hay un destino negro por delante... Pero no te preocupes. Mañana habrá pasado. Y nos olvidaremos también de esto (*Los inocentes de la Moncloa* 1968: 168).[10]

Ricardo Doménech objects that the work presents an incomplete picture, since 'para ser absolutamente real, debería haber en ella, cuando menos, un personaje universitario que tomase clara conciencia de la situación y, consecuentemente, se rebelase contra ella' (1962: 48).[11] Doménech appears to be missing the point, though, which is that the rebelliousness has been drained out of this generation. The main character, José Luis, is concerned only with getting through his exam; the women express strong empathy for the destitute student from Córdoba and others like him but feel completely powerless. Paco Ruiz is the most politically aware but resigns himself to making sardonic, fatalistic pronouncements: 'Morirse a los veinte años. Eso es ganar una oposición' (*Los inocentes de la Moncloa* 1968: 175).[12] Unlike the middle-class intellectuals who appear in some of the history plays (*El círculo de tiza de Cartagena*, *El vano ayer* and *Flor de Otoño*), these young people lack passion and commitment to action, and have no real contact with the *pueblo* (here represented only fleetingly by the young man from Córdoba).

As a result of the way in which the characters' frustration and anger are dissipated, the text was approved relatively easily by the censors. José María Cano's report in 1961 notes the occasional politically charged reference in the text but decides that 'todo concluye con un gesto optimista, con reacciones de juventud esperanzada' (Ministerio de Información y Turismo 1961),[13] playing down the sense of hopelessness that remains in the air despite the protagonist's success in his examination. The 1961 production was approved for audiences over the age of eighteen, with eight lines cut and two altered. A few of these changes are provoked by indecorous language, while others are for political reasons: Ana Mari's bitter remark about 'sufriendo como la mayoría de los españoles' (*Los inocentes de la Moncloa* 1968: 147) ('suffering like the majority of Spaniards'); Paco's excitement at a character known as Trotsky having been to Moscow (159–60); and Paco's comment about 'un destino negro por delante' (168) ('a dark future ahead of us'), which was changed to 'una vida negra' ('a dark life'). In the early 1960s, official propaganda was increasingly directed towards the celebration of Francoism's achievements in maintaining peace and building prosperity, and gloomy remarks such as these were considered to project an unacceptably negative view of the prospects on offer to the young people who were supposed to be benefiting from those achievements.

La vendimia de Francia (*French Harvest*, written in 1961 and first performed in 1964) shifts the focus from disaffected middle-class youth in an urban setting to a much grittier working-class milieu – a group of migrant workers alleviating the hardship of rural life in Spain by working as grape pickers in southern France. There are historical echoes in the situation, since the two main male characters (González and Márquez) were amongst the Republican refugees who fled across the border into France in early 1939 ahead of the Nationalist invasion of Catalonia and were in many cases received with hostility and treated harshly in internment camps.[14] Returning some twenty years later with his wife, Candelas, González now focuses on Márquez (who remained in France) all the resentment generated by these experiences and by the hardship he has suffered while life in exile has turned out to be easier. The contempt he shows for Márquez as a coward and a 'franchute' ('Frenchy') is mixed with envy; the chauvinistic patriotism he repeatedly declares is undermined by his own recognition of the harshness of conditions in Spain and by the exiles' determination not to return. At the end, humiliated by his wife's affair with Márquez and the failure of his attempt to exact revenge, he is a broken man limping home without pride and without hope: '¿Por qué he tenido que caer de rodillas lleno de sangre? Otra vez más... Y siempre de rodillas' (*La vendimia de Francia* 1961: 40).[15] Up to this point, and especially when he is drunk, González has displayed a particularly aggressive, authoritarian and intolerant brand of *machismo*, which he associates with his identity as a working-class Spaniard (in contrast with the supposedly effeminate French). In this desperate, bullying *chulería* there is none of the charm, creativity or social rebelliousness of the various versions of *machismo español* that emerge from the history plays, and even the women in this case seem to lack the courage and resilience of their predecessors. Candelas is left weeping and begging her departing companions not to leave her there. The bitterness of the ending is underlined by the sinister old French beggar woman muttering 'l'Espagne...' and spitting contemptuously.

The censors do not seem to have been worried about this play casting an unfavourable light on social conditions in Spain. A report written in 1967 by Florencio Martínez Ruiz regards the play as having little relevance to contemporary circumstances: 'Quiere ser una denuncia de la España topiquera, pobre y violenta. El recuerdo de postguerra es mínimo y pueden pasar algunos matices intencionados. La obra es ya vieja y no puede suponer problema' (Ministerio de Información y Turismo 1967).[16] The production was authorized for audiences over eighteen years of age, with an instruction to local officials that they should conduct a careful inspection of the dress rehearsal paying attention to possible implications of both a political and an 'erotic' nature (Ministerio de Información y Turismo 1967). Only one cut was imposed: an ambiguous line in which González, who has been drunkenly shouting '¡Viva España!', muddles his words and comes out with '¡Viva Fran... digo, ¡viva España y muera ...!' (*La vendimia de Francia* 1961: 26) ('Long live Fran... I mean, long live Spain and death to...!')[17]

In the meantime, pieces written for La Pipironda explored the suburban working-class environments familiar to the audiences that the group was aiming to reach.

While containing some elements of comedy, they show communities in the process of disintegration and the spirit of *machismo* ground down by the economic and ideological pressures of industrialization and an authoritarian state. The most substantial of these works, *La batalla del Verdún* (*The Battle of El Verdún*, written in 1961 and first performed in 1965) is the first of Rodríguez Méndez's works to be set in Barcelona. El Verdún (or Verdum, in the district now known as Nou Barris) is a working-class quarter in the northern suburbs overlooking the city centre and the sea, developed from the early 1950s primarily for migrant workers from other parts of Spain, especially Andalucía. As the author explains in his introduction to the edition of the play, 'lo de la "batalla del Verdún" es una pobre ironía alusiva a la batalla diaria de estas gentes por salir adelante, a base de destajos, horas extras y chapuzas' (Rodríguez Méndez 1966: 9).[18] Predecessors of these 'other Catalans' feature amongst the secondary characters of *Flor de Otoño*, mixing in the centre of the city with the Catalan bourgeoisie, but here the focus is limited to an uprooted, alienated Andalusian community on the periphery. While there are still signs of the linguistic verve and community spirit of the groups portrayed in the history plays, the mood is more subdued and the collective identity that emerges is rootless and fragmented, lacking cultural distinctiveness.

The characters of *La batalla del Verdún*, crammed into overcrowded housing, either worn out by long days at work, frustrated by the search for work, or bored by aimless idleness, spend much of the time bickering pointlessly. The young despise the nostalgia felt by the old for their place of origin, but have no real sense of belonging in their adopted city; some escape abroad, while others dream of taking possession of Barcelona: 'Sí que bajaremos un día a la ciudad... La conquistaremos, la llevaremos nuestra alegría' (*La batalla del Verdún* 1966: 48).[19] The men cling to notions of patriarchal authority no longer validated by the customs and working patterns of traditional community life, while the aspirations of their long-suffering wives are more and more circumscribed by the ideal of the self-contained nuclear family. Andrés and Carmela, the couple newly arrived in the city at the beginning of the play, have by the end achieved a degree of prosperity, yet he works twelve hours a day and she complains that she is 'entre paredes todo el día. En el pueblo, mujer, era otra cosa... Salías a la puerta, charlabas con una y con otra... qué sé yo... aquí se aburre una' (53).[20] Although the material conditions of life are improving to some extent, the fight has clearly been knocked out of the *pueblo* and their sense of community is fading.

Since it can be read as an unproblematic, largely apolitical portrait of working-class people getting by thanks to hard work and humility, presented in a conventional dramatic form, *La batalla del Verdún* caused the Junta de Censura Teatral no concern. There is no record in the censorship files of an application for approval of the 1965 production, but the 1966 edition was quickly approved without cuts. José María Zárate's report sees the text as entirely harmless: 'Lo principal en él, como sainete, es la pintura de tipos, situaciones y ambiente, de gran realismo y colorido. [...] Nada que ataque a la moral o al régimen' (Ministerio de Información y Turismo 1965).[21]

In contrast, the next play dealing with the lives of working families in the new capitalist economy was judged to be politically and socially problematic. Although La Pipironda was allowed to perform *El ghetto, o la irresistible ascensión de Manuel Contreras* (*The Ghetto, or the Irresistible Rise of Manuel Contreras*, written in 1964) in Barcelona in 1966, an application for an amateur production in Barcelona in 1972 was turned down. The play is set 'en España y en plena época de desarrollo' (*El ghetto* 1964: title page) ('in Spain, with economic development in full swing'), in a new housing estate built on the outskirts of a large city by an international manufacturing company to house its workers, who are delighted by the material comforts and modern conveniences that industrialization has brought them. However, they are drawn into new forms of solitude, servitude and alienation, since they are cut off from the solidarity of traditional community life and find that the company demands absolute loyalty.[22] Material conditions for these labourers and their families are massively different from those endured by the characters of *La Mano Negra* fifty years earlier, yet they are tied into very similar structures of corruption and subservience. The action centres on the dilemma of Manuel, an honest worker who on being appointed as a union official is persuaded to collaborate with the unfair dismissal of two politically suspect (but otherwise blameless) employees, and on his wife Marisa's growing awareness of the moral price they are paying for prosperity. Towards the end, she remarks: 'Si es que una vive vendida, vendida vive una en estos sitios' (36).[23] While the men still convince themselves that they share a kind of working-class camaraderie, it is the women who see most keenly what has been lost.

The only trade union structure permitted by the Franco regime was the official Organización Sindical developed and run by the Falange, which claimed to bring employers and employees harmoniously together in *sindicatos verticales* in the service of the state, rather than acting as vehicles for collective negotiation and 'horizontal' solidarity between workers.[24] By the time of the application for approval of a performance of *El ghetto* in 1972, the role of the unions had become a politically sensitive one for the regime: in an attempt to regain control in the face of increasing infiltration of the Organización Sindical by the Communist-led Comisiones Obreras, the Ley Sindical (Trade Union Law) of 1971 had given the official unions a slightly more meaningful role in defending the interests of workers. The censors' reports clearly indicate that the problem now posed by the text is its inconvenient reminder of the coercive function of the *sindicatos verticales* at a time when they are supposedly acquiring a more democratic status. Sebastián Bautista de la Torre's report is the most specific:

> La intención crítica del autor pudiera admitirse si el tono del enfrentamiento se redujera al concepto estricto patrono-obrero, y a sus respectivas reivindicaciones; pero al dar entrada al complejo sindical y sus consiguientes derivaciones oficiales, el tema toma un cariz de acusaciones muy definidas y concretas que resultan muy delicadas en nuestro contexto actual (Ministerio de Información y Turismo 1972).[25]

Having returned to his cultural roots and injected new energy into his work with *Bodas que fueron famosas del Pingajo y la Fandanga* in 1965, Rodríguez Méndez used a similar setting and an even more flexible dramatic structure in *Los quinquis de Madriz* (*Down and Out in Madrid*, written in 1967). The world of the exotic lumpenproletariat of Madrid in 1898 has turned into the shanty towns sprawling around the edges of industrial Madrid in 1967. Just as the period of the earlier play is evoked through its structuring in picturesque *estampas* and its references to the *género chico*, so this text, subtitled 'reportaje dramático en diez momentos' ('dramatic news report in ten moments'), refers to modern mass culture by means of techniques that suggest the visual language and narrative structures of film and television (swift cuts between acting spaces on different parts of the stage, sound effects offstage, and a series of flashbacks in *momentos* 8 and 9), together with references to photography and recorded popular music on a juke box.[26] The characters, all known by nicknames, living in *chabolas* (shacks) and drinking in scruffy bars in Vallecas, are reminiscent of the marginalized community of *Bodas*: Trueno, like Pingajo, a delinquent recently returned from military service overseas and hoping to make easy money; Lurdes, the girlfriend with pretensions to respectability; Tranvi, Chungui and Caribe, Trueno's drinking companions and partners in crime; and Puma and Chato, two thugs turned policemen, more vicious and considerably less amusing than the lieutenant in *Bodas*.[27] Their language is as distinctively colloquial and colourful as that of the characters in *Bodas*, if not quite so rich in metaphor: 'Me enchufé en automovilismo y me pulía la gasolina a base de bien. [...] ¡Menúo macho está hecho! Ni reaños tie el gachó. [...] ¡Qué tío, la mare que lo echó!' (*Los quinquis de Madriz* 1982: 61–63).[28] There are still echoes of the arrogant, flamboyant *majeza* of Manolo and his kind, but they are even fainter now than they were in 1898.

The *machismo* performed by Trueno and his friends in the 1960s is represented as having been degraded by the homogenizing effect of consumerism and by the increasingly efficient penetration of the mechanisms of economic and ideological control into every corner of social existence. Trueno makes no significant rebellion against the hegemonic system, not even a gesture as futile as that made by Pingajo. Although he adopts the traditional anti-employment pose of the *macho*, his aspirations are primarily materialistic and conventional, fed by advertising and the cult of celebrity:

> TRUENO – (*Imitando un anuncio de la televisión.*) 'No me llores, no me llores, que te compraré una nevera super-ser.' Anda, atontoliná. Que nos amos a casar por la iglesia. [...] Y que me voy a comprar un seiscientos, pa llevarte a Benidorm (54).[29]

He shows generosity towards his friends, but the party he throws in the sixth scene is a small-scale, private affair in comparison with the genuinely communal festivities dramatized in *Bodas* and *Historia de unos cuantos*. His obsession with cameras and photography may be seen as a form of creativity, yet it is significant that this particular cultural practice is dependent upon technology and that he values it primarily as a means of imitating images from celebrity magazines and pornography. Rather than enriching popular culture, consumerism and the mass media drain it of both distinctiveness and dissidence, as well as acting as accomplices of a repressive system that has become much more efficient and ruthless than in the past.[30] Caribe is picked up by the police almost as soon as he leaves Trueno's house with the packet of hashish and quickly disintegrates under torture, while Trueno himself is wrongly blamed for the murder of Puma and hunted down with dogs: neither of them gets the chance to make a heroic gesture, however futile. The execution of the protagonist at the end is a moment of horror unalleviated by the kind of positive factor represented by the solidarity of the group of women at the close of *Bodas*.

The censors who wrote reports on *Los quinquis de Madriz* in response to an application for approval of a production in 1970 were unanimously opposed to the play being performed, even with cuts. This was partly on the grounds of the overall impression created by the text: Antonio de Zubiaurre asserts that 'el tono dominante es de gran crudeza' ('the dominant tone is extremely crude'), while Padre Artola complains that the text glorifies the figure of the *quinqui* (Ministerio de Información y Turismo 1970b). However, there are also more specific objections. All three reports identify the unfavourable representation of the authorities as the factor that makes the text completely unacceptable: as Soria accurately points out, Franco's police force as represented by Puma and Chato emerges as 'zafia, brutal e inhumana' (Ministerio de Información y Turismo 1970b) ('rough, brutal and inhumane'). Zubiaurre identifies some specific passages that would need to be cut if authorization were given, including Tranvi's remarks about Puma's steel-tipped whip and his own desire to get rid of 'tos los creminales de la brigaílla' ('all those criminals in the CID') (*Los quinquis de Madriz* 1982: 63); the student's denunciation of social injustice (106–107); Puma's sinister threats of violence (109); and the whole of the last scene (113–14), in which the *quinquis* are summarily condemned and Trueno is executed by the dead Puma, who has come to represent the entire system. However variable censors' readings of the general moral and political implications of plays might be, the insistence on protecting the reputation of the institutions of the regime (the Church, the armed forces, the police and the Falange) remained a constant feature of theatre censorship throughout the dictatorship.

The fading of the defiant and creative *machismo español* of the past into the passive consumerism of the present is confirmed in other plays of the late Franco years. *La Andalucía de los Quintero* (*Andalusia with the Quintero Brothers*, written in 1966) satirizes the flashy vulgarity of migrant workers who have made money in Germany and return to their village to show off their new-found prosperity. *Comedia clásica* (*Classical Comedy*, written in 1970) is a light-hearted, rather clumsy pastiche in verse of a Golden Age *comedia* in the trendily modern setting of a tourist resort on the Costa del Sol. *Las estructuras* (*Structures*, also written in 1970) is more interesting: an expressionistic drama featuring a building site as a metaphor for an absurd social hierarchy, satirizing the impact of accelerated economic development on an unsophisticated, confused people.

Individuals and communities are represented as alienated, homogenized, under increasingly strict control, and less and less able to resist the ideological power of the state. What is more, the silencing of the distinctive voice of the *pueblo* in these texts was matched by the stifling of the playwright's own voice by censorship. *Los quinquis de Madriz* is the most powerful articulation of this vision of contemporary

Spain, but has never been performed: unlike the history plays that were rescued from oblivion by productions during the transition to democracy, the perceived relevance of this text faded quickly once the dictatorship had disappeared.

Disillusionment and disorientation after Franco

Rodríguez Méndez's cynical attitude towards the liberal, postmodern, free-market, pro-European society of post-Franco Spain has been summed up in Chapter 1. The social, cultural and economic trends he deplored in the 1960s – consumerism, the triumph of the mass media, cultural imperialism and ideological control – were consolidated in the 1980s as the dominant globalized features of contemporary life, confirming the displacement of traditional forms of popular cultural production.

In this environment, the characters in Rodríguez Méndez's plays are more alienated and rootless than ever. *La sangre de toro* (*Bull's Blood*, written in 1980 and staged in 1985) presents a bitterly ironic contrast between traditional Spanish popular culture and the glossy cosmopolitanism that was beginning to dominate the official cultural aspirations of post-Franco Spain. The members of a flamenco group representing Spain at an international arts festival are determined to do justice to the passion and creativity of their musical heritage, yet find themselves treated with indifference. Although they express their defiance as vibrantly as any of Rodríguez Méndez's *machos españoles*, they seem resigned to the fact that little notice will be taken of their protests:

> ¿Sabes lo que te digo? Si fuéramos de verdad la sangre de toro, si fuéramos españoles como es de ley, tendríamos que ir delante de todos ellos y decirles: se meten ustedes por donde saben su dinero, que aquí la Trini y los suyos no necesitan nada de ustedes. [...] ¡Hijos de mala madre!, ¡nos basta con haber demostrado lo que somos!, ¡nuestro arte, coño!, ¡nuestra sangre y nuestra raza! (quoted in Barea 1986: 9–10).[31]

The author underlines this sense of defeatism in his programme notes for the Bilbao premiere, making explicit the function of the bull as a symbol for Spain: 'El toro ibérico, el mítico toro hispánico, apenas tiene ya sangre. Soltó mucha sangre a través de la historia [...]. Ahora es sólo un torillo, enjuto de carnes, que apenas se sostiene en sus remos, que cae de rodillas constantemente por las arenas del mundo' (quoted in Barea 1986: 8).[32] As is usually the case with this writer, the tone with which he uses such traditionally right-wing phrases as 'el toro ibérico, el mítico toro hispánico' is difficult to pin down. While the intention may be partly ironic, there is undoubtedly some sincerity in the lament for the decay and cheapening of a notion of Spanishness defined by the stereotypes of proud, fiery flamenco performers and fighting bulls, at least insofar as these are associated with popular culture. Although the 1985 production of *Sangre de toro* in Bilbao (directed by Enrique Belloch) was moderately successful, the aim of transferring it to Madrid was not realized.

Other plays written and set in the 1980s continue in a mode of bitter, disillusioned satire, highlighting some dramatically promising contradictions in post-Franco Spanish society but generally failing to find effective theatrical structures through which to

La marca del fuego, Real Coliseo Carlos III (San Lorenzo de El Escorial), November 1986. *Photograph by Chicho, courtesy of Centro de Documentación Teatral, Madrid.*

explore them. *El sueño de una noche española* (*Dream of a Spanish Night*, written in 1982) echoes *Última batalla en El Pardo* in its focus on the historical role of the military. However, the officers featured here – imprisoned participants in the failed coup of 1981 – represent an institution that has become socially irrelevant and has lost its ideological coherence and confidence. The plot is based on a rather inconclusive confrontation between a young, apparently gung-ho Civil Guard captain (el Tete) and a gloomily introspective colonel (Francisco de Paula Benítez de Castro), who looks back with sadness on the terrible casualties suffered by both sides in the civil war. He asks not to be addressed by his rank, since 'ya no somos eso. Ni tú eres capitán ni yo soy eso. [...] Aquí no somos más que presidiarios, hijo, ya lo sabes' (*El sueño de una noche española* 1982: 11).[33] Tete claims to be planning to join the Sandinistas in Nicaragua when he gets out, in order to have a cause to fight for, regardless of what that cause might be: 'Pues cuando se ha nacido pa luchar, como yo he nacido, viejo, hay que luchar. Y yo si aquí, en mi patria, no puedo, no me permiten realizarme, habrá otros lugares' (22).[34] He expresses contempt for what he sees as the cowardice and defeatism of the colonel, blaming him and other senior officers for the failure of the *23-F* coup. In the end, however, the conflict is defused by the unexpected death of the colonel from a heart attack, it turns out that Tete's plan to become a mercenary in Nicaragua is a fantasy, and the remaining prisoners resign themselves to their insignificance. Neither the character development nor the outcome of the action makes clear to what extent the text should be read as a lament for the decline of social values traditionally associated with the military and to what extent it is an acerbic satire on the historical irrelevance of a previously hegemonic institution.

La Restauración (*Restoration*, written in 1984 and revised in 2001) refers to the 1981 coup in a more comical way, using it as the focus for a satire of parliamentary democracy. The tone is signalled clearly in the sardonic stage direction that opens the first scene, set at the opening of the first parliament of the transition to democracy:

> En el gran hemiciclo se apiñan los nuevos prohombres de la muy nueva DEMOCRACIA MONÁRQUICA PARLAMENTARIA. Todos ellos, ahítos de emoción y salpicados por el flujo misterioso de la historia, esperan al augusto MONARCA, motor del cambio según los medios de comunicación, quien va a ser el encargado de volver a poner en marcha el GRAN RELOJ DE LA HISTORIA (*La Restauración* 1984: 1).[35]

Instead of dramatizing the political processes taking place in the legislative chamber itself, the play adopts a quirkily unusual perspective: the action is set in the members' lavatories, so that the events of the opening session of 1979 and of the session of 23 February 1981 are seen from the alienated point of view of the attendants down below. Apart from a contrast between the down-to-earth scepticism of the workers and the hypocritical opportunism of the various politicians who pass through, very little of substance or dramatic impact emerges from the situation, however. Once again, the text appears to be affected by the same confusion and disorientation that the author sees as characteristic of contemporary Spanish society.

With *La marca de fuego* (*The Mark of Fire*), also known as *El Equis* (*X*, written and first staged in 1986), Rodríguez Méndez returns to gritty social realism and the familiar surroundings of the traditionally working-class Madrid district of Lavapiés, but in this devastatingly grim drama of drug addiction there is no sign of the creative popular culture that once characterized the area. Even the degraded *machismo* displayed by the *quinquis* of the 1960s has drained away as life at the bottom of the social hierarchy has become dominated by drug abuse and its accompanying culture of violence and exploitation. Yimy and Pepa, the young couple at the centre of the play, hope to regain control over their lives and escape from addiction, but become helplessly entrapped in the ruthless manipulations of El Equis, the drug dealer who also turns out to be involved in child trafficking and the white slave trade. None of the characters shows the slightest compassion or sense of solidarity, not even towards Yimi and Pepa's baby, who is given away in exchange for money to buy drugs. The kind of community that provides support to individuals in plays set in earlier periods seems to have collapsed altogether, and all social relationships have been reduced to ruthless commercial transactions and violent sado-masochistic gratification. The fact that Yimi walks out on Equis at the end vowing to give up drugs appears to offer an element of hope; however, the ruthless Equis has the last word: 'Yo sé que volverás... tarde o temprano. Nadie puede escapar de su destino... Y el tuyo está ya marcado... con fuego' (*Teatro escogido* 2005, vol. 1: 552).[36]

The author's comments in the programme for the premiere of *La marca de fuego* in Alicante emphasise that the play is intended as a condemnation not only of the drug trade itself but of society as a whole: 'Una sociedad proclive y entregada satánicamente a la destrucción. La droga es sólo un elemento entre muchos. Lo peor es la degradación no ya moral, sino física, humana; la degradación de la especie, tal vez' (quoted in B. B. 1986: 31).[37] Such widening of the social and moral relevance of the action is indicated by the fact that an accomplice of Equis poses as a social worker, yet it is not convincingly built into the dramatic structure. The play expresses a powerful, heartfelt cry of anguish at the social effects of the expansion of the culture of drug abuse in Spanish cities in the 1980s, but does little to establish the implied argument that this is symptomatic of the general degradation of Spanish society and the whole human species.

La hermosa justicia (*Beautiful Justice*, written in 1986) switches the point of view to that of the materially comfortable but politically and socially insecure middle classes. The vacuous existence of a judge's family is briefly thrown into turbulence by the intrusion into the exclusive enclosure of their luxury suburban housing estate of a convict on weekend leave innocently hoping for an interview with the judge – a representative of the real, dirty urban world from which the privileged attempt to insulate themselves. As the title ironically indicates, the main point of the play is to satirize the judiciary, revealing a lack of vocational commitment and seriousness and suggesting improper political interference in judicial processes. Don Fernando and a fellow judge who comes for lunch dream of taking early retirement and setting up lucrative businesses, while their wives prattle hysterically about how dangerous society has become: 'Que una está que no vive las veinticuatro horas del día y de la noche' (*La hermosa justicia* 1986: 17).[38] However, both the critique of the judicial system and the ironic portrait of a social class remain superficial, and no substantial dramatic tension is created. The satire of bourgeois pretentiousness and moral panic is reminiscent of parts of *El vano ayer* (which may perhaps hint at parallels between the two Borbón restorations of 1875 and 1975); as was concluded in the discussion of that play in Chapter 3, this is not the kind of dramatic environment in which Rodríguez Méndez's talent is most at home.

Leyenda Áurea (*Golden Legend*, written in 1988) returns to more familiar territory. The first scene is set amongst blocks of flats in Vallecas, a working-class suburb to the east of Madrid, where 'enormes y monstruosos barrios dormitorios albergan a viejas familias chabolistas que han pasado de la barraca sumaria a los pisos con dos baños y grandes ventanales abiertos a la terrible meseta castellano-manchega' (*Leyenda Áurea* 1998: 295).[39] The play is in part an updated representation of the kind of social environment explored by *La batalla del Verdún* and *Los quinquis de Madriz*. Although the language is as colourfully down-to-earth as in those earlier texts, the overall impression created of the way of life of the Spanish *pueblo* is not a positive one. The proletariat has now moved further out from the city centre and is housed and cared for by the welfare state, but seems to have gained material well-being at the cost of vitality, individuality and humanity: 'El enjambre de andaluces, manchegos y extremeños que habitan esos lugares aparece guarecido en sus nichos mortuorios especialmente preparados para acompañar sus absortas vidas de trabajo y bienestar' (295).[40] In the distance, the enormous statue of the Sacred Heart of Jesus on the Cerro de los Ángeles south of Madrid can be seen on the skyline, serving as a reminder of 'la tradición que se bate en retirada ante el empuje progresista del gran edificio de viviendas y el coche utilitario' (295).[41] The monument is an icon of conservative traditions of both nationalism and Catholicism: it stands on the spot regarded as the precise geographical centre of the Iberian peninsula and is a replacement, inaugurated by Franco in 1965, for an older statue destroyed in the civil war (a notorious photograph of a firing squad of Republican militiamen aiming at the statue was widely circulated by the Nationalists). Stage directions specify the visibility of the statue in only two of the text's twelve scenes, yet the implication seems to be that its mysterious, nostalgic presence should be felt in some way throughout the play.

An ambitious dramatic structure involving multiple locations and simultaneous actions extends this sense of vacuousness, tedium and uniformity to various other social groups: hospital staff more interested in a football match on television than in the patients arriving in the casualty department; bored police officers engaging in idle banter with assorted felons who wander into the station from the street; a sanctimonious middle-class family and a squabbling working-class one. The various strands of the action are linked together by the mysterious appearances of a gypsy bootblack who seems to bring about miraculous turns of events: first his own rescue from a beating when his assailant suffers a heart attack, and later the recovery of the same assailant, who has turned out to be a renegade priest whose wavering faith is restored as a result. The transformed priest purges the scroungers, junkies and delinquents from the Christian *comunidad de base* (collective) he has been running as a kind of liberation theology project and reinstates the traditional Latin mass.

Leyenda Áurea is one of the plays with which Jiménez Sánchez illustrates his argument that Rodríguez Méndez's theatre is increasingly devoted to the construction of archetypes of traditional Christian values as an antidote to the loss of spirituality in contemporary society. He takes a rather simplistic approach to this text, however, taking the gypsy seriously as a saintly figure capable of working miracles and overstating the extent to which the return to Tridentine liturgy is proposed as the answer to society's ills:

> De la lectura de *Leyenda áurea* se desprende una clara visión de lo que debe de ser la Iglesia y su misión. La Iglesia es lugar de oración, a través del cual el creyente llega a Dios, otras funciones – nos dirá el autor – no han hecho más que desdibujar su función primordial y para la que fue instituida como se verifica en la historia. Por eso, frente a un catolicismo político, reclama un catolicismo místico, cobrando así importancia de modelos arquetípicos las obras de *El oratorio de Teresa de Ávila* y *El pájaro solitario* (1998: 185).[42]

What Jiménez Sánchez seems to be underestimating, however, is the extent to which Rodríguez Méndez's treatment of Santa Teresa and San Juan de la Cruz – as I have argued in Chapter 5 – emphasizes a religiosity that is both mystical and political, inspired not by conventional liturgical forms but by visionary experience and a desire to communicate that experience to ordinary people in ordinary vernacular language. He also makes a rather naive connection between this play and the original *Legenda Aurea* on which its title is based, referring to a 'clara intención, por parte del autor, de acercarnos a arquetipos de santidad hoy que, como en el siglo XIII hiciera Santiago de la Vorágine, sirvieron de modelos de vida para tantos creyentes' (1998: 131–32).[43] Since almost all the stories retold in the *Legenda Aurea* contain highly fantastical material (prompting Luis Vives and other Humanist scholars to condemn it for encouraging superstition amongst the credulous), it would be wise to assume that Rodríguez Méndez's use of the title is at least partly ironic rather than straightforwardly devotional. Sherry L. Reames concludes that Jacobus de Voragine's approach 'would inadvertently have made it easy for untrained readers to cherish the marvellous and the sensational for their own sakes'; instead of presenting 'ordinary laymen and women with examples they might reasonably be expected to imitate, the *Legenda* effectively told them that they could only revere and obey the saints' (1985: 209).

In Rodríguez Méndez's play, neither the gypsy nor the reformed priest constitutes an unambiguously exemplary model of saintliness. The former certainly represents humility and a traditionalist form of Catholic faith, but the question of whether he brings about the recovery of the priest is left open to interpretation. For his part, the priest rejects the ill-conceived social project that appears to have brutalized him and done nothing for the intended beneficiaries and rediscovers the traditional sacerdotal role of ritually offering the sacrament to the faithful, yet the mass he celebrates at the end is a far from triumphant event: he has trouble remembering the script, and his congregation consists only of the gypsy *limpiabotas* and the old grandmother who in an earlier scene had been prevented by her family from watching a Latin mass on television. A feeling that contemporary society (defined by globalized capitalism, consumerism, mass-mediated culture, social democracy and the decline of traditional communities) is spiritually, morally and culturally empty is undoubtedly expressed in this text and in other writings by Rodríguez Méndez, and his cynicism about the public services and material comforts provided by the welfare state is more corrosive here than ever. In none of them, however, does he propose clear solutions, either religious or political. His introduction to *Leyenda Áurea* makes clear that his interest is not in institutions but in the suppressed potential of ordinary, obscure human beings: he expresses a desire that 'frente al mundo maligno y terrible que nos circunda – tan materializado y destructivo – se ponga de manifiesto el alma secreta y limpia de algunos seres que vagan por el mundo y tal vez sin saberlo dan testimonio de bondad y aun de santidad' (Rodríguez Méndez 1998: 291).[44]

De Voragine's collection of legends is referred to again in the title of another Rodríguez Méndez text, *Otra leyenda áurea* (written in 1992), but the two plays have little else in common. In this case the tone is clearly playful and the action fanciful, consisting essentially of two religious jokes for which the playwright fails to find satisfactory punchlines. In the first part, the devil in the guise of a business executive visits the Pope to complain that he has been made redundant by the rampant wickedness of the modern world and to ask His Holiness to pay him unemployment benefit. The Pontiff refuses, arguing that the USA should foot the bill, in recognition of services rendered: 'En América del Norte tiene usted su terreno de juego, amigo mío' (*Otra leyenda áurea* 1992: 12).[45] In the second part, a resentful Satan attempts to obtain revenge by signing a deal with the pop star Madonna to work together against the Vatican, yet she too turns him down. While this bizarre and inconclusive text may lend some support to Jiménez Sánchez's general argument about the playwright becoming increasingly preoccupied with religion, it is certainly not an example of such interest being expressed with sincerity or conventional piety.

Something like a sincere expression of religious belief is contained in Rodríguez Méndez's most recent play, *Estoy reunido* (*I'm in a Meeting*, 2004), a fantasy with a melancholy, valedictory tone. This text draws together some of the central preoccupations of his work and places the author himself at the heart of them. In a series of encounters with the ghost of Lope de Vega, the world-weary playwright José María Rodríguez Méndez reflects on mortality and the significance of his work, contrasting his reverence for the classic literature of the Golden Age and his love of the traditional popular culture of Madrid with the trashy commercialism of the present, as exemplified by the cocktail bars proliferating around his flat on the Calle Huertas and the tourists queuing to visit Lope's house nearby. The two playwrights wander the streets of the *barrio de las letras* (writers' quarter) and comment dismissively on the mediocrity of the modern age in comparison with Lope's. The only traces that Lope can find of the 'donaire' (charm, wit, spark, character) that used to characterize the popular culture of Madrid are in the cats and dogs in whose form the colourful characters of his time seem to have been reincarnated (2005: 29). *Estoy reunido* appears to signal a desire to withdraw definitively from the world. Its protagonist dismisses his writings as insignificant and hopes only to join Lope in eternal peace in the afterlife. The master agrees that his disciple's work does not add up to much: 'Total cuatro cosillas' (2005: 32) ('A few bits and pieces, that's all'). Nevertheless, this self-effacement on Rodríguez Méndez's part is to some extent an ironic rhetorical pose, in the best tradition of the Golden Age, and in Lope's parting words to the protagonist, the author reasserts his claim to be engaged on an important project:

> Y seguir con tu defensa del idioma español, ese idioma que construimos entre todos y que ha triunfado en el mundo entero. [...] Sigue defendiendo a España, que es lo que odian tus contemporáneos, esos que se sientan en el Congreso, en los sillones de la Academia de la Lengua, en las embajadas y en muchas cátedras... Contra todos ellos, ¡Santiago y cierra España como se dijo siempre en estos lares! (2005: 33)[46]

In case anyone is tempted to take the use of the medieval crusaders' battle cry entirely seriously, the brief final scene of the play leaves a highly ambiguous impression. Rodríguez Méndez's apartment is seen piled high with documents, newspapers and bags of rubbish, and a television report is heard announcing a sad case of 'Diogenes syndrome': an elderly man has been found dead in his home, surrounded by rubbish but smiling serenely. The term Diogenes syndrome, named after the ancient Cynic philosopher who renounced all comfort and wordly ambitions in pursuit of a natural, virtuous existence, was coined in a medical study of elderly patients who insisted on living alone in a state of squalor and hoarding rubbish despite having adequate resources and high levels of education and articulacy (Clark, Mankikar & Gray 1975), and has been used with increasing frequency in press reports in Spain. The author may be associating himself with an icon of integrity and scourge of pretentiousness and hypocrisy, but the clinical identification of Diogenes syndrome indicates that sufferers tend to be aggressive, emotionally unstable, 'reality-distorting individuals' who refuse to recognize their condition (Clark, Mankikar & Gray 1975: 367). The ironic elusiveness is given a further twist at the end, when it is suggested that the protagonist is still very much alive. The voices of both characters are heard; Lope's comes from above, while Rodríguez Méndez's is 'perfectamente terrenal' (*Estoy reunido* 2005: 34) ('entirely earthly'), and the laughter of the two of them fills the theatre.

Conclusions

In the plays discussed in this chapter, the possibility of defining and representing a vital, positive, authentically popular sense of Spanish cultural identity has become more and more remote. The hegemony of the powerful is shown to be reinforced by unprecedented means of coercion and persuasion, and the masses as passive and alienated. The history plays discussed in Chapters 3, 4 and 5 demonstrate in a dazzling variety of ways the proposition that resistance to ideological hegemony and social homogenization is only effective through traditional, participative popular culture (and literary culture with genuine popular roots). In contrast, the plays with contemporary settings implicitly reject the modern consensus amongst Gramsci-inspired cultural studies theorists that the reception of mass culture can be 'a process of contestation and resignification' (Graham & Labanyi 1995b: 4), suggesting instead that modern mass-mediated culture irremediably stifles resistance and promotes conformity and consumerism. The ways in which the texts written during the dictatorship indicate that this effect of mass culture exacerbates the oppressive social impact of an authoritarian political system amount to a telling critique of Francoism. In the process, unfortunately, some of the portraits of individuals and communities which emerge are far from constructive in political terms. The dramatist's mordant cynicism about the benefits of political and social change since 1975 and the possibilities for cultural participation in contemporary society makes the post-Franco plays even more negative, while his nostalgia for what has been lost is at times expressed in alarmingly reactionary terms.

Despite this generally pessimistic outlook, Rodríguez Méndez's work does propose some positive, progressive values. In one of the essays discussed in Chapter 2, he argues that the prime objective of contemporary theatre as a cultural practice constituted by and constitutive of social realities should be 'sacar al hombre de la masa y hacerle consciente de sí mismo y solidario de sus semejantes' (Rodríguez Méndez 1968d: 90).[47] That is, to combat alienation, counter the effects of ideological apparatuses and propose models of identity not determined by dominant power groups. For Rodríguez Méndez, theatre can only achieve this if it reflects and engages with the everyday cultural activity of ordinary people. It is his history plays that respond in the most effective and stimulating ways to the challenges involved in the exploration of the liberating possibilities of theatre, since they show people embedded in communities in which distinctive cultural identities are still active and creative. The kind of history they dramatize is social and cultural rather than political, focusing primarily on the relationship between individuals and the popular cultural environments they inhabit. Those environments are placed at the core of Spanishness, providing multiple ways of 'imagining the community' (in Anderson's terms as discussed in Chapter 1) at national and local levels which challenge both the centralized, authoritarian nationalism of the dictatorship and the internationalizing aspirations of post-Francoist social democracy. In principle, Franco's censors were prepared to tolerate the general thrust of Rodríguez Méndez's theatre and, at times, recognized that in some respects it was not incompatible with the social and cultural values of the regime. However, their tolerance was subject to two basic conditions that his work was bound to flout: a prudish notion of decorum totally at odds with his commitment to the reproduction of colloquial speech, and a respect for the institutions of the Francoist Establishment to which his emphasis on identities arising from popular culture is fundamentally opposed. Thus, while many of the particular decisions made by censors may seem relatively trivial or incidental, the overall effect of censorship on Rodríguez Méndez's work in the 1960s and 1970s went to the heart of his cultural project and had a devastating effect on the development of his career as a playwright.

The stories told in the history plays do not conform strictly to one or other of the generic forms of emplotment referred to by Hayden White; instead, they tend to combine elements of Tragedy, Satire, Comedy, Epic and Romance in various ways. The key component holding the mixture together is the emphasis on the creative performance by individuals and groups of culturally mediated identities – expressions of nationhood, neighbourhood, class, religion, gender and language community all summed up in the various manifestations of *machismo español*. Along the way, audiences and readers of Rodríguez Méndez's plays are offered a fascinating and unorthodox series of insights into the relationship between the history and the *intrahistoria* of Spain, and treated to moments of striking visual, linguistic and emotional impact. The best of his texts generate theatrical structures that synthesize the historical moment, the cultural environment, the characters and the action in highly distinctive and effective ways. The loose collection of *estampas* in *Bodas que fueron famosas del Pingajo y la Fandanga* offers glimpses of a society in ragged confusion, and its blend of folksiness and grittiness is transformed at the end into disconcerting tragicomedy. In *Historia de unos cuantos*, a more solid sense of place and chronological perspective convincingly historicizes and individualizes the *género chico* source material, building Mari Pepa into a powerful image of popular endurance. The outrageous, protean protagonist of *Flor de Otoño* embodies the decadence, effervescence and instability of Barcelona at the end of 1920s, but in the final scene shares a moment of exquisitely poignant understanding with his mother. *El pájaro solitario* sets up vivid contrasts between the stark purity of Juan's mysticism and the promiscuous hubbub of popular street life, while creating mysterious, fecund links between them.

The resistance enacted by the individuals and communities in historical settings is not necessarily any more effective in practical terms than that of the characters in contemporary settings. Rebellions are crushed and power structures remain in place. Nevertheless, what emerges strongly from the history plays is a sense of autonomy, vitality and creativity enabled by the continuity and renewability of popular culture. For ordinary members of the *pueblo*, distinctive modes of speech, gesture and behaviour are collectively passed on and individually reworked, providing both a sense of belonging and a means of challenging the status quo. For dissident members of the elite, a connection with popular culture is the only way to maintain humanity and avoid being absorbed into the machinations of power. And for the writers who mediate between elite and popular cultures, active engagement with the linguistic and cultural practices of particular communities in particular places at particular times is essential. The simple fact of theatrical representation draws attention to the performative nature of these processes, and this is reinforced both by the sense in almost all Rodríguez Méndez's plays that the characters' utterances are as much to do with display as with communication and by the presence of explicitly metatheatrical or intertextual elements. By embodying in theatrical form a set of variations on the notion that all social interaction and cultural activity is performative (in the sense expounded by Geertz and Turner, as set out in Chapter 2), Rodríguez Méndez's theatre implicitly proposes that all identities, while gaining strength from collective historical precedents, are open to innovation. Judith Butler's conclusions about gender can therefore be applied to the representation of various forms of identity in Rodríguez Méndez's work: to expose them as performative is to contest their reified status and open up new ways of acting them. The diverse forms of *machismo español*, played by both men and women, are subversive performances with the potential to 'expand the cultural field' (Butler 1990: 282) – bodily, linguistically, intellectually and emotionally.

Notes

1. 'When I gave the text to a few people to read, I noticed that it made them very uneasy. They kept on saying the same things: "We've got to forget the civil war", "These things are too recent, it's too soon", and so on.'
2. For information about the 2001 production and the author's connections with Ávila, see the special issue of *El Diario de Ávila* published to mark the city's tribute (Ayuntamiento de Ávila 2001). The success of this production prompted the publication of a new edition (*Última batalla en El Pardo* 2003).
3. The gradual development of the dramatic structure is traced in detail in my introduction to the play (Thompson 1991: 13-15).
4. 'As soon as I began to write the play, the figure of Franco imposed himself more and more, taking over as if winning the war again, so I decided that Franco should be portrayed in full detail. When it came to the defeated general, however, I found it impossible to convey a clear picture of him, and even less to endow him with a vigour that he showed no evidence of.' This process was obscured to some extent in the 2001 production by the tendency of the actor playing Franco, Pep Sais, to emphasize the comic effect of the dictator's mannerisms.
5. 'He is portly. His form is rotund and catlike, with an aquiline nose and bright eyes. He almost leaps onto the stage, like a cat pouncing onto a mouse. He carries his cap in his hand and moves with tremendous agility.'
6. 'If only it was possible to steer History and even put right past mistakes in the same way as you can lead armies. I've managed to do something towards that, but unfortunately History often takes its own path.'
7. 'We're living in a period when the jails are full.'
8. 'Care should be taken in the final scene to avoid confusion over the role of the priest.'
9. See Martí Farreras (1961) and Halsey (1980: 9–49) for discussion of the context and the impact of the play in Madrid.

10. 'These things need to happen, don't you see? Little things like this, so that we notice something. So that we realize we're just poor suckers who have no idea where we're heading. So that we realize there's a dark future ahead of us... But don't worry, it'll be all right tomorrow, and we'll forget about this.'

11. 'For it to be absolutely real, there ought to have been at least one of these student characters who showed a clear understanding of the situation and rebelled against it accordingly.'

12. 'Dying at the age of twenty. They ought to give him a distinction for that.'

13. 'It all ends on an optimistic note, with the reactions of hopeful young people.'

14. For a moving account of these events, see Stein (1979).

15. 'Why do I have to end up on my knees and covered in blood? Again... Always on my knees.'

16. 'It is intended to be a denunciation of the clichéd Spain of poverty and violence. There is some evocation of the postwar period, and a few politically charged implications can be allowed to remain. It is an outdated work and poses no problem.'

17. Presumably, the point is that the character's drunkenness almost makes him mix up 'Francia' and 'España'. But perhaps the censors suspected that what is abbreviated here – possibly with satirical intent – is 'Franco'.

18. 'The business about the "battle of El Verdún" is a rather desperate piece of irony referring to the daily battle waged by these people to get on, on the basis of piecework, overtime and odd jobs.' The battle of Verdun (1916-17) was a prolonged episode of trench warfare in which French forces eventually prevailed over the Germans, with heavy casualties on both sides.

19. 'We'll go down to the city one day... We'll take it over, we'll show 'em how to have a bit of fun.'

20. 'Between the four walls of the house all day long. It was different back in the village, wasn't it? You used to go out on the front doorstep and have a bit of a chat with the neighbours... I don't know, you get so bored here.'

21. 'As a *sainete*, it relies principally on portraying character types, situations and atmosphere, with a high degree of realism and colourfulness. [...] Nothing that goes against morality or the regime.'

22. Pérez-Pineda emphasises the 'testimonial' value of *El ghetto* in drawing attention to 'la deshumanización del hombre mediante el trabajo alienado' (1994-95: 9) ('the dehumanization of man by means of alienated labour').

23. 'We've sold out in these places, we've really sold out.'

24. See Balfour (1990) and Grugel & Rees (1997: 107-108).

25. 'The author's critical intention could be tolerated if the focus of the dramatic conflict was limited to the basic relationship between employer and worker, and the respective demands of the two parties. But with the involvement of the union and the official implications this brings with it, the theme of the play ends up incorporating very specific accusations, which are rather delicate in the current context.'

26. Balboa Echevarría offers a sophisticated analysis of the visual texture of *Los quinquis de Madriz*, concluding that 'en la España de los sesentas, el diálogo y la posibilidad del diálogo eran inexistentes, de allí la producción de un teatro cuya estructura no es dialógica sino visual y gesticulante' (1987: 74) ('in the Spain of the 60s, dialogue and the possibility of dialogue were non-existent, hence the creation of a theatre whose structure is not dialogic but visual and gesticulatory').

27. The marginalized world of the *quinquis* (literally, tinkers or scrap metal dealers, but in practice anyone living in slums or shanties and scraping a living in the black economy), including some of these same characters, also appears in two of the author's narrative works: the story 'Vida de un quinqui' in *Pobrecitos pero no honrados* (Rodríguez Méndez 1972: 13–42) and the novel *El cisne de Cisneros* (Rodríguez Méndez 1981).

28. 'I got a posting in the transport corps and made a tidy bit on the side by "losing" petrol supplies. [...] They've really made a man of him, haven't they? The lad's got no guts any more. [...] Yeah, that's the way to do it!'

29. 'TRUENO – (*Imitating a TV advertisement.*) "Don't cry now, don't have a care, I'll buy you a frigidaire." Come on, silly, we're gonna get married in church and all that. [...] And I'll buy a Seat 600 to drive you to Benidorm.'

30. This point is made more explicit in an early version of *Los quinquis de Madriz* by the inclusion of a parodic final scene imitating a television discussion programme, in which a panel of experts comments without compassion on Trueno's case.

31. 'You know what I think? If we really had bull's blood in us, if we were real Spaniards, we'd go out there in front of everybody and tell 'em where to stick their money, tell 'em we don't need anything from them. [...] Bastards! For us it's enough just to have shown what we're made of! Shown our art, sod it, our blood and our pedigree!'

32. 'The Iberian bull, the mythical Hispanic bull, has hardly any blood left. It has lost a great deal of blood during the course of history [...]. Now it's merely a bullock, a scrawny creature that can barely stay on its feet, constantly falling to its knees in the sand [of bullrings] around the world.'

33. 'That's not what we are now. I'm not that any more and you're not a captain. [...] In here, we're just prisoners, my boy. You know that.'

34. 'Look, old man, when you were born to fight, like I was, you've got to fight. And if I can't do that here in my homeland, if they don't let me be myself, I'll have to find somewhere else where I can.'

35. 'The great chamber fills up with the new dignitaries of the ever so new MONARCHO-PARLIAMENTARY DEMOCRACY. Overcome with emotion and marked by the mysterious flux of history, they are all awaiting the arrival of the august MONARCH, the motor of change according to the media, the man who is to be responsible for setting in motion once again the GREAT CLOCK OF HISTORY.'

36. 'I know you'll be back... sooner or later. Nobody can get away from their destiny... And yours is marked on you... with fire.'

37. 'A society given over satanically to destruction. Drugs are just one element amongst many. The worst thing is not so much the moral degradation as the physical, human degradation; the degradation of the species, perhaps.'

38. 'Life is just impossible these days, isn't it? You can't feel safe at any hour of the day or night.'

39. 'Enormous, monstrous dormitory suburbs house former shanty-town families who have graduated from improvised shacks to apartments with two bathrooms and large windows looking out over the harsh plains of Castilla-La Mancha.'

40. 'The swarm of incomers from Andalucía, La Mancha and Extremadura who have settled in these places huddle in their mortuary niches, specially designed to accommodate lives devoted to work and welfare.'

41. 'The tradition forced to beat a retreat in the face of the modern, progressive advance of the blocks of flats and the compact cars.'

42. 'A reading of *Leyenda áurea* conveys a clear vision of what the Church and its mission should be. The Church is a place of prayer, by means of which the believer comes closer to God; any other functions – the author will tell us – have only obscured the primordial function for which the Church was established, as history demonstrates. Consequently, in opposition to political Catholicism, he advocates a mystical Catholicism, which gives his plays *Teresa de Ávila* and *El pájaro solitario* crucial importance as archetypal models.'

43. 'A clear intention on the part of the author to offer us modern-day archetypes of saintliness like those which, in the thirteenth century, Jacobus de Voragine created as models of conduct for so many believers.' The original Latin text of the *Legenda Aurea* compiled between 1260 and 1275 by Jacobus de Voragine became the most widely read book in medieval Europe after the Bible. It is an anthology of accounts of the lives and miracles of numerous saints, based to some extent on verifiable historical records but clearly mythical and apocryphal in many parts.

44. 'In contrast to the terrible, malign world around us, so materialistic and destructive, a glimpse should be offered of the secret, pure soul of a few beings who wander the earth and, perhaps without realizing it, give an example of goodness and even sanctity.'

45. 'Your field of play is in North America, my friend.'

46. 'And stick to your defence of the Spanish language, the language that we made between us all and which has triumphed the world over. [...] Continue to defend Spain, to defend what is hated by your contemporaries, those people sitting in parliament, in the Royal Academy, in embassies and universities... To the devil with them all, cry "Saint James and Spain as one!", as people always said around these parts.'

47. 'To lift the individual out of the mass and endow him with consciousness of self and solidarity with others.'

BIBLIOGRAPHY

Texts of Rodríguez Méndez's plays
Bodas que fueron famosas del Pingajo y la Fandanga; Flor de Otoño (1979), Madrid: Cátedra, ed. José Martín Recuerda.
Comedia clásica (1995), Murcia: Escuela Superior de Arte Dramático, ed. Antonio Morales.
El círculo de tiza de Cartagena (1964), Barcelona: Occitania.
El ghetto, o la irresistible ascensión de Manuel Contreras (1964). Unpublished typescript.
El milagro del pan y de los peces (1953). Unpublished typescript.
El pájaro solitario (1993), Ávila: Diputación Provincial de Ávila, ed. José María Muñoz Quirós.
El pájaro solitario (2004), Madrid: Iberautor/Fundación Autor, ed. Robert Muro; other supporting material by Michael
    Thompson, Paloma Pedrero and José Monleón.
El sueño de una noche española (1982). Unpublished typescript.
El vano ayer (1963). Unpublished typescript.
En las esquinas, banderas (1964). Unpublished typescript.
Estoy reunido (2005), Madrid: Caos. Available online at <http://www.caoseditorial.com>.
Flor de Otoño (1974), *Primer Acto* 173: 22–47. [With various pieces of supporting material about the author and the
    historical background].
Flor de Otoño (1979). [In the same volume as *Bodas que fueron famosas del Pingajo y la Fandanga*].
Historia de unos cuantos (1982). [In the same volume as *Los quinquis de Madriz*].
Isabelita tiene ángel (1994), *Estreno* 20.1: 10–28. [With an introduction by Antonio Fernández Insuela].
La batalla del Verdún (1966), Barcelona: Occitania (Colección 'El sombrero de Dantón', 14). [With an introduction
    by the author].
La Chispa (1999). [In the same volume as *Reconquista*].
La hermosa justicia (1986). Unpublished typescript.
La Restauración (1984). Unpublished typescript.
La tabernera y las tinajas; Los inocentes de la Moncloa (1968), Madrid: Taurus/Primer Acto, ed. José Monleón; other
    supporting material by the author and María Aurelia Capmany.
La vendimia de Francia (1961), typescript. [First published in *Yorick* 2 (1965)].
Leyenda Áurea (1998). Unpublished page proofs.
Literatura española (1989), Murcia: Universidad de Murcia. [With an introduction by the author].
Los inocentes de la Moncloa (1968). [In the same volume as *La tabernera y las tinajas*].
Los inocentes de la Moncloa (1980), Salamanca: Almar, ed. Martha T. Halsey.
Los quinquis de Madriz; Historia de unos cuantos; Teresa de Ávila (1982), Murcia: Godoy, ed. José Martín Recuerda.
Otra leyenda áurea (1992). Unpublished typescript.
Reconquista; La Chispa (1999), Madrid: Universidad Nacional de Educación a Distancia, ed. José Romera Castillo.
Soy madrileño (1998), Murcia: Escuela Superior de Arte Dramático, ed. Virtudes Serrano.
Teatro escogido (2005), Madrid: Asociación de Autores de Teatro, ed. Domingo Miras, volume 1: *Vagones de madera,
    Los inocentes de la Moncloa, La vendimia de Francia, La batalla del Verdún, La Mano Negra, Los quinquis de
    Madriz, La marca de fuego*; volume 2: *Bodas que fueron famosas del Pingajo y la Fandanga, Flor de Otoño, Historia
    de unos cuantos, El pájaro solitario, El rincón de don Miguelito, Última batalla en El Pardo, Soy madrileño, La banda
    del 'Tisi' habla de literatura, El marqués de Sade en Usera, Novios de la muerte, Real Academia*.
Teresa de Ávila (1982). [In the same volume as *Los quinquis de Madriz*].
Última batalla en El Pardo (1991), Madrid: El Público/Centro de Documentación Teatral, ed. Michael Thompson, with
    an introduction by the author.
Última batalla en El Pardo (2003), Madrid: Iberautor/Fundación Autor.
Vagones de madera (1963), *Primer Acto* 45: 38–55.

Other sources cited
Abella, Rafael (1973), *La vida cotidiana durante la guerra civil: la España Nacional*, Barcelona: Planeta.
————— (1975), *La vida cotidiana durante la guerra civil: la España Republicana*, Barcelona: Planeta.
————— (1985), *La vida cotidiana en España bajo el régimen de Franco*, Barcelona: Argos Vergara.
Abellán, José Luis (ed.) (1968), *Visión de España en la Generación del 98: antología de textos*, Madrid: Magisterio
    Español.
Abellán, Manuel L. (1980), *Censura y creación literaria en España (1939–1976)*, Barcelona: Península.
————— (ed.) (1987), *Censura y literaturas peninsulares*, Amsterdam: Rodopi.
Abós Santabárbara, Ángel Luis (2003), *La historia que nos enseñaron (1937–1975)*, Madrid: Foca.
Adamson, Walter L. (1980), *Hegemony and Revolution: A Study of Antonio Gramsci's Political and Cultural Theory*,
    Berkeley/Los Angeles/London: University of California Press.
Adorno, Theodor W. (1991), *The Culture Industry: Selected Essays on Mass Culture*, London: Routledge.
Aguirre, José María (1974), '¡Barrio Chino!' *Primer Acto* 173: 20–22, originally published in *Mundo Gráfico*
    (29/11/1933).
Alier, Roger (2002), *La Zarzuela*, Teià: Ma Non Troppo.
Althusser, Louis (1984), *Essays on Ideology*, London/New York: Verso. (First published in French 1970).
Álvarez Pérez, A. (1959), *Enciclopedia intuitiva, sintética y práctica: Tercer Grado*, Valladolid: Miñón (1st ed. 1954),
    facsimile ed. Madrid: EDAF, 1997.
Anderson, Benedict (1991), *Imagined Communities: Reflections on the Origins and Spread of Nationalism*, 2nd ed.
    London/New York: Verso.
Aszyk, Ursula (1999), 'La cuestión de la vanguardia en el teatro español durante el período de la transición política'
    in Martha T. Halsey & Phyllis Zatlin (eds), *Entre Actos: Diálogos sobre teatro español entre siglos*, University Park,
    PA: Estreno, 137–46.
Ayuntamiento de Ávila (2001), *El Diario de Ávila*, Edición Especial: *José María Rodríguez Méndez: Última batalla en*

el Pardo (14/2/2001), (some of the contents were published at the same time in *Revista Cultural de Ávila y Segovia* 20 (2001): 40–41.)

Aznar Soler, Manuel (ed.) (1996), *Veinte años de teatro y democracia en España (1975–1995)*, Barcelona: Cop d'Idees/CITEC.

B. B. (1986), '*La marca del fuego*: conflicto sin esperanza', *El Público* 39: 30–31.

Balboa Echevarría, Miriam (1987), 'Lenguaje teatral: voz e imagen en *Los quinquis de Madriz* de José María Rodríguez Méndez', *Gestos* 3: 67–75.

Balfour, Sebastian (1990), 'From Warriors to Functionaries: The Falangist Syndical Élite, 1939–1976' in Frances Lannon & Paul Preston (eds), *Élites and Power in Twentieth-Century Spain*, Oxford: Oxford University Press, 229–48.

———— (2002), *Deadly Embrace: Morocco and the Road to the Spanish Civil War*, Oxford: Oxford University Press.

Bárbulo, Tomás (2002), *La historia prohibida del Sáhara español*, Barcelona: Destino.

Bardasano (1937), '¡Fuera el invasor!' (poster). *Carteles de la Guerra Civil*. Accessed online 25/11/2004 at <http://guerraespana.turincon.com>.

Barea, Pedro (1986), '*Sangre de toro*, banderillas de fuego', *El Público* 28: 8–10.

Benach, Joan-Antón (2003), 'Inmarchitable flor otoñal', *La Vanguardia* 1/12/2003. Accessed online 2/8/2004 at <http://www.artenbrutteatre.com>.

Beramendi, Justo G. (2000), 'Identity, Ethnicity and the State in Spain: 19th and 20th Centuries' in William Safran & Ramón Maiz (eds), *Identity and Territorial Autonomy in Plural Societies*, London/Portland: Frank Cass. 79–100.

Blanco Aguinaga, Carlos, Julio Rodríguez-Puértolas & Iris Zavala (1983), *Historia social de la literatura española*, vol. 3, Madrid: Castalia.

Bottomore, Tom (ed.) (1983), *A Dictionary of Marxist Thought*, Oxford: Blackwell.

Boyd, Carolyn P. (1979), *Praetorian Politics in Liberal Spain*, Chapel Hill: University of North Carolina Press. Available online at LIBRO (Library of Iberian Resources Online) <http://libro.uca.edu/boyd/praetorian.htm>.

———— (1989), 'History in the Schools and the Problem of Spanish Identity' in Richard Herr & John H. R. Polt (eds), *Iberian Identity: Essays on the Nature of Identity in Portugal and Spain*, Berkeley, CA: Institute of International Studies, University of California, Berkeley, 181–93.

Brandeis Libraries (2003), *Spanish Civil War Posters: A Checklist*, Brandeis University, accessed online 12/9/2003 at <http://library.brandeis.edu/specialcollections/SpanishCivilWar/posters.html>.

Brecht, Bertolt (1963), *The Caucasian Chalk Circle*, trans. J. & T. Stern & W. H. Auden, London: Methuen.

Brooksbank Jones, Anny (1997), *Women in Contemporary Spain*, Manchester: Manchester University Press.

Buero Vallejo, Antonio (1994), *Obra completa*, 2 vols. Madrid: Espasa Calpe.

———— (1980–81), 'Acerca del drama histórico', *Primer Acto* 187: 18–21.

Butler, Judith (1990), 'Performative Acts and Gender Constitution: An Essay in Phenomenology and Feminist Theory' in Sue-Ellen Case (ed.), *Performing Feminisms: Feminist Critical Theory and Theatre*, Baltimore/London: Johns Hopkins University Press. 270–82.

Cabal, Fermín & José Luis Alonso de Santos (eds) (1985), *Teatro español de los 80*, Madrid: Fundamentos.

Cabanellas, Guillermo (1977), *Cuatro generales (2): la lucha por el poder*, Barcelona: Planeta.

Cámara Villar, Gregorio (1997), 'Prólogo' in Andrés Sopeña Monsalve, *El florido pensil: Memoria de la escuela nacionalcatólica*, Barcelona: Círculo de Lectores, 13–22.

Candel, Francisco (1968), 'Con "La Pipironda"'in José María Rodríguez Méndez, *La tabernera y las tinajas; Los inocentes de la Moncloa*, Madrid: Taurus/Primer Acto, 74–81.

Capmany, María Aurelia (1968), 'José María Rodríguez Méndez, irreconciliado y minucioso' in José María Rodríguez Méndez, *La tabernera y las tinajas; Los inocentes de la Moncloa*, Madrid: Taurus/Primer Acto, 56–62.

Carr, Raymond (1980), *Modern Spain, 1875–1980*, Oxford: Oxford University Press.

———— (1982), *Spain 1808–1975*, 2nd ed. Oxford: Oxford University Press.

Carr, Raymond & Juan Pablo Fusi Aizpurúa (1981), *Spain: Dictatorship to Democracy*, 2nd ed. London: Allen & Unwin.

Castellet, José María (1957), *La hora del lector*, Barcelona: Seix Barral.

Centro de Información Administrativa (2003), *Constitución Española de 1978*. Accessed online 21/10/2003 at <http://www.igsap.map.es/cia/dispo/constitu.htm>.

Centro de Investigaciones Sociológicas (2002), *Instituciones y Autonomías, II*, Estudio n° 2455 (Septiembre 2002). Accessed online 14/5/2003 at <http://www.cis.es/ novedades/estudios.html>.

Certeau, Michel de (1984), *The Practice of Everyday Life*, trans. Steven Rendall. (Berkeley/Los Angeles/London: University of California Press.

Clark, A. N., G. D. Mankikar & I. Gray (1975), 'Diogenes Syndrome: A clinical study of gross neglect in old age', *The Lancet* 7903: 366–68.

Conversi, Daniele (1997), *The Basques, the Catalans and Spain: Alternative Routes to Nationalist Mobilisation*, London: Hurst.

Cornago Bernal, Óscar (1996), *La vanguardia teatral en España (1965–1975): Del ritual al juego*, Madrid: Visor.

———— (2000), *Discurso teórico y puesta en escena en los años sesenta: La encrucijada de los 'realismos'*, Madrid: Consejo Superior de Investigaciones Científicas.

Díaz, Elías (1995), 'The Left and the Legacy of Francoism: Political Culture in Opposition and Transition' in Helen Graham & Jo Labanyi (eds), *Spanish Cultural Studies: An Introduction*, Oxford: Oxford University Press, 283–91.

Díaz, Luis (1989), 'La manipulación de la cultura popular en España: entre el folklorismo homogeneizador y la búsqueda de señas de identidad' in Richard Herr & John H. R. Polt (eds), *Iberian Identity: Essays on the Nature of Identity in Portugal and Spain*, Berkeley, CA: Institute of International Studies, University of California, 98–111.

Díaz del Moral, Juan (1969), *Historia de las agitaciones campesinas andaluzas*, Madrid: Alianza. (First published 1929).

Doménech, Ricardo (1962), 'Lectura de *Los inocentes de la Moncloa*, de Rodríguez Méndez', *Primer Acto* 34: 47–48.

Doménech Rico, Fernando (1998), *La zarzuela chica madrileña*, Madrid: Comunidad Autónoma de Madrid.

Du Gay, Paul, Jessica Evans & Peter Readman (eds) (2000), *Identity: A Reader*. London: Sage/Open University.

Edelvives (1958), *Historia de España: Primer Grado*, Zaragoza: Luis Vives.

El País (1982), 'El polémico montaje de *Flor de Otoño*, de Rodríguez Méndez, en el Teatro Español, de Madrid', *El País* (10/12/1982). [Report based on interviews with Rodríguez Méndez and Díaz Zamora; name of interviewer not given.]

Enciclonet (2004), 'Luis Candelas', Madrid: Micronet. Accessed online 18/8/2004 at <http://www.enciclonet.com>.

Espina, Antonio (1929), *Luis Candelas: El bandido de Madrid*, Madrid: Espasa-Calpe. (Latest edition 1996).

F. T. D. (1940), *El libro de España*, 2nd ed. Zaragoza: Luis Vives.

Fernández Insuela, Antonio (1981–82), '*Bodas que fueron famosas*...: degradación e ironía', *Archivum* 31–32: 289–304.

————— (1994), 'Un peculiar drama histórico de Rodríguez Méndez: *Isabelita tiene ángel*', *Estreno* 20.1: 7–9.

Fernández Torres, Alberto (1983), 'Un espectáculo no consumado: *Flor de Otoño*, de Rodríguez Méndez', *Ínsula* 434: 14.

Fiske, John (1987), *Television Culture*, London: Methuen.

Fontana, Josep (ed.) (1986), *España bajo el franquismo*, Barcelona: Crítica.

Gabriele, John P. (1997), 'Diálogo con José María Rodríguez Méndez, cronista teatral' (interview), *Iberoamericana* 21.2: 75–83.

Gabriele, John P. & Candyce Leonard (eds) (1996a), *Panorámica del teatro español actual*, Madrid: Fundamentos.

————— (eds) (1996b), *Teatro de la España demócrata: Los noventa*, Madrid: Fundamentos.

García Barrientos, José Luis (1991), *Drama y tiempo: Dramatología I*, Madrid: Consejo Superior de Investigaciones Científicas.

García de la Concha, Víctor (1978), *El arte literario de santa Teresa*, Barcelona: Ariel.

García Gómez, Manuel (1996), *El teatro de autor en España, 1901–2000*, Madrid: Asociación de Autores de Teatro.

García Lorca, Federico (1943), *Romancero gitano*, Buenos Aires: Losada.

Gardiner, Patrick (1959), *Theories of History*, New York/London: Free Press/Collier Macmillan.

Geertz, Clifford (1975), *The Interpretation of Cultures*, London: Hutchinson.

Gómez, José Luis (1978), 'Notas para una concepción de puesta en escena', programme notes for *Bodas que fueron famosas del Pingajo y la Fandanga*, Teatro Bellas Artes (Madrid).

González, Agustín (2001), 'Grupo de teatro Barcense de Castilla la Vieja', *Diario de Ávila*, Edición Especial (14/2/2001): 8–9.

González Ruiz, Nicolás (1987), 'Una gran tarea de dignificación del teatro' in Manuel L. Abellán (ed.), *Censura y literaturas peninsulares*, Amsterdam: Rodopi, 173–75.

Graham, Helen (1995), 'Gender and the State: Women in the 1940s' in Helen Graham & Jo Labanyi (eds), *Spanish Cultural Studies: An Introduction*, Oxford: Oxford University Press, 182–95.

————— (1996), 'Community, Nation and State in Republican Spain, 1931–1938' in Clare Mar-Molinero & Ángel Smith (eds), *Nationalism and the Nation in Iberian Peninsula: Competing and Conflicting Identities*, Oxford/Washington DC: Berg, 133–47.

Graham, Helen & Jo Labanyi (eds) (1995a), *Spanish Cultural Studies: An Introduction*, Oxford: Oxford University Press.

————— (1995b), 'Introduction. Culture and Modernity: The Case of Spain' in Helen Graham & Jo Labanyi (eds), *Spanish Cultural Studies: An Introduction*, Oxford: Oxford University Press, 1–19.

Gramsci, Antonio (1971), *Selections from the Prison Notebooks*, trans. and ed. Quintin Hoare & Geoffrey Nowell Smith, London: Lawrence & Wishart.

Granja, José Luis de la, Justo Beramendi & Pere Anguera (2001), *La España de los nacionalismos y las autonomías*, Madrid: Síntesis.

Grugel, Jean & Tim Rees (1997), *Franco's Spain*, London: Arnold.

Gubern, Román (1981), *La censura: función política y ordenamiento jurídico bajo el franquismo (1936–1975)*, Barcelona: Edicions 62.

Hall, Stuart (1980), 'Encoding/decoding' in S. Hall, D. Hobson, A. Lowe & P. Willis (eds), *Culture, Media, Language*, London: Hutchinson, 128–38.

————— (1990), 'Cultural Identity and Diaspora' in Jonathan Rutherford (ed.), *Identity: Community, Culture, Difference*, London: Lawrence & Wishart, 222–37.

Halsey, Martha T. (1977), 'La generación realista: A Select Bibliography', *Estreno* 3.1: 8–13.

————— (1980), 'Prólogo' in José María Rodríguez Méndez, *Los inocentes de la Moncloa*, Salamanca: Almar, 9–49.

————— (1987), 'History "From Below": The Popular Chronicles of José María Rodríguez Méndez', *Revista de Estudios Hispánicos* 21.2: 39–58.

————— (1988a), 'The Politics of History: Images of Spain on the Stage of the 1970s' in Martha T. Halsey & Phyllis Zatlin (eds), *The Contemporary Spanish Theater: A Collection of Critical Essays*, Boston: University Press of America, 93–108.

————— (1988b), 'Introduction to the Historical Drama of Post-Civil-War Spain', *Estreno* 14.1 (special issue on *El drama histórico español contemporáneo*): 11–17.

————— (1988c), 'Dramatic Patterns in Three History Plays of Contemporary Spain', *Hispania* 71: 20–30.

Hamilton, Paul (2003), *Historicism*, 2nd ed. London/New York: Routledge (The New Critical Idiom).

Hatzfeld, Helmut A. (1969), *Santa Teresa de Avila*, New York: Twayne.

Hennessy, C. A. M. (1962), *The Federal Republic in Spain: Pi y Margall and the Federal Republican Movement 1868–74*, London: Oxford University Press.

Hoggart, Richard (1957), *The Uses of Literacy*, London: Chatto & Windus.

Isasi Ángulo, Amando (1974), *Diálogos del teatro español de la postguerra*, Madrid: Ayuso.

Jiménez Sánchez, Gonzalo (1998), *El problema de España. Rodríguez Méndez: una revisión dramática de los postulados del 98*, Salamanca: Universidad Pontificia.

Jones, Margaret E. (1977), 'The Modern Spanish Theater: The Historical Perspective', *Revista de Estudios Hispánicos* 11: 199–218.

Jordan, Barry (1990), *Writing and Politics in Franco's Spain*, London/New York: Routledge.

Juan de la Cruz, San (1968), *Poesías completas y comentarios en prosa a los poemas mayores*, ed. Dámaso Alonso & Eulalia Galvarriato de Alonso, Madrid: Aguilar.

————— [John of the Cross, Saint] (1991), *The Spiritual Canticle*, trans. Kieran Kavanaugh & Otilio Rodríguez, Washington DC: ICS Publications. Accessed online 9/1/2005 at <http://www.karmel.at/ics/john/cn.html>.

Juliá, Santos, Javier Pradera & Joaquín Prieto (eds) (1996), *Memoria de la transición*, Madrid: Taurus/El País.

Jutglar, Antoni (ed.) (1982), *História de Catalunya*, vol. 8, Madrid: CUPSA.

Kavanaugh, Kieran (1991), *General Introduction to the Collected Works of St. John of the Cross*, Washington DC: ICS Publications. Accessed online 9/1/2004 at <http://www.karmel.at/ics/john/gen.html>.

Labanyi, Jo (1989), *Myth and History in the Contemporary Spanish Novel*, Cambridge: Cambridge University Press.

———— (1995a), 'Censorship or the Fear of Mass Culture' in Helen Graham & Jo Labanyi (eds), *Spanish Cultural Studies: An Introduction*, Oxford: Oxford University Press, 207–14.

———— (1995b), 'Postmodernism and the Problem of Cultural Identity' in Helen Graham & Jo Labanyi (eds), *Spanish Cultural Studies: An Introduction*, Oxford: Oxford University Press, 396–406.

———— (2002), 'Introduction: Engaging with Ghosts; or, Theorizing Culture in Modern Spain' in Jo Labanyi (ed.), *Constructing Identity in Contemporary Spain: Theoretical Debates and Cultural Practice*, Oxford: Oxford University Press, 1–14.

Lafuente, Isaías (1999), *Tiempos de hambre: Viaje a la España de la posguerra*, Madrid: Temas de Hoy.

Lázaro Carreter, Fernando (1974), 'Sobre *Flor de Otoño*', *Primer Acto* 173: 16–18. Originally published in *Gaceta Ilustrada* (23/9/1973).

León Solís, Fernando (2003), *Negotiating Spain and Catalonia: Competing Narratives of National Identity*, Bristol/Portland: Intellect.

Lewis, Jeff (2002), *Cultural Studies: The Basics*, London: Sage.

Ley, Pablo (2003), 'Barcelona, retrato de época: *Flor de Otoño*', *El País* 1/12/2003. Accessed online 2/8/2004 at <http://www.artenbrutteatre.com>.

Lida, Clara (1972), *Anarquismo y revolución en la España del XIX*, Madrid: Siglo XXI de España.

Lindenberger, Herbert (1975), *Historical Drama: The Relation of Literature and Reality*, Chicago/London: University of Chicago Press.

López Mozo, Jerónimo (1999), 'El "Nuevo Teatro Español" durante la transición: una llama viva' in Martha T. Halsey & Phyllis Zatlin (eds), *Entre Actos: Diálogos sobre teatro español entre siglos*, University Park, PA: Estreno, 17–22.

López Sancho, Lorenzo (1982), '*Flor de Otoño*, un gran personaje dentro de un marco rococó', *ABC* 17/12/1982: 59.

Luján, N. (1994), *Cabaret catalán*, Barcelona: Planeta.

Lukács, Georg (1963), *The Meaning of Contemporary Realism*, trans. J. & N. Mander, London: Merlin.

———— (1969), *The Historical Novel*, trans. H. & S. Mitchell, Harmondsworth: Penguin, 1969.

Lyon, John (1983), *The Theatre of Valle-Inclán*, Cambridge: Cambridge University Press.

———— (2001), 'History and Opposition Drama in Franco's Spain' in Kenneth Adams, Ciaran Cosgrove & James Whiston (eds), *Spanish Theatre: Studies in Honour of Victor F. Dixon*, London: Tamesis, 91–109.

Machado, Antonio (1998), *Poesías completas*, 28th ed., Madrid: Espasa Calpe.

Madariaga, María Rosa de (2000), *España y el Rif, crónica de una historia casi olvidada*, Melilla: Ayuntamiento de Melilla.

Maestre Alonso, Juan (1975), *El Sáhara en la crisis de Marruecos y España*, Madrid: Akal.

Malefakis, Edward (1970), *Agrarian Reform and Peasant Revolution in Spain*, New Haven, CT: Yale University Press.

Mar-Molinero, Clare (2000), *The Politics of Language in the Spanish-Speaking World: From Colonisation to Globalisation*, London/New York: Routledge.

Mar-Molinero, Clare & Ángel Smith (eds) (1996), *Nationalism and the Nation in the Iberian Peninsula: Competing and Conflicting Identities*, Oxford/Washington DC: Berg.

Marcuse, Herbert (1964), *One Dimensional Man: Studies in the Ideology of Advanced Industrial Society*, London: Routledge & Kegan Paul.

Martí Farreras, C. (1961), 'La crítica de Barcelona juzga *Los inocentes de la Moncloa*', *Primer Acto* 24 (1961): 22.

Martín Recuerda, José (1969), 'Manifiesto de *El caraqueño* o la deshumanización de un hombre de España', *Primer Acto* 107: 32–34.

———— (1979), *La tragedia de España en la obra dramática de José María Rodríguez Méndez*, Salamanca: Universidad de Salamanca.

Martín Recuerda, José & José María Rodríguez Méndez (1975), 'Carta a la Sociedad General de Autores y Editores', *Informaciones de las Artes y las Letras* 12/6/1975: 5.

Martínez-Michel, Paula (2003), *Censura y represión intelectual en la España franquista: el caso de Alfonso Sastre*, Hondarribia: Hiru.

Marx, Karl (1999), *The Eighteenth Brumaire of Louis Napoleon*, Marx and Engels Internet Archive. (First published 1852). Accessed online 21/9/2005 at <http://www.marxists.org/archive/marx/works/1852/18th-brumaire>.

Massip, Francesc (2003), 'Merescut rescat', *Avui* (1/12/2003). Accessed online 2/8/2004 at <http://www.artenbrutteatre.com>.

Medina Vicario, Miguel (2003), *Veinticinco años de teatro español (1975–2000)*, Madrid: Fundamentos.

Menéndez-Reigada (2003), *Catecismo patriótico español*, ed. Hilari Raguer, Barcelona: Península. (First published in 1939).

Méndez Moya, Adelardo (1991), 'Una nueva etapa en el teatro de José María Rodríguez Méndez', *Canente* 9: 225–34.

Millás, Jaime (1982), 'La ruptura de un maleficio,' *El País* 10/12/1982.

Ministerio de Cultura (1978), 'Expediente de calificación de obras teatrales 692–78: *Bodas que fueron famosas del Pingajo y la Fandanga* de José María Rodríguez Méndez', Alcalá de Henares: Archivo General de la Administración. Caja 85551 (Topográfico 83/57).

———— (1982), 'Expediente de calificación de obras teatrales 545–82: *Flor de Otoño* de José María Rodríguez Méndez', Alcalá de Henares: Archivo General de la Administración. Caja 88994 (Topográfico 83/57).

Ministerio de Información y Turismo (1960), 'Expediente de censura teatral 311–60: *Vagones de madera* de José María Rodríguez Méndez', Alcalá de Henares: Archivo General de la Administración. Caja 71715 (Topográfico 83/57).

———— (1961), 'Expediente de censura teatral 20–61: *Los inocentes de la Moncloa* de José María Rodríguez Méndez', Alcalá de Henares: Archivo General de la Administración. Caja 71722 (Topográfico 83/51).

———— (1962), 'Expediente de censura teatral 106–62: *El círculo de tiza de Cartagena* de José María Rodríguez Méndez', Alcalá de Henares: Archivo General de la Administración. Caja 71724 (Topográfico 83/51).

———— (1965), 'Expediente de censura de libros 5818–65: *La batalla del Verdún* de José María Rodríguez Méndez', Alcalá de Henares: Archivo General de la Administración. Caja 16499 (Topográfico 21).

————— (1966), 'Expediente de censura teatral 268–66: *El vano ayer* de José María Rodríguez Méndez', Alcalá de Henares: Archivo General de la Administración. Caja 85148 (Topográfico 83/55–56).
————— (1967), 'Expediente de censura teatral 6–67: *La vendimia de Francia* de José María Rodríguez Méndez', Alcalá de Henares: Archivo General de la Administración. Caja 85169 (Topográfico 83/55).
————— (1970a), 'Expediente de censura teatral 0/3–70: *Bodas que fueron famosas del Pingajo y la Fandanga* de José María Rodríguez Méndez', Alcalá de Henares: Archivo General de la Administración. Caja 85334 (Topográfico 83/55–56).
————— (1970b), 'Expediente de censura teatral 413–70: *Los quinquis de Madriz* de José María Rodríguez Méndez', Alcalá de Henares: Archivo General de la Administración. Caja 85320 (Topográfico 83/55–56).
————— (1971a), 'Expediente de censura teatral 581–71: *El milagro del pan y de los peces* de José María Rodríguez Méndez', Alcalá de Henares: Archivo General de la Administración. Caja 85393 (Topográfico 83/55).
————— (1971b), 'Expediente de censura teatral 91–71: *La tabernera y las tinajas* de José María Rodríguez Méndez', Alcalá de Henares: Archivo General de la Administración. Caja 85343 (Topográfico 83/55).
————— (1972), 'Expediente de censura teatral 555–72: *El ghetto* de José María Rodríguez Méndez', Alcalá de Henares: Archivo General de la Administración. Caja 85465 (Topográfico 83/55).
————— (1973), 'Expediente de censura teatral 251–73: *Historia de unos cuantos* de José María Rodríguez Méndez', Alcalá de Henares: Archivo General de la Administración. Caja 85506 (Topográfico 83/55).
Miralles, Alberto (1977), *Nuevo teatro español: Una alternativa social*, Madrid: Villalar.
————— (2001), 'Nada en las alforjas para caminar ligero' in Juan Casamayor & Encarnación Molina (eds), *La lucidez de un siglo*, Madrid: Páginas de Espuma, 185–88.
Miras, Domingo (2005), 'Introducción. José María Rodríguez Méndez: vivir para escribir' in José María Rodríguez Méndez, *Teatro escogido*, vol. 1, Madrid: Asociación de Autores de Teatro, 11–60.
Monleón, José (1962), 'Nuestra Generación Realista', *Primer Acto* 32: 1–3.
————— (1968a), 'Teatro popular: la respuesta de Rodríguez Méndez' in José María Rodríguez Méndez, *La tabernera y las tinajas; Los inocentes de la Moncloa*, Madrid: Taurus/Primer Acto, 21–55.
————— (1968b), 'Pequeña historia de "La Pipironda"' in José María Rodríguez Méndez, *La tabernera y las tinajas; Los inocentes de la Moncloa*, Madrid: Taurus/Primer Acto, 65–8.
————— (1971), *Treinta años de teatro de la derecha*, Barcelona: Tusquets.
————— (1974a), 'Rodríguez Méndez y Martín Recuerda', *Triunfo* 611 (15/6/1974): 78.
————— (1974b), 'Teatro último de Rodríguez Méndez: Biografía', *Primer Acto* 173: 10–14.
————— (1975), '*Historia de unos cuantos*: otro grito de teatro español', *Triunfo* (26/4/1975): 88–89.
————— (1976), 'España amarga: Valle, Mediero y Rodríguez Méndez, tres dramaturgos frente a la Historia', *Triunfo* 676 (10/1/1976): 46–49.
————— (1978a), 'Comparsas y personajes', programme notes for *Bodas que fueron famosas del Pingajo y la Fandanga*, Teatro Bellas Artes (Madrid).
————— (1978b), 'Centro Dramático Nacional: Rodríguez Méndez, para empezar', *Triunfo* 2/12/1978: 73–74.
Morales y Marín, Antonio (1998), 'El bandolero, personaje obligado' in José María Rodríguez Méndez, *Soy madrileño*, Murcia: Escuela Superior de Arte Dramático, 9–13.
Muñoz Cáliz, Berta (2005), *El teatro crítico español durante el franquismo, visto por sus censores*, Madrid: Fundación Universitaria Española.
Muñoz Quirós, José María (1993), 'José María Rodríguez Méndez: las virtudes del pájaro solitario' in José María Rodríguez Méndez, *El pájaro solitario*, Ávila: Diputación Provincial de Ávila, i–xxiii.
Neuschäfer, Hans-Jörg (1994), *Adiós a la España eterna: la dialéctica de la censura. Novela, teatro y cine bajo el franquismo*, Barcelona: Anthropos.
Nieva, Francisco (1975), *Teatro furioso y Teatro de farsa y calamidad*, Madrid: Akal.
O'Connor, Patricia (ed.) (1992), *Plays of the New Democratic Spain, 1975–1990*. Lanham, MD: University Press of America.
O'Connor, Patricia & Anthony Pasquariello (1976), 'Conversaciones con la Generación Realista', *Estreno* 2.2: 8–28.
O'Leary, Catherine (2005), *The Theatre of Antonio Buero Vallejo: Ideology, Politics and Censorship*, Woodbridge: Tamesis.
Oliva, César (1978), *Cuatro dramaturgos 'realistas' en la escena de hoy: sus contradicciones estéticas*, Murcia: Universidad de Murcia.
————— (1979), *Disidentes de la generación realista: Introducción a la obra de Carlos Muñiz, Lauro Olmo, Rodríguez Méndez y Martín Recuerda*, Murcia: Universidad de Murcia.
————— (1988), 'Breve itinerario por el drama histórico español', *Estreno* 14.1 (special issue on *El drama histórico español contemporáneo*): 7–10.
————— (1989), *Historia de la literatura española actual*, vol. 3: El teatro desde 1936, Madrid: Alhambra.
————— (1999), 'Teatro histórico en España (1975–1998)' in José Romera Castillo & Francisco Gutiérrez Carbajo (eds), *Teatro histórico (1975–1998): textos y representaciones*, Madrid: Visor, 63–72.
Olmo, Lauro (1997), *Luis Candelas: El ladrón de Madrid*, Alcalá de Henares: Universidad de Alcalá.
Orozco, Lourdes (2004), 'El impacto de la política teatral en el teatro de la ciudad de Barcelona (1980–2000)', Ph.D. thesis, University of Durham.
Ortega y Gasset, José (1947), *Obras completas*, vol. 3, Madrid: Revista de Occidente.
Oxford English Dictionary (1994), *OED2 on CD-ROM*, Version 1.11. Oxford/Rotterdam: Oxford University Press/Software BV.
Palacios Buñuelos, Luis & José Luis Rodríguez Jiménez (2001), *Para acercarnos a una historia del franquismo*, Madrid: Ediciones Académicas.
Pedraza Jiménez, Felipe B. & Milagros Rodríguez Cáceres (1995), *Manual de literatura española*, vol. XIV: *Posguerra: dramaturgos y ensayistas*, Pamplona: Cénlit.
Pemán, José María (1938), *La historia de España contada con sencillez*, Madrid: Escelicer.
Perales, Liz (2001), 'Rodríguez Méndez: "El público de ahora es el peor que hemos tenido"' (interview), *El Cultural* 14/11/2001: 42–43.

Pérez Coterillo, Moisés (1982), 'Rodríguez Méndez, en el Español', *ABC* 10/12/1982: 59.
Pérez Fernández, H. (1978), 'Crítica de teatro: *Bodas que fueron famosas del Pingajo y la Fandanga*', *ABC* 24/11/1978: 53–54.
Pérez-Pineda, Federico (1994–95), '*El ghetto o la irresistible ascensión de Manuel Contreras*: un caso de alienación', *Explicación de Textos Literarios* 23.1: 3–9.
Pérez-Stansfield, María Pilar (1983), *Direcciones de teatro español de posguerra*, Madrid: José Porrúa Turanzas.
Perriam, Chris, Michael Thompson, Susan Frenk & Vanessa Knights (2000), *A New History of Spanish Writing, 1939 to the 1990s*, Oxford: Oxford University Press.
Pörtl, Klaus (ed.) (1986), *Reflexiones sobre el Nuevo Teatro Español*, Tübingen: Max Niemeyer.
Powell, Charles (2001), *España en democracia, 1975–2000*, Barcelona: Plaza y Janés.
Prades, Joaquina (1997), 'La historia ¿era ESO?' *El País* 2/11/1997: *Domingo* 8–10.
Preston, Paul (1986), *The Triumph of Democracy in Spain*, London: Methuen.
——— (1993), *Franco: A Biography*, London: Harper Collins.
Primo de Rivera, José Antonio (1972), *Selected Writings*, ed. Hugh Thomas, trans. Gudie Lawaetz, London: Jonathan Cape.
Ragué-Arias, María José (1996), *El teatro de fin de milenio en España (De 1975 hasta hoy)*, Barcelona: Ariel.
Ramos Gascón, Antonio (ed.) (1991), *España hoy*, Madrid: Cátedra, vol. 1: *Sociedad*, vol. 2: *Cultura*.
Real Academia de la Historia (2000), *Informe sobre los textos y cursos de Historia en los centros de Enseñanza Media*, Madrid: Real Academia de la Historia. Accessed online 19/5/2003 at <http://www.filosofia.org/his/h2000ah.htm>.
Real Academia Española (1992), *Diccionario de la lengua española*, 21st ed. Madrid: RAE/Espasa Calpe, 2 vols.
Reames, Sherry L. (1985), *The Legenda Aurea: A Reexamination of its Paradoxical History*, Madison: University of Wisconsin Press.
Rebollo Sánchez, Félix (1994), 'El realismo de Rodríguez Méndez' in Joaquín María Aguirre (ed.), *Teatro Siglo XX*, Madrid: Universidad Complutense, 315–24.
Reilly, Bernard F. (1988), *The Kingdom of León-Castilla under King Alfonso VI, 1065–1109*, Princeton University Press, 1988. (Accessible online at <http://libro.uca.edu/alfonso6/alfonso.htm>).
Riaza, Luis (1978), 'Prólogo' in Luis Riaza, *El desván de los machos y el sótano de las hembras; El palacio de los monos*, Madrid: Cátedra, 96–116.
Richards, Michael (1996), 'Constructing the Nationalist State: Self-Sufficiency and Regeneration in the Early Franco Years' in Clare Mar-Molinero & Ángel Smith (eds), *Nationalism and the Nation in the Iberian Peninsula: Competing and Conflicting Identities*, Oxford/Washington DC: Berg, 149–67.
——— (1998), *A Time of Silence: Civil War and the Culture of Repression in Franco's Spain 1936–1945*, Cambridge: Cambridge University Press.
——— (2000), 'Collective Memory, the Nation State and Post-Franco Society' in Barry Jordan & Rikki Morgan-Tamosunas (eds), *Contemporary Spanish Cultural Studies*, London: Arnold, 38–47.
Rodríguez Méndez, José María (1963), 'Cuando las literaturas se enfrentan', *Primer Acto* 45: 5–8.
——— (1966), 'Aclaración' in José María Rodríguez Méndez, *La batalla del Verdún*, Barcelona: Occitania, 9–11.
——— (1968a), 'La tradición burguesa frente al realismo', *Primer Acto* 102: 30–31.
——— (1968b), 'Lo poco que yo puedo decir' in José María Rodríguez Méndez, *La tabernera y las tinajas; Los inocentes de la Moncloa*, Madrid: Taurus/Primer Acto, 15–18.
——— (1968c), 'Mis estrenos en "La Pipironda"' in José María Rodríguez Méndez, *La tabernera y las tinajas; Los inocentes de la Moncloa*, Madrid: Taurus/Primer Acto, 69–73.
——— (1968d), 'El teatro como expresión social y cultural' in José María Rodríguez Méndez, *La tabernera y las tinajas; Los inocentes de la Moncloa*, Madrid: Taurus/Primer Acto, 85–100. (First published in 1966 in *Primer Acto* 71).
——— (1968e), 'Belleza y realismo' in José María Rodríguez Méndez, *La tabernera y las tinajas; Los inocentes de la Moncloa*, Madrid: Taurus/Primer Acto, 101–104. (First published 24/1/1964 in *El Noticiero Universal*).
——— (1969), 'Martín Recuerda, allá en Granada' in José Martín Recuerda, *Teatro*, Madrid: Taurus, 37–39.
——— (1971a), *Ensayo sobre el machismo español*, Barcelona: Península.
——— (1971b), *Los teleadictos: La sociedad televisual*, Barcelona: Estela. (2nd ed. Barcelona: Laia, 1973).
——— (1972a), *Ensayo sobre la 'inteligencia' española*, Barcelona: Península.
——— (1972b), *Comentarios impertinentes sobre el teatro español*, Barcelona: Península.
——— (1972c), *Pobrecitos pero no honrados*, Barcelona: Laia.
——— (1973), *Carta abierta a Televisión Española*, Madrid: Ediciones 99.
——— (1974a), 'Conmigo mismo', *Primer Acto* 173: 14–16.
——— (1974b), *Pudriéndome con los árabes*, Barcelona: Península.
——— (1974c), *La incultura teatral en España*, Barcelona: Laia.
——— (1974d), *Ciudadanos de tercera*, Barcelona: Plaza y Janés.
——— (1977), untitled contribution in Fundación Juan March, *Teatro español actual*, Madrid: Cátedra, 93–97.
——— (1979), *Los herederos de la promesa*, Barcelona: Plaza y Janés.
——— (1981), *El cisne de Cisneros*, Barcelona: Plaza y Janés.
——— (1987), *La Generación Realista y la incultura teatral en España*, Bristol: University of Bristol.
——— (1989), 'Prólogo' in José María Rodríguez Méndez, *Literatura española*, Murcia: Universidad de Murcia, 17–20.
——— (1991), 'Aprovechamiento de la victoria' in José María Rodríguez Méndez, *Última batalla en El Pardo*, Madrid: El Público/Centro de Documentación Teatral, 21–25.
——— (1993), *Los despojos del teatro*, Madrid: J. García Verdugo.
——— (1998), 'Presentación' in José María Rodríguez Méndez, *Leyenda Áurea*. Unpublished page proofs, 291.
——— (1999), 'Mi teatro historicista (la interpretación histórica en el teatro)' in José Romera Castillo & Francisco Gutiérrez Carbajo (eds), *Teatro histórico (1975–1998): textos y representaciones*, Madrid: Visor, 39–48.
——— (2001), 'El poder sin la gloria y la razón sin la fuerza', programme note for *Última batalla en El Pardo*, Teatro Caja de Ávila. Also published in *Diario de Ávila*, Edición Especial (14/2/2001): 4.
Rodríguez Puértolas, Julio (1986), *Literatura fascista española*, vol. 1: *Historia*, Madrid: Akal.
——— (1987), *Literatura fascista española*, vol. 2: *Antología*, Madrid: Akal.

Ruibal, José (1977), 'Notas de producción' in José Ruibal, *El hombre y la mosca*, Madrid: Fundamentos, 110–17.
———— (1984), *Teatro sobre teatro*, Madrid: Cátedra.
Ruiz Ramón, Francisco (1978), *Estudios sobre teatro español clásico y contemporáneo*, Madrid: Fundación Juan March/Cátedra.
———— (1986), 'Apuntes sobre el teatro español de la transición' in Klaus Pörtl (ed.), *Reflexiones sobre el Nuevo Teatro Español*, Tübingen: Max Niemeyer, 90–100.
———— (1988), *Celebración y catarsis: leer el teatro español*, Murcia: Universidad de Murcia.
———— (1989), *Historia del teatro español: Siglo XX*, 8th edition, Madrid: Cátedra.
Salvat, Ricard (ed.) (1995), *Drama i Realisme*. Special issue of *Assaig de Teatre* 2–3.
———— (2005), 'Introducción: *La batalla del Verdún*' in José María Rodríguez Méndez, *Teatro escogido*, vol. 1, Madrid: Asociación de Autores de Teatro, 263–70.
Sastre, Alfonso (1974), *Anatomía del realismo*, 2nd edition, Barcelona: Seix Barral.
Shaw, Donald L. (1975), *The Generation of 1898 in Spain*, London: E. Benn.
———— (1997), *La generación del 98*, Madrid: Cátedra. [Revised translation of Shaw (1975)].
Sinova, Justino (1989), *La censura de prensa durante el franquismo (1936–1951)*, Madrid: Espasa-Calpe.
Sopeña Monsalve, Andrés (1994), *El florido pensil: Memoria de la escuela nacional-católica*, Barcelona: Crítica.
Spang, Kurt (1998), 'Apuntes para la definición y el comentario del drama histórico' in Kurt Spang (ed.), *El drama histórico: Teoría y comentarios*, Pamplona: EUNSA, 11–50.
Stein, Louis (1979), *Beyond Death and Exile: The Spanish Republicans in France, 1939–1955*, Cambridge, MA: Harvard University Press.
Thompson, Michael (1989), 'The Unity of the Historical Theatre of José María Rodríguez Méndez', Ph.D. thesis, University of Bristol.
———— (1991), 'El teatro histórico de Rodríguez Méndez' in José María Rodríguez Méndez, *Última batalla en El Pardo*, Madrid: El Público/Centro de Documentación Teatral, 9–17.
———— (1994), 'Introduction' in Antonio Buero Vallejo, *Un soñador para un pueblo/A Dreamer for the People*, ed. & trans. Michael Thompson, Warminster: Aris & Phillips, 1–30.
———— (1996), '*Iberismo* and *machismo español* in the theater of Martín Recuerda and Rodríguez Méndez', *Estreno* 22.2: 35–44.
———— (1999), 'Cultural identity in the theatre of Rodríguez Méndez' in Martha T. Halsey & Phyllis Zatlin (eds), *Entre Actos: Diálogos sobre teatro español entre siglos*, University Park, PA: Estreno, 293–300.
———— (2004a), 'Rodríguez Méndez en el laberinto de la censura: el confuso expediente sobre *Historia de unos cuantos*', *Estreno* 30.1: 19–27.
———— (2004b), 'José María Rodríguez Méndez, tenaz paladín de la lengua española' and 'Cronología' in José María Rodríguez Méndez, *El pájaro solitario*, Madrid: SGAE/Fundación Autor, 17–56.
———— (2005), 'Introducción: *El pájaro solitario*' in José María Rodríguez Méndez, *Teatro escogido*, vol. 2, Madrid: Asociación de Autores de Teatro, 273–78.
Toynbee, Arnold J. (1935), *A Study of History*, 2nd ed., vol. 1: *Introduction*, Oxford: Oxford University Press.
———— (1961), *A Study of History*, 2nd ed., vol. 12: *Reconsiderations*, Oxford: Oxford University Press.
Tuñón de Lara, Manuel (ed.) (1981), *Historia de España*, vol. 9. Barcelona: Labor.
Turner, Victor (1988), *The Anthropology of Performance*, New York: PAJ.
Tusell, Javier (1988), *La dictadura de Franco* (2nd ed. 1996), Madrid: Alianza.
———— (1990), *Manual de historia de España: Siglo XX*, Madrid: Historia 16.
———— (2001), *Historia de España: la España actual, 1982–2000*, Barcelona: Labor Ediciones 2000.
Unamuno, Miguel de (1943), *En torno al casticismo*, Madrid: Espasa-Calpe. (First published in 1916).
Valle-Inclán, Ramón María del (1985), *Martes de carnaval*, 10th ed. Madrid: Espasa-Calpe.
Valls, Rafael (1987), *La interpretación de la Historia de España y sus orígenes ideológicos en el Bachillerato franquista (1936–1951)*. Valencia: Universitat de Valencia.
Vega, Ricardo de la (1943), *La verbena de la Paloma* in Federico Carlos Sainz Robles (ed.), *El teatro español: Historia y Antología*, vol. 7, Madrid: Aguilar, 1079–1117.
Vergara, Alexander (1998), *The Visual Front: Posters of the Spanish Civil War from UCSD's Southworth Collection*, University of California San Diego. Accessed online 12/9/2003 at <http://orpheus.ucsd.edu/speccoll/visfront/index.html>.
Versteeg, Margot (2000), *De Fusiladores y Morcilleros: El discurso cómico del género chico (1870–1910)*, Amsterdam/Atlanta, GA: Rodopi.
Vilches de Frutos, María Francisca (1999a), 'La generación simbolista en el teatro español contemporáneo' in Martha T. Halsey & Phyllis Zatlin (eds), *Entre Actos: Diálogos sobre teatro español entre siglos*, University Park, PA: Estreno, 127–36.
———— (1999b), 'Teatro histórico: la elección del género como clave de la escena española contemporánea' in José Romera Castillo & Francisco Gutiérrez Carbajo (eds), *Teatro histórico (1975–1998): textos y representaciones*, Madrid: Visor, 73–92.
Villanueva, Darío (ed.) (1992), *Historia y crítica de la literatura española*, vol. 9: *Los nuevos nombres: 1975–1990*, Barcelona: Crítica.
Webber, Christopher (2002), *The Zarzuela Companion*, Lanham: Scarecrow.
Wellwarth, George (1970), *The New Wave Spanish Drama*, New York: New York University Press.
———— (1972), *Spanish Underground Drama*, University Park, PA: Pennsylvania State University Press. (Published in Spanish in 1978).
White, Hayden (1973), *Metahistory: The Historical Imagination in Nineteenth-Century Europe*, Baltimore/London: Johns Hopkins University Press.
Yáñez, María-Paz (1993), 'La doble función del catalán en *Flor de Otoño* de José María Rodríguez Méndez' in Elvezio Canónica & Ernst Rudin (eds), *Literatura y bilingüismo: Homenaje a Pere Ramírez*, Kassel: Reichenberger, 253–68.